RECORD LINKAGE IN MEDICINE

Record Linkage
in Medicine

Proceedings of the
International Symposium
Oxford, July 1967

Edited by

E. D. ACHESON

Nuffield Department of Clinical Medicine, Oxford

E. & S. LIVINGSTONE LTD.
EDINBURGH AND LONDON
1968

©

E. & S. LIVINGSTONE LTD
1968

SBN 443 00577 x

PREFACE

THIS book publishes the proceedings of a symposium which was held in Oxford on 17th and 18th July 1967. The title 'Record Linkage in Medicine' is derived from a term which came of age in 1967, having first been used 21 years previously by H. L. Dunn. However, the concept underlying record linkage is at least one hundred years old and there is a clear exposition of it dating from 1865.

Systems of linked medical records limited to a single hospital or clinic, to the collection of data about a single class of disease (e.g. psychiatric or cancer registers), or set up 'ad hoc' for the execution of a particular research study, have been familiar on the medical scene for many years. With the development of high speed electronic data processing, considerable interest has arisen in the idea of *systematic record linkage for certain classes of medical records extending to whole populations.*

It was with the problems and potentialities of systematic record linkage in mind that this symposium was planned. The time was ripe, it was felt, to bring together some of the principal people working in the field in the hope that an exchange of views would accelerate progress. In addition to specialists in the use of electronic computers, and in statistics, genetics, chronic disease epidemiology, and the law, the participants included a number of persons with more general interests including senior administrators in the health and social services at home and abroad, and clinicians. In all, 29 papers were presented by 31 contributors from 8 countries.

The proceedings were opened by Sir George Godber, Chief Medical Officer of the Ministry of Health. They are set out in nine parts, one for each session, following the chronological sequence in which these took place at the symposium. The discussion which followed each paper is given as it took place with minor alterations for the sake of clarity or brevity.

Parts I and II are concerned with some general aspects of systems of linked records in existence or projected in Britain and elsewhere. Parts III and IV are devoted to methodology. Included here are a number of papers on allocated personal numbers, and on techniques for record linkage where unique personal numbers are not available. There is also a paper on the statistical theory of record linkage procedures. These papers together made up the work of the first day of the symposium.

The second day (Parts V to IX) began with a session on the applications of linked files in the study of the epidemiology of chronic disease. This was followed by a group of papers about various aspects of *family record linkage* or family reconstitution as it is sometimes called. Results were discussed from widely contrasting populations in Pennsylvania, Italy, and Oxfordshire.

Medical record linkage carries with it inescapable ethical and legal issues. For this reason a whole session (Part VII) was devoted to a discussion of confidentiality and related problems. In addition to papers by a clinician and an epidemiologist, this session includes a unique account of the law of England in this field.

The symposium closed with a final general session (Part VIII) and a period of discussion and summing up, with contributions from the standpoint of a health administrator (Dr. J. Brotherston, Scotland), an epidemiologist (Dr. J. Mosbech, Denmark), and a geneticist (Dr. C. Carter, England).

April 1968   E. D. ACHESON

ACKNOWLEDGEMENTS

THIS Symposium was financed by a grant from the Nuffield Foundation. This grant, which was a generous one, in addition to meeting the usual administrative expenses of a conference of this sort, made it possible for a number of distinguished visitors to be invited from abroad. The Oxford Regional Hospital Board acted as hosts to the Symposium and, at considerable inconvenience, made their Board and Conference Rooms available for the scientific meetings. The participants of the Symposium are also grateful to the Provost and Fellows of The Queen's College for making accommodation available to them.

LIST OF PARTICIPANTS

DR. M. E. ABRAMS, Department of Medicine, Guy's Hospital Medical School, London.
DR. E. D. ACHESON, Oxford Record Linkage Study.
DR. A. M. ADELSTEIN, General Register Office, Somerset House, London.
PROFESSOR P. ARMITAGE, London School of Hygiene and Tropical Medicine, London.
DR. ANITA K. BAHN, Women's Medical College of Penn, Philadelphia, U.S.A.
DR. J. A. BALDWIN, Department of Mental Health, Aberdeen University.
DR. A. BARR, Oxford Regional Hospital Board, Oxford.
PROFESSOR I. BARRAI, Istituto di Genetica, Universita di Pavia, Italy.
DR. J. C. BARRETT, Department of Medical Statistics and Epidemiology, London School of Hygiene and Tropical Medicine, London.
DR. B. BENJAMIN, Greater London Council, London.
DR. A. E. BENNETT, Department of Clinical Epidemiology and Social Medicine, St. Thomas's Hospital Medical School, London.
PROFESSOR J. M. BISHOP, Department of Medicine, Queen Elizabeth Hospital, Birmingham.
MR. J. BOGOD, British Computer Society, London.
DR. P. W. BOTHWELL, Automotive Safety Research Unit, Birmingham University, Birmingham.
DR. A. J. BOYCE, Department of Human Anatomy, University of Oxford.
DR. F. BRIMBLECOMBE, Royal Devon and Exeter Hospital, Exeter.
DR. J. H. F. BROTHERSTON, Scottish Home and Health Department, Edinburgh.
PROFESSOR NEVILLE BUTLER, Department of Child Health, University of Bristol.
PROFESSOR W. J. H. BUTTERFIELD, Department of Medicine, Guy's Hospital Medical School, London.
MR. R. G. CARPENTER, Department of Human Ecology, University of Cambridge.
DR. C. O. CARTER, Clinical Genetics Research Unit, Medical Research Council, London.
PROFESSOR R. A. M. CASE, Chester Beatty Institute, London.
PROFESSOR E. A. CHEESEMAN, Department of Medical Statistics, The Queen's University of Belfast.
DR. J. R. CONNELLY, Ministry of Social Security, London.
MISS PAULA J. COOK, Statistical Research Unit, Medical Research Council, London.
DR. C. B. COPE, Department of Medicine and Surgery, Veterans Administration, Central Office, Washington D.C., U.S.A.
DR. H. E. CROSS, Division of Medical Genetics, The Johns Hopkins Hospital, Baltimore, U.S.A.
DR. K. CROSS, Department of Medical Statistics, Queen Elizabeth Hospital, Birmingham.
MR. A. A. CROXFORD, Department of Education and Science, London.
DR. J. O. F. DAVIES, C.B.E., Oxford Regional Hospital Board, Oxford.
DR. W. R. S. DOLL, O.B.E., Statistical Research Unit, Medical Research Council, London.
DR. J. DONNELLY, Scottish Home and Health Department, Edinburgh.
DR. J. H. DOUGHTY, Division of Vital Statistics, British Columbia.
MR. G. DRAPER, Department of Social Medicine, University of Oxford.
DR. H. C. EBBING, Human Genetics Unit, World Health Organization, Switzerland.
DR. W. EDGAR, Department of Public Health, Northampton.
DR. J. EDWARDS, Department of Social Medicine, University of Birmingham.

ix

Dr. J. G. Evans, Medical Unit, Wellington Hospital, Wellington, S.I., N.Z.
Dr. A. S. Fairbairn, Oxford Record Linkage Study.
Mr. J. Fisher, 20a Woodstock Road North, St. Albans.
Mr. J. A. Ford, General Register Office, Edinburgh.
Dr. F. Clarke Fraser, Human Genetics Section, McGill University, Canada.
Dr. S. Fridriksson, University Research Institute, Reykjavik, Iceland.
Dr. T. McL. Galloway, County Health Department, Chichester, Sussex.
Dr. A. Gatherer, Health Department, Reading, Berkshire.
Mr. P. R. Glazebrook, Jesus College, Cambridge.
Mrs. A. M. Hailey, Institute of Psychiatry, Medical Research Council, London.
Dr. P. J. S. Hamilton, London School of Hygiene and Tropical Medicine, London.
Mr. M. J. R. Healy, Clinical Research Centre, Medical Research Council, London.
Dr. M. A. Heasman, Scottish Home and Health Department, Edinburgh.
Dr. M. S. T. Hobbs, Oxford Record Linkage Study.
Dr. J. Howlett, Atlas Computer Laboratory, Chilton, Berks.
Mr. M. R. Hubbard, Oxford Record Linkage Study.
Dr. George Innes, Department of Mental Health, University of Aberdeen.
Dr. Seymour Jablon, National Academy of Sciences, Washington D.C.
Dr. A. Johnson, Office of the High Commissioner for Australia, London.
Miss G. M. Jones, Ministry of Social Security, London.
Mr. P. Duncan Jones, Nuffield College, Oxford.
Dr. J. M. Kennedy, University of British Columbia, Canada.
Professor N. Kessel, Department of Psychiatry, University of Manchester.
Dr. L. J. Kinlen, Oxford Record Linkage Study.
Miss C. F. Kuchemann, Department of Human Anatomy, University of Oxford.
Dr. Katherine Levy, Headquarters, Medical Research Council, London.
Dr. A. Lindgren, Swedish National Board of Health, Stockholm.
Dr. R. F. L. Logan, Department of Social Medicine, University of Manchester.
Professor M. Magnusson, Computer Centre, University of Iceland.
Dr. T. Meade, Social Medicine Research Unit, Medical Research Council, The London Hospital.
Mr. H. W. Melhuish, Central O. & M. Unit, Ministry of Health.
Mr. David G. Millar, Department of Obstetrics, University of Newcastle-upon-Tyne.
Mr. R. Milne, Computing Services Ltd., Birmingham.
Dr. J. R. A. Mitchell, Radcliffe Infirmary, Oxford.
Miss B. Morrison, Department of Applied Statistics, University of Reading.
Professor S. L. Morrison, Department of Public Health and Social Medicine, University of Edinburgh.
Dr. J. Mosbech, Danish National Health Service, Copenhagen, Denmark.
Dr. T. G. C. Murrell, General Practitioner Research Unit, Guy's Hospital Medical School, London.
Dr. N. Nevin, Population Genetics Research Unit, Medical Research Council, Oxford.
Dr. H. B. Newcombe, Atomic Energy of Canada Ltd., Chalk River Nuclear Laboratories, Canada.
Dr. M. Newhouse, London School of Hygiene and Tropical Medicine, London.
Dr. H. Nielsen, Ministry of the Interior, Denmark.
Dr. D. M. Nitzberg, Bio-Dynamics Inc., U.S.A.
Mr. M. W. Oakes, Population Genetics Research Unit, Medical Research Council, Oxford.
Dr. M. Ounsted, Nuffield Department of Obstetrics and Gynaecology, The Radcliffe Infirmary, Oxford.
Dr. R. Owen, Her Majesty's Medical Inspectorate of Factories, Ministry of Labour, London.
Dr. K. M. Parry, Wessex Regional Hospital Board, Winchester.

Dr. R. J. C. Pearson, Department of Social Medicine, University of Manchester.
Mr. W. Phillips, Jnr., National Institute of Mental Health, Baltimore, Md., U.S.A.
Dr. R. T. C. Pratt, National Hospital for Nervous Diseases, London.
Dr. H. C. Price, Fulham Chest Clinic, London.
Mr. M. Reed, C.B., General Register Office, London.
Dr. J. Renwick, Department of Genetics, University of Glasgow.
Dr. Fraser Roberts, Guy's Hospital Medical School, London.
Mr. B. Rowe, London School of Hygiene and Tropical Medicine, London.
Dr. R. C. Sanders, Radcliffe Infirmary, Oxford.
Professor R. Schilling, London School of Hygiene and Tropical Medicine, London.
Dr. W. H. Schutt, Royal Hospital for Sick Children, Bristol.
Mr. R. F. A. Shegog, Nuffield Provincial Hospitals Trust, London.
Dr. B. Smedby, Research Associate, Department of Social Medicine, Stockholm, Sweden.
Professor Alwyn Smith, Department of Social and Preventive Medicine, University of Manchester.
Mr. M. E. Smythe, 32 Swallowdale, Basildon, Essex.
Dr. C. C. Spicer, Computer Unit, Medical Research Council, London.
Dr. A. L. Stevenson, Population Genetics Research Unit, Medical Research Council, Oxford.
Dr. Alice Stewart, Department of Social Medicine, Oxford.
Mr. A. Sunter, Dominion Bureau of Statistics, Ottawa, Canada.
Sir Ronald Tunbridge, Department of Medicine, University of Leeds.
Dr. W. Tünte, Institut fur Humangenetik, Universitat Munster, W. Germany.
Mr. A. Waaler, Helsedirektratet, Oslo, Norway.
Professor G. Wagner, Institut fur Dokumentation, Heidelberg, W. Germany.
Mr. G. Watts, O.B.E., Oxford Regional Hospital Board.
Mr. A. Weber, World Health Organization, Copenhagen, Denmark.
Dr. R. Deans Weir, Department of Public Health and Social Medicine, University Medical Buildings, Aberdeen.
Mr. D. White, Ministry of Health, Alexander Fleming House, London.
Dr. Charles Whitty, The Radcliffe Infirmary, Oxford.
Dr. J. M. G. Wilson, Ministry of Health, London.
Dr. Lorna Wing, Medical Research Council, Institute of Psychiatry, London.
Dr. C. B. Winsten, Nuffield College, Oxford.
Professor L. J. Witts, C.B.E., Oxford.

Mrs. S. Watts, Oxford Record Linkage Study.
Mr. John Sargent, Oxford Record Linkage Study.

CONTENTS

OPENING REMARKS

SIR GEORGE GODBER

MY function is to open these proceedings and to welcome you here, and it's a pleasure and privilege to be invited to do that.

We all know something about records because we all start doing our medical work by inscribing at great length, in longhand, records of very little use to posterity. But really it goes back much further than that because I suppose the statistics of morbidity and mortality began to be of some moment in public health, in this country, just over a century ago. Of course it's an even further cry back to John Graunt and the Bills of Mortality in the City Vestries, but William Farr just over a century ago was the first to advocate a cumulative personal file giving the health record of the individual. Now he was never able to see that, but it is my guess that his successor Dr Adelstein, who is here, may well see at least the beginning of the realization of that objective.

We started with medical records as personal things for the individual patient and they were supposed to be there for reference about the treatment and subsequent care of that patient. Vast piles of paper exist in all our hospitals and I wonder how much they are really used. I believe a recent study discovered that not one in fifty is used more than two years after the patient was in hospital. Yet one person in ten in the population of this country, one in seven in Sweden or the States, and one in five in the USSR, or even more than one in five in Saskatchewan, goes into hospital every year, at least that is the proportion of admissions to population, uncorrected for readmission.

On the other hand, in this country the general practitioner has got a continuous record and that record, ever since National Health Insurance began in 1911, has followed the patient wherever he went—at least it has followed him to his doctor. But how far is it really of any value for recall? Even a totally unsuitable size has been riveted on us by custom for nearly half a century. We are stuck with a record in its most primitive manuscript form that is almost useless for later reference, largely because all the general practitioners have their cabinets for storing records in the particular size of record that is used. That doesn't really seem to me a valid method for deciding how medical records should be kept in general practice over half a century later. I know the Royal College of General Practitioners has

1

been working on the subject and Dr Cross, who has done so much for them, is here, but we have simply got to work out a more useful method of dealing with general practitioners' records.

Local health authorities and local education authorities also have their own records for public health service, and there is some continuity between them, but it has not always been arranged that there should be any continuity with general practice or even continuity between the maternity and child welfare records and those of the school health service. Even the state of immunization of the patient may not be known to the Medical Officer of Health fully or to the general practitioner fully. Indeed the only real assurance that the Medical Officer of Health has reasonably complete information was obtained by the fact that he had to pay the general practitioner a fee for the record. Now the way in which automation of this sort of thing can secure continuity has been well shown by Dr Galloway's work in West Sussex, using a computer not only for the record but actually for doing the necessary work of making appointments for subsequent immunizing procedures. It is not coincidental that he is about the only Medical Officer of Health in the country, aside from Dr Warin of this city, who manages to get about 90 per cent. of the children immunized with all the procedures that we are trying to get carried out on them. But apart from that most of our permanent records in this country are of episodes like birth, death and marriage, and notification of infectious disease.

Then of course the Ministry of Social Security, which is also represented here, has its records of sickness absence of which remarkably little use can be made for any epidemiological or medical purpose, although they did reveal to us for the first time the strikingly high proportion of the population that had dropped out of the working force for health reasons long before retiring age. Now some of these records tell us something about incidence, something about causes, and some of them hardly do either of these things. We have brought so much disease under control in all the countries with sophisticated services, that our future interests are bound to be increasingly in congenital abnormalities, trauma, the chronic and especially the degenerative conditions. We have got the technology to make longitudinal analyses and input from many sources practicable for the first time.

The first rather primitive attempt in the National Health Service to improve our record keeping for central analysis was the Hospital Inpatient Enquiry, which was concerned only with inpatient records. That enquiry was born in 1944 in the basement of the old Ministry of Health building in Whitehall. It had a very curious parentage

2

because in fact Dr Percy Stocks, Dr Adelstein's predecessor at the General Register Office and I are the parents, though I don't think I have ever confessed publicly to that before. It took twelve years to sell that scheme completely to the hospitals of this country although it only involves taking a summary from one in ten of the records of all admissions. As I said, it was worked out in its original form in the Ministry of Health. I am not sure that the Registrar General didn't come into this in one of his earlier incarnations at a fairly early stage, but I am still going to claim the real parentage for Dr Percy Stocks and myself. The only trouble about the Hospital Inpatient Enquiry, which contains an extraordinary amount of information about what goes on in our hospitals, is that hardly anybody in this country looks at it closely. It is quite well known abroad, but it seems to me that not more than maybe fifty people in this country pay any serious attention to it.

Now we are moving on to Hospital Activity Analysis with an abstract from every record and we hope then to be able to feed back to the individual consultant in each hospital information much more contemporary than the just published 1963 Report of the Hospital Inpatient Enquiry. In this way perhaps we will get more active interest concerning what we are trying to do from the practising clinicians.

Then along came the Record Linkage Study in Oxford and I think the real parentage of that can be attributed jointly to Professor Leslie Witts and Dr Donald Acheson. Certainly they are the people who have pushed it hardest and brought it to the level where it is really beginning to give us some return now. I hope Acheson will forgive me if I describe it as a pretty primitive example of record linkage. I am sure he would accept that description of it in its present form. It is restricted of course to inpatients. Its greatest help so far, I think, has been in providing some detailed analyses of maternity work which ought to be extremely valuable to us in future planning.

The National Health Service since it first began, as everybody knows, has been subdivided into three parts and whenever anybody talks about our National Health Service almost the first thing they say is that the tripartite organization ought to be brought to an end. They are talking about the administration. What we really want is surely functional continuity and administration is intended to get round the difficulties in producing that. I would regard administrative continuity as a purely secondary object even if it becomes a necessary means. But the Record Linkage Study fully developed really does give us an opportunity of hastening the achievement of functional continuity. After all hospital work is only part of the

3

whole pattern of medical care and things like the Hospital Inpatient Enquiry only touch the fringe. We've got to look forward to a change from possessiveness about patients and secrecy about what happens in one phase of their treatment. It is absurd that there is not an exchange of information much more promptly and much more readily than now occurs. In future we have just got to have access to a continuous personal record. I know it is expensive. Nuffield generosity once more started this ; so often new developments have started in this way and Exchequer funds, as here, have followed on. Oxford Regional Hospital Board has been the sponsor of this particular scheme. It wouldn't have got off the ground if this Reginal Hospital Board hadn't been the leader, as so often, in thinking about what we do next with the hospital service.

We should really be extremely grateful in this country to Nuffield and to Leslie Witts and Donald Acheson for their pioneer work. I don't see that there is any need for further argument as to whether a complete system of linked records should be achieved—the argument really should only be about when we can achieve it. I believe that this Conference can carry us a long step forward in our thinking in this country to the achievement of that unity.

PART I

GENERAL SESSION I

Chairman : DR ALICE STEWART (Oxford)

PRODUCTS FROM THE EARLY STAGES IN THE DEVELOPMENT OF A SYSTEM OF LINKED RECORDS

HOWARD B. NEWCOMBE

NEARLY a decade has passed since the possibility of using computers to integrate, or 'link', health records from a variety of sources into personal and family histories on a large scale was first seriously discussed. It is perhaps timely, therefore, to ask what useful products have been derived so far, and what indications there are of the likely value in the near future of more extensive applications of the technology of record linkage.

For those who are interested primarily in the research uses of the medical and biological information contained in the various health records, it is necessary to remember that the custodians of the source files have as a primary responsibility either the production of routine statistics, the administration of schemes of health insurance and social welfare, or the maintenance of the files for legal purposes. In these circumstances it is natural that acceptance of proposals for changing the existing methods of file upkeep so as to facilitate linkage on any substantial scale is likely to depend upon the demonstration of benefits relating either to the existing recognized uses of the files, or to essentially new uses such as the extraction of data in quantity for research purposes. In the latter case, however, the responsible agencies are apt to ask if the research products will be worth the additional cost.

This poses a difficult problem for the investigator interested in making extensive use of the records, partly because he may not be used to making cost-value judgments, but more especially because pronouncements on the matter are unlikely to carry weight in the appropriate circles unless they come from officially constituted authorities, such as research councils or departments of health. There is also the inevitable question of whether the needs of research cannot be met in cheaper ways, as by the use of conventional, clerical methods of follow-up through visual and manual searches of the files in their present forms. Unfortunately, authoritative opinions on these matters are hard to come by, partly because experience with record linkage is still fairly limited, but even more because officially constituted authorities on matters of research have so far devoted only slight attention to the subject, and the results of their deliberations are for the most part not generally available for scrutiny and discussion.

7

In the account which follows I shall suggest a possible way out of this dilemma. The solution has less to do with assessment of the likely money value of the research products than with the multiplicity of uses of the files of health records that become possible when they are integrated into personal and family histories of events.

There is, for example, no reason to suppose that the present and future administrative needs are in fact adequately taken care of by the current methods of processing the records, which in most instances were designed before modern computers became available or at least before their capabilities were fully understood. Similarly, there is ample testimony to the effect that routine health statistics fall grossly short of meeting the recognized and important needs for which they are produced. Often this is not because the relevant facts have failed to be recorded, but is instead because of apparent difficulties of extracting the required information from the accumulated files.

The case which I shall make for linking and integrating various source records will be that better use can thereby be made of them, simultaneously, for administration, for demographic studies, for the provision of health statistics, and for research into the causes of ill health. To support this case I shall give examples of uses and potential uses of each of these kinds, based on work with vital and health records from the Canadian province of British Columbia. Since this study is still in its early stages, and since a quick return on any investment is always of special interest, the emphasis throughout will be on the early products of a linkage operation.

I shall start by mentioning briefly some of the more conspicious deficiencies in the utilization of routine records for the purposes of health statistics, administration, and research, where improvement is possible through integration and linkage of the source material.

Current deficiencies in health statistics

At least three major functions of a system of vital and health statistics are generally recognized, if one omits from consideration the commercial, demographic and administrative uses of the annual tabulations of births, deaths and marriages. The statistics should serve to indicate the health status of a population, to point to needs for programs of disease control, and to make possible the evaluation of the success and adequacy of such health measures as are instituted (United Nations, 1953).

Few would claim that current practices satisfy these requirements. In Canada, the recent Royal Commission on Health Services (1965) that successfully advocated legislation on 'medicare', deplored the mcagreness of the health statistics on which it had to base its recommendations. Its plea that better information on health matters would be needed in the future attracted unfortunately little comment, largely because of the more spectacular nature of the recommendations concerning services themselves.

A substantial section of the report dealt with specific deficiencies and the means for their correction. In particular, the Commission pointed to (a) a need to consolidate information from the various sources to derive better statistics on the incidence and prevalence of diseases ; (b) the importance of longitudinal studies of such conditions as tuberculosis, cancer, mental disease, and physical and mental handicaps, for which the causal factors may be widely separated in time from the full expressions of the diseases ; and (c) a need for information on the courses which various diseases run and on the prognoses under different circumstances. Throughout this section of the Report it was emphasized that the required data could often be obtained from existing records by linking those from a number of sources, derived at different times in the individual histories.

Specific examples will be mentioned later in connection with attempts to determine the frequency of congenital anomalies and to devise ways of detecting future changes in incidence such as occurred in the past at the time of the thalidomide incident.

In addition, an important deficiency that was mentioned only briefly by the Royal Commission exists because of a tendency to think of ill health as something apart from, and unrelated to, the other kinds of problems encountered by the same individuals. For example, Canada is currently engaged in a campaign against poverty and for this reason is seeking better socioeconomic statistics. And yet there has been no apparent move to investigate the extent to which poverty influences the risk of disease and the use made of health services.

At least three lines of evidence from British Columbia indicate that the effects of social and economic differences are large and important. The North American Indians make nearly twice as much use of the hospital services per capita as do the rest of the population. Our own linkage studies of the incidence of disease among illegitimate children indicate a substantial correlation which is almost certainly environmental in origin. And, non-specific associations of diseases have been found in different members of the same families that would be difficult to explain if they are not due to a greater tendency for the children of poorer homes to become ill. Currently, however, there are no statistics on the importance of poverty as a

9

predisposing factor, such as could be obtained by linkage of health records with others that describe the social and economic characteristics of the same people.

If we accept that disease is not an isolated phenomenon, statistics relevant to its social correlates could be derived from existing records, wherever the identifying information is adequate for linkage, treating either the individual or the family as the important unit. Many of these records are already partially transcribed into machine readable form, such as those of census enumerations, labour force surveys, unemployment insurance, delinquency, crime, and so on, and where changes in the identifying information are needed these would in most instances be minor.

This sort of ecological approach could be reflected in the early statistical products of a linkage operation. The possible impediments have little to do with the availability of the records, the technology of linkage, or the existence of appropriate mathematical procedures for multivariate analysis. Instead, the chief limiting factor is probably a traditional tendency when compiling health statistics to ignore the social variables, except perhaps as relating to occupation.

As the means for improvement of health statistics become available it is to be hoped that a changing attitude will demand a better understanding of the ecology of human health and disease.

Current deficiencies in the administrative uses of the source records

It might be thought, since many of the routine records are created primarily for administrative purposes, that little improvement in the administrative uses could result from changes in the methods of processing the files, such as would be needed for linkage on any substantial scale. In general, however, this is unlikely to be the case except where the upkeep and use of a file is already fully automated, where the file is entirely self-contained and the individual records do not require updating, or where no advantage would result from taking cognisance of repeat contacts with the same individuals.

Such circumstances are uncommon. Frequently there is a need to confirm certain facts such as those of birth, age, family composition, change of name at marriage, and dead-or-alive status, by reference to other files. This is true of the files kept by schools, passport authorities, immigration departments, insurance schemes, pension plans, and the authorities which administer schemes of family allowances, superannuation, old age pensions, and so on. Such operations commonly make use of the vital registrations, sometimes in a manner that pieces together parts of the individual and family histories, and for the most part they are carried out by

10

conventional clerical methods. Since the vital records of many countries have for some time been transcribed routinely into machine readable form for indexing and statistical purposes, this fact makes the substitution of machine methods for existing manual linkage relatively simple in a number of instances. The advantage for scientific purposes arises from the resulting more rapid access to the partial histories which these linked files contain.

Examples of possible financial savings and increased convenience through conversion to more modern methods of linkage with the vital records will be mentioned later.

Current deficiencies in the research uses of health records

A major deficiency in the current research uses of health records relates to the failure to extract from these records the information they frequently contain about related events that have occurred at different and often widely separated times in the lives of the same individuals. To illustrate the range of applications of the approach, examples have been chosen of a variety of studies that have made use of manual linkages of health records (Table I). These have dealt with such diverse topics as

— the consequence of cousin marriage,
— the effects of selection on stature, and on intelligence,
— correlation of the causes of death in husbands and wives,
— virus infections as causes of congenital malformations,
— prenatal irradiation as a cause of leukaemia,
— premarital conceptions as influencing the risk of divorce,
— descriptions of the patterns of inbreeding in human populations, and
— risks to relatives of persons with hereditary diseases.

The examples serve also to illustrate the practical limitation on the quantity of data that can be extracted where the linkages have to be carried out manually. The importance of this deficiency has to do, in part, with the difficulties of demonstrating statistically significant relationships where the data are limited. Less widely recognized, however, is the loss of insight into possible causal relationships where the data are too few to permit the effects of a number of variables to be examined simultaneously because not enough of the cells in a multiple cross tabulation are filled. For some of the above studies, for example, it might well have been important to show that the comparisons were not biased by population heterogeneities with respect to parental ages, birth rank, social circumstances and so on.

The refinements of a multivariate approach depend upon the

Table I. *Examples of manual linkage of information from two or more independently derived records concerning the same individuals*

	Nature of the study	Records linked	Information extracted	Reference
1.	Parental consanguinity	Catholic Church dispensations; Birth registrations; School records	Consanguinity; Birth weight; Intelligence scores	Slatis et al., 1961
2.	Parental consanguinity	Catholic Church dispensations; Conscription records	Consanguinity; Physical fitness	Barrai et al., 1960
3.	Selection for stature	Conscription records; City population register	Stature; Deaths of sibs	Cavalli-Sforza, 1959; Conterio et al., 1960
4.	Selection for intelligence	School records; Pedigree (from interviews)	Intelligence scores; Fertility	Higgins et al., 1962
5.	Mortality in spouses	Death registration—husbands; Death registration—wives	Cause, spouse; Cause, spouse	Ciocco, 1940
6.	Viruses and malformation	Sickness benefit; Maternity benefit	Virus infection; Malformations	Hill et al., 1958
7.	Radiation and leukaemia	Hospital (radiology); Hospital (maternity); Death registration	Pelvic irradiation; Maternity; Leukaemia (child)	Court Brown et al., 1960
8.	Divorce and premarital conception	Marriage registration; Birth registration	Date of marriage; Date of birth	Christensen, 1960
9.	Breeding structure	Family record (Koseki); Related family records	Family identification; Pedigree	Ohkura, 1960; Yanase, 1962; Moroni, 1962
10.	Breeding structure	Catholic Church dispensations; Parish registers of baptisms, marriages, deaths	Consanguinity; Vital events	
11.	Breeding structure	Mormon geneological records	Pedigrees	Woolf et al., 1956
12.	Disease inheritance	Genetic register (routine reports from physicians)	Diagnosis, pedigrees	Kemp, 1951
13.	Sibling risks, central nervous system defects	Birth registrations; Birth registrations of siblings	Diagnosis, family; Diagnosis	Milham, 1962

availability of an abundance of data. And these are unlikely to be obtained at reasonable costs for studies of the above kinds without resorting to automatic methods.

Products from linkages of British Columbia vital and health records

As examples of early products from the British Columbia linkage study I shall mention separately those from the compilations of individual histories, and those from histories of family groups. Both kinds of product will be treated briefly because they have already been reviewed elsewhere (Newcombe, 1967).

The personal histories were built up from records of births, registerable handicaps and deaths over the six year period 1953–58 during which there were about 35,000 births per year. Information on parental ages, birth orders and legitimacy from the birth records was thus linked with diagnostic information from the handicap and death records.

A number of correlations of the risks of various diseases with maternal age, paternal age and birth order have been demonstrated (Table II). Some of these are of possible genetic interest, and others appear to be indicative of socioeconomic influences on health. The occurrence of mongolism, which is a genetic condition, showed the expected strong correlation with age of mother. The risk of strabismus, or 'squint', on the other hand, was unexpectedly increased among children of higher birth ranks, independent of mother's age, indicating the influence of a hitherto unrecognized environmental cause ; this must act to reinforce an existing genetic predisposition, however, since the condition is also strongly clustered in family groups. The study also showed a curious correlation between deaths from respiratory disease and elevated paternal age. The increased risk could in this instance hardly be due to any accumulation of genetic changes, or mutations, in aging fathers, and confirmation that the correlation must be a product of social heterogeneities was obtained when it was shown largely to disappear where data for North American Indians and non-Indians are treated separately.

There is also evidence that unfavourable social circumstances can influence mortality well beyond the first year of life. Thus, there is a tenfold increase in the risk of death among children of high birth rank as compared with low, and the expressions of this effect do not become apparent until after the first week of life when the mother and child have returned home from hospital. Furthermore, the effect continues to be important in the period from the second to the sixth year (Fig. 1). Whatever social differences are responsible for the elevated risk of death in children of higher birth ranks, they do not

13

Table II. *Summary of special risks associated with birth order and parental ages. Data from British Colombia handicap and death records linked with birth records, and from stillbirth records* (From Newcombe, 1965 b.)

Disease category	Code	Total cases	Relative risk	χ^2 (DF = 1)
Firstborn children (vs. 2nd)				
(excluding maternal age effects)	760–776	58	2·16	10·6
Certain diseases of early infancy	760	123*	1·80	9·1
Intracranial and spinal injury at birth				
Higher birth orders (3rd and over vs. 1st and 2nd)				
(excluding maternal age effects)	001–138	146	1·76	9·9
Infective and parasitic diseases	384	285	1·58	11·7
Strabismus	753	175*	1·84	12·1
Other c.m. of nervous system and sense organs	762	773*	1·70	39·2
Postnatal asphyxia and atelectasis				
Children of very young mothers (0–19 vs. 20–24)				
(excluding birth orders effects)	400–716	58	2·44	8·6
Categories VI–XII	760	72*	2·19	9·6
Intracranial and spinal injury at birth	762	413*	1·66	15·4
Postnatal asphyxia and atelectasis				
Children of older mothers (35 and over vs. 0–34)				
(excluding birth order effects)	325·4	191	7·68	172·6
Mongolism	351	215	1·84	11·6
Cerebral palsy	754	868*	1·66	29·1
C.m. of circulatory system				
Children of older fathers (40–99 vs. 0–39)				
(excluding maternal age effects)	470–527	955*	1·61	17·8
Diseases of the respiratory system	750–759	1727*	1·28	9·1
Congenital malformation	135	753*	2·07	7·8
Other c.m. of nervous systems and sense organs				

* Includes cases ascertained through death and/or stillbirth records.

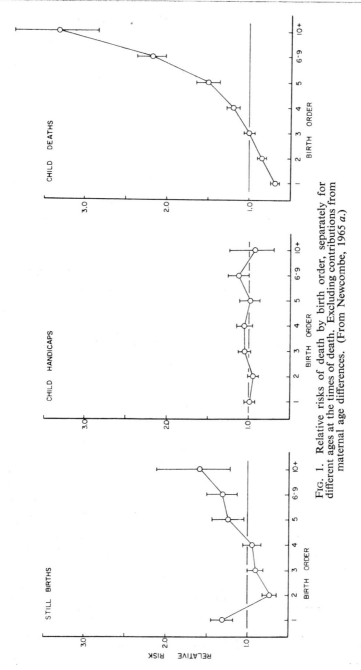

FIG. 1. Relative risks of death by birth order, separately for different ages at the times of death. Excluding contributions from maternal age differences. (From Newcombe, 1965 *a*.)

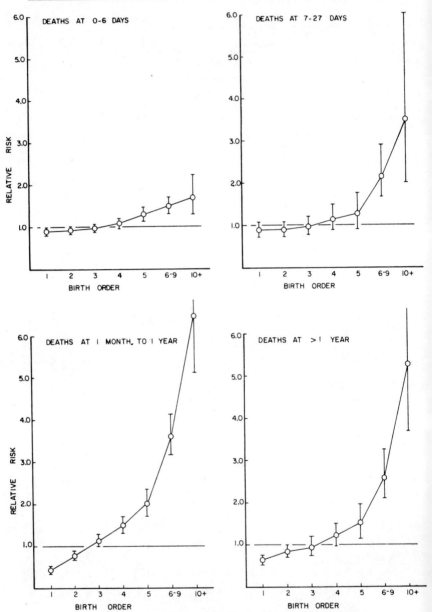

FIG. 2. Relative risks of stillbirth, handicap, and death, by birth order. Excluding contributions from maternal age differences. (From Newcombe, 1965 *a*.)

alter detectably the risk of registerable handicaps (Fig. 2) except of course in the special case of strabismus.

In addition to these observations there are unpublished data from the British Columbia study which likewise point to a large effect of social factors on the risk of death during childhood, and indicate a much smaller effect on the risk of handicapping conditions. A few years ago we were asked by the Department of Sociology of Sir George Williams University for statistics on the risk of death and of handicap among illegitimate as compared with legitimate children. Appropriate tabulations, broken down by birth order and maternal age, took only a few minutes of computer time using the files that had already been linked for the other studies. The illegitimate children showed a 70 to 80 per cent. increase in risk of death, and an increase in the risk of handicapping conditions of about one quarter of this percentage (Table III). Both effects remained after the

Table III. *Risks of handicaps and deaths among illegitimate as compared with legitimate children*

Ratio of illegitimate/legitimate children, among
liveborn (1955)	4,387/32,076
handicapped (1953–58)*	684/ 5,732
dead (1953–58)†	237/ 2,104

Relative incidence of illegitimacy
(no allowance made for differences in maternal age or birth order) among
handicapped/liveborn	$1\cdot14$ $(\chi^2 = 4\cdot2,\ P = \cdot03)$
dead/liveborn	$1\cdot82$ $(\chi^2 = 167,\ P < 1/10^6)$

Relative incidence of illegitimacy
(allowing for differences in maternal age and birth order) among
handicapped/liveborn	$1\cdot18$ $(\chi^2 = 7\cdot0,\ P = \cdot008)$
dead/liveborn	$1\cdot68$ $(\chi^2 = 112,\ P < 1/10^6)$

* Children born in 1953–58 and dying in the same period.
† Children born in 1953–58 and registered as handicapped by 1960.

removal of contributions from differences in maternal age and birth order, and both are statistically highly significant. The analysis was also carried out by computer using an existing program and likewise required only a matter of minutes. To have carried out the linkage and the analysis by hand would have been prohibitively laborious and expensive.

A further, quite small use of the linked files is worth noting. One of the recognized functions of a system of health statistics mentioned earlier is to provide evidence of the health status of the population. A special case of this function is represented by the emphasis, since the thalidomide incident, on the desirability of keeping track of the numbers of children born with congenital malformations. What has become increasingly apparent, however, is that no single kind of record is adequate for the purpose because a large proportion of anomalies fail to be detected and reported at the time of birth. Thus, the physicians' notices of births, which in Canada are separate from the birth registrations, provide very incomplete reporting.

Even where a number of sources of information are used to supplement one another, further cases may still be ascertained through yet another source. The register of handicapped children in British Columbia, for example, makes use of the physicians' notices and a variety of other sources to achieve a high level of ascertainment of congenital anomalies. Until recently, however, it has not been the custom to take note in the handicap register of malformations that are reported for the first time on the death certificate.

To determine how many of the malformations reported at the time of death had not been brought to the attention of the registry earlier, a small linkage study was carried out relating to the 31,746 live births and 375 stillbirths in the year 1953. The numbers of known cases of congenital malformations are given below:

— from the handicap registrations to
    1960   334

— from the stillbirth registrations   46

— from the death registrations to
    1959 (not registered as handicapped) 81

— total from all sources   461
    (= 14·4 per 1,000 total births)

Thus, inclusion of cases of congenital malformation from the death registrations increased the total by 21 per cent. (*i.e.* by 81/380).

Some of this increase may represent malformations of internal organs, detectable only at autopsy, but some could be indicative of oversights in the other source files. Just how many further cases might be ascertained through yet other record files such as those of Canada's scheme of universal hospital insurance, or of 'medicare' when this becomes operational, will not be known until records of congenital malformations from these sources have been linked into a common pool. It is doubtful whether sensitive means for detection of changes in the rate of occurrence of malformations can be set up in any other way.

The research products from the British Columbia Study have been concerned primarily however with family histories as distinct from individual histories. Over the past few years, data have been extracted from an integrated family file based on 10 years of marriages (1946–55), six years of births (1953–58) and the deaths and registered handicaps among these children. Currently, the files are being extended to cover a 20-year period (1946–65) and methods are being developed for linking the records into multi-generation pedigrees.

Examples of the early products from these family linkages include studies of *twins*, risks of disease in *siblings* of affected children, *maternal fertilities* following the births of children with various diseases, and a *demographic study* of the early productivity of a cohort of marriages.

Unpublished results from the twin studies have shown :

(*a*) elevated risks of stillbirths, handicaps and deaths among twins as compared with singletons,

(*b*) especially high risks among twin pairs of like sex as compared with those of opposite sex (Table IV), and

(*c*) a much stronger tendency for both members of a pair to be similarly affected when they are of like sex (Table V), this being true for all causes of disease studied with the notable exception of diseases peculiar to early infancy (Table VI).

Table IV. *Risks among twins* from like-sexed pairs as compared with opposite sexed pairs*

Events	Twins from		Relative risk (like/ opposite)
	Like sexed pairs	Opposite sexed pairs	
All twin born children . .	3,096	1,508	—
Stillbirth	106	33	1·59
Handicap only	87	28	1·46
Death only	273	119	1·08
Handicap and death . . .	19	5	1·79
Combined.	485	185	1·29

* Born in British Columbia 1953–58.

Differences in both the intrauterine environments and the hereditary influences are probably involved so that this sort of study has implications for epidemiology, genetics, and teratology.

Table V. *Risks to co-twins of stillborn, handicapped, and dead twins, among like sexed as compared with opposite sexed pairs*

Events	Like sexed prs. (concordant/ discordant)	Opposite sexed prs. (concordant/ discordant)	Relative risk (like/ opposite)
Stillbirth	21/64	1/31	10·2
Handicap only	12/56	1/33	7·1
Death only	74/125	33/53	1·0
All kinds of events* . . .	189/207	44/97	3·4

* *I.e.* treated as concordant even when members of a twin pair are affected by dissimilar events.

The present data on twins are too few to permit useful breakdowns by particular diseases but this deficiency can be readily repaired when more extensive files are linked.

Considerably larger amounts of information have been obtained concerning the risks of disease in brothers and sisters of 'affected' children. Geneticists have been interested in this sort of study from the beginning but have tended to confine themselves to those diseases that they believed in advance to be hereditary or partially so. We, on the other hand, were able to get data on all recorded diseases and groups of diseases, across the board, and to measure the strengths of the family associations regardless of the origins of the conditions (*e.g.* see Table VII).

A number of conclusions may be drawn from this study :

(*a*) Many conditions that are obviously environmental in origin show strong familial associations, which are presumably indicative of social influences on the risks of disease.

(*b*) Although particular malformations may tend to repeat in families, congenital malformations as a class are less likely to repeat in later born brothers and sisters of affected children than are any other broad category of disease for which we have adequate data.

(*c*) Even where a family has a case of a disease of a kind that is known to repeat, the increased risk to the later born brothers and sisters from stillbirths, deaths and handicaps due to other causes is generally at least as great as the risk from the disease in question. This last finding seems to indicate that some families are especially vulnerable to diseases of a wide variety of seemingly unrelated kinds.

Other examples of this sort of study might be mentioned. Unpublished data from the British Columbia files on the risk of repeat

Table VI. *Risks to co-twins of handicapped and dead children* (Data from Newcombe, 1966)

International code	Broad category of disease	Concordant/Discordant		Ratio like/opposite
		like sexed pairs	opposite sexed pairs	
001–138	Infective and parasitic diseases	1/2	0/2	
140–239	Neoplasms	0/6	0/5	
240–289	Allergic, endocrine, metabolic, etc. . .	0/1	0/2	
290–299	Blood and blood forming organs . .	0/0	0/0	
300–326	Mental, psychoneurotic, etc. . .	4/13	0/6	
330–398	Nervous system and sense organs . .	3/17	0/7	
400–468	Circulatory system	0/0	0/0	
470–527	Respiratory system . . .	1/16	0/7	
530–587	Digestive system	1/5	0/1	
590–637	Genito-urinary system . . .	0/1	0/0	
690–716	Skin and cellular tissue . . .	0/0	0/0	
720–749	Bones and organs of movement . .	2/7	0/7	
750–759	Congenital malformations . . .	4/44	0/14	
780–795	Symptoms and ill-defined conditions .	0/0	0/1	
800–999	Accidents, poisonings, and violence .	1/2	0/2	
Y30–Y39	Stillbirths, all causes . . .	21/61	1/29	
—	Other (except diseases of early infancy)	1/209	0/99	
	Combined	39/384	1/182	18·5
760–776	Diseases of early infancy . . .	68/88	32/34	0·8

Table VII. *Risks to later siblings of handicapped and dead children*

Internation code	Broad category of disease	Sibs affected/unaffected	Birth Population affected (vs 202,968 unaffected)	Relative Risk sibs/population
780–795	Symptoms and ill-defined conditions	1/27	27	192·8
240–289	Allergic, endocrine, metabolic, etc.	2/78	142	36·7
800–999	Accidents, poisonings, and violence	32/359	502	36·0
530–587	Digestive system	8/190	297	28·8
001–138	Infective and parasitic diseases	4/195	313	13·3
300–326	Mental, psychoneurotic, etc.	16/398	724	11·3
470–527	Respiratory system	40/715	1083	10·5
760–776	Diseases of early infancy	218/1399	3027	10·4
720–749	Bones and organs of movement	7/269	561	9·4
330–398	Nervous system and sense organs	20/538	962	7·8
140–239	Neoplasms	1/134	274	5·5
750–759	Congenital malformations	38/1044	2330	3·2
690–716	Skin and cellular tissue	0/39	54	...
400–468	Circulatory system	0/21	51	...
590–637	Genito-urinary system	0/23	40	...
290–299	Blood and blood forming organs	0/9	24	...
	Weighted mean relative risk			10·4

occurrences of stillbirths to mothers who have already had two stillborn children, were extracted in response to a request from the University of Michigan (Table VIII). Family clusters of central

Table VIII. *Risks to later siblings of stillborn children*

Following two stillbirths (35 later sibs observed)

Stillborn   5 = 14·3% ⎫
Handicapped   0 =   ⎬ 34·3%
Dead   7* = 20·0% ⎭

Following one stillbirth (1,265 later sibs observed)

Stillborn   85 = 6·7% ⎫
Handicapped   29 = 2·3% ⎬ 15·4%
Dead   81 = 6·4% ⎭

Among all births (217,795 live plus stillbirths)

Stillborn   2403 = 1·1% ⎫
Handicapped   3987 = 1·8% ⎬ 6·8%
Dead   8437 = 3·9% ⎭

* The causes of death following two stillbirths include international codes
    421   chronic endocarditis,
    493   pneumonia,
    752   hydrocephalus,
    762   postnatal asphyxia and atelectasis
           (two cases), and
    776   immaturity (two cases).

nervous system malformations have been studied in New York State, using manual linkages of their vital records, in a search for a possible tendency for adjacent birth ranks to be affected (Milham, 1962). The approach has been used also in California to investigate the familial nature of Hashimoto's disease as indicated by sibship groupings of hospital records (Masi, Sartwell and Shulman, 1964).

A further use of the British Columbia files has been to study the fertilities of mothers of children with hereditary diseases. Such information has long been of interest to geneticists as indicating the likely prevalence of the causal genes in the next generation. In particular, the study sought to find out whether mothers whose children died of erythroblastosis, or from various other kinds of early illnesses, tended to 'compensate' for their losses by having another child sooner than would have been expected in view of their ages and parities. The result differed with the different diseases, and need not be described here (Table IX). This is the first time that it has been possible to subject the widely held 'compensation theory' to a direct and simple test.

Table IX. *Under- and over-fertility following infant mortality and morbidity (measured over a 4-year period)* (From Newcombe, 1965 *b*, and Newcombe and Rhynas, 1962)

Condition	Cases*	Subsequent births		
		obs.	exp.	ratio
Stillbirths . . .	269	136	146·0	0·93
Erythroblastosis . .	52	22	22·1	0·99
Haemorrhagic disease .	29	14	14·0	1·00
Mongolism (living) .	118	45	35·4	1·27
Postnatal asphyxia .	97	111	66·0	1·68

* Stillbirths in 1953, and births in 1953–55 of children with other conditions.

A different kind of undertaking was a demographic study of the early productivity of a cohort of marriages, made possible by the inclusion of the marriage registrations in the family groups of records (Minet, 1964). It will be noted, for example, that the timings of the births of first children with respect to the marriages, and in particular the proportions of premarital conceptions, varies widely with the age of the mother (Fig. 3).

Demographic studies may provide one of the strongest and earliest reasons for extensive linkages of the vital records into family groups. There are a number of reasons for this. Detailed studies of the patterns of family formation cannot be carried out solely through the use of census enumerations because these commonly (*a*) lack information about the date of marriage, (*b*) fail to take account of stillbirths, (*c*) do not distinguish twins from pairs of siblings born in the same year, and (*d*) lack information about the deaths of children.

The unique advantages of linked vital records for such purposes were pointed out 17 years ago by the Statistical Committee of a British Royal Commission on Population (1950). They took the matter seriously enough to propose that the necessary linkages be carried out for the whole of Britain as a continuous clerical operation, indicating that 'It would be possible to study fertility with a thoroughness and detail which could never be achieved under the existing system'. The proposal was later dropped because it would have been a difficult undertaking using conventional manual procedures. Somewhat curiously, the published discussions make it clear that no one then foresaw that within seven or eight years the operation could be performed with reasonable rapidity by electronic computers, and that by a decade after that the speeds of these instruments would have increased as much as 5000-fold so that the cost and the time required for the linkage operation proper would have become almost trivial.

A small bonus to be had with the use of the vital records in this manner for fertility studies is worth mentioning. Canadian marriage registrations, and those of some other countries, record all three of

FIG. 3. Legitimate first births, by duration of marriage and maternal age. First marriages of the mothers. (From Minet, 1964.)

the religions associated with a marriage, namely those of the groom, the bride, and the officiating clergyman. These are fortunately entered also into the statistical punchcards. Until fertility data from the linked records become available it will be difficult to guess which of the three has the strongest influence on the patterns of family building and on the temporal changes in these patterns.

Other files that might be used to extend the individual and family histories

The experience with the linkages into individual and family histories has indicated other improvements in health data that could be achieved at little expense by simple extensions of the procedures already carried out. Of the files that could be used to supplement these histories, mention has already been made of those of the *hospital insurance* and *medicare* schemes. In addition, detailed information concerning the circumstances of deliveries, as indicating possible causes of disorders that do not develop until later, could be added from the *physicians' notices* of births, and details of migrations of families into and out of a province may be derived from a number of sources of which the family allowance *change-of-address* forms are the most readily available. A large part of the relevant information from most of these sources is already transcribed into machine language.

The merits and difficulties of using the Canadian hospital records are worth a few comments. The wealth of diagnostic information which the hospital insurance records contain may be illustrated by reference to the congenital malformations. Over the first year of life there are 15 discharges per 1000 children in British Columbia with a primary diagnosis of congenital malformation, and the corresponding figure over the first 10 years is 44 per 1000. It is not known to what extent these represent repeat hospitalizations of the same children, or to what extent the hospital files and those of the handicap registry overlap, but manual studies are in progress which will provide the answers. The studies have already served to establish, also, that the labour involved is sufficient to rule out any extensive use of the hospital records for such purposes except where electronic methods of linkage are employed.

There are calculations and tests to show, however, that the cost of mechanized integration of the hospital insurance records with those from other sources need not be great. Of an annual 300,000 hospital discharges in British Columbia, between 15,000 and 20,000 relate to children under age 15 who have conditions that may be regarded as of special interest. The cost of punching name cards for this number of events, to be joined up with the diagnostic information that is already on magnetic tape, should not greatly exceed $2,000 per year provided that manual, clerical steps in the operation are strictly avoided. This is in fact quite possible. Serial numbers for discharge of special interest can be derived by a computer scan of the existing magnetic tapes and supplied direct to the keypunch operators. The additional time required by the operators to find the records thus indicated would add only about 20 per cent. to the usual cost of keypunching. Tests have shown that this would be true for punching either from paper files or from microfilm images, provided the density of records actually used is in the vicinity of one in 30, or higher.

One current impediment to extensive use of the Canadian hospital insurance records after the fashion of the Oxford Record Linkage Study (Acheson and Barr, 1965) arises because in most provinces the schemes are not administered by health departments, and the insurance authorities have no statutory responsibilities for research except as it bears on the running of an efficient insurance scheme. A solution to this problem is currently being sought.

Opportunities offered by possible extensions of the British Columbia study

In addition to the products that have already been obtained from the linkages there are others that could readily be obtained at small cost in the near future. Mention has already been made of the possibility of improved ascertainment of congenital malformations, and I shall describe one other such application to illustrate the point.

It would be a simple matter to look for correlations between the risks of serious central nervous system defects, as reported to the British Columbia Registry of Handicapped Children and Adults, and various circumstances of the births as described in detail in the physicians' notices of births. Both sorts of records exist in punchcard form, both carry the birth registration number so that they can easily be linked to one another, and only a few thousand such linkages would need to be performed. A study of this general kind, linking obstetrical data to records of school performance has just recently been completed in Birmingham (J. H. Edwards, personal communication).

The amount of material available for study is substantial. According to the most recently published counts, the children 15 years of age or under who are known to be affected by cerebral palsy, epilepsy, and mental retardation, number 996, 837, and 3,133 respectively, or about 5,000 in all (British Columbia Registry, Annual Report, 1965). If impaired hearing, blindness and strabismus are also included the total becomes 7,862. The physicians' notices of births cover approximately 35,000 births per year from 1953 onwards, *i.e.* over half a million births to the present time.

A considerable part of the physicians' notice form is devoted to questions which have a bearing on the possibility of brain injury due to anoxia, mechanical manipulation during birth, jaundice, immaturity, and congenital malformation. The questions include :

1. weight
2. was resuscitation necessary
3. number of weeks' gestation

27

4. was the mother's blood tested for Rh (results available elsewhere by manual search)
5. was the labour spontaneous or induced
6. name of anaesthetic and/or sedative used
7. describe operative procedure
8. describe complications of pregnancy
9. describe any birth injury to child
10. describe any congenital malformation

The answers, because they are recorded at the time of the birth, will be unbiased by the later diagnoses of cerebral palsy, epilepsy, etc.

The numbers of cases are sufficient to make possible a multivariate approach with a view to distinguishing the separate contributions from the different recorded variables even where these are correlated with each other. Such a study would be based on nearly half a million pregnancies for which there are data concerning the deliveries. But the total cost would be trivial by comparison with even the *annual* budgets for similar investigations of more elaborate design being carried out elsewhere on very much smaller total birth populations.

Extensions of these family linkages of the British Columbia vital records to include various additional sources of diagnostic and other information would also be technically simple provided that appropriate identifying information is made available in machine readable form. The possible early products from the incorporation of hospital insurance records, medicare records, census enumerations, and so on are too numerous, and many of them too obvious, to be catalogued here. Instead, I shall describe as an example of this sort of thing a possible use of medical records of veterans from the armed services that would be of special interest to geneticists.

The relationships between fertility and normal variations of human characteristics have long been of interest as indicating the operation of selective forces which alter the hereditary endowments of future generations. Towards the end of World War II the results of medical examinations of new recruits were summarized in the form of so-called PULHEEMS scores, the word being an acronym for various body parts or functions, under the individual letters of which may be indicated numerically the states of fitness including mental ability and emotional stability. Taken as a whole the score gives a detailed picture of the suitability of the individual for various kinds of military service. In addition, recruits were all measured for uniforms. The bulk of the later conscripts would be young, unmarried men who subsequently returned to their home provinces, married, and raised families there.

When the vital records for British Columbia have been linked into family groupings back to 1946 there will be no great technical difficulty in linking the information about physical fitness and mental ability from the military records with the information about marriage and reproduction from the family groups of vital records. A few thousand such linkages would be sufficient to provide a wealth of data that could not be obtained in any other way.

Routine linkages that are already being carried out manually

Still further opportunities to obtain early products are provided by certain linkages of personal records that are already being carried out on a large scale by conventional clerical means, and which in the natural course of events will be automated anyway in the interests of economy. Examples of such operations include (a) the routine linkages of infant death records to birth records for statistical purposes ; (b) the registrations of handicapping conditions from a diversity of source records including physicians' notices of births, public health nurses' reports, and records of voluntary health societies, private physicians, and so on ; and (c) the verifications of statements made on the application forms for a universal scheme of family and youth allowances paid to all mothers from the time their children are born until they reach age 19.

Not only does the mother's statement that there has been a birth have to be verified by comparison with a listing of registered births derived from the birth index punchcards, but the fact of death of a child is also verified by manual linkage with the files of death registrations. Thus the family allowance administration duplicates, and extends, the death-to-birth linkages that are being carried out elsewhere to derive statistics on infant mortality.

In fact, the manual linkages of the family allowance files with the vital records system do more than produce individual histories of birth and death ; they serve also to establish family composition in the form of histories of birth and death within sibship groups.

Multiple uses of family groupings of vital arecords

The potential multiplicity of uses for linked files of vital and health records has been emphasized earlier as providing the most generally acceptable case for embarking on a substantial linkage operation. To illustrate the point I shall summarize briefly some of the administrative, demographic, and statistical uses, in a Canadian setting, of an integrated family file which would contain initially just the vital records but could later be expanded to include other health records.

In its early stages such a linked file could provide :

(a) mechanized verifications of family compositions for the family allowance administration, which currently uses manual methods of linkage,

(b) verifications of ages, changes of name at marriage, and dead-or-alive status, for the central index of social insurance numbers and for Canada's portable pension plan,

(c) automation of the current manual linakges of infant death records with birth registrations for statistical purposes, and possible extensions of these statistical uses,

(d) demographic data on fertility and the patterns of family building, of kinds not obtainable from the census enumerations above.

The list is by no means exhaustive, because a large number of other agencies already make use of information from the vital records system, or could profitably do so if the mechanics of access to it were simpler ; possible examples include the department of immigration, passport authorities, school systems, electoral offices, welfare schemes and so on.

Later, with the inclusion of other records containing diagnostic information the linked files could provide

(e) health statistics in the form of unduplicated counts of the numbers of people making use of the various health services, and the extents of these uses,

(f) statistics on the courses run by the chronic diseases and the prognosis at various stages,

(g) nearly complete ascertainment of cases of particular diseases for special registers of handicapping conditions, cancer, diabetes, and other conditions of special interest, for purposes of rehabilitation, and for schemes of surveillance, and

(h) data for epidemiological and genetic studies of the environmental and hereditary factors contributing to disease, including such social phemomena as poverty.

The critical requirement, if the potential value of the health records is to be realized in practice, is that the initial linkage scheme be capable of justifying its existence on a continuing basis. One proposal that is currently receiving serious consideration in Canada is that the vital records be linked into family groups, initially for the purpose of demographic studies. The currently estimated costs of such an undertaking do not appear large, and if the initial purpose can justify continuation of the operation without becoming its only objective the rest should follow.

National Health statistics versus specialized research

Those responsible for maintaining the source files may well attach greater weight to the potential usefulness of record linkages for the variety of recognized purposes served by a national system of health statistics, than as relating to the seemingly more specialized research applications. For this reason it is worth considering briefly how great the need is for health statistics of the kinds which linkage can provide.

In the past, when highly lethal epidemic diseases represented the most serious source of concern for the health of a community, annual tabulations of causes of death provided a good indication of the state of health of the population and of the needs for special measures of disease control. Today, with the shift in emphasis in the direction of the chronic diseases, no single set of records is sufficient to provide a parallel kind of statistics that deals in a similar manner with simple counts of the numbers of seriously affected people. The problem is generally recognized (Sullivan, 1966), but the currently accepted solutions based on survey techniques are particularly unsuitable as applied to the chronic diseases. Thus, a disease that becomes severe only during the latter part of its course will fail to be counted in an individual if the survey is conducted too early, or after the person is already dead.

There is no special difficulty in imagining how simple counts of chronic diseases might be derived if the source files were integrated to yield individual histories of illnesses to the time of death. For example, tables of cumulative risks of serious illnesses to various ages could be regarded as closely analogous to cumulative risks of death and, more important, they would provide in the same manner simple and readily interpretable indicators of the state of health of the population and of sub-groups within the population.

The same histories could likewise provide information on the extents of the uses by different people over a period of time of such health services as 'medicare' and hospital insurance, and measures of the successfulness of the treatments received in terms of the needs for repeated medical attention or hospitalization and the risks of subsequent deaths.

The competing alternative to this seemingly simple-minded approach is the unsatisfactory one of accepting instead the statistics that can be drawn most directly from the operational records, that is with a minimum of manipulation and processing. A good example of this is the tabulation of hospital admissions and of the lengths of stay in hospital, without regard to the number of people involved or their subsequent fates when they leave.

31

There seems, in fact, to be a real danger that for national health statistics we may come to accept as important the tabulations that are most readily obtained but least readily interpreted. And we may question the value of those kinds of data that require for their production new patterns of organization of the source records, but that bear more directly on the recognized bread-and-butter uses of a health statistics system.

REFERENCES

ACHESON, E. D. & BARR, A. (1965). Multiple spells of in-patient treatment in a calendar year. *Br. J. prev. soc. Med.* **19**, 182–191.

BARRAI, I., CAVALLI-SFORZA, L. L. & MAINARDI, M. (1960). Studio pilote per determinazione degli effetti della consanguineita su caratem esaminati alla visitada di leva. *Atti Riun. scient. Ass. genet. ital.* pp. 1–14.

British Columbia Registry for Handicapped Children and Adults (1965). Annual Report, Special Report No. 92. Division of Vital Statistics, Health Branch, Victoria, British Columbia.

CAVALLI-SFORZA, L. L. (1962). Demographic attacks on genetic problems. In. *The Use of Vital and Health Statistics for Genetic and Radiation Studies*, pp. 221–232. United Nations Publications, Sales No. 61, XVII, 8, New York.

CHRISTENSEN, H. T. (1960). Cultural relativism and premarital sex nouns. *Am. sociol. Rev.* **25**, 31–39.

CIOCCO, A. (1940). On mortality in husbands and wives. *Hum. Biol.* **12**, 508–531.

CONTERIO, F. & CAVALLI-SFORZA, L. L. (1960). Selezione per carretteri quantitativi, nell'uomo. *Atti Riun. scient. Ass. genet. ital.* pp. 294–304.

COURT BROWN, W. M., DOLL, R. & HILL, R. B. (1960). Incidence of leukaemia after exposure to diagnostic radiation *in utero. Br. med. J.* **2**, 1539–1545.

HIGGINS, J. V., REED, E. W. & REED, S. C. (1962). Intelligence and family size : a paradox resolved. *Eugen. Q.*, **9**, 84–90.

HILL, A. B., DOLL, R., GALLOWAY, T. McL. & HUGHES, J. P. W. (1958). Virus diseases in pregnancy and congenital defects. *Br. J. prev. soc. Med.*, **12**, 1–7.

KEMP, T. (1951). *Genetics and Disease.* Edinburgh: Oliver and Boyd.

MASI, A. T., SARTWELL, P. E. & SHULMAN, L. E. (1964). The use of record linkage to determine familial occurrence of disease from hospital records (Hashimoto's disease). *Am. J. publ. Hlth.* **54**, 1887–1894.

MILHAM, S. (1962). Increased incidence of anencephalus and spina bifida in siblings of affected cases. *Science*, **138**, 593–594.

MINET, P. (1964). Fertilité precocé d'une cohorte de marriages dans une province canadienne. *Acta genet. Statist. med.*, **14**, 186–196.

MORONI, A. (1962). Sources, reliability and usefulness of consanguinity data, with special reference to Catholic records. In *The Use of Vital and Health Statistics for Genetic and Radiation Studies*. United Nations Publications, Sales No. 61, XVIII, 8, New York.

NEWCOMBE, H. B. (1965 a). Environmental versus genetic interpretations of birth order effects. *Eugen. Q.*, **12**, 90–101.

NEWCOMBE, H. B. (1965 b). The study of mutation and selection in human'populations. *Eugen. Rev.* **57**, 109–125.

NEWCOMBE, H. B. (1966). Familial tendencies in diseases of children. *Br. J. prev. soc. Med.* **20**, 49–57.

NEWCOMBE, H. B. (1967). Present state and long-term objectives of the British Columbia population study. In *Proceedings of the Third International Congress of Human Genetics*, 291–313, Baltimore : Johns Hopkins Press.

NEWCOMBE, H. B. & RHYNAS, P. O. W. (1962). Child spacing following stillbirth and infant death. *Eugen. Q.*, **9**, 25–35.

OHKURA, K. (1960). Use of family registration in the study of human genetics in Japan. *Jap. J. hum. Genet.* **5**, 61–68.
Royal Commission on Health Services, Vol. II (1965). Ottawa : Queen's Printer.
Royal Commission on Population. Vol. II (1950). *Reports and Selected Papers of the Statistics Committee*, London : H. M. Stationery Office.
SLATIS, H. M., REIS, R. H. & HOENE, R. E. (1958). Consanguineous marriages in the Chicago region. *Am. J. hum. Genet.*, **10**, 446–464.
SULLIVAN, DANIEL F. (1966). Conceptual problems in developing an index of health. Vital and Health Statistics. P.H.S. Publication No. 1000, Series 2, No. 17. Washington, D.C. : U.S. Gov. Printing Office.
United Nations (1953). *Principles of a Vital Statistics System.* New York : United Nations.
WOOLF, C. M., STEPHENS, F. E., MULAIK, D. D. & GILBERT, R. E. (1956). An investigation of the frequencies of consanguineous marriages among the Mormons and their relatives in the United States. *Am. J. hum. Genet.*, **8**, 236–252.
YANASE, Y. (1962). Use of the Japanese family register for genetic studies. In *The Use of Vital and Health Statistics for Genetic and Radiation Studies.* United Nations Publications, Sales No. 61, XVII, 8, New York.

DISCUSSION

Dr Acheson : I would like to ask Dr Newcombe a question about the Handicapped Children's Register of British Columbia. I am intrigued by the association which he has found between strabismus and other abnormalities in members of the same family. I would like to ask him whether there is any question of a systematic bias entering into this material ; whether if one member of a family is registered with the Handicapped Register there is a greater chance of another member being registered than a member of another family.

Dr Newcombe : This question ought perhaps to be directed to Mr Doughty who is here and who runs the Handicapped Register, but I would like to make just one comment on it. It is certainly true of the non-lethal conditions that where one member of a family has been brought to the attention of the health services another one who is also affected may stand a better chance of also coming to their attention. But we get similar correlations with lethal conditions, and we certainly hope that when one member of a family dies and becomes known to the health services that this knowledge does not make the other one more likely to die also.

Dr Adelstein : I want to ask Dr Newcombe if the effect of later birth on squint is dependent on social class because this itself has a great effect.

Dr Newcombe : We would like to test for such an effect. The occupation of father has in the past been on the birth record although it has never been entered on the federal statistical punch cards. Recently, however, there has been a federal-provincial committee

D

which has decided to leave it off the registration forms. This was a matter of some regret to myself. The reasoning was that better statistics on occupation could be derived from other sources, but of course it then couldn't readily be linked with the diagnostic information. The source of the information is drying up just as we might have made use of it.

Dr Bahn : What access to your research data bank do university and other research investigators have who are not concerned directly with the maintenance of the system?

Dr Newcombe : The matter of confidentiality was handled in a special way. We were sworn in under the Vital Statistics Act in the same fashion as the provincial and federal people who handle the records routinely. It was a special arrangement which has not been extended to other groups. Thus the personal information has remained confidential. The statistical information, however, has not been confidential. We have had various visiting workers who have been sworn in and have worked with us as attached staff. They have extracted statistical information and we have always sent copies of this to both the Dominion Bureau of Statistics and the Provincial Health Department—the records belong to the Health Department—so that they would know exactly what these workers were using the files for. Such people have gone away with tables in their pockets but not personal information.

A CENTRALIZED NATION-WIDE PATIENT DATA SYSTEM

C. B. COPE

AN attempt will be made to describe the storage and retrieval of medical record data, past, present and planned, of a large executive agency of the United States government. This agency is charged with administering a diverse benefits programme for United States' veterans, of whom there are 26 million. This number increases enormously to 94 million if immediate dependents and surviving relatives are included.

In the medical care area on any given day there may be in excess of 120,000 patients in its 165 hospitals. In a given year there may be as many as 5 million visits to its 202 outpatient clinics and another 1·2 million to authorized private physicians. In addition there are domiciliaries, restoration centres, nursing care units, and contract beds in non-agency institutions. In a single year there may be as many as 30,000 post-mortems completed in the hospitals of the Veterans Administration, a total that rivals the number performed by the renowned Rokitansky during his lifetime.

An efficient medical record keeping system is therefore not only desirable but essential. It must be functionally oriented, reflect the system's intent, and permit facility of access and egress. In addition it must honour the requirements of user acceptability, flexibility to receive modifications and reliability of information content.

At this point I will pose very briefly a few searching questions. Why are we attempting to collect a mountain of data? Are we in the same position as the mountain climber when confronted with an analogous question? Are we merely collecting data for data-collection's sake or, as one discerning commentor has put it, because it is the 'neurotic thing to do'? Perhaps if the question is reoriented or rather rephrased, one may ask for what purposes are data in the clinical records used. Each user will state his special interest in the matter but a system's designer unfortunately cannot afford such luxury. He must honour all recognizable requirements in so far as his available resources will permit and integrate them into a practical, functional system observing sound economic practice. The following are four of the principal fields in which data about patients are used : (1) care of the individual patient, (2) teaching, (3) research and (4) administrative management. In addition it is necessary that they should satisfy legal requirements and third-party inquiries, such as those of insurance groups and accreditation bodies.

The linkage of records of the individual patient has evolved through a number of stages. In the distant past, the patient's name was the principal parameter by which successive or relevant records were identified. At one time in our own system a different hospital number was assigned for every admission of the same patient. This eventually gave way to a relatively permanent unit number which was peculiar only to one hospital. At the regional or national level of record keeping an eight-digit claim number (C. No.) identified each beneficiary. The C. No. permitted cross reference of the individual's records. The social security number (SSN), assigned by another governmental agency, is now replacing the previous numerical identifiers in interrelating records for all administrative and medical purposes. Because of anticipated difficulties both the C. No. and SSN will continue to identify all records until the transition period has been successfully completed.

The ADP number, although specific for an individual at a given time, may be assigned at a later date to another. It is a convenient

35

and often necessary symbol permitting greater operational efficiency by the data processor.

May I point out that once the data are machine-coded for input and the record fields properly identified, which is standard operating procedure in automatic data processing, the records can be interrelated for any field of interest. They can be individual-linked, age-linked, diagnosis-linked, procedure-linked or community-linked.

The remainder of this paper will refer to two national files that contain machine assimilable, medically relevant data about individual patients : The Patient Treatment File (PTF) and the Compensation and Pension File (CPF).

The CPF is concerned with recording information about individuals who receive compensation for their medical disabilities. In 1966 there were two million veterans receiving compensation for disabilities incurred in or aggravated by military service and 1·2 million receiving pensions for non-service connected infirmities.

The file itself consists of seven basic ADP records varying from 35 to 90 characters each and dealing with a variety of subject matter including vital statistics, functional loss, clinical aetiologies, and transaction records. Disability designations mirror functional limitations of members, organs or systems. The classification is designed in such a way that a group of clinical conditions can be compounded into a single coded four-digit integer.

The PTF consists of three on-going systems, each operating virtually independently and each satisfying requirements not satisfied by the others. These will eventually be merged into a single integrated system with a greatly expanded data base and elimination of overlapping data.

The Inpatient Discharge Data System (IDDS) is the largest PTF component and contains a record on every inpatient hospitalization. It is generated on discharge of the patient and consists of summary information relative to his identity, as well as demographic, clinical and statistical data. The clinical record serves as the source document for the preparation of formalized code sheets which are converted locally to machine acceptable input. These are forwarded to a centrally located digital computer where they are subjected to editing and error detecting routines. Invalid records are returned to the originating institution for correction. All valid records are submitted to further processing including additional computations.

The Annual Census is taken during the latter part of the year and up to the present time has been based on a 40 per cent. sample of inpatients. A 20 per cent. sample will be used for the 1967 Census. It is more than a census in that more information than is required for a simple enumeration of patients is obtained. It includes information about topics to which the attention of the profession, public, or management, has been directed. It may, for example, request data concerning schemes of treatment, abuse of drugs, etc.

The third component, the Longitudinal File, was begun in 1957. Although it was originally intended as a 10-year study, it will undoubtedly be extended until the total PTF is unified. The file's data are individually oriented and all inpatient treatment episodes are listed in temporal sequence. The file is based on samples derived from the terminal digit of a patient's identifying number, those patients whose numbers end in the digits one and five being included. The IDDS contributes and accounts for a significant amount of its data. Other independent sources also contribute to it. The data have been or will be used in cohort studies related to the study of admission rates, length of stay, diagnostic relationships, effect of treatment, etc.

Recently an attempt has been made to extend significantly the data recorded in the PTF. Five segments have been included :

Admission, Diagnostic, Surgical, Disposition and Turnaround. Amongst other things the admission diagnoses are converted into two digit recodes and entered into the Admission Segment. The operative procedure(s), surgical specialty involved, anaesthetic technique, and identity of the surgeon are included in the Surgical Segment. Data relevant to the patient's disposition (income source, monthly amount, manner of disposal, level of self care, ambulation, and mental status, etc.) are summarized in the Disposition Segment. These have been tested and the results are now under evaluation by management as to acceptance, revision and/or modifications.

So much for the past and the present. What of the future? The data base will be progressively expanded to include more fields. Duplication in the current files will be eliminated when possible. Frequent, periodic evaluation of the content of the data fields as to validity and effective use in clinical or administrative management is a *sine qua non*. It is planned to generate each record on admission to the hospital rather than at disposition. Eventually the bulk of all data will be entered in real time to an online digital computer located regionally.

Some of the current needs and problems of those involved in data processing in the medical field are listed below :

1. An increase in computer capabilities, in respect both of hardware and software, of several orders of magnitude. In addition to

massive on-line memories, there is a need for more adaptable input/ output devices, universal terminals, that are poly-functional and psychologically acceptable.

2. More interest and willing participation in the evolution of these information systems is required from the users and intermediaries.

3. Objective criteria are needed with which to evaluate the subject matter of data fields.

4. We need a discipline-oriented computer language which out-performs the present procedural or problem-oriented languages and omits the infinite detail required for knowledge of machine language itself.

In conclusion, we are grappling with the complex problem of developing an effective information and retrieval system based on medical records. The data base will be progressively expanded with each subject data field being frequently reviewed and evaluated for its usefulness. Fields of doubtful usefulness will be dropped and re-placed by those likely to be more meaningful.

DISCUSSION

Dr Mosbech : There is one question in which I am interested. How are these files used at the moment? Is any form of publication made? Is there any feedback to the hospital and the institution which give this information?

Dr Cope : At present these files are used principally for the preparation of statistical data for many agencies, departments and legislative bodies in the nation. The clinical investigator in the field uses them mostly as a case-locator, since the superficial nature of the data is such that any conclusions drawn from their immediate manipulation would be risky. The research worker has the option, however, of going to the field and getting the complete record and in those institutions having microfilming equipment he can have the complete case histories sent directly to him for permanent use. We have no formal feedback mechanisms although this is certainly one of the avenues that will have to be explored. We do get requests from State agencies but principally for listings of individuals with a minimum of collateral information. We have no feedback from them as a rule.

Dr Bahn : I would like to ask Dr Cope if he has any comments about his experience with the transition from the various case numbers and claim numbers previously in use to the social security number and also whether he plans to include outpatient information on his longitudinal files.

Dr Cope : Transition from one numbering system to another always presents difficulties. If one remembers that many of these files have an economic relationship to the individual beneficiary, you can well imagine that we are preserving both numbers (C. No. and SSN) until this transitional period is an avowed success. We expect to include outpatient clinic data in the Patient Treatment file, which will be a conglomerate of the three files mentioned in my paper. However one can also predict that it will be a tremendous job to include this information in any depth. We have estimated, on the basis of past experience, that records of 500 Holerith characters or their equivalent would require 150 magnetic tapes.

Dr Acheson : I had the pleasure of working at the Veterans Administration (V.A.) in Washington in 1959, and when Sir George Godber was talking about the progenitors of the Record Linkage Study he should have mentioned the records system of the Veterans Administration. At that time the V.A. was far ahead in the field of large scale medical data processing, and it has made further rapid progress. There is one point in particular from which we can learn in this country. As Dr Cope says, in the last 18 months the Veterans Administration abandoned a carefully prepared personal identification number universally used in that department, in favour of a national number, the social security number of the United States. I think this was a remarkable administrative decision as it must have involved considerable inconvenience and expense in the short term with the Administration, in the general interest.

Dr Newhouse : May I ask Dr Cope who is financing him? Is his research a Federal project from Washington or V.A., or an independent research group?

Dr Cope : Our funds come indirectly from the taxpayer.

Dr Mosbech : I notice that you include the diagnosis on admission in your national file. I wonder what use could be made of that in view of the fact that the diagnoses made at admission are often found later to be incorrect?

Dr Cope : Our regulations specify that if there is a change from the admission diagnosis, whether it becomes more specific or more general than what had been included on the admission sheet, it must be reported within an arbitrary period so that it can be entered on our record.

Dr Bahn : Because you are dealing with such large masses of data, you must have problems of quality. How do you handle this?

Dr Cope : Our problems are more horrible than one can possibly imagine. At the ward level we use the Standard Nomenclature for Disease and Operations sponsored by the A.M.A. but not revised since 1961. As soon as a diagnosis reaches the level of the record custodian it is converted to the International Classification of Diseases so that it can be assimilated by other statistical groups in Washington and locally. In this process information is lost. For example, a clinical investigator recently asked for a listing of all cases of Kleinfelter's syndrome. By the time this diagnosis gets into the files it is unceremoniously lumped into category 9 (the classifier's paradise, and the retriever's nightmare), and is classified under 'polyglandular syndromes and other diseases of endocrine glands'. Luckily, based on our estimate, there are only 128 entries in this category, so we should not have too much of a problem in retrieving the information manually.

THE OXFORD RECORD LINKAGE STUDY
THE FIRST FIVE YEARS

E. D. ACHESON

RECORD linkage is concerned with integration of data about people, families and communities (Acheson, 1967). As far as medicine is concerned it is based on the following elementary premises : that the past medical experiences of a person may be relevant to his present situation ; that the experience of his brothers or sisters may be relevant to his own ; and that when we are considering an event such as birth, or the diagnosis of tuberculosis or carcinoma of the cervix, there are advantages in assembling all the data for the community regardless of which clinic, authority or hospital is responsible for it.

The basic ideas underlying record linkage are not new (Farr, 1861 ; Stocks, 1944). What is new is that a practical attempt should be made to assemble, as an outgoing operation, selected medical data from a population prospectively and to arrange it with the person, the family and the community rather than different classes of event as the working units.

In this area, thanks to a generous grant from the Nuffield Foundation, we started to collect data and assemble them along these lines on 1st January 1962. The population covered by the study was originally that of Oxford City, and Oxfordshire (1962–64) but now includes Reading and much of Berkshire, and consists of about

750,000 people, including 57 hospitals and four public health authorities (Fig. 1).

For this population we collect elementary data concerning each birth, each obstetric delivery (whether at home or in hospital), each discharge from hospital, and each death. An abstract relating to each event is coded, punched on cards, and read on to magnetic tape. At this point each new record is compared with the master file to determine whether it relates to a person already known to the study or a new person, the existing magnetic tape record being updated

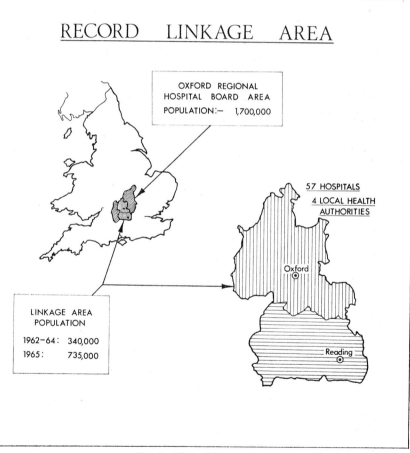

RECORD   LINKAGE   AREA

OXFORD REGIONAL
HOSPITAL BOARD AREA
POPULATION:— 1,700,000

57 HOSPITALS
4 LOCAL HEALTH
AUTHORITIES

Oxford

LINKAGE AREA
POPULATION

1962–64 : 340,000
1965 : 735,000

Reading

FIG. 1. Map of the area.

or a new file being created as is appropriate. The techniques used at present are described in more detail in Mr M. Hubbard's paper (p. 157).

In the space remaining to me I cannot hope to deal adequately with all the different types of output from the files. My colleagues, Dr A. S. Fairbairn and Dr M. S. T. Hobbs describe two projects illustrating applications of personal and family record linkage on pages 215 and 358 respectively.

Studies have been published on the epidemiology of self-poisoning in the Oxford Area (Evans, 1967) ; the relationship of sex ratio to the incidence of bleeding in pregnancy (Hobbs and Acheson, 1966 a) and comparisons between the diagnoses on death certificates and on hospital inpatient summaries (Alderson & Meade, 1967).

In all of these projects personal, family or community record linkage was involved to a greater or lesser degree. In some, all the data used came from the study's files. In others the files were either used as a starting point for a field study or provided follow-up data for an *ad hoc* survey commenced in the field.

If a project carried out on the scale of the Oxford Record Linkage Study is to justify a permanent place for itself or merit extension, it must provide in addition to research material assistance to the medical community in the familiar day-to-day problems met with in planning and running a Health Service. I will devote the remainder of this paper to a consideration of some of the operational and service applications of the material.

In a detailed analysis of the obstetric services in this area, my colleague Dr M. S. T. Hobbs uncovered striking differences in the proportions of mothers having their first baby selected for delivery in fully equipped obstetric units in the two principal cities in the area (Fig. 2). In City A 80 per cent. of the primigravidae are selected for confinement in consultant units while in City B only 18 per cent. are selected for this type of care. Conversely the proportion of primigravidae who require emergency transfer in late pregnancy or labour is 20 per cent. in City B and 2 per cent. in City A. These figures came as a surprise to the authorities concerned because of the way in which the responsibility (and therefore the data) for the domiciliary and hospital services in obstetrics are split in this country. No manipulation of the conventional material available to either party could have yielded these findings. Hobbs has also shown that in the Oxford area small maternity homes without equipment for Caesarean section, blood transfusion, etc. are sometimes used for risky cases (Hobbs and Acheson, 1966 b). Both these results are influencing the planning of the maternity services.

Health Services are inclined to be divided administratively into more or less watertight compartments between which communications may be poor. From its very nature a system of linked records

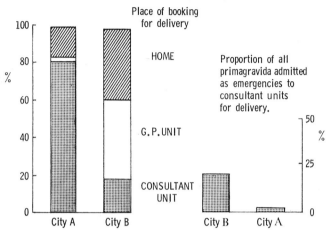

ARRANGEMENT OF OBSTETRIC CARE FOR PRIMAGRAVIDA IN TWO CITIES IN THE O.R.L.S. AREA

FIG. 2. Booking and emergency transfer patterns for the care of primigravidae in two cities within the area.

provides a means whereby such communications may be improved. Mr M. Hubbard has developed a computer programme which reports to the hospitals in our area the names, dates of death, and coded causes of death of persons who have died after being discharged home or transferred to another hospital. To our astonishment (and that of the hospitals) we found that only one-third of all deaths occurring within two years of discharge had been recorded in the hospital notes. Further, only one-half of the deaths occurring within *one month* of discharge were recorded in the hospital notes (Fig. 3). We hope soon to survey a sample of these unrecorded deaths and to classify them from the point of view of the hospital clinician into cases which are

1. irrelevant, or

2. inevitable (and no doubt these two categories will constitute the majority) or

3. clinically relevant to the diagnosis, treatment, or prognosis reached in the hospital concerned.

The provision of these listings is to become a regular service.

43

In this country many local Medical Officers of Health maintain Registers of babies born in their area who require special surveillance because of immaturity, or for some other reason. I am not concerned with the merits of those Registers which are controversial but rather with their mechanics, which can be used to illustrate a general principle. The data necessary to define these groups have to be collected laboriously from many sources. For us, it is simple to provide such listings mechanically and we are currently experimenting

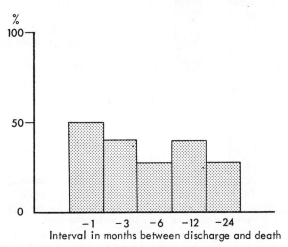

FIG. 3. Proportions of deaths taking place within two years of discharge from hospital, by interval between discharge and death.

with lists which select babies on the basis of birthweight, means of delivery, presence of foetal anoxia, etc., for two local Medical Officers of Health, omitting babies who died in the first week of life. This is an example of an application which comes close to providing a direct service to the patient. The principle could be extended to the definition of groups especially at risk in adult life requiring medical surveillance.

To plan services and to operate them efficiently various other types of feedback are needed some of which require linked and some unlinked data. For example we supply data about carcinoma of the cervix to the Medical Director of the local Cytological Laboratory to check against his positive and negative screening test results : we also supply information about cases of non-pulmonary tuberculosis to the local Medical Officer of Health to check against the statutory notification which he should have received. Here again we have been able to help with a problem which had not been recognized ; our experience shows that a substantial proportion of cases of non-pulmonary tuberculosis had not been notified. This is now a standard service. We also provide local hospitals and physicians and surgeons with elementary statistics about their work ; diagnostic and operations indices, and so on.

The provision of accurate estimates of the load of sickness due to chronic disease is one of the principal contemporary problems in medical statistics. At present the study is limited to dealing with diseases which generally cause admission to hospital. Nevertheless it can make a contribution to morbidity statistics. Mrs Sheelagh Watts has written a programme which counts a patient only once in any one year for any one diagnosis no matter how many times he is admitted to the same or different hospitals with the same complaint. Figure 4 shows a piece of the tabulation dealing with discharges

MORBIDITY ANALYSIS LISTING FOR 1963 IN
OXFORD RECORD LINKAGE STUDY AREA
(EXCLUDING OXFORD CITY)

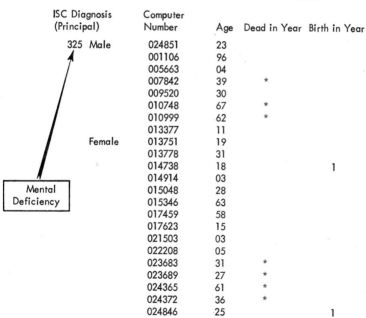

ISC Diagnosis (Principal)	Computer Number	Age	Dead in Year	Birth in Year
325 Male	024851	23		
	001106	96		
	005663	04		
	007842	39	*	
	009520	30		
	010748	67	*	
	010999	62	*	
	013377	11		
Female	013751	19		
	013778	31		
	014738	18		1
	014914	03		
	015048	28		
	015346	63		
	017459	58		
	017623	15		
	021503	03		
	022208	05		
	023683	31	*	
	023689	27	*	
	024365	61	*	
	024372	36	*	
	024846	25		1

FIG. 4. Part of a tabulation showing number of persons discharged once or more, number of deaths, and number of births according to diagnosis.

45

from hospital for patients suffering from *Mental Deficiency*. Each person appears once, and this ingenious tabulation also shows if this person died anywhere within the area within the year, and, if female, whether she was delivered of a baby. Note how this tabulation gives away no secrets about the identity of the patients concerned.

The frequency of readmissions naturally varies considerably according to the diagnosis. Using another programme we have made systematic tabulations for all the three-figure diagnostic codes in the International Statistical Classification. Table I shows a portion dealing with some common cancers. In the case of carcinoma of the cervix a morbidity rate based on *discharges* rather than *persons discharged* would be about double the corrected figure and the hospital fatality rate would be about one-half the correct figure. Derived over a five-year period this type of tabulation would provide sufficiently accurate estimates of incidence of most cancers for practical purposes.

In a system of health care without rationing such as exists in Britain where costs are mounting it is important to know how much of the work load is due to a few people who make repeated calls for service. If such people exist and can be located could their demands be anticipated by some alternative approach? Without cumulative personal data it is very difficult to study these problems. We have recently ventured into the field of general practice and have obtained elementary computer accessible records about each of 7,000 patients who comprise a practice within the area. For a period of nine weeks a note of each demand for urgent ambulatory treatment in which the patient felt he could not wait for a regular appointment with the Doctor was kept. The demand for this type of treatment cannot be planned for and disrupts the general pactitioner's work and reduces efficiency. By linking up the notes it was found that almost half the demand for urgent care came from a small number of importunate families who appeared again and again often with different complaints (Table II). I give this as an example on a small scale of the use of the idea of record linkage (in this case carried out manually) in operational research.

One point remains of such importance that it cannot be passed over. This concerns the confidential nature of the material with which we deal. I must stress that every reasonable precaution is taken to maintain its security. Clerical staff are carefully selected and are required to promise to maintain secrecy. We have devised a system whereby personal data are linked only on magnetic tape within the computer so that a cumulative paper dossier no longer exists. Any communications made about patients are made by doctors to doctors.

Table I. *Corrected and uncorrected morbidity rates for certain cancers, Oxford Area, 1963–4.*

Principal diagnosis ISC Code		Uncorrected discharge rate per 10⁵ per annum	Corrected discharge rate per 10⁵ per annum	Uncorrected fatality rate per cent. per annum	Corrected fatality rate per cent. per annum	Reduction factor
162,163	Cancer of Bronchus	71·3	50·2	13·3	18·9	29·6
170	Cancer of Breast	51·3	41·1	4·8	5·9	19·9
171	Cancer of Cervix Uteri	29·9	14·7	3·4	6·9	51·0

Table II. *Demand for urgent ambulatory treatment by families*

	Items of service		Families	
	No.	Per cent.	No.	Per cent.
No member attended	...	...	1508	75·1
One member attended	413	53·3	354	17·6
Two or more members attended .	362	46·7	146	7·3
Totals	775	100·0	2008	100·0

47

In spite of all these careful precautions it may be argued that in setting up this file the patient has surrendered a particle of his privacy without his prior consent. There are important precedents, fortunately, both in the National Cancer Register, and the Mental Health Enquiry in both of which the patients consent is assumed rather than required. The processing of identifiable material outside the hospital of origin has in this country once again recently received the imprimatur of the Ministry of Health in the Tunbridge Report on the standardization of hospital records. It forms a key part of the procedure for the notification of drug reactions to the Dunlop Committee.

Although there are obvious differences in scale, for myself I do not see any difference in principle between a system of medical records in which identifiable material suitably protected crosses the barriers *between* the branches of the Health Service in the patient's interest, and one in which such material crosses the boundaries *between departments within a hospital* or between hospitals in a group. The issue of principle would come, in my view, only if the data were accessible to persons other than the medical profession or their agents. As we integrate our health services to serve the community so must we integrate the system of medical information. As specialization within hospitals made necessary the development of the Unit Hospital Record System in the first half of this century, so may the complexity of the community Health Services lead to medical record linkage between hospitals and other administrative units in the Health Service in the second. From the patient's point of view —and he is also the taxpayer—an integrated system of medical records with proper safeguards is likely to be the only solution which will serve the interest both of his health and his pocket.

ACKNOWLEDGMENTS : The work of the Oxford Record Linkage Study was initiated in 1961 following a benefaction from the Nuffield Foundation. Subsequently it has received financial support from the Ministry of Health and the Nuffield Provincial Hospitals Trust. Help essential to its work also comes from the Oxford Regional Hospital Board and the General Register Office.

REFERENCES

ACHESON, E. D. (1967). *Medical Record Linkage.* Published by the Oxford University Press for the Nuffield Provincial Hospitals Trust. London.

ALDERSON, M. & MEADE, T. (1967). Accuracy of diagnosis on death certificates compared with that in hospital records. *Br. J. prev. soc. Med.* **21**, 22–29.

EVANS, J. (1967). Deliberate self-poisoning in the Oxford area. *Br. J. prev. soc. Med.* **21**, 97–107.

FARR, W. (1861). In *Report on Army Medical Statistics,* by Lord Herbert, Sir A. Tulloch and Dr Farr. Parliamentary Paper No. 366.

HOBBS, M. S. T. & ACHESON, E. D. (1966 *a*). Secondary sex ratio following bleeding in pregnancy. *Lancet*, **1**, 462.
HOBBS, M. S. T. & ACHESON, E. D. (1966 *b*). Obstetric care in the first pregnancy. *Lancet*, **1**, 761.
STOCKS, P. (1944). Measurement of morbidity. *Proc. R. Soc. Med.* **37**, 593–608.

DISCUSSION

Dr Doll : In opening this discussion I would like first to acknowledge how much all of us who are interested in medical research in this country owe Dr Acheson for his initiative in introducing this record linkage pilot study. It is unthinkable that we should have to conduct medical research without a linked system of medical records in the future and this is entirely due to Dr Acheson's energy in following up suggestions which Professor Witts, Sidney Truelove and he made in a letter to the medical press some years ago (Acheson, Truelove & Witts, 1961).

My own interests have been particularly in the research aspects of the system, particularly the enormous assistance it would provide in follow-up studies of groups of people defined as having different amounts of exposure to different noxious factors in their environment ; this, to my mind, is alone sufficient to justify the introduction of such a system. But what Dr Acheson has brought out in his paper to-day is the enormous advantage for the Health Service itself. When we have such a system we shall, I believe, regard the period when hospital records, G.P. records, and local authority records were maintained in watertight compartments as belonging to the era of prescientific medicine.

At present, Dr Acheson has not managed to include the recording of drugs in his system and I am sure he was right to begin simply. First, we need to get a system organized on a simple basis and then, as machinery and the science of computing advance, we shall be able to expand it. But at the present time there are few things which are more urgent for medicine than the bringing together of knowledge about what doctors are doing to patients in one place and what is happening to the same patient weeks, months, or years later, in another place as a result of that treatment. Irradiation and the prescription of oral contraceptives provide two examples of treatments whose major effects could have been discovered much more quickly and efficiently if a system of linked records had been available, and I have recently come across another which may be almost insoluble in its absence. In the last six years the deaths from asthma in children aged 10 to 14 years have risen so greatly that they now account for 5 per cent. of all deaths in this age group. This, it seems,

E

may well be an iatrogenic effect demonstrating itself by death in one hospital (or on the road to hospital) as the result of treatment recommended in another hospital and prescribed by a general practitioner.

Dr Acheson has pointed out that there is no logical difference between having a unit system for a group of hospitals and a unit system for the National Health Service ; and if we want to bring general practitioners and local authorities into a unified Health Service with the hospitals so that all are playing their part efficiently and in an informed way, surely we must make the records of one available to the other. And in this way too the Ministry itself should be able to assess the relative efficiency of its operation in different fields of the National Health Service.

Dr Benjamin : I want to follow up the last sentence of what Dr Doll has said by asking Dr Acheson whether he doesn't think that we make life unnecessarily difficult for ourselves by accepting records as they are and by doing our best to match them ; whether we shouldn't make an all-out effort, given the technical means which now exist to ensure that records are integrated as they are made, *i.e.* by joining general practitioners, hospitals and public health departments together into a proper community health record system.

Dr Acheson : May I answer Dr Benjamin first and say that in an ideal situation one should start with organization and finish with records. Records only *reflect* organization. To start in the way we have done, trying to piece the records together in a disintegrated health service is illogical. One ought to go about it the other way. On the other hand it is just possible that our efforts may bring the integration of the Health Service a step nearer. When an integrated health service exists with the person, the family and the community as units, it won't be necessary to link records in the sense in which we are doing it at the moment.

If I could just take up Dr Doll's point about drugs. We would very much like to bring prescriptions into the system. However, in our initial population of 350,000 people there were one million prescriptions a year made outside hospital by general practitioners alone. The processing of data on such a scale is beyond our capabilities. One solution might be to introduce a special form which doctors would have to use for certain specified drugs including all new drugs, and link these into the main file.

Dr Davies : I would like to take up the point that Dr Benjamin has made and illustrate it by saying that we have in this Region a handsome brand-new health centre in which we have the hospital service, the general practitioner and the local authority service all together. The records reflect the fact that they are not integrated although they are all under one roof and in many ways they behave in exactly the same way as they would if they were 15 miles apart. The real thing to do is to have integrated organization. The intergrated records would then follow in the way Acheson has suggested.

My other point is that in this region we have a remarkably good obstetric record over the region and we thought ourselves extraordinary clever and far in advance of all other regions for that reason. Acheson has in fact shown, from some of the things that you have in fact seen on the board and a whole lot of other things that you haven't seen, how remarkably haphazard some of our arrangements are. And his findings I must say are uncomfortable to those of us who have to organize the obstetric service. Good though our record is, we shall have to make changes so that he is unable to reflect the pattern that he has been doing to date.

Mr White : I only want to make a comment arising from Dr Benajamin's proposal, which I don't think many people here would disagree with in principle. I think what we have to remember is the vast scale of expenditure entailed if we were to attempt this on a national basis. We have estimated that there may be a couple of hundred hospital groups over the country as a whole which would justify and would need for this kind of purpose a major computer installation. Now that, at approximately half a million pounds a time, which is what it is likely to cost for remote access facilities on a computer in a hospital, is £100 million to start with. At the moment the cost of a really good on-line access point for a G.P.—that is, a visual display unit with a keyboard and the necessary equipment to attach it to a distant computer—is of the order of £5,000. I hope they will be very much cheaper than that in a few years' time, but at the moment that is the cost. If you take only 10,000 G.Ps., another £50 million is involved. Now that isn't only a question of finding the money, as everyone here will realize. It is a question of possibly having to sacrifice other National Health Service needs to find the money. And while agreement over objectives is one thing, impetus in implementing such a system is going to demand even more effort.

REFERENCES

Acheson, E. D., Truelove, S. C. & Witts, L. J. (1961). National epidemiology. *Br. med. J.* **1**, 668.

PART 2

GENERAL SESSION II

Chairman : SIR RONALD TUNBRIDGE (Leeds)

THE INTRODUCTION OF RECORD LINKAGE
IN NORTH EAST SCOTLAND

R. Deans Weir

The first point that I must make is that this morning I am speaking on behalf of a group concerned with Record Linkage in the North-East of Scotland, and this includes many people outside the three research units which function in this area. I would like to deal with the practical problem of introducing record linkage into an existing service and particularly with the difficulty of making certain that the costs of record linkage are seen to be justified.

Certainly so far as Aberdeen was concerned there were few problems in convincing people about the ultimate benefits and need for record linkage, and the fact that this was coupled with a population of manageable size in an area with certain geographical and administrative advantages was encouraging. Plans for the phased introduction of linkage were produced and approved. It was agreed that the immediate needs were firstly, a reorganization of patient identification on a regional scale making certain that enough information was being collected ; secondly, an improvement in the methods of recording and, thirdly, a study of the feasibility of linkage and its likely costs. No one knew what this would involve ; initially it might involve more cost and perhaps no saving at all because if the system could then do more, more would be asked of it and as a result running costs would be even greater. Paradoxically the advantages of linkage were at the same time likely to be the greatest drawbacks to its introduction. Simply to argue that the system would be more efficient is not enough.

The means by which record linkage could be used and exploited seemed at that time obvious and therefore of less importance and their consideration was postponed. It would now appear that we have misjudged our priorities and are in danger of being accused either of proposing facilities we cannot fully justify or, if successful, of developing facilities we will be unable to exploit.

The purpose of record linkage is to bring together reliable and related items of information. Techniques to achieve this goal will very soon be available, and it will be possible to apply these techniques if wished on a national scale. Against this is the cost and the fact that we are not in a position to make use of such facilities. It would not be far from true to say that records officers, clinicians and administrators are neither willing, ready nor able to utilize record linkage, and this has very serious implications. There is a grave danger that the only people who will use record linkage are the ones who are advocating it, and without the active support of the people creating records the value and accuracy of the data being linked will be considerably reduced.

Despite the logic of the case and the goodwill of those planning health services there will be, in the foreseeable future, heavy competition for money in which record linkage is unlikely to be a popular or particularly successful contender. The main reason for this is the lack of immediate return on the effort and money required for record linkage. The quickest way to win over both the public and the profession to the relatively urgent need for record linkage facilities is to show its potential and value in the immediate clinical care of patients.

It is against this background that the developments in the North East of Scotland have to be seen.

1. Techniques for matching have been developed.

2. Existing recording methods have been improved and new ones devised—this is particularly true of the psychiatric services.

3. The feasibility of linkage has been examined.

4. The costs of linkage have been estimated. The cost of introducing linkage to the area would be about £25,000–£30,000 and would cost about £7,000 a year to maintain. This works out at approximately nine pence per admission or hospital attendance. However as a result it would be possible to do away with eight separate indices currently held within the region and the saving in this respect could be set against the expenditure on the new index.

5. Not enough has been done to demonstrate the immediate value of linkage to the local health services. This was brought home fairly forcibly when the records officers declared that linkage at this stage would be of no benefit to them and in fact would merely involve them in more work. If we have failed to convince records officers then the present tacit approval of doctors may vanish at the first sight of the bill—indeed this very sentiment is expressed in greater or lesser degree by board members and clinicians. Everyone can see the advantages of the full system once it is operational but no one is willing to justify the expenditure in the face of other developments.

This is a ridiculous and serious situation—data linkage cannot exist on its own or in addition to (even in opposition to) existing systems and the truth is that we have failed to sell the idea to the majority of our colleagues. There is a gap that needs to be filled (and quickly) between the establishing of linkage techniques and the long term benefits to research and planning. A number of years will elapse before the advantages, so far detailed, will be seen in terms of patient care. Planners, administrators and research workers are used to thinking ahead in terms of five or ten year units but this will have little attraction for the clinician and less for the general practitioner. So far few people have suggested that linked data can be used in clinical care—and some have implied that they cannot—yet if this could be achieved there would result a very convincing argument in favour of linkage and one which would have the support of clinicians particularly if they could use it in looking after their patients.

There are a number of ways in which potential linkage techniques can be developed for use in patient care. Some of these are :

1. improvement in the facilities for the follow-up of patients ;

2. ways of overcoming the effects of the shortage of doctors and ancillary staff ; and

3. influencing prescribing methods and through this the monitoring of adverse drug reactions.

It is possible to devise ways of helping with these problems which are *not* initially dependent upon record linkage but which if successful and were then to be extended would require linked data.

'Give me a fulcrum and I will move the world'. Over the last two thousand years these words have been paraphrased by many people but the significance of that original claim is unchanged. For the next two years in Aberdeen the less ambitious task of developing a lever to move a small part of the National Health Service will be attempted. Certainly in the North East of Scotland without a stronger case such as linkage as an aid in patient care we cannot count on sufficient local support and record linkage may founder despite all our advantages. This I suspect may prove to be the case in other areas. It is not possible at this stage to do more than outline the problems and it would appear that if these difficulties are to be overcome it will be necessary (for the immediate future) to change our priorities.

Over the past three years the work in Aberdeen has concentrated on three areas :

1. Record matching—leading to record linkage and the creation of a regional index.

2. Improved methods of recording—so that reliable data (in a suitable form) would be available for addition to the regional index.

3. The development of data handling methods—automatic coding ; creation of dictionaries ; up-dating routines ; validity checks and so on.

A fair measure of success has been achieved with matching and methods of recording. In addition an urgent effort is needed for the further development of handling methods as this will be the only way of reducing costs. The cost of processing is causing some anxiety and most of this expense is due to the abstracting of existing records. In addition a much more vigorous attempt must be made in the application of these methods to specific clinical problems. I now believe that if linkage is ever to become more than a separate or academic exercise then a practical application of these techniques must be demonstrated. In an attempt not only to recognize but to rectify this omission efforts are now being made to change the emphasis of the work to meet specific clinical problems.

In the short time that remains I would like to outline very briefly one of the projects that is being undertaken. This deals with the automatic follow-up of patients deemed for one reason or another to be at risk, a variant of the ' at risk ' register theme. Thousands of patients in this country undergo therapeutic procedures in hospital which many years later can result in morbidity which frequently goes undetected because of a breakdown in communications between the hospital and general practitioner services. Two examples are :

1. the late onset of hypothyroidism after radioactive iodine therapy for thyrotoxicosis ; and

2. nutritional complications following a partial gastrectomy—anaemia and bone disease.

The problem is initially one of data processing and in respect of the follow-up of patients who have received radio-iodine therapy a mechanical process of follow-up has been devised. Basically the steps are as follows :

1. a register of all patients receiving a particular type of treatment is maintained by a secretary with no medical training ;

2. each year a letter is sent to the general practitioner enclosing a form listing 12 symptoms and signs (with the relevant criteria) and an iodine-free syringe. The patient is notified by post-card to attend the doctor who completes the form and obtains the blood sample ;

3. when the form and the blood are returned to the hospital, the secretary makes a provisional diagnosis on the basis of previous discriminant function analysis of signs and symptoms and the laboratory measurement of blood protein bound iodine.

This system has been working very well in Aberdeen for nearly two years ; essentially doctors are being provided with a service—information relevant to the care of their patients is being produced with the minimal involvement of their staff.

This has encouraged further developments :

1. the inclusion of another group of patients—those who have had a gastrectomy ;

2. experiments with questionnaires sent directly to patients ; these would increase considerably the range of information presented to the general practitioners—*e.g.* time off work, unreported illness, etc. ;

3. blood sampling in outpatients or local authority clinics (when it is otherwise inconvenient for the general practitioner) ; and

4. the preparation of computer programmes to handle the routine parts of the follow-up. Once the system is handled automatically by computer then the scope can be greatly increased.

By changing the disease or treatment and the tests, all types of follow-up could be undertaken and information from many different sources could then be brought together. This would provide a strong case for the development of linkage with the additional argument that it provided a valuable technique in patient care without excessive use of medical resources.

Another area for the development of similar techniques is in the prescription of drugs (since this is likely to be one of the most potent sources of the need for follow-up). Here again information from a number of sources and obtained in a variety of ways must be brought together and then be presented as rapidly as possible to the doctors responsible for the care of these patients.

In conclusion, I genuinely believe that the success of record linkage (certainly in the North East of Scotland and perhaps elsewhere for that matter) is in jeopardy because of a failure to convince our colleagues of its immediate and practical applications. This is a real deficiency which must be, at least in part, remedied before further general linkage schemes are proposed. For this reason in the North East of Scotland the establishment of a Regional Register will be delayed (although the data that will ultimately be fed to the Register will still be collected) and the immediate tasks are :

1. more efficient and cheaper methods of recording and handling ; and

2. applications of linkage such as follow-up and monitoring.

There is a danger of getting out of phase with our developments (if in fact we are not already out of phase) and in consequence there is a temptation to hide behind or within the techniques of linkage and recording and leave the more mundane tasks of implementation and application to others. This is a temptation and deficiency that must be avoided if record linkage is to obtain both rapid and general approval.

DISCUSSION

Mr White : I seem to detect a mild persecution complex among people who believe fervently in record linkage. I am thinking of Dr Weir's fears that he has got to justify enormous expenditure on record linkage ; even, if I may say so, Dr Doll's insistence that research alone will justify the cost of record linkage. Is there not an alternative approach to this? The Health Service is about to enter the era of multi-access, multi-programming computers. If we are going to put this kind of computer into a hospital, since practically every activity of the hospital either contributes to or uses the patient record in some way or the other, the nucleus of any multi-access system in a hospital is going to be the patient record. If we are to give assistance to general practice it is most likely to be by getting G.Ps. linked to multi-access computers, possibly at the nearest hospital. The kind of assistance that we can give to them includes among its foremost objectives, helping them to keep their records. Local authorities believe that the administrative efficiency of local health services would be substantially increased by getting health records on to computers. These things are going to be pursued for the reasons of better patient care in hospitals and surgeries, improved hospital administration, increased clinical efficiency—things that are likely to show rapid returns. All of them will facilitate record linkage as an obvious by-product. Therefore it seems to me that we are not obliged to justify record linkage *per se* as the reason for substantial capital expenditure. Capital expenditure ought to arise for much more immediate reasons and give facilities for record linkage much more automatically.

Professor Logan : If I can continue this dialogue with my neighbour, I think your remarks were to a converted audience, whereas what Weir was saying is that we really have to be missionaries or the thing is in jeopardy. This takes us back to the Oxford Conference on Computers a couple of years ago, when we had the same kind of problem. It seems this is the chicken and the egg again. Deans Weir is worried that we won't have the egg to sell while we are struggling to keep this chicken alive. It comes down to the practical point that records officers don't like it. In our experience in trying to get Hospital Activity Analysis across half of the Liverpool Region we came right up against this and the size of the missionary job there is enough to jeopardize any research. But while we have been here this morning the cost of running the Oxford Regional Hospitals would more than pay in these last three hours for the whole of a record linkage system going on year in year out. So we have to get this point of cost into proportion. Regional Hospital boards are not spending peanuts. Most of them spend a million pounds per week. They are spending this without top management, with very little even in the middle layers of management. They are struggling to keep the thing going in the old quill-pen stage. This is what we are right up against. We are bringing along a jet machine when they don't know how to ride a bicycle.

How can we hope to try to keep this small chicken going? It seems to come back to a massive educational exercise. It was the same kind of thing that hit other major industries, *e.g.* the Coal Board and the Railways. That is the kind of area that we are into and what bothers me is that we have been talking so far of how can we sell this to the clinicians as if they are the only people who will be using it. There is another large group of consumers and these are the managers, and surely if we can get it over to them that here is an aid, a tool to modern management, then as a by-product of this system we can get the clinical research aspects that many of us are interested in.

Dr Benjamin : I couldn't agree more with what Deans Weir has said. He emphasized I think two things which I have been trying to preach for some time. First, that if you really want to get not only records officers but consultants and all kinds of personnel in the Health Service involved in integrated records then you have got to provide some kind of immediate dividend to them. They have got to have a feedback from their experience so that they can see the value of the system in helping them to do their job much better. That leads on to the second point, that we have got to get away from the idea that research is something luxurious and expendable and recognize that it is an integral part of running a good system of medical care. It comes back to the point which Professor Logan has just mentioned about getting through to managers. If we can get over the idea that in order to operate a system efficiently in the interests of the patient, research is an integral part of good management then I think we shall have a better lever for getting this thing on the move.

Dr Weir : Mr White must remember that the Scots have always been persecuted (especially by the English), and we have also a great regard for money. Therefore my anxiety is I think a genuine one that we must be able to justify this expenditure, and particularly I feel this in regard to patient care.

61

RECORD LINKAGE IN A SELF-CONTAINED COMMUNITY

O. BJARNASON, S. FRIDRIKSSON and M. MAGNUSSON

In the treatise on Icelandic Cultural History : ' Islenzk menning' it is stated that the Icelanders are the only nation in Europe who recollect their origin (Nordal, 1942). However, opinions still differ with regard to the ethnology of the original settlers and inhabitants of Iceland.

It is generally accepted that in the ninth century, when the first Norse settlers came to Iceland, the island was uninhabited except for Irish monks who are believed to have fled from the country when they became aware of the heathen Vikings. Until recently it has been assumed that the majority of the settlers came from Norway with the exception of those few who came from other Scandinavian countries, mainly Sweden. One hypothesis, however, maintains that the majority of the Norwegian settlers had previously migrated to Norway from the south-eastern part of Europe, *i.e.* the area around the Black Sea, and were of the Herulan tribe (Gudmundsson, 1959). Actually the names of many of the chieftains who formed the original Icelandic community are on record in the Book of Settlement. It is also realized that the first inhabitants originated in part from northern Scotland and Ireland but it is hard to estimate their proportion in the total population. Recent blood group and anthropological studies seem to indicate that the Scottish and Irish element may have been larger than previously assumed (Steffensen, 1946 ; Donegani *et al.*, 1950).

The first settlers came over around 870 A.D. and the country is supposed to have been fully settled in some 60 years, *i.e.* all inhabitable land had been occupied although the inhabitants and their homesteads increased in numbers as time went by (Johannesson, 1956). It may even be assumed that the population was steadily increasing until the end of the twelfth century. The changes in the growth of the population of Iceland through the ages as calculated by Steffensen (1963), are shown by the curve in Figure 1. The first part of this curve may not be altogether accurate, but from the beginning of the eighteenth century reliable data concerning the population changes are on record, e.g. the national census of 1703 and as a whole the curve may be said to be soundly based.

The irregularities and frequent dips in the population curve from

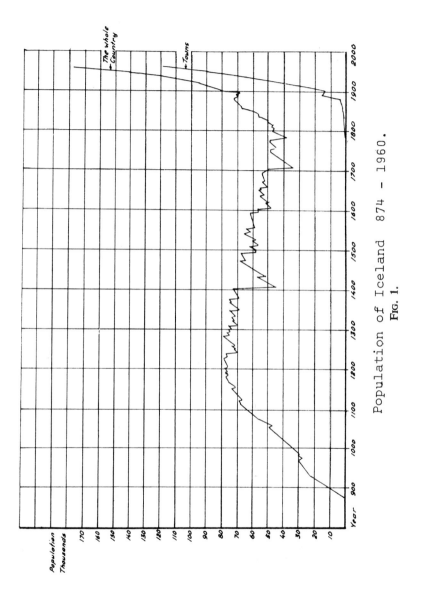

Population of Iceland 874 – 1960.

Fig. 1.

63

the thirteenth century until the beginning of the nineteenth century have been caused by frequent epidemics, natural disasters and famine, but immigration into Iceland has been negligible from the end of the settlement period. Neither has emigration had any influence on the population structure except in the last decades of the nineteenth century when a number of people emigrated to North America. In spite of the isolation of the Icelandic population, the consanguinity rate has not been found to differ significantly from that of the other Scandinavian countries or the Protestants of Northern Ireland (Helgason, 1964).

At the present time the population is 196,549 individuals according to preliminary official figures from the National Register of December 1st 1966.

The relatively small population of Iceland and its isolation through the ages seem to render it very advantageous for a study of human genetics. Detailed records of births, deaths and marriages are available from 1816 onwards in parish registers which could be collected on punch-cards for processing by a computer. Demographic records of the conventional type are available in printed forms and publications from 1916. Since 1952 punched cards have been used for every living resident of the country. In this National Register the individuals are defined by their name, their birth date and a two-digit number as well as sex, marital status, nationality and religion. Their address, and if over 12 years of age, their occupation and a name identification number, are added.

Some work with general genetical information in view is already in progress under the supervision of the Genetics Committee of the University of Iceland. The transfer of the demographic data of the Icelandic population to punch cards suited for analysis and linkage by a computer started in 1965.

The first step in the programme was the punching of all live-birth records from 1951 to 1960 which amounted to 45,000 individuals. Then followed the punching of approximately 99,000 birth cards for live births during the period 1916 to 1950 as well as 3,000 stillbirths from 1916 to 1965. Individuals were identified on birth cards by punching three initial letters in each name of child and parents as well as date of birth. These were punched in addition to other demographic data.

Prior to 1940, however, only parents' age is in most cases recorded on birth certificates instead of birth date, causing great difficulties in linking such parents with their own birth cards. Therefore, when punching older records, six initial letters had to be used. Even this is not sufficient in all cases to identify the individual.

64

In order to aid the identification further and the linking up of the individuals the birth places were punched. For the same reason marriage licenses as well as adoptions will be used.

In addition to the regular demographic data, reliable records of cause of death are available for 70,000 individuals and are being added to the previous material by the punching of death certificates for the period 1916 to 1966. Such records also include information on occupation. These have been identified by a two digit code based on the International Labour Office Occupational code, which, however, had to be altered slightly to meet the form of the local recorded information. The occupation of individuals on the death certificates as well as the occupation of parents can be used as a further aid in linking the families, *i.e.* through the occupation and birthdates on the death certificates the number of names competing for parentage on the birth certificates can be narrowed down and others rejected. All this information is made available by the Icelandic Bureau of Statistics.

By the courtesy of the Icelandic Blood Bank information on blood groups was made available and is being included in the present programme. Already data on 12,000 blood donors who attended the Blood Bank since 1953 have been punched with regard to ABO and Rh blood groups, haemoglobin, systolic pressure and diastolic pressure. In addition available data on blood groups of 14,800 recipients and 18,900 pregnant women have also been punched.

The processing of the collected data is being done mainly at the University of Iceland Computing Centre. The centre is equipped with an IBM-1620 Model II computer with 40k fast storage (40,000 decimal digits) and two disc drives, each with a removable magnetic disc pack containing two million decimal positions.

The first phase of the work consisted of putting into disc packs records of all those individuals in the National Register as of December 31st 1965 and born during the period January 1st 1925 to December 31st 1950. In this age group there were 36,391 males and 35,490 females, or 71,881 individuals. The contents of each individual record was as follows :

1. The first three letters of the first name, the middle name and the surname.

2. The year, month, day of birth and the birth number, which is a two digit number distinguishing the different births occurring on the same day. This sequence of eight decimal digits identifies the individual uniquely and will be used as the basic individual identification in this and associated studies.

3. The personal, or name number, which is derived from the person's name and is used extensively in Iceland in connection with medical and other services.

4. The place of birth, both county and district.

5. Sex.

6. Marital status.

In all 40 decimal positions are required. The records of the males and the females were put on separate disc packs, each capable of containing up to 40,000 individual records. There are 10 digits available for additional data concerning each individual, such as blood groups.

In the second phase the ABO and Rh blood group data collected at the Blood Bank from donors, recipients and pregnant women were linked to the age group born from 1925 to 1950 which was in the National Register on December 31st 1965. Of the 45,700 blood group cards about 24,000 fell within the age group. The number of individuals linked to the National Register was 17,577 or 24·4 per cent. of the age group, 17·2 per cent. of the males and 31·9 per cent. of the females. Further work needs to be done on these linkages.

The blood group material for the 17,557 individuals has been analysed and grouped according to towns, counties and the country as a whole, the percentages of the different blood groups worked out and the results tabulated. Further work is in progress on this material. In addition material has been collected for more detailed blood analysis.

Work has already started on the third phase which is based on the birth certificates. As mentioned previously the birth certificates from 1916 to 1960 have already been punched, about 144,000 cards in all. Birth certificates for the period 1961 to 1966 are being punched, about 26,000 cards. Thus in the near future all births from 1916 till 1966 will be available for processing, about 170,000 births in all. The data on each card are as follows. Date of birth, sex, birth order, single or multiple birth, birth place, name of child and names and dates of birth (or ages) of parents. Sixty-five positions are required on the disc pack for each birth, so that about 30,000 can be accommodated on each pack. Thus six disc packs are required for this rather extensive material. Later this can be compressed considerably.

Programmes have been written to read the birth certificates on to disc packs and this will be done during the summer. The next step is to link the birth records with the National Register and extract the birth number, and give those not in the Register a birth number so that each individual born has a unique identification, *viz.* an eight digit number consisting of the year, month, day and birth number. From this one will proceed to the linking of the parents to their own birth records and build up an ancestral file. This file can then be compressed by using only the unique identification number for each individual. From the ancestral file it is planned to build up a descendant file based on the mother and including the father, or fathers, and children. Furthermore it is envisaged to build up an individual file or register incorporating social and medical data, in effect an expanded National Register.

It is clear that considerable difficulties will arise in the linking process. Additional material, such as marriage and death certificates will therefore be used, as described previously. In addition Iceland is in the perhaps unique position of having well-nigh exhaustive and reliable genealogical records and a host of willing and able genealogists only too eager to help out when the computer must give up. Thus there is a reasonable hope that the files can be satisfactorily built up, even extending well back into the nineteenth century.

As mentioned before, previous blood-group studies indicate that the Icelanders originate in part from Scottish and Irish settlers, (Donegani *et al.*, 1950). The extensive blood-group investigation performed by the Icelandic Genetics Committee confirm these findings (Bjarnason, V., personal communication).

Previous nosographical studies have indicated that further genetical approach to some of the diseases in question should be feasible. These investigations comprise mental disorders (Helgason, 1964), malignant tumours of the uterus (Bjarnason, 1963), carcinoma of the breast (Snaedal, 1965), epilepsy (Gudmundsson, 1966) and glaucoma (Björnsson, 1967). Some such genetical studies are already in progress and others are planned. Of those in progress may be mentioned : studies on hereditary cerebral haemorrhages, osteopsatyrosis and mongolism.

A nation-wide cancer registration has been carried out in the country under the auspices of the Icelandic Cancer Society since the beginning of the year 1954. This registration has for instance confirmed previous findings of an exceptionally high incidence of carcioma of the stomach in Iceland (Dungal, 1961). A peculiar high incidence of thyroid carcinoma in women has been shown to occur, although thyroid cancer is relatively infrequent, being the seventh most common cancer in women (Bjarnason, 1967). A close contact has been established between the Icelandic Genetic Committee and the Cancer Registry and genetical aspects of the malignant diseases mentioned above and others will be studied in the near future.

67

The Icelandic Heart Association which now is in the process of collecting extensive data pertaining to cardio-vascular diseases in Iceland has also shown great interest in collaboration with the Genetics Committee. Their initial survey concerns Icelandic males in the age group 45–49 (inclusive) living in Reykjavik, the capital city, and the neighbourhood. These individuals account for about 50 per cent. of the age group.

SUMMARY

A few points concerning the ethnology of the Icelanders have been described, as well as changes in the Icelandic population through the ages from the settlement of the country and onwards.

The advantages of geneticial studies in Iceland are stressed and some of the work already in progress under the auspices of the Genetics Committee of the University of Iceland is mentioned. Some problems regarding record linkage and computer processing are discussed.

The feasibility of further genetical investigations concerning some mental and somatic disorders, already studied from other points of view in Iceland, is put forward.

ACKNOWLEDGMENTS : This work has been supported by a grant from the Atomic Energy Commission, Contract No. AT (30-1)-3548.

REFERENCES

BJARNASON, O. (1963). Uterine Carcinoma in Iceland (Thesis), Reykjavík.

BJARNASON, O. (1967). Cancer incidence in Iceland. In *Racial and Geographical Factors in Tumour Incidence*. University of Edinburgh, Pfizer Medical Monograph No. 2, pp. 117–131.

BJÖRNSSON, G. (1967). Primary glaucoma in Iceland (Thesis) *Acta ophthal*. Suppl. 91.

DONEGANI, J. A., DUNGAL, N., IKIN, E. W. & MOURANT, A. E. (1950). Blood groups of Icelanders. *Ann. Eugen*. **15**, 147.

DUNGAL, N. (1961). The special problem of stomach cancer in Iceland. *J. Am. med. Ass*. **178**, 789–798.

GUDMUNDSSON, B. (1959). Uppruni Íslendinga (The Origin of the Icelanders). Bókaútgáfa Menningarsjóðs.

GUDMUNDSSON, G. (1966). Epilepsy in Iceland (Thesis). *Acta neurol. Scand*. Suppl. 25. Vol. 43.

HELGASON, T. (1964). Epidemiology of mental disorders in Iceland (Thesis). *Acta psychiat. scand*. Suppl. 183.

JOHANNESSON, J. (1956). *Íslendinga saga* (The History of the Icelanders), pp. 27 and 47. Almenna Bókafélagið. Ísafoldarprentsmiðja.

NORDAL, S. (1942). *Íslenzk menning* (Icelandic culture), p. 42. Mál og Menning, Reykjavík.

SNAEDAL, G. (1965). Cancer of the breast (Thesis). Acta chir. scand. Suppl. 338.

STEFFENSEN, J. (1946). Uppruni Íslendinga (The Origin of the Icelanders) In : *Samtíð og saga 3*. Reykjavík.

STEFFENSEN, J. (1963). Islands folkemaengde gennem tiderne. *Medsk Forum*, **16**, 129–152.

DISCUSSION

Mr Healy : Are you intending to take the family linkage beyond parents and sibs, as far as cousins ? This might compensate to some extent for lack of information on grandparents.

Professor Magnusson : The data we have at present only reaches back to 1916, but we are hoping to go back eventually into the last century and even further. In that way we are hoping to build up pedigrees of several generations.

Mr Healy : Will you do it sideways as well in the current generation ?

Professor Magnusson : Yes, we are trying to build up this ancestral file, going from child to parents, and then from the other file which I mentioned we shall be able to go sideways. We haven't reached that stage yet as there are quite a lot of difficulties.

Dr Adelstein : I wonder if you could tell us what the response of the community has been to all this personal material being put together in this file ?

Professor Magnusson : I think that the community is very interested in this project. Many of the Icelanders have an interest in genealogy and they are very enthusiastic about a project which will enable them to trace their ancestors and the ancestors of other people.

Dr Bahn : I don't believe I heard you say anything about migration out of Iceland. How would you get information on this ?

Professor Magnusson : I think that emigration is insignificant and immigration also. We are pretty self-confined. I haven't got exact data on immigration but from the end of the settlement period it has been very small.

MEDICAL RECORD LINKAGE IN NORTHERN IRELAND—RECONNAISSANCE AND PROPOSALS WITH PARTICULAR REFERENCE TO PROBLEMS OF IDENTIFICATION

E. A. CHEESEMAN

MEMBERS of the Faculty of Medicine of the Queen's University of Belfast are involved in most of the medical research done in Northern Ireland and they give advice on the problems which, from time to time, arise in the Northern Ireland health services. This situation is almost inevitable because there is no other medical school or medical research unit in Northern Ireland. In 1964 some members of the Faculty decided to stimulate a greater awareness of the potential value of the records kept by the government departments and statutory bodies concerned with the health services. We felt that the time had come for a national system of linked medical records because, without it, neither our research nor our advice could be fully efficient. It was no coincidence that some of us who made this decision were then members of a committee concerned with re-developing genetic research. We were disturbed by the considerable amount of tedious work invariably required to organize the abundant recorded data into individual or family groups. Many present will recognize that, in effect, we were reacting to the frustration which arises in attempts to cross departmental boundaries in search of data when individuals or families, rather than single events in their lives, are the appropriate units to study.

The timing of our first positive step along the path to a national system was influenced by two factors. By 1964, of course, Howard Newcombe's admirable pioneer work had convinced us that, in addition to being desirable, record linkage was also feasible on the scale which we should have to adopt. In that year, moreover, we first learnt that within a few years there would be sufficient accessible electronic computing power in Northern Ireland for a linkage scheme of the size envisaged. An appreciation of the problems facing Donald Acheson in the Oxford region led us to believe that, as an area for successful linkage operation, Northern Ireland had several advantages over most other regions in the United Kingom. I must mention three of these in order to clarify what follows. At the same time I shall attempt to sketch in the administrative background in so far as it differs from that in Great Britain.

70

The size of the population (about 1·5 million), and the annual numbers of births (33,000), marriages (10,000), and deaths (15,000) are very similar to those of British Columbia. In our view, communities of this size are convenient not only for linking records (as has been shown by Howard Newcombe) but also for most epidemiological and genetic studies (as past contributions from Northern Ireland in these fields have shown).

The area (about 5,000 square miles) and geography of Northern Ireland facilitate communications of all kinds and the rapid and easy data transmission which should result is a prerequisite of successful record linkage. The country has a continuous natural sea boundary to the east and north and a political boundary to the south and west. This compact area of responsibility is convenient for record linkage. About 35 per cent. of the Northern Ireland population live in one large conurbation (Belfast) ; sited in it are the four major hospital groups ; the headquarters of three of the eight local health authorities ; all the government departments and statutory bodies concerned with the health services ; and the only computer installations to which easy access is assured. It is possibly relevant that the Belfast hospitals have about 35 per cent. of the total hospital bed complement of Northern Ireland (18,000) and deal with about 40 per cent. of all inpatient admissions (190,000) and 60 per cent. of all outpatient attendances (1·2 million). This concentration results in easy personal contacts between people with common medical and para-medical interests and should minimize technical problems when, as we hope, computer data links or a computer grid system are established to transmit medical data.

But probably the greatest advantage which Northern Ireland enjoys, as a potential area for successful medical record linkage, is due to the fact that the number of statutory bodies and government departments maintaining relevant records is very small and that none of them has responsibilities for services outside the area now proposed for the national linkage scheme. Thus, there is only one body (the Northern Ireland Hospitals Authority) responsible for the administration of virtually all the hospital services, the laboratory services, the ambulance service, the blood transfusion service, and the mass radiography service. Again, there is only one body (the Northern Ireland General Health Services Board) responsible for the administration of virtually all general practitioner medical and dental services, the pharmaceutical service, and the supplementary eye services. Although there are eight local health authorities with functions relating to public health, maternal and child health, school health, and vaccination and immunization, their medical officers meet frequently and this has resulted in appreciable standardization of records. One government ministry (the Ministry of Health and Social Services) has overall responsibility for the Northern Ireland health services and one of its branches administers the National Health Insurance scheme in much the same way as does the Ministry of Social Security in Great Britain. Finally, Northern Ireland has its own Registrar General with functions similar to those of England and Wales, and of Scotland.

In 1964, I had a series of talks with senior officials of relevant government departments and statutory bodies. At each, I outlined what I should now like to call Newcombe's principles of record linkage and emphasized the benefits which would accrue from a national system in Northern Ireland. All whom I approached agreed to take part in a joint discussion which the secretary of the Human Genetics Committee organized in May 1964. This discussion was almost unique in that the participants included senior permanent officials and medical advisers of all the relevant government departments and statutory bodies, senior members of those bodies, the Dean and members of the Faculty of Medicine, and representatives of the University and Government computer installations. The discussion concluded with acceptance in principle of a national system of linked medical records. Except for a slight reservation on the part of those responsible for the payment of sickness benefits, the conclusions were unanimous. A Steering Committee was set up, consisting of senior officers of the statutory bodies and government departments, and representatives of the Faculty of Medicine. The importance of involving, at this stage, senior members of the bodies whose records we hoped to link cannot be over-emphasized—this representation enabled the Steering Committee to carry out a reconnaissance and make an appreciation of the situation quickly and at no cost.

In November 1965 the Steering Committee presented a report to the Ministry of Health and Social Services outlining, with provisional costs, proposals for a detailed scheme. These proposals were referred to, and obtained approval from, several independent assessors from outside Northern Ireland. The Ministry proposes to finance the first four years of record linkage, as a research project associated with the Departments of Medical Statistics and Computing Science of the University, and we hope to start work within the next twelve months.

One of the Steering Committee's first tasks was to consider ways in which the confidential nature of medical records could be preserved. There are two safeguards which we shall adopt. First, we propose that the administrative and computer operations involved

72

in linking records will be carried out by members of a Medical Records Linkage Unit, and all members of this Unit who are not already employees of, or holding contracts with, one of the statutory bodies will be granted honorary appointments with the Hospitals Authority to bring them within the ambit of the Northern Ireland Health Services Acts. Second, in certain circumstances (*e.g.* for some medical and genetic research projects), research workers must interview individual members of the population. We propose that when an interviewee is ascertained from the Unit's files, the research worker's initial approach will be to the practitioner associated with, or responsible for, that individual's health ; the practitioner will then explain the research to the individual and obtain consent to an interview. This procedure sounds cumbersome but, from past experience, we believe it will work. We do know that it will give satisfaction to general medical practitioners and should help to secure their co-operation which is often essential in such studies.

Early in their work the members of the Steering Committee each prepared a detailed schedule of the data included in their departmental records. Some 26 personal records were documented and for all of these we took particular note of the information which would enable us to identify individual members of the population. In all, some 32 items of identification were enumerated although very few of these were common to all, or even to a majority, of the records.

At this stage I must explain the unique contribution which the General Health Services Board can make to identification problems. Since 1948 the Board has maintained a card index for all patients (virtually the whole population) registered with the 750 general practitioners in Northern Ireland. This could clearly be a key document and, indeed, the origin of a master file because each card records in full the subject's names (including maiden surname where applicable), sex, marital state (for women), date of birth, National Health Service number, usual address, and identity of general practitioner. The Steering Committee were advised that there were some omissions in the information on some of the cards, particularly those relating to older members of the population. We therefore examined a random sample of about 5,000 cards. Among other results, this study showed that dates of birth were missing from 0·3 per cent. of the sample cards and that this proportion was not much affected by the sex of the persons to whom the cards related ; marital status was missing from 8 per cent. of the sample cards relating to women ; and maiden names were missing from 5·5 per cent. of the sample cards relating to women who were known to be married. From this, after estimating 95 per cent. confidence limits, we concluded that :

1. there were probably not more than 7,000 cards in the index from which dates of birth were missing ;

2. there were probably not more than 70,000 cards in the index relating to females and having no entry about their marital state ; and

3. there were probably not more than 22,000 cards in the index relating to women known to be married and having no entry of their maiden surnames.

The officers of the General Health Service Board have since been making every effort to rectify omissions. They recently reported that there were now very few dates of birth omitted.

Some of us then had doubts about the ability of members of the population to report identification information accurately and a small experiment was carried out among 115 patients in four wards of the Royal Victoria Hospital. We asked the nurses to collect a number of items of identification by questioning their patients. We limited our enquiry to those items which either had been used or had been proposed for use in record linkage schemes. The patients were told that they could refer to any documents which they normally carried but the nurses were advised not to help the patients in any other way. There is no need for me to detail all the results but I should draw attention to a few which surprised some of us and confirmed the worst suspicions of others.

1. Few patients had any difficulty in reporting their own dates and places of birth and their present addresses. Three gave only their year of birth and five misunderstood the question about place of birth. What was reported agreed with their hospital records.

2. About 60 per cent. of the patients could not state their National Health Service number and of the 40 per cent. who tried to do so many gave numbers which were obviously National Insurance numbers. In fact only about 12 per cent. reported numbers which could have been National Health service numbers.

3. Just over 30 per cent. of patients were able to give the full dates of birth of their parents.

4. About 80 per cent. of patients were able to give the places of birth of their parents in sufficient detail for the localities to be identified as being in specific county boroughs or counties.

5. Just over 95 per cent. of patients were able to give their parents' first names and their mothers' maiden surnames.

We were able to trace 91 or 79 per cent. of the patients on the General Health Services Board card index, and the officer in charge of the index assured us that he would probably have been able to trace most of the others if we had allowed him more time. Most of the untraced patients were over the age of 60 and this, of course, ties up with earlier information that we have had about omissions from the General Health Services Board records. Of the traced patients, there were relatively few differences between the information given by the patients and the information recorded on the Board's index. For example, there were differences in only seven of the first names in 91 of the traced patients, but in most cases these were such that further first names could be added. There were differences in dates of birth of 10 of the patients. National Health Service numbers were found in the General Health Services Board list for 48 patients who gave no reply to this question and for 29 who gave National Insurance numbers.

From such a limited study only tentative conclusions can be drawn but the proportion of apparent errors in reporting dates of birth is a matter for some concern. On the other hand, the study suggests that most patients are likely to know their mothers' maiden names and that this could, therefore, be a useful item of identification in Northern Ireland. We were not surprised by the confusion which arose about the National Health Service and National Insurance numbers—why must we have both ?

By now you will have come to the conclusion that in Northern Ireland we have talked a lot and, I hope, thought a lot about medical record linkage. You will also have come to the conclusion that we have achieved very little in practice. In a sense this is true but shortly money and facilities will be available for practical work to be done by a full-time staff with no other commitments. Meanwhile, the Steering Committee's activities have done nothing but good because they have forced most organizations keeping medical and para-medical records to make re-appraisals of their systems. I shall conclude by referring to three examples. First, the Hospitals Authority, with the help of members of the University Departments of Medical Statistics, Computing Science, and Social Medicine, has made a complete review of the way in which it collects its statistical information, the medical records system used in its hospitals, and the need for computer support for these activities. There is now under way a pilot study of a standardized record system which takes the needs of medical record linkage into full account. Second, the Registrar General has under consideration ways and means of substituting dates of birth for ages in all registration procedures. Third, an experimental scheme for processing the outpatient records of the Northern Ireland skin clinics has proved so successful that it is being

75

kept going by mechanical data-processing methods until such time as it can be incorporated into a comprehensive linkage system. These examples typify the great advantage which Northern Ireland enjoys when any integrated scheme is planned—it is so easy to secure collaboration between individuals or organizations with very different functions and backgrounds. This we hope augurs well for the future of a national system of linked medical records.

I am indebted to the Northern Ireland Medical Records Linkage Steering Committee for permission to describe their work.

DISCUSSION

Professor Morrison : I am very grateful for this opportunity to congratulate Professor Cheeseman on his success in organizing a system of linkage in Northern Ireland. His skill as a negotiator must have been severely tried during the last three years. I must also congratulate him on getting this grant—obviously Northern Ireland is going to complete with Oxford in the next few years in producing some very interesting data. I was particularly interested in the point he made about the National Health Insurance difficulties, because in this country we have had trouble in getting information from this source about the return of patients to work. It would be of very great administrative and research interest if information about return to work could be linked routinely to hospital inpatient data : in other words if some of Ferguson's research work in this field (' Hospital and Community ') could be made part of routine statistics. Dr Acheson told us that he was able to report the subsequent death of patients to the hospital ; the addition of subsequent mortality and of return to work data to the hospital inpatient enquiry would be very helpful indeed.

The vexed question of confidentiality came up in Professor Cheeseman's paper. He worried me when he mentioned research workers interviewing individuals who had been ascertained from the Unit's files. I wonder whether this is a snag in the whole system of record linkage. It is one thing to do a field study and then to be able to get subsequent mortality and morbidity data on these individuals. It seems to me quite another to approach individuals in the first place with the backing of a large file not only of medical records but of social security and so on as well. I don't think I would like to be approached by a research worker armed not only with my medical history from the cradle but also with full details of all my brushes with official bodies. It is only a matter of time perhaps before information about skirmishes with the law are added in and I would like this even less. Probably we will discuss this area tomorrow.

May I end with a question : In Northern Ireland emigration must be a very big problem. Is there any way of linking this in, because without data on emigration the linked record system is surely going to have a large hole in it ?

Professor Cheeseman : Can I just reply to two points : the first concerns the confidential aspects when a survey is being carried out and a research worker approaches a member of the population. We have had considerable difficulty with this. We have discussed the matter with officials in the Ministry of Health and Social Services and with legal people. The approach which we are putting forward seems to be most generally acceptable to everybody ; it is that the research worker will deal first of all with the medical practitioner, although not necessarily with the general practitioner because it could be a hospital consultant if at the time the consultant has care of the patient. And then—and here is where we depend upon the general practitioner and the consultant's goodwill—it is really up to him to get the support of the interviewee. I think this is not difficult. We have tried it successfully in the past, using records which we have been maintaining mechanically. The final point—emigration : the answer is easy if only Great Britain will get on and get its record linkage organized then we can link in with them.

Dr Bahn : You spoke about the usefulness of this pre-study survey in terms of the various agencies reviewing the adequacy of their records. Do you think that some standardization of these records will be accomplished before the register gets under way ?

Professor Cheeseman : Yes. This gives me the opportunity to put in some emphasis that I had to miss out because the bell rang. The Hospital Authority, with the help of the University Departments of Medical Statistics, Computing Science, and Social Medicine, have, as a matter of fact, made a complete review of the way in which it collects its statistical information and of the medical records systems used in hospitals and of its need for computer support for these activities. We now have under way a pilot scheme on a standardized record system. Perhaps I may take the opportunity of putting one other point : our Registrar General is considering the ways and means of entering dates of birth instead of ages on all registration certificates.

Dr Weir : The question of confidentiality raised by Professor Morrison hinges on my disagreement with Mr White in that we are going to be dependent on consultants and general practitioners. While the money may be promised, unless we show them it is being properly used and for their benefit then the scheme will fail. I am sorry to reiterate this.

Professor Cheeseman : You are a pessimist. So little money has been promised so far that I can easily justify the expenditure on a very large number of other aspects of linked records.

Dr Acheson : May I make a comment about cost ? In the first five years of our study we spent a good deal of money and I don't think there was very much we could put on the positive side in respect of services rendered which saved other people money. The point here is that if you think of a system of linked records as something that is *superimposed* on the records systems that are already in existence, and doesn't change any of these systems, it will always be expensive. But since the end of the fifth year various interesting things have begun to happen. For example, two of the large hospitals in the area are closing their manual diagnostic and operations indices, which I reckon together must cost something in the order of £5,000 a year to maintain purely in clerical wages, and we will provide the data for these indices and more beside. Again, I think it is quite likely that we may be able to take over for the Medical Officers of Health, as I mentioned this morning, the provision of lists of persons for the at-risk register. This again is costly when it is done on a manual basis. And so we hope gradually to offset by savings to our colleagues in the area the costs which we expend. There is another category of output of course which is very difficult to cost, and that is the expense of services which could not be offered unless one had a system of linked records. This is an entirely different point which perhaps we will have an opportunity to discuss later.

Dr Spicer : Dr Cheeseman's reply to the previous question calls forth an immediate request for information : if you have been granted so little money is it enough, because if so it means that record linkage is very cheap ?

Professor Cheeseman : I particularly don't want to go into great detail about the ways in which we are getting the grant and how much is promised at the moment. It is enough, and the sums we are getting for recurrent expenditure will meet the proposals which we have for the records which are to be linked. One of the very big savings which we have in our operation is the use of the University's computer. When Queen's University made its submission to the Flowers Committee for computer hardware and software we did include in it the research needs of the Department of Medical Statistics and included in them were a number of proposals for medical record linkage.

Dr Benjamin : I wondered if I might say that it is possible to demonstrate the usefulness of linkage before you have a formal system of record linkage. With help from the Registrar General in

England and Wales I have already, with others, completed a follow-up study of mortality of a sample of widowers to relate their mortality to the effect of bereavement. Now with even more help from the Registrar General I am engaged with Professor Yudkin in a longitudinal study of the relationship between sugar intake and mortality, particularly mortality from heart disease, based on a sample of middle-aged men in the London area. The sample will be drawn from Census records. In the same sampling operation we shall record a number of demographic characteristics about these individuals. We intend to obtain information about their sugar intake from a postal questionnaire which has already been demonstrated to be efficient. We will follow these people until they die, getting events from the National Health Service Central Register and then referring back to the Death Register for the cause of death. None of this involves any formal system of record linkage but it does involve drawing information about the same individuals from different registers and I think it will certainly indicate the usefulness of the idea of linkage. Incidentally it really is quite cheap in the sense that total costs of the sugar survey are not likely to be much more than £5,000.

Dr Bahn : Dr Benjamin brings up an interesting point—the potentiality of record linkage. In some of our discussions in the United States about the desirability of linking various kinds of vital statistics and health records, many of us have come to the conclusion that it might be a more feasible goal to be ' able ' to link records than to actually put all the data together on a national basis. As yet we do not have a unique number that would make it feasible to carry out linkage on any large geographic scale. Various attempts to link death certificates and other records with the Census have not been very successful. A second point relates to cost. Are some of the medical record linkage studies we have been discussing sufficiently similar so that the computer programmes can be exchanged ?

Professor Alwyn Smith : This idea that Dr Bahn offers of making records linkable rather than linked has already been adopted quite extensively in Britain, for example the Registrar-General for Scotland punches a linkage code on all punch cards relating to all vital registration events in Scotland. The problem has been to persuade research workers to make any use of it. All the stillbirth records (with causes) for the last 20 years have now been assembled into families and it is extremely difficult to find anyone who would want the data. In a large part of the North-East of Scotland, marriages since 1951 have had the children of those marriages added so that there is a considerable amount of demographic data on family building and the way it has changed over the last nearly 17 years. Again it seems very difficult to interest demographers in this kind of data even when it has already been supplied and provided by a Government department.

MEDICAL RECORDS AND RECORD LINKAGE IN LOCAL GOVERNMENT

T. McL. Galloway

THE major local governments in the United Kingdom store medical records of many kinds. These relate to the life, sickness and death experience of their populations and the increasingly comprehensive preventive and other health services provided for these populations. A small but growing number of local governments are using electronic data processing (E.D.P.) methods to make better use of this information and to improve their administration of local health services. The working party of the Local and Public Authorities Computer Panel and the Society of Medical Officers of Health recently confirmed that 62 major authorities had a computer in use or on order and were carrying out, or considering its use for, public health work. The applications varied from straightforward statistical analyses to comprehensive record keeping and simulations of administrative/clerical routines.

In this short paper I propose to deal briefly with two applications involving record linkage which were developed in my department. The first is the scheme of administration of vaccination and immunization for infants and schoolchildren. This was begun in 1962 and has been described in some detail elsewhere (Galloway, T. McL. 1963, 1966). A magnetic tape file of over 60,000 participating children and their current records is maintained. This central record is accessible to any interested clinician and by a monthly programmed procedure, appointments are made for the beneficiaries to attend their chosen service source (either family doctor or county clinic) as the vaccinations and immunization become due, to suit the convenience of the clinicians. The arrangements provide for the monthly up-dating of the file, the necessary statistical appreciations and the production of lists of payments due to the family doctors for the work done by them.

The up-dating of the records is done from the information returned by the clinicians at the end of each vaccination and immunization session. The link used is the code number of the family doctor

80

or county clinic and the schedule line number. This is a quite primitive linkage system but it has worked well and as an early example may be of some interest.

The second application has been described recently (Saunders & Snaith, 1967) by two departmental colleagues and is an E.D.P. scheme of administration for cervical cytology. The master file in this case is the list of females from the electoral register. From this file, personal invitations to submit to cervical cytological diagnosis are addressed (as laboratory resources permit) to every woman (over 35 years of age) in the county at five-yearly intervals. The laboratory reports are stored centrally and it will be possible to analyse the results of this recent public health measure in due course as particulars of age, social class of husband and wife, marriage and obstetric history, and contraceptive technique are included in every record. By diligent follow-up of women who refuse the offer of a test and of those who fail an appointment, it is hoped to achieve a high proportion of acceptances as it is well known that the women who are most likely to benefit from this service are those least likely to accept the offer of it. This scheme is a recent development and the records of successive services are brought together using link numbers allocated to beneficiaries by the County Health Department for this purpose.

These examples of record linkage are functioning now, and the third generation machine brings nearer the prospect of integrating in a more useful way, the records of individuals now held in hospitals and family doctors' offices. The special purpose files now held by the E.D.P. Unit in West Sussex are likely to be assimilated in a data bank before long. Identification links are likely to be at least duplicated for services, things and people ; one identification will be a derivation of the item description, and the other will be an alphabetical/numerical identification with a distribution point significance.

REFERENCES

GALLOWAY, T. McL. (1963). Management of vaccination and immunization procedures by electronic computers. *Med. Offr*, **109**, 232.
GALLOWAY, T. McL. (1966). Computers : their use in local health administration. *R. Soc. Hlth J*. **86**, 213.
SAUNDERS, J. & SNAITH, A. H. (1967). Cervical cytology : a computer assisted population screening programme. *Med. Offr*, **117**, 299.

DISCUSSION

Dr Parry : It is no accident that Dr Galloway's scheme has been mentioned by several speakers here to-day. There is a tendency to

G

consider that the application of the computer is only appropriate in the most complex organizational problems. The outstanding merit of Dr Galloway's application to the immunization programme is its simplicity. The objectives are very clear and its achievement impressive, and I certainly think it has given value for money. He claims that it is no more than common sense, but this is obviously a subject which must be included in the Diploma of Public Health if we are going to see a national immunization programme as good as that in West Sussex. I think the objective of the cervical cytology programme is also quite clear and it will no doubt be as successful as that for immunization. We shall all watch Dr Galloway's venture into general practitioner records with much interest. I would like to ask him what he had in mind to record in his data bank. So much of general practitioner records are merely records of patient–doctor contact and we shall be interested to see objectivity applied to general practitioner records.

Secondly, I wonder if a local authority area is in fact the right one on which to think in terms of record linkage. As a cyclist in Professor Logan's Jet Age (p. 61), I am a little reluctant to suggest that Hospital Boards are ready to launch into this field. However as the Regional Boards have already started Hospital Activity Analysis and they rely so much on comparability within their larger administrative areas for epidemiological statistics—I think it is perhaps these Boards which should take the initiative in record linkage.

Dr Galloway : The question of what to record from the point of view of the family doctor is a difficult one, of course, and this must take into account not only what a family doctor himself wants to record—and this is important because I think we must always try to be sure that we are giving the clinician a service—but also what is capable of being recorded succinctly with reasonable economy. I was careful to say, I think, that I hold no particular brief for the local health authority doing this kind of thing and when I was talking about what we hope we may be able to do with the general practitioners who come into our health centres, initially it is no more than a feasibility study. It might become viable in the long term, but we would like to show that this can be done. We visualize links not only between the data bank and the general practitioners and our own records in the data bank, but with the hospital as well. Clearly if the family doctors cannot communicate with the hospital and vice versa through the data bank, the thing is of comparatively little interest to them. I would be delighted to see the Boards really take the initiative in this, but as things are at the moment I think that the local health authorities are more likely to take the initiative in respect of the interests of domiciliary medical care.

Dr Edgar : I should like, on behalf of my colleagues, as a Medical Officer of Health, to pay tribute to Dr Galloway and his department's pioneer work in the application of computers by local health authorities. I think it might perhaps be assumed by some amongst the audience, from Sir George's introductory remarks, that the very high acceptance rate for infant vaccination and immunization to which he referred which obtains in West Sussex is purely attibutable to the use of a computer. I am perfectly certain that this is not so. It underestimates the ability of Dr Galloway and his department, because there are an increasing number of medical officers of health who are fortunate to have access to computers, who don't get anything like the acceptance rate that Dr Galloway has in his area.

Medical Officers of Health are increasingly interested in the possibilities of computer assistance for various records kept by them, yet they have available to them a very heterogeneous collection of data processing machinery and computers, some obviously more advanced than others. There are two points that I am a little apprehensive about.

Firstly, although an authority like my own is very willing to proceed in this matter, computer time is not available to us. Secondly I am not sure that some of our colleagues are not a little too narrow in their vision with regard to the possibility of computer assistance not only for local health authorities but also in the very much wider context that we have been discussing this morning. For example, I think too many are thinking purely and entirely in the field of vaccination and immunization. I know of other schemes—Dr Galloway has himself mentioned one this morning—another was one record for the whole of the maternity services—hospital, general practitioner and local authority, with a particular view to looking at the vexed question of perinatal mortality. Further, we are very fortunate in the Oxford region in having the Oxford Regional Hospital Board working our cervical cytology recall service for us.

I would like to ask Dr Galloway three questions. Firstly, how does he account for his very high acceptance rates for vaccination and immunization ? Secondly, most local authorities in England and Wales have been obliged to hand over these records to the executive councils on the 1st April. Is he one of the privileged few who have managed to retain his well-established system ? Thirdly, to what extent would he be prepared to forgo his very efficient and excellent records sytem based on the local authority computer in favour of a central, multi-access, multi-programme computer provided, say, by the Regional Hospital Board.

Dr Galloway : I would agree with Dr Edgar that the E.D.P.

method is only one factor in producing good protection indices. Other things contribute to this, not least the fact that our health visiting staff are attached to general practices and when they go seeking a consent they go with the authority of their family doctor. They are also obliged to return this consent form whether or not they secure a consent, and very few of them are prepared to confess their failure on the back. It may interest you to know that in a consecutive series of 12,000 births we only had seven forms returned as failures to consent and I think the statisticians would confirm that seven exotics in a population of 24,000 is to be expected.

The change on 1st April consequent on the new charter for general practice was a subject of some brief correspondence with the Ministry, who were extremely helpful both on the audit as well as on the medical side. The Executive Council were in any case overwhelmed with other work and only too delighted that we should continue to do as we were doing. The family doctors would have insisted on this anyway and the Executive Council have no resources to carry out a scheme of this kind had they wished to. The arrangement that we arrived at is that instead of the computer being programmed to write the cheques for the family doctors it now writes a list of payments due by the Executive Council to the individual family doctors, and those lists take into account not only vaccination and immunization but cervical cytology as well.

Finally, I was asked how would I react to a central takeover on this ? Well I think most of us here look forward to the day when we have a national organized scheme of information storage and retrieval and I would like to emphasize that what I have been talking about are quite clearly small laboratory experiments, and I would like very much to see this established as a national going concern and we can fade out and do something else, because there are a lot of interesting things that we would like to do.

Mr Healy : May I ask Dr Galloway the extent to which his existing and projected programmes can be taken over by other interested parties ? It is vital at present to make the fullest possible use of computer personnel such as programmers and systems analysts. In this connection, I would urge a more widespread use of high-level machine languages which are to some extent machine independent. The efficiency of these languages is often underrated in this country.

Dr Galloway : The Society of County Treasurers and the Institute of Municipal Treasurers and Accountants have for some years past foreseen the likelihood of waste in the development of new applications and for some years now a register of potential and operational programmes has been maintained by the County

Treasurer of the West Sussex County Council. There is a mutual aid scheme by the local authorities whereby they can have those programmes and are in fact encouraged to take them rather than compete among themselves for scarce personnel. There is of course a problem of translation from one language to another. I am not a computer expert but I understand that those difficulties are comparatively small, having regard to the difficulties inherent in producing something quite new. For some time we have had a working party to which I alluded early in my presentation and we have recommended to the senior authorities that a small central research unit should be established somewhere with a view to developing possible applications which will be available to any of the local authorities, because we recognize that many agencies, not only Government agencies, are competing very wastefully for those scarce people. This suggestion was made to overcome this difficulty and we are hopeful that it may be accepted.

Mr White : I think there is, as has been implied, a substantial need for co-ordination in the whole of this field. Three of the areas in which co-ordination is beginning to develop are, firstly, the general content and format of records, of which there is an increasing amount of public and semi-public discussion. Secondly, the area of computer languages—the Ministry has recently established a medical computing language committee which is going to consider the possibility of a computing language that will enable all Health Service computer users to use the computer in the same way wherever that computer comes from. This in itself will help to promote compatibility of systems. And, thirdly, I think there is probably a need for what one might call ' system auditors ', a group of people who are well informed about the different ways in which computers are being used in the field of health records and begin to pick the best of the bones out of these systems and devise model systems for the country as a whole,—model systems that can be adapted to local circumstances without a serious sacrifice of compatibility.

Dr Edwards : If I could just draw attention to the severity of this problem : I know of some regions in which computers actually provided by the same manufacturers are incompatible, and in which the manufacturer has succeeded in recommending the use of a very primitive language. This is extremely unfortunate so far as the taxpayer is concerned as it is quite impossible to avoid the duplication of programming activity in which so many computer firms do in fact have a considerable vested interest. There has been a precedent at the Government level for getting over this problem as the Central Electricity Generating Authority have bought an integrated series of computers for use throughout the country. There has got to be clear guidance quickly as to whether one has a standard type of computer or a standard language or both ; the cost of indecision is rising very rapidly in this field.

PART 3

METHODOLOGY I

Chairman : Dr B. BENJAMIN (London)

A STATISTICAL APPROACH
TO
RECORD LINKAGE

A. B. SUNTER

INTRODUCTION

WHILE a number of reports on particular linkage operations have been published very little progress has been made so far towards developing a suitable theoretical framework for the procedures used. In most of the published reports the criteria used to decide whether pairs of records should be linked have been a set of more or less arbitrary rules justified partly on intuitive and partly on empirical grounds.

Notable contributions towards a general theory have been made by Tepping (1955), Tepping and Chu (1958), Nathan (1964), and duBois (1964). It would be impossible to overstate the importance of the work done over a period of several years by Newcombe and his associates (Newcombe *et al.*, 1959) at Chalk River. The approach of this paper is perhaps best justified on the grounds that it is more general than that of the first three authors above and that it formalizes the essentially intuitive approach of Newcombe. This formalization makes explicit the underlying assumptions of the linkage criterion and makes possible the systematic investigation of its properties.

There will be two distinct but interrelated parts of a complete theory for record linkage. The first part is concerned with the purely statistical problem of deciding whether a particular pair of records, once brought together for comparison, should be linked. The second part is concerned with the design of efficient (computer) systems to bring records together for comparison and, although this part has a significant statistical content, it will be intimately concerned with the particular computer hardware available. This paper will be concerned with the first part of the theory.

Two records which relate to the same unit (*e.g.* person or event) are said to be *matched*. If a decision is made that the records do in fact relate to the same unit the records are said to be *linked*. Obviously there are two kinds of error possible : (1) non-matched records are linked, and (2) matched records are non-linked. It appears that it is sometimes difficult for the non-statistician to accept the idea that levels of error should be pre-specified in a linkage operation, particularly an administrative one. And yet it is clear that no system could give an absolute guarantee that there will be no linkage errors of either type. In any event the concepts of levels of error of the two types is essential for the theory to be developed in this paper.

THEORY

1. The mathematical model

Two files or lists, L_A and L_B, contain N_A and N_B records respectively. Each record of each file may be regarded as an information *vector*, of dimensionalities K_A and K_B respectively, and which we may write as :

$$a_\alpha = (a_{\alpha 1}, a_{\alpha 2}, ..., a_{\alpha \kappa_A}) ; \qquad \alpha = 1, 2, ..., N_A \qquad (1)$$

and

$$b_\beta = (b_{\beta 1}, b_{\beta 2}, ..., b_{\beta \kappa_B}) ; \qquad \beta = 1, 2, ..., N_B \qquad (2)$$

respectively.

The components of these two vectors are items of identifying information such as surname, given name(s), age, sex, marital status, etc. in the case of persons or date of event, primary diagnosis, secondary diagnosis, etc., in the case of, say, medical events.

Two records, one from each file, brought together generate a *comparison* (α, β) described by a *comparison vector*

$$\gamma (\alpha, \beta) = (\gamma^1 [\alpha, \beta], \gamma^2 [\alpha, \beta], ..., \gamma^\kappa [\alpha, \beta]) \qquad (3)$$

of dimensionality K, not necessarily the same as either K_A or K_B.

The components of the comparison vector may be numerical codes representing simple item by item comparisons of the components of a_α and b_β but may be much more complicated. They may be for example, numerical codes representing agreement on particular values (such as a particular surname) of the entries in the original records or they may represent ' cross-comparisons ' of the original components. (For example, Newcombe has found that two initials are sometimes switched around in a record and has found it useful to make each of four possible comparisons of first initial of one record with first of the other, second initial of one record with first initial of other, etc.). The specification of the comparison vector may be, in fact, perfectly general the only requirement being that its components be capable of being numerically coded—a very mild restriction.

A formal requirement of the theory that is being developed here is that we must state how records are selected for comparison. Either

90

of two alternative specifications will suit our purpose equally well and, in practice, it will not matter which one we choose.

Alternative 1 : a record is selected from each file at random and with equal probability.

Alternative 2 : an inference will be made about all possible N_A . N_B comparisons.

We now define the *comparison space* Γ as the set of all possible realizations (whether actually realized or not) of the comparison vector, *i.e.*

$$\Gamma = [(\gamma^1, \gamma^2, ..., \gamma^\kappa)] \tag{4}$$

and on this space we define two probability measures

$$m(\gamma) = Pr \{\gamma = (\gamma^1, \gamma^2, ..., \gamma^\kappa)|(\alpha, \beta)\varepsilon M\} \tag{5}$$

and

$$u(\gamma) = Pr \{\gamma = (\gamma^1, \gamma^2, ..., \gamma_\kappa)|(\alpha, \beta)\varepsilon U\} \tag{6}$$

where M and U denote the set of matched comparisons and the set of unmatched comparisons respectively.

Equation (5), for example, is read as ' $m(\gamma)$ is the probability that the random (vector) variable γ takes on the value $(\gamma^1, \gamma^2, ..., \gamma^\kappa)$ given that the records which generated it are matched '.

From now on we drop the argument (α, β) except where needed for explicit reference.

Corresponding to each possible observable value of γ we would like to have a rule, say L, which enables us to make one of the two following inferences :

A_1 : the records which generated γ are matched.

A_3 : the records which generated γ are non-matched.

However, since we also want to specify the probabilities that the inferences A_1 or A_3 are in error, it is clear that we must allow a third inference, namely :

A_2 : we cannot infer A_1 or A_3 at the pre-specified levels of error.

It is convenient to refer to the set $[A_1, A_2, A_3]$ as the *action space*. Now, in general, the inference from γ to the action space need not be certain. We could specify a set D of probability measures on $[A_1, A_2, A_3]$, one set corresponding to each $\gamma\varepsilon\Gamma$.

A *linkage rule* is defined as a mapping from the comparison space Γ onto a set of random decision functions $D = [d(\gamma)]$. Corresponding to each $\gamma \varepsilon \Gamma$ there is a decision function $d(\gamma)$ which is itself a random variable on the action space.

$$d(\gamma) = [Pr(A_1|\gamma), Pr(A_2|\gamma), Pr(A_3|\gamma)] \tag{7}$$

where $\sum_{i=1}^{3} Pr(A_i|\gamma) = 1$

In less formal terms, the linkage rule might be described as consisting of a set of appropriately weighted probability devices (*e.g.* a set of roulette wheels whose perimeters are divided into three sections of appropriate lengths). Having observed a particular γ we select the probability device corresponding to that γ and operate it (*i.e.* spin the roulette wheel). It will then lead to one of the actions A_1, A_2, or A_3 with probabilities specified by (7). We admit 'degenerate' random decision functions (*i.e.* decision functions in which one of the probabilities is 1 and the other two are 0) and in fact it will turn out that the decision function corresponding to nearly every $\gamma \ \varepsilon \ \Gamma$ is degenerate under our optimal linkage rule.

As mentioned above there are two types of errors whose levels $u, \lambda (0 \leqslant \mu \leqslant 1 \ ; \ 0 \leqslant \lambda \leqslant 1)$ are given by

$$u = Pr(A_1 | U) = \sum_{\gamma \epsilon \Gamma} u(\gamma) \, Pr(A_1 | \gamma) \qquad (8)$$

and

$$\lambda = Pr(A_3 | M) = \sum_{\gamma \epsilon \Gamma} m(\gamma) \, Pr(A_3 | \gamma) \qquad (9)$$

The first of the equations above, for example, may be read as ' the probability, denoted by μ, of linking a comparison when the records are non-matched is calculated by summing, over all $\gamma \ \varepsilon \ \Gamma$, the product of the probability of realizing that γ, given that the records are non-matched, and the probability of the inference A_1, using the decision function corresponding to that γ".

The parameter μ and λ are said to be the levels of the linkage rule L which we now denote by $L(\mu, \lambda, \Gamma)$. It remains to give a basis for comparing linkage rules.

The inferences or actions A_1 and A_3 may be described as *positive dispositions* of a comparison. The action A_2 is, from a practical point of view, an undesirable one since it leaves us with the necessity either of making an arbitrary disposition (in which case we lose control of the error levels) or of incurring the expense of an extended comparison, usually a clerical examination external to the computer system. Thus it seems reasonable to judge the relative merits of two linkage rules at the same error levels by their relative numbers of failures to make positive dispositions.

Formally, a linkage rule $L(\mu, \lambda, \Gamma)$ is said to be *better* than $L'(\mu, \lambda, \Gamma)$, another linkage rule at the same error levels and on the same space, if

$$Pr(A_2 | L) \leq Pr(A_2 | L') \qquad (10)$$

and to be *best* among the class of linkage rules at the levels (μ, λ) if the inequality (10) holds for every linkage rule L' in the class.

If the levels (μ, λ) are set too high it is not hard to see that it may be the case that no linkage rule at these levels is possible, *i.e.*, it may be impossible to satisfy the equations (8) and (9) simultaneously. However, it is very unlikely that, in practice, one would set μ and λ high enough for this to occur and hence we will not discuss this problem here.*

2. A fundamental theorem

In this section we define a linkage rule $L(u, \lambda, \Gamma)$ which is best, in the sense given above. That is, no other linkage rule can be produced which satisfies the relationships (8) and (9) and which has a higher probability of a positive disposition.

Assume that : $m(\gamma) > 0$ and $u(\gamma) > 0$ for every $\gamma \, \varepsilon \, \Gamma$. This assumption will simplify our construction and is a perfectly reasonable one since, if $m(\gamma)$ and $u(\gamma)$ are both zero we might as well exclude γ from Γ, while if only one of them is zero the disposition of the comparison is obvious and error-free.

We now assign our ordering of the values of γ by requiring that the corresponding sequence of the ratio

$$l(\gamma) \,=\, m(\gamma)/u(\gamma) \tag{11}$$

be monotone decreasing.

When the value of (11) is the same for two or more γ we order these arbitrarily. Thus, if we index the ordered set of γ by the subscript i, writing $l_i = l(\gamma_i)$, $u_i = u(\gamma_i)$, we have

$$l_i \leqslant l_{i'} \text{ if } i > i' \tag{12}$$

Now, given μ and λ, choose n and n' such that

$$\sum_{i=1}^{n} u_i \leqslant \mu < \sum_{i=1}^{n+1} u_i \tag{13}$$

$$\sum_{i=n'-1}^{n} m_i > \lambda \geqslant \sum_{i=n'}^{N} m_i \tag{14}$$

where N is number of points $\gamma \, \varepsilon \, \Gamma$. We assume for our present purposes that when (13) and (14) are satisfied we have $1 \leqslant n < n'-1 < N$. This ensures that the levels (μ, λ) are admissible.

Let $L(\mu, \lambda, \Gamma)$ denote the linkage rule defined by :

---

* A definition of an ' admissible ' pair (u, λ) and an extension of the theorem given in the next section are given in a paper to be presented by the author and I. P. Fellegi at the 36th Session of the International Statistical Institute, 1967.

$$d(\gamma_i) = \begin{cases} \{1, 0, 0\} & i \leqslant n & (15\ a) \\ \{P_\mu, 1-P_\mu, 0\}\ ; & i = n+1 & (15\ b) \\ \text{where } P_\mu \text{ is determined by the solution to} \\ \qquad u(\gamma_{n+1})\ . P_\mu = \mu-u_n \\ \{0, 1, 0\}\ ; & n+2 \leqslant i \leqslant n'-2 & (15\ c) \\ \{0, 1-P_\lambda, P_\lambda\}\ ; & i = n'-1 & (15\ d) \\ \text{where } P_\lambda \text{ is determined by the solution to} \\ \qquad m(\gamma_{n'-1})\ . P_\lambda = \lambda-m_{n'} \\ \{0, 0, 1\}\ ; & i \leqslant n' & (15\ e) \end{cases}$$

The random decision functions (15 b) and (15 d) are necessary to ensure that the error levels (μ, λ) are exact. In practice, as will be seen in a corollary to the theorem, we will not find it necessary to use them. The effect of the decision functions (15 a), 15 c) and (15 e) is to partition Γ into three subspaces in the first of which we always link, in the second of which we cannot make a decision, and in the third of which we always non-link.

THEOREM Let $L(\mu, \lambda, \Gamma)$ be the linkage rule defined by (15). Then L is a best linkage rule on λ Γ at the levels (μ, λ).

The proof is straight forward, but rather lengthy, and will not be given here. It consists, of course, in showing that if L' (μ, λ, Γ) is any other linkage rule at the levels (μ, λ) on Γ then

$$Pr\{A_2 | \Gamma \lambda\} \leqslant Pr\{A_2 | \Gamma'\}$$

The theorem is of considerable interest to a mathematical statistician. Its practical importance is contained in the following two corollaries which are, mathematically, almost trivial.

Corollary 1

If $\mu = \sum\limits_{i=1}^{n} u_i$, and $\lambda = \sum\limits_{i=n'}^{N}$, then

the optimal linkage rule becomes

$$d(\gamma_i) = \begin{cases} \{1, 0, 0\}\ ; & i \leqslant n \\ \{0, 1, 0\}\ ; & n < i < n' \\ \{0, 0, 1\}\ ; & n' \leqslant i \end{cases} \qquad (16)$$

Corollary 2

Let T_μ and T_λ be any two positive numbers such that

$$l_1 \geqslant T_\mu > T_\lambda \geqslant l_N$$

94

Then the linkage rule

$$d(\gamma_i) = \begin{cases} (1, 0, 0) & \text{if } l_i \geqslant T_\mu \\ (0, 1, 0) & \text{if } T_\mu < l_i < T_\lambda \\ (0, 0, 1) & \text{if } T_\lambda \geqslant l_i \end{cases} \qquad (17)$$

is a best linkage rule at the levels (μ, λ) determined by summing μ_i and m_i over the appropriate subspaces.

The second corollary assures us that whatever the levels of the rule (17) it is best at these levels. In practice the theorem will be used in this form. Thus we try to get an estimate of the distribution of l_i and choose the *threshold values* T_μ and T_λ so as approximately to satisfy our specified error levels and apply the linkage rule given by (17).

3. Some simplifying assumptions

In most linkage problems the number of $\gamma \, \varepsilon \, \Gamma$ (if Γ is to be large enough for reasonably low error levels to be possible) will be so large that the enumeration of the corresponding probabilities $m(\gamma)$ and $u(\gamma)$ would be completely impracticable. Fortunately, it appears that we can make some simplifying assumptions which will make an implicit enumeration practicable.

We assume that the components of γ can be grouped in such a way that γ can be written

$$\gamma = (\gamma^1, \gamma^2, ..., \gamma^\kappa) \qquad (18)$$

and that these components are mutually statistically independent with respect to each of the two probability measures m and u separately ; *i.e.*

$$m(\gamma) = m_1(\gamma^1) \cdot m_2(\gamma^2) \cdot \; ... \; m_\kappa(\gamma^\kappa) \qquad (19)$$

and

$$u(\gamma) = u_1(\gamma^1) \cdot u_2(\gamma^2) \cdot \; ... \; u_\kappa(\gamma^\kappa) \qquad (20)$$

where

$$m_i(\gamma^i) = Pr\{\gamma^i \,|\, M\} \qquad (21)$$
$$u_i(\gamma^i) = Pr\{\gamma^i \,|\, U\}$$

For simplicity we will drop the subscripts and write $m(\gamma^i)$ and $u(\gamma^i)$ instead of $m_i(\gamma^i)$ and $u_i(\gamma_i)$.

It is important to understand the exact nature of the assumption (21) or it will not seem a reasonable one. An example of the first part of the assumption is that if two records are matched (*i.e.* they do in fact relate to the same person) then the configuration of the component relating to, say, surname is independent of the configuration relating to, say, address. Disagreement would usually be due in this case to errors in reporting, transcribing, key-punching, etc., and the assumption implies that these errors are independent for different components. Similarly the second part of (21) would assume that accidental agreements of components of unmatched records are statistically independent. It is also important to understand that we do *not* assume anything directly relating to the two files to be linked. It is quite clear, for example, that given name and sex are *not* statistically independent and we do not assume them to be. It is the components of the *comparison* vector which are assumed to be independent. Note that the assumption is made separately, so to speak, for each of the two probability measures m and u.

Clearly any monotone increasing function of $m(\gamma)/u(\gamma)$ would serve equally well as a test statistic. In particular, it is convenient to use the logarithms and define the *weight* as

$$w^\kappa(\gamma^\kappa) = \log m(\gamma^\kappa) - \log u(\gamma^\kappa) \tag{22}$$

We can then write

$$w(\gamma) = w^1(\gamma^1) + w^2(\gamma^2) + \ldots + w^\kappa(\gamma^\kappa) \tag{23}$$

and use $w(\gamma)$ as our test statistic. It is a convenience for intuitive interpretation of the linkage process that the weights defined above are positive for those configurations for which $m(\gamma^\kappa) > u(\gamma^\kappa)$, and that this property is preserved by the weights associated with the total configuration γ.

The components γ^κ of γ are, in general, themselves vectors the different values of which we have referred to as *configurations*. If the number of configurations which can be realized γ^κ is n_κ the number of *total configurations* which can be realized by γ is obviously $n_1 . n_2$. $\ldots . n_\kappa$. However, because of the additive properties of the weights defined for components, which depend on the postulated independence, it will be sufficient to determine $n_1 + n_2 + \ldots + n_\kappa$ weights. We can always determine $w(\gamma)$ by employing this additivity.

4. Calculation of weights

The estimation of the probabilities $m(\gamma^\kappa)$ and $u(\gamma^\kappa)$ and hence of the weights w^κ requires considerable ingenuity and a thorough understanding of the principles involved.* Some general techniques can be discerned, however, and an outline is given here. This discussion will be presented in terms of the surname component, but the techniques apply to any component. In order to obtain the information

---

* An algorithm for the calculation of weights based only on the assumptions of section 3 and which does not make the same demands on the ingenuity of the statistician, is given in the paper by the author and I. P. Fellegi already cited.

necessary for the approach given below it will usually be necessary to do some preliminary analysis of the files being linked although over time one would hope to build up sufficient experience to proceed in a particular case without this preliminary analysis.

The surname component of the comparison may be specified as a simple scalar function of the agreement status (*e.g.* it has a single sub-component which has the value 0, 1, or 2 corresponding to disagree on surname, one or both missing in file records, or agree on surname) or it may be a more complicated vector function such as the one specified in the next part of this paper. A typical realization might be a set of numerical codes corresponding to ' records agree on Soundex code ; the Soundex code is B650 ; the first five characters are in character by character agreement ; the second five characters are in character by character agreement ; the surname is BROWNING.'

Now assume that we could list all error-free realizations of all surnames in the two files, and also the frequencies of each surname in each file. Let the respective frequencies in L_A and L_B be

$$f_{A1}, f_{A2}, ..., f_{Am} ; \qquad \sum_{j=1}^{m} f_{Aj} = N_A$$

$$f_{B1}, f_{B2}, ..., f_{Bm} ; \qquad \sum_{j=1}^{m} f_{Bj} = N_B$$

Let the corresponding frequencies among the matched records be

$$f_1, f_2, ..., f_m ; \sum_{j=1}^{m} f_j = N$$

The following additional notation is needed :

e_A or e_B the respective probabilities of a name being misreported in L_A or L_B (we assume that the probability of misreporting is independent of the particular name).

e_{Ao} or e_{Bo} the respective probabilities of a name not being reported in L_A or L_B (we assume that the probability of name not being reported is independent of the particular name).

e_T the probability the name of a person is differently (though correctly) reported in the two files (this might arise, for example, if L_A and L_B were generated at different times and the person changed his name).

Finally we assume that e_A and e_B are sufficiently small that the probability of an agreement on two identical, though erroneous, entries is negligible and that the probabilities of misreporting, not reporting and change are independent of one another.

H

We shall first give a few rules for the calculation of m and u corresponding to the following configurations of γ : name agrees and it is the j-th listed name ; name disagrees ; name missing on either record.

m (name agrees and is the j-th listed name)

$$= \frac{f_j}{N}(1-e_A)(1-e_B)(1-e_T)(1e-_{Ao})(1-e_{Bo})$$

$$\doteq \frac{f_j}{N} \quad (1-e_A-e_B-e_T-e_{Ao}-e_{Bo}) \tag{24}$$

m (name disagrees)

$$= [1-(1-e_A)(1-e_B)(1-e_T)](1-e_{Ao})(1-e_{Bo})$$
$$\doteq e_A+e_B+e_T \tag{25}$$

m (name missing on either file)

$$= 1-(1-e_{Ao})(1-e_{Bo}) \doteq e_{Ao}+e_{Bo} \tag{26}$$

u (name agrees and is the j-th listed name)

$$= \frac{f_{Aj}}{N_K}\frac{f_{Bj}}{N_B}(1-e_A)(1-e_B)(1-e_T)(1-e_{Ao})(1-e_{Bo})$$

$$\doteq \frac{f_{Aj}}{N_K}\frac{f_{Bj}}{N_B}(1-e_A-e_B-e_T-e_{Ao}-e_{Bo}) \tag{27}$$

u (name disagrees)

$$= [1-(1-e_A)(1-e_B)(1-e_T)\sum_j \frac{f_{Aj}}{N_A}\frac{f_{Bj}}{N_B}](1-e_{Ao})(1-e_{Bo})$$

$$\doteq [1-(1-e_A-e_B-e_T)\sum_j \frac{f_{Aj}}{N_A}\frac{f_{Bj}}{N_B}](1-e_{Ao}-e_{Bo}) \tag{28}$$

u (name missing on either file)

$$= 1-(1-e_{Ao})(1-e_{Bo}) \doteq e_{Ao}+e_{Bo} \tag{29}$$

The proportions f_{Aj}/N_A, f_{Bj}/N_B, f_j/N may be taken, in many applications, to be the same. This would be the case, for example, if two large files are listed, both of which are thought to have a distribution of names similar to the national distribution. These frequencies may be estimated from the files themselves.

We should emphasize that it is not really necessary to list all the possible names for the validity of formulae (24) to (29). We might only list a group of names, e.g. grouping all names which have the same Soundex code or listing the more common names separately, grouping all the remaining names. In the case of groupings the appropriate formulae in (24) to (29) have to be summed over the corresponding values of the subscript j.

In the specification of the comparison vector components for surname comparison it is not feasible, and would not be efficient even if it were, to specify every particular surname. However, it will usually be efficient to specify some in accordance with our intuitive notion that agreement on a comparatively rare name will have a higher weight than agreement on a relatively common one and in fact the rarer the name the higher the weight. In order to apply the differential weighting implied we have to carry in the system a library of surnames. If a surname in the library (we call these 'specified names') occurs in an agreement configuration we can apply the appropriate weight. If the surname in agreement configuration is not in the library it has to receive a weight reserved for any surname not in the library (we call this 'agreement on an unspecified name'). In the case of such groupings of unspecified names the appropriate formulae in (24) to (29) have to be summed over all names in the group. The question thus arises as to how one should group the individual comparisons or how one should collapse groups into larger groups.

Clearly the object of the weighting system is to 'discriminate' between comparisons by giving high weights to as many as possible of the comparisons which are likely to arise from matched records and low weights to as many as possible of those which are likely to arise from unmatched records. If we have listed n'_k configurations (some of these may already refer to groups), it seems reasonable to measure the discrimination corresponding to the particular list of configurations by the function

$$G = \sum_{j'=1}^{n'_k} m(\gamma_{j'}^k)\, w_{j'}^k - \sum_{j'=1}^{n'_k} u(\gamma_{j'}^k)\, w_{j'}^k, \qquad (30)$$

where γ_j^k denotes the j-th configuration of γ^k.

Since the numbering of the configurations is arbitrary, we can look at the problem of choosing a subset of them to collapse into one configuration as one of numbering the configurations in a suitable order and combining the last $(n'_k - n_k + 1)$ configurations into one (which we now number n_k). We do this in such a way as to maximize

$$G^* = \sum_{j=1}^{n_k-1} m(\gamma_j^k) + w_j^k + m(\gamma^{k*})\, w^{k*}$$

$$\sum_{=1}^{n_k-1} u(\gamma_j^k)\, w_j^k - u(\gamma^{k*})\, w^{k*} \qquad (31)$$

where γ^{k*} is the collapsed configuration and

$$m(\gamma^{k*}) = \sum_{j=n_k}^{n_k'} m(\gamma_j^k) \tag{32}$$

$$u(\gamma^{k*}) = \sum_{j=n_k}^{n_k'} u(\gamma_j^k) \tag{33}$$

$$w^{k*} = \log m(\gamma^{k*}) - \log u(\gamma^{k*}) \tag{34}$$

In less formal terms we might say that we pick out the subset of configurations which, in the sense made precise above, contributes least to the discrimination of the characteristic.

5. Calculation of threshold values

Having specified all the relevant configurations γ_j^k and determined their associated weights w_j^k; $k = 1, 2, ..., K$; $j = 1, 2, ..., n_k$ it remains to set the threshold values T_μ and T_λ corresponding to given μ and λ and to estimate the number or proportion of failures to make a positive disposition of comparisons.

As shown before, the number of weights to be determined is equal to $n_1 + n_2 + ... + n_K$. The total number of different configurations is, however, $n_1, n_2 ..., n_K$. Since the number of total configurations will, in most practical situations, be too large for their complete listing and ordering to be feasible we have restorted to sampling the configurations in order to estimate T_μ and T_λ.

The problem is made considerably easier by the independence of the component vectors γ^k. Thus, if we sample independently the component configurations $\gamma_{j_1}^1, \gamma_{j_2}^2, ..., \gamma_{j_K}^K$ respectively, we will have sampled the total configuration $\gamma_j = (\gamma_{j_1}^1, \gamma_{j_2}^2, ..., \gamma_{j_K}^K)$. Hence, we do not need to list all configurations of γ for sampling purposes, only all configurations γ^k for each k. From the sample of total configurations we estimate the values of T_μ and T_λ corresponding to given μ and λ.

We have written a computer programme for the pilot project described below which, working from a list of configurations for each vector component selects a sample of total configurations, orders the sample by decreasing values of $m(\gamma)/\mu(\gamma)$, calculates estimates of μ and λ corresponding to each γ in the sample (i.e. it estimates the μ and λ that would correspond to γ if the whole set of γ in Γ had been listed), and finally prints out the whole list giving for each total configuration its associated λ, μ, T_λ, T_μ. The statistician or administrator is then free to make a choice of appropriate error levels since the programme also gives an estimate of the number of failures to make a positive disposition that corresponds to each pair of error levels.

100

1. Description of the project

At the Dominion Bureau of Statistics we are presently engaged in pilot project involving the linkage by computer of two administrative files of about 10,000 and 800,000 records, respectively. About 5000 records are expected to be common to the two files. In order to be certain of at least comparing the 5000 matched records we would have to compare every record in one file against every record in the other file—a total of 8×10^9 comparisons. Since this is a very large number of comparisons even for a large computer we have decided to ' block ' the files by the Soundex coded surnames and to make comparisons only between records in the same blocks. This still runs to about 2×10^8 comparisons and depending on the speed of comparisons and the amount of computer time we have available we may have to break at least the large blocks down even further. By so doing, of course, we may fail to compare matched records and hence contribute to the error λ in a way which may not be optimum in light of the theorem of Part II. It may happen that disagreement on Soundex will automatically produce such a high negative weight that it would preclude linkage by itself. This, then, would not represent a departure from the theorem. In any event, the probability of matched records resulting in disagreement on Soundex (or other characteristic) can be estimated, hence also the contribution of blocking to λ. The usefulness of Soundex for blocking lies exactly in the fact that it is explicity designed to minimize this type of error.

We are willing, as is usual in such pilot projects, to tolerate considerable inefficiency in order to obtain the information necessary for more efficient designs. For example, in practical linkage procedures and particularly where the files are known to contain no duplications, one would probably be willing to cease further comparisons on a particular record if the weight for some comparison was ' high enough ' that the probability, in some sense determined by the file sequencing, of finding another comparison with a weight high enough to be considered a 'competitor' for linkage was 'low enough'.

In a preliminary operation to the linkage procedure itself we must prepare the files for linkage. This preparation includes translating the surnames into Soundex codes, resequencing the files by Soundex code, and attempting to edit and standardize addresses written in free form (*i.e.* to identify the components of addresses and put them into fixed fields). We also tabulate the distributions of a number of characteristics in order to obtain the information necessary for the estimation of the sets of probabilities $\{m \, (\gamma_j^k)\}$ and $\{u \, (\gamma_j^k)\}$.

Following this we prepare the input for the programme described in Section 5 of Part II. The output from that programme provides information necessary to determine reasonable values of the error levels μ and λ and the corresponding threshold values T_μ and T_λ.

Table I. *Comparison components for record linkage pilot project*

Component (γ^k)	Subcomponents
1 Surname	Agreement status on 1. Particular Soundex surname 2. First 5 characters of surname 4. Second 5 characters of surname 4. Particular surname in Soundex code class
2 First Name	Agreement status on 1. Initial 2. First 5 characters 3. Particular initial
3 Second Name	Agreement status on 1. Initial 2. First 5 characters 3. Particular initial
4 Sex	Agreement status on 1. Particular sex
5 Marital Status	Agreement status on 1. Particular marital status 2. Initial of spouse 3. Particular initial of spouse 4. Name of spouse (first 4 characters)
6 Day of Birth	Agreement status on 1. Day of birth
7 Month of Birth	Agreement status on 1. Month of Birth
8 Year of Birth	Agreement status on 1. Particular year of birth 2. Age difference
9 Address	Agreement status on 1. Positions 1 through 4 of edited address 2. Positions 5 through 10 of edited address 3. Positions 11 through 13 of edited address 4. Positions 14 through 19 of edited address 5. Positions 20 through 21 of edited address 6. Positions 22 through 24 of edited address

The output from the linkage programme itself will be a printed list showing for each record α in one file the set of records β in the other file for which $w(\gamma(\alpha,\beta)) > T_\gamma$, the lower threshold value. That is, we will print out all records β which are linked or possibly linked to α. The records will be ordered by decreasing values of $w(\gamma(\alpha,\beta))$. In addition we will obtain, in a form suitable for further processing, data for certain investigations concerned with the cost and efficiency of the linkage operation itself.

Table II. *Surname component*

Subcomponent	Code values
1. Particular Soundex	0 if the Soundex codes for surname disagree 1 if one of both surnames are missing 2 if the Soundex codes agree on 1st specified code 3 if the Soundex codes agree on 2nd specified code . . . $T+1$ if the Soundex codes agree on t-th specified code $T+2$ if the Soundex codes agree on an unspecified code
2. First 5 characters	0 if the first 5 characters diagree 1 if one or both surnames are missing 2 if the first 5 characters agree
3. Second 5 characters	0 if the second 5 characters disagree 1 if one or both surnames are missing 2 if the second 5 characters agree
4. Particular surname within Soundex Code class (say t-th specified code class)	0 if the surnames disagree 1 if one or both surnames are missing 2 if surnames agree on 1st specified name in t-th specified Soundex class . . . V_t+1 if surnames agree on V_t—the specified name in t-th specified Soundex class V_t+2 if surnames agree on unspecified name in the t-th specified Soundex class

The list putput will be intensively examined in an attempt to ascertain our success in predicting the error levels and to resolve contradictions in the output (*e.g.* a record in one file might be ' positively linked ' to more than one record in the other file).

2. Specification of the comparison vector

The two files being used for the pilot record linkage project generate the comparison vector whose components are given in Table I.

In order to clarify some of the concepts introduced in Part II we will describe the surname component, in detail, as an example.

In Table II, T denotes the number of specified Soundex codes (possibly, $T = 0$) and V_t ($t = 1, 2, ..., T$) the number of specified names in the t-th specified Soundex code (possibly, $V_t = 0$).

In our pilot project, missing surnames and hence missing Soundex coded surnames do not occur since the presence of surname was a condition of entry in the file. Also, records whose Soundex codes do not agree will not be compared. These codes, impossible within our project, are included in Table II for the sake of completeness.

Not only some particular codes but also some combinations are impossible. For example, if either the second or third subcomponent is coded zero then the fourth subcomponent must be coded zero. Table III exhibits the possible configurations.

Table III. *Possible configurations for surname component γ^1*

Subcomponent			
1	2	3	4
0	0	0	0
0	0	2	0
0	2	0	0
2	0	0	0
2	0	2	0
2	2	0	0
2	2	2	2
2	2	2	3
.	.	.	
2	2	2	$V_t + 2$
.	.	.	
$T+2$	0	0	0
.	.	.	
$T+2$	2	2	$V_{t+2} + 2$

The total number of configurations for the surname component is easily seen to be

$$3(T+2) + \sum_{t=1}^{T+1} (V_t + 1).$$

Unsolved problems

The theory given in this paper is a framework for an operational approach and possibly for a more complete theory. It has nothing to say, for example, on the resolution of situations such as that shown diagrammatically below, in which solid lines represent 'positive linkages', broken lines represent 'possible linkage', and the absence of a connection implies a 'positive non-linkage'.

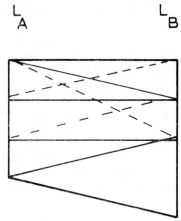

FIG. 1. Links, non-links and possible links.

Clearly there is an interaction between the levels of μ and λ and the occurrence (and the resolution) of situations such as that shown in the Figure. We will be examining this interaction in the light of the results from our pilot project.

Soundex coded surnames are one method of 'blocking' a file containing personal records (Note : while Soundex appears to be quite efficient for Caucasian surnames, Newcombe has pointed out its inefficiency for names of oriental origin) but it has some definite disadvantages. It results in a very uneven distribution of records to blocks and in large files many blocks will still be intolerably large. Also, like any other blocking method, it contributes to the error λ in that matched records in different blocks will not be compared, hence they will not be linked. Thus, we need to develop some theory for optimal blocking methods. As part of this theory and in the light of the costs involved we should consider the possibility of re-blocking the files on the basis of another characteristic and repeating the linkage operation. This would recover some of the losses caused by the original blocking. We should also consider the relative advantages of large blocks and a single file arrangement as opposed to small blocks with multiple file arrangements.

If the files are known to be substantially free of duplications we might expect to include in a practical linkage procedure a rule under which positively linked records are removed from further comparison as soon as they are discovered. All comparisons which fail to result in a positive link are, in a sense, wasted and we need to develop sensible rules as to the order in which records in corresponding blocks should be compared in order to minimize the number of ' wasted comparisons '.

We have made some progress in relation to the problems described above. Our approach has been to develop a fairly simple mathematical model which we will build into a computer programme to carry out the necessary prelinkage analyses.

Finally, there is a class of problems, intimately connected with the preceding ones, but on which we have made very little progress and which therefore, we do no more than mention here. These are concerned with efficient use of the particular computer hardware available and include such problems as optimal allocation of memory space to records from the two files, of lists of specified configurations of the comparison vector and the corresponding weights.

ACKNOWLEDGEMENTS : The author would like to express his gratitude to the Dominion Bureau of Statistics for providing the opportunity for the research leading to the present paper. Dr I. P. Fellegi of D.B.S. has been a close collaborator and Dr H. B. Newcombe has been generous in lending his vast experience and his encouragement.

REFERENCES

DU BOIS, N. S. D. Jr. (1964). On the problem of matching documents with missing and inaccurately recorded items. *Ann. math. Statist.* **35**, 1404. (Abstract).

NATHAN, G. (1964). On Optimal Matching Processes. Unpublished Doctoral Dissertation, Case Institute of Technology.

NEWCOMBE, H. B. & KENNEDY, J. M. (1962). Record linkage : making maximum use of the discriminating power of identifying information. *Communs Ass. Comput. Mach.* **5**, 563.

NEWCOMBE, H. B., KENNEDY, J. M., AXFORD, S. J. & JAMES, A. P. (1959). Automatic linkage of vital records. *Science*, **130**, 954.

NEWCOMBE, H. B. & RHYNAS, P. O. W. (1962). Family Linkage of Population Records. Proc. U.N./W.H.O. Seminar on Use of Vital and Health Statistics for Genetic and Radiation Studies. United Nations Sales No. 61, XVII 8. New York.

NITZBERG, D. M. & SARDY, H. (1965). The methodology of computer linkage of health and vital records. *Proc. Am. Statist. Ass.*, Soc. Statist. Sect.

A STATISTICAL APPROACH TO RECORD LINKAGE

PHILLIPS, W. Jr. & BAHN, A. K. (1965). Experience with computer matching of names. *Proc. Am. Statist. Ass.*, Soc. Statist. Sect.
TEPPING, B. J. (1955). *Study of Matching Techniques for Subscriptions Fulfilment.* Philadelphia : National Analysts Inc.
TEPPING, B. J. & CHU, J. T. (1958). *A Report on Matching Rules applied to Readers Digest Data.* Philadelphia : National Analysts Inc.

DISCUSSION

Professor Armitage : The calculations I have seen on these odds ratios have always assumed that the probabilities of errors for different attributes are independent, so that they can be multiplied together. I would like to ask Mr Sunter to what extent this assumption is made and to what extent it is justified.

Mr Sunter : We do in fact make that assumption but we are very careful about it. We make the assumption about the components of the comparison vector and not the components of the original records, and we make it independently for the class of matched comparisons and the class of unmatched comparisons. If you take these precautions I think it is a reasonable assumption. This is why I said that the components may themselves have to be vectors because we want the components to be statistically independent.

Mr Healy : I think Mr Sunter's paper is closer to the main stream of statistical research than is immediately apparent. His ratio M/U is in fact a ratio of likelihoods, and in statistician's jargon, he has shown that a likelihood ratio technique gives rise to a set of rules that are *admissible*. Is if of interest that, having fixed the risks of error, a wide range of admissible procedures is still available, and some of these are preferable to others.

I also am a little worried about the various assumptions of independence made in the paper. For example, the probability of non-agreement between first names may well be independent of sex in the linked records, where one is in fact dealing largely with recording errors ; but it is unlikely to be so in the unlinked records. I would be interested to know whether the effects of failure of these assumptions can be assessed quantitatively.

Mr Sunter : I am rather sorry about that example. We noticed ourselves that sex and given name are not going to be statistically independent even in the class of unmatched comparisons. In order to get around it we can combine them into one component and make sure they are statistically independent or reasonably so. It is quite true that this whole idea can be expressed in the classical terms of statistical hypothesis testing ; in fact at first this is the way we

107

developed it but it turned out to be too awkward to express it that way. I am not claiming any originality for the theory, at least in the context of mathematical statistics, although I have not found any theory that corresponds precisely to this in the sense that you have this symmetry between two ends of the scale.

The question of statistical independence of course does not arise in anything I said here to-day. It has something to do with deriving the weights to be used in practice and it is concerned with the necessity for enumerating, in some sense anyway, all possible observable configurations. If you have 10 components with, just for argument's sake, 10 possible configurations on each component then this gives you a total of 10^{10} observable configurations which is an uncomfortably large number. But if they are statistically independent then it turns out you only have to worry actually about 100 of them. The weights become additive and the problem becomes tractable.

Dr Nitzberg : I would like to comment on the question of statistical non-independence and its practical effect. In the work that I did, I ran into this problem very early and what I did was to lump first and last names together as one component, and considered full date of birth and address as two other components. I then assumed independence of these components to develop weights. Empirically I had results that were way beyond my expectations ; my error rates due to some degree of nonindependence between the items assumed to be independent were far below 1 per cent. For instance, in New York City different ethnic groups live in different sections of the city, but although I assumed the address and name components to be independent, even though there is some correlation between them, the assumption did not foul up my results to any appreciable level.

An unidentified member of the audience : One question which occurs to me over this problem of matching the two properties mu and lambda is that in certain circumstances you may set a very small lambda and still get a very large number of records which should be brought together but are not because you may be looking for a very small number of actual matches in a very large number of tries ; you may thus get a large number of missed matches even though the probabilities are small. I think this probably relates to the second part of the system which the speaker didn't talk about, which is how you bring the record together. I wonder if we could know a bit more about that and whether in fact small error rates could lead to large numbers of missed matches.

Mr Sunter : There are sure to be an enormous number of chances to make the second kind of error and the lambda has to be set very low indeed. In practice of course we don't make all possible comparisons because this would lead to an impossibly large number of comparisons to make even in a very large computer with a file of any size. This is another statistical problem that we are looking into. Obviously we must break the files down in some way and only make comparisons within the sub-divisions of the file. When this is done some of the records will find their way into the wrong blocks and they will never get compared with the record with which they match. This means that you use up some of your lambda in your initial sub-division of the file and one of the problems that I am working on at the moment is some kind of theory for an optimal way of breaking the file up. The method we are using at the moment in our experimental work is on a Soundex code but it is not really very satisfactory since it still leaves very large blocks in very large files.

Professor Wagner : I would like to ask the speaker if the theoretical probability functions take into account or are influenced by the clumping phenomena within our material, e.g. in the coding of family names. We used the Swiss family name code which has 900 possibilities, but only 536 possibilities were realized in material from 20,000 patients. The most common *eight* names made up 10 per cent. of the sample. A Lorenz curve for the distribution of the birth dates of our patients shows that about 50 per cent. of our sample were born within one birth decade. Regarding the distribution of births over the year, we also have very big deviations from equal distribution. It is interesting to note that the distribution of birth months in the north of Germany is quite different from that in the south and the west.

Mr Sunter : There is nothing in what you say that contradicts any part of our approach. In fact if you will let me have the frequency diagrams I can use them to derive the probability distributions that we need.

FILE STRUCTURES FOR THE AUTOMATIC MANIPULATION OF LINKED RECORDS

J. M. KENNEDY

As this year marks the tenth anniversary of my collaboration with Dr H. B. Newcombe on record linkage, it is perhaps an appropriate time to review some of the techniques that have evolved for the manipulation of linked files by a computer. My own activity in this field has not been continuous ; it has been concentrated into two periods during 1958 and 1963. Our early studies used what is now known as a first-generation computer, while more recent work has used a second-generation machine. Now that the third-generation machines are said to be upon us, it is time to look at the whole problem again to see how improvements in computer technology and computer science might be exploited. In most of what follows I shall be thinking of files with some hundreds of thousands or even millions of records in them. Hence a high degree of mechanization of all processes is essential.

There are three phases to any system for linking and maintaining files of linked records. The first of these is the confrontation of potentially linkable records from whatever source they may occur. The second is the decision-making part—the examination of points of comparison from pairs of records to decide whether or not they should be associated with each other. The third introduces the retrieval problem : how should files be structured in order to record the linked information in the most convenient manner for subsequent examination and extraction. These phases are not all independent of each other of course, and the answers to the various questions depend on the size and nature of the files under study as well as on the cost of performing certain types of operation in the computer. Because these costs change from year to year with changes in computer design the schemes that are feasible also change. Fortunately use of computers is one of the few areas in which the cost per operation decreases as time goes on. Thus projects that appear too costly now may well become economically feasible after a few years have elapsed.

The three generations of computers

Before turning to the evolution of our ideas about the structure of linked files it might be worth reviewing the evolution of computers over the past 15 or 20 years. It has become fashionable to divide the period into three generations. Machines of the first generation, including most of those available commercially up until the late fifties, were characterized by calculating speeds of several hundred basic operations per second, and a memory that was capable of holding a few thousand words. The hardware of these machines was composed mainly of tubes or valves for the electronic circuits and magnetic drums for memory. Many people now regard this period as the ' heroic age ' of computation. Scientists communicated with machines in the language of the machines ; they sat at the consoles of the machines and nursed them through the calculations ; they

110

took an intimate interest in the health of their machine from day to day ; they also lavished considerable ingenuity on circumventing some of the hardware limitations of the early computers. In this connection I might mention that our early record linkage studies were held up by the fact that the machine on which we were working was incapable of reading alphabetic input from cards. We managed to overcome this difficulty by a combination of a rather tricky piece of programming together with the insertion of a piece of cardboard in a vital part of the computer every time we were going to do some calculations using the record linkage programme.

In the second generation of computers, the speed was increased to perhaps a hundred thousand or more operations per second. The size and speed of the memory also increased, and memories containing some tens of thousands of words became common. The hardware of the machine was composed of transistors and magnetic cores. There was also a change in the operating philosophy of the computers of this period. As the machines became larger, the cost per hour for running them became large enough that one could no longer afford to let scientists sit and think while the machine was idle. The idea of a ' batch processor ' manned by staffs of full-time operators became common. People with problems simply left them in an anteroom and in the fullness of time (usually a few hours to a day) the results would emerge. At the same time the idea of the computer as a information processor rather than a giant calculator became popular as methods were devised for the manipulation of nonnumeric information. The second generation machines are still with us, and the bulk of the computing work that is done at the present time is handled in the way that I have just described.

Within the last few years, however, the so-called third generation has begun to appear. Computers of this era are characterized by such phrases as ' multiple access ', ' multi-programming ', ' time sharing', or ' conversational computing ', all of which described parts of a 'computer utility '. The idea here is that a person who wishes to make use of a computer need not have one close by him but should simply be able to communicate with a suitable computer just as he can make use of such public utilities as the telephone, electricity, or a water supply. The machines of the third generation usually have speeds that are greater than those of the second generation computers, and memories which are larger by a factor of ten or so, containing perhaps a hundred thousand to even a million words. They are also supported by back-up storage in the form of some hundreds of millions of words on drums, discs, and other semirandom access devices. Because these machines make it possible for persons at diverse locations to have access to the same central computer and central memory system, the notion of integrated files of material derived from a number of sources can be exploited in the third generation machines in a manner that has been impossible up to now. I shall return to this point shortly.

Maintenance of linked files

Next I want to turn to the file maintenance problem itself. My main concern to-day is in the first and the last of the three phases I referred to earlier. Before going on to these I would like to say a little about how we have handled the decision-making process. As in other information retrieval problems, we wish to have both a high rate of recall, and a high rate of precision. ' Recall ' refers to the ability to obtain linked records from the files without losing information that ought to have been linked. ' Precision ' refers to the obtaining of this information in a form that is uncontaminated by irrelevant information which has erroneously been linked into the file. These properties are somewhat incompatible and the design of any information retrieval system involves the balancing of the one against the other.

Throughout our work we have done the comparisons and decisions about linkages in a stratified manner. At the first level we make a decision that if certain features of the information disagree, then the attempt to link is abandoned forthwith. In our studies of vital statistics records this decision has been based on something called a Double Soundex Code. This is an approximate representation of a pair of surnames. Thus we establish what might be called a ' super-family ' which consists of all individuals with the same double soundex code. Thus in our files a super-family includes ordinary families—parents and their children—and all other families in which the parents have the same surnames, or surnames that sound about the same. Once we have matched a new record to its super-family, we then try to select the correct family by a second comparison that considers the agreement or disagreement of six prime items of information. If all six of these items agree, we accept the records as linked without further decisions. If too few agree we reject the linkage. If we are still undecided we consider the remaining information on the record in more detail. About a dozen items are considered at this third detailed level of scrutiny, and some rather complex tables that are associated with the information content and reliability of these items are used in making the final determination of whether the records ought to be linked or not.

The details of this process depend, of course, on the particular study. Various types of information have various degrees of discriminating power depending on the population being considered. The two final levels of comparison could well be integrated into a single sequential comparison. Our own methods have not changed very much here in the 10 years that we have been working on the study. It turned out that the original scheme was both good enough and cheap enough for the statistical purposes that we were interested in, giving levels of recall and of precision that were both 98 per cent. or better.

File organization

Now I would like to turn to the file organization problem. In our pilot study this was very simple in its conception. We began with a single magnetic tape containing marriage records, and a number of other tapes, each of which contained birth records pertaining to a single year. Each tape was individually sorted into sequence by super-family. Our plan was to produce a cross-reference output tape by submitting a birth tape and the marriage tape to the computer simultaneously and keeping a record of the identification of linked pairs. We had no detailed plan about how to organize the results. It turned out that considerable manipulation of the cross-reference file was needed to produce useful information in the form of family grouping of records. One difficulty was that the recording of the linkage of successive births to the same marriage would appear on different output tapes, and that these files must be merged and sorted to bring the families together. A second more serious difficulty was that many groups of siblings appeared to be ' orphans ' ; their parents were not in the files because of a marriage outside the period of time being considered, or outside the province of British Columbia. To bring these siblings together we were obliged to perform matchings of birth tapes against each other as well as birth tapes against the marriage tape. Thus as our study expanded to consider more annual birth files the number of pairs of tapes to be compared increased very rapidly.

It appeared to us that the whole process would be much simplified by moving to a single integrated file of all events. The linkage of events would then correspond to the insertion of the new record into the master file at a suitable spot, just as one would do by hand. Thus all records for a given individual would be adjacent to each other, surrounded by other members of the same family. The family records in turn would be contained within a super-family group and finally the super-families would remain in their quasi-alphabetic order. The operation of this system has proved to be straightforward in principle. New records of any type are collected and sorted on to a single input tape. This tape and the master file are then run through the computer for the linkage process. The output from this process is a single new master tape in which all new records have been inserted in their proper places.

In practice there are a number of technical difficulties to overcome. These arise from the fact that computers and people have rather different views about what is easy and what is hard. While it is very simple to imagine a human person inserting a new record in the form of a new card between two existing records in a card file, it turns out to be more difficult for a computer to insert new information into a long file that has already been written. To avoid large amounts of copying of information within the computer memory to create space for new records we have found it prudent to use a somewhat complicated indexing system that allows us to keep the files logically in one order, although physically in a different one. The ideas for this have come from what is known to computer scientists as List Processing, and in what follows I shall discuss the extension of this type of indexing system to maintenance of files whose structure becomes more complex.

The complexity increases when we decide to expand the treatment of families to include more than one generation of individuals. So far we have been using a family as synonymous with a household—a typical grouping includes a married couple and the children of that marriage. What we would like to do next is to allow for the possibility of the children getting married and establishing households of their own.

If we set aside certain technical difficulties for the time being it is not too difficult to see how to add information to the population file that will make it useful as a file for tracing pedigrees as well as for scrutinizing linked records pertaining to the same generation. The essential linkage step is the identification of the two partners to a marriage. Assuming this can be done, a cross-reference must be inserted in the personal file of each of the two individuals. This points to the new family, and at the same time a cross-reference entry must be made on the marriage record itself referring back to the personal files of the individuals concerned. Once this has been done it is possible in principle to trace family trees in both the forward and the backward directions.

In the past few months I have performed some experiments with a file of artificial events linked together in this fashion. We started with a few hundred simulated individuals who were then allowed to breed, so to speak, inside the computer for several generations, until

114

the total population was several thousand. At each stage cross-reference information about the marriages as well as the birth were recorded in the manner that I have described. Programmes were then written to scrutinize these files. As the population was not very interesting of itself, we did not attempt to do more than create family trees of ancestors and of descendants. However, these programmes proved to be quite feasible, and not too difficult to write. We could ask for a list of all the descendants of a given person for a specified number of generations or, conversely, for a list of all the ancestors for a specified number of generations. It is clear that once these operations are in hand it is possible to discover the relationship between any pair of individuals in the file by asking for ancestor lists and then having the computer look for common entries in these two lists. However, we have not pursued that point. I might remark in passing that this set of programmes was connected up to a graph plotting programme (written for another purpose) that allowed the computer to draw the family trees as names of individuals connected by lines containing their relationships. Any situation in which there were marriages of cousins or other relatives would be exhibited by lines crossing at the normal tree-like relationships. The pilot system allows for multiple marriages by the same individual, and of course allows for the possibility that one or both partners to a marriage do not have personal histories already in the files. As things stand at the present, we have trouble with individuals who contrive to become their own ancestors by marrying their grandmothers, but this is a very mild technical difficulty that can readily be eliminated.

It therefore appears that there are no serious problems of principle in forming a complete linked file covering several generations of a large population. The additional cross-reference information can be handled by indexing procedures of the type that were used in the original master files : that is, we avoid frequent copying of the same information by a certain amount of ingenuity in the cross-referencing system. However there are rather serious difficulties of cost connected with the implementation of this type of system on a large scale on present-day equipment. This is because the file no longer has any natural order once one begins to introduce the multi-generation cross-references. The ' straight-line ' system breaks down as soon as we begin to allow inter-family relationships to enter, and in fact the file that we produce cannot be less complicated in its structure than a family tree. As a result, magnetic tape is no longer an appropriate medium for retaining these files when they are being used by the computer, even though tape will almost certainly remain the medium on which the archive files are recorded. The fact that the records for two partners to a marriage may be located many hundreds of yards apart on a spool of magnetic tape means that the cost of hunting about at random in files of this type is too great to be contemplated.

We must therefore exploit the large-scale random-access backup stores of the third-generation computer. As I mentioned earlier, these are capable of holding some hundreds of millions or even thousands of millions of words of information. Therefore if we can keep our active files on a disc storage device during the scanning by the computer, we will be able to hunt for items at random in the file without a long lapse of time between retrieval of items whose geographical location is somewhat distant. However, even on a modern computer it is doubtful that we can keep the whole file of information randomly accessible to the machine. In fact, it appears that we must provide two separate files closely related to each other, the one actually being a genealogical index to the other. Thus I envisage the main file of personal information of birth, illness, death, and other events relating to an individual remaining in very much the same form as it does at present. However, this file will be supplemented by a second file, which contains only the pedigree information—that is, it will be concerned with brief records of marriages and births. The complete life history of one person would contain fewer than one hundred words of information in the index file, and we can therefore contemplate keeping these files for tens of millions of individuals simultaneously accessible to the computer on a suitably large storage device. Then if one wishes to study the incidence of a particular disease, and have a number of persons now suffering from that disease, it would be possible to use the index file alone to find the ancestors of the affected persons and, in turn, all descendants of these ancestors. The list so obtained could then be sorted into a suitable order for a detailed scrutiny of the main files to extract the personal information.

The process of scanning the index file is still too expensive to be used on a second-generation computer. The storage devices with capacities adequate for the index file do not permit accesses more rapidly than a few per second, and therefore even a few hundred or a few thousand searches in the index file can be an expensive process. We must exploit the modern idea of multiprogramming of computers in order to keep the costs within reasonable bounds. The point is that during most of the elapsed time during a search of the index file the main computer is unused while an access arm moves into position to read a particular piece of information. However, in a third-generation computer utility, the computer system as a whole

116

contains several problems at any time, each of which has differing requirements. During delays while access arms are moving, searching files needed for one problem, the intervening time can be spent performing arithmetical calculations or printing results on paper for some quite different problem. The machine is supposed to be organized in such a way that the switching between these problems is carried out without the various users of the system being aware of any interruption in their own work. The consequence of this is that the cost of the searching process is not based on the elapsed time for execution of the whole job. It is rather concerned only with those times in which the computer is paying attention to the work on that job, and this may be as small as 1 per cent. of the total time used.

If one combines the information retrieval possibilities of a file of the type that I have described with the advantages of remote access to this file from stations that may be located quite a distance from the computer itself, there appear to be very great possibilities for expansion of record linkage and record retrieval processes in the next few years. However, there are still several problems that must be solved before a really satisfactory system is achieved. One of these is that limitations of memory size force us to keep the index file and the main file separate. This means that studies of the main files cannot be made instantaneously even though our time-shared computer is available for their use, as the main files will continue to be on magnetic tape and sequential searches will have to be performed on them after the identification of the individuals of interest has been made by scrutiny of the index file. One may hope that as the cost of memory devices diminishes we may see a day in which the whole file might be held in the system at once and the process of scanning the files would be correspondingly simplified.

A second limitation is that one cannot consider doing these studies for only a few individuals at a time. Even the index file cannot be kept permanently inside the computer system to be called on whenever wanted, as the cost of the disc storage is too great to allow permanent storage of files with low activity. Thus in updating the files or scanning them it is still necessary to accumulate material or inquiries until there is enough to justify transferring the index file from magnetic tape into the computer to perform the retrieval operations. Keeping these files permanently in the machine could be contemplated only if their uses expanded to the point at which they were being queried frequently throughout every day of the year.

There are persons who believe this type of activity will come to pass. As more and more files are collected on larger and larger utility computers, it will become technically feasible to retain universal files of material of all sorts for a large number of purposes. However, the social consequences of this type of file maintenance have been called into question recently, and I think it will be some time before it is clear just how far it is proper to go in this direction.

DISCUSSION

Mr Carpenter : In commenting on Dr Kennedy's paper, I would like to raise a few anxieties in the hope that he will be able to allay them. My first anxiety is the cumulative effect of linkage errors that arises with multi-generation studies. We are impressed by the fact that in Dr Kennedy's studies only 2 per cent. links are missed. Nevertheless if you start considering say four generations of people, that is the parents, the grandparents and the great grandparents, you find 14 ancestors of the one person connected by seven marriage links and seven birth links. Then each of these 15 people identified in the genealogical file must also be correctly linked to the corresponding records in the medical file. Thus to get the complete picture of a case and three generations of ancestors some 29 links have to be established. If at each stage 2 per cent. of links are missed you end up with less than 60 per cent. of complete family histories. You get up to 87 per cent. correct if you only make a half per cent. error at each stage. I can envisage such errors introducing considerable bias into a genetic study.

My second anxiety is the enormous size these data files are likely to become, especially if we introduce medical records into them. Without going into details, we would need approximately one computer word per head of the total population per year if we include a medical history. Thus, if we start using a population like England and Wales, we will have to store up to fifty million words of data a year which will fill about the biggest disc file that is readily available in two years. The very problem of loading this with data becomes considerable.

My third anxiety concerns the third generation computers which are said to be upon us. We have a fully time shared machine working in Cambridge. It was announced originally as being 100 times faster than the previous machine, and I believe that this is the internal speed of the machine. But the actual performance has only improved by a factor of about 10 and the time used by the peripherals is only divided by three. It seems that just the sheer organization of the machine itself is consuming an enormous amount of its own time. I therefore have some anxieties about the future. Nevertheless I suspect that the people actually involved in record linkage—I am rather remote from doing it myself—are probably not so worried about these difficulties as the onlookers.

Dr Kennedy : I don't know that I can allay all your fears in the time that is likely to remain for discussion. As far as the error in the multi-generation pedigrees is concerned I think that certainly is a danger and one that one has to assess. However I feel that you will not have too much difficulty about accuracy in the marriages. At the time of the marriage you know who the individuals are and practically everybody has some kind of a number. So we have always found that our difficulties were in building up family histories ; discovering that one person is somebody else's brother is the difficult thing because they don't give the social security number or any number pertaining to their parents and so you have to use this unreliable stuff. But at the time at which they get married you can make them declare unequivocally who they are and therefore in principle you should be able to keep that part of it running accurately enough and be left only, again, with these problems of who is who's son rather than who is who's wife. So that I think—I haven't worked it all out—but I think it might turn out that it is only going to be a problem fourfold rather than fifteenfold in the things that one is worrying about.

The size of the data file : yes, it is really going to get quite large but as I remarked, I can't envisage one keeping the medical information and the genealogical information in the same file. I feel that one must have the master file, the one that is going to be on discs read in from tape, presumably when one wants to do some work with it. This would contain only a few words per member of the population, just enough to say who he is and what connections he has with other individuals in the population. If one decides that a certain person is interesting because he is the cousin of a man who is sick one must then go back to the medical files and go through these to pull out the information about the individuals concerned. It would be nice to think of disc files. I am sure the computer manufacturers would like to think of selling you disc files big enough to keep the whole population and all its medical records, but that is costly.

As far as the third-generation computers are concerned, they are not as effective as they are supposed to be. I am in a state of some trepidation because we are changing from second- to third-generation (getting something that is supposed to operate in a fully time-shared mode) at the University of British Columbia next year. This is a problem of computer science.

RECORD LINKAGE FOR A CHRONIC DISEASE REGISTER

WILLIAM PHILLIPS, JR.

IN the past the electronic digital computer was regarded as a super speed calculator by some persons and as a super ' electronic brain ' that would replace the human brain by others. My favourite definition of a computer is : ' a moron which does exactly what it is told to do with phenomenal speed and accuracy and regardless of the consequences '.

With the realization that an electronic computer was not a device with super intelligence and ability for independent judgement also came the realization of its capabilities as a tool to perform many tasks that are a drudgery to man. Present day computers are being designed and manufactured with this purpose in mind.

Many tasks that were not feasible in the past are definitely a possibility with modern day computers. Among these tasks is the linkage of data from recorded events in the life of individuals who lack an assigned unique number tattoed on their forehead or some other part of their anatomy. While many studies would be enhanced by the availability of longitudinal information, the expense and amount of time required to link recorded events or episodes for a given person have been deterrents. The present day electronic computers with their tremendous speed and decision-making capabilities seem to offer a solution.

The methods for utilization of computers and data banks to accumulate and analyse data are fairly well advanced. Not so well advanced at present is the linkage of events that pertain to the same person. The project which will be discussed here is the linking of episodes of service for patients of psychiatric facilities. The purposes and uses of this register or data bank have been described in several publications (Gorwitz *et al.*, 1963 ; Bahn, 1960, 1965, 1966).

On 1st July, 1961, the Maryland Psychiatric Case Register was established as a joint project of the Biometry Branch, National Institute of Mental Health and the Maryland State Department of Mental Hygiene. The Register included all patients treated in psychiatric clinics in Maryland and all Maryland residents receiving service in psychiatric clinics of the adjacent District of Columbia. In short, the objective was a statewide register covering all Maryland residents who received service in a psychiatric inpatient or outpatient facility. Reports for non-residents of Maryland who receive service

120

Fig. 1. *Number of facilities by type*
(as of May 1, 1967)

	Number of facilities	Fiscal 1966 admissions
All facilities which report patient data	137	31,333*
Psychiatric hospitals and institutions which report		
Public mental hospitals	8	9,917*
Private mental hospitals	11	1,877
General hospitals accepting psychiatric patients . .	11	2,021
Veterans administration hospitals	2	1,064
State institutions for mental defectives . . .	2	417
Private homes for mental defectives (children) . .	2	8
Total	36	15,304*
Psychiatric outpatient facilities which report		
Psychiatric day care centres	11	351
State mental hospital preadmission clinics . . .	2	409
State mental hospital aftercare clinics . . .	3	1,690
State mental hospital alcoholic clinics . . .	2	169
County health department alcoholic clinics . .	6	263
County health department clinics (other than alcoholic)	37	5,254
Hospitals operated outpatient units in Baltimore City .	15	4,713
Hospitals operated outpatient units in counties . .	3	439
Alcoholic clinics in Baltimore City	2	412
All other clinics in Baltimore City	6	1,249
All other clinics in counties	3	751
Clinics in District of Columbia	11	329
Total	101	16,029

Known facilities in Maryland currently not reporting .   6 (est)   400
Edgemeade Youth Rehab. Centre
Middle River Day Care—Baltimore County
Fort Meade Psychiatric Outpatient Clinic
Emergency Clinic, Johns Hopkins Hospital
Baltimore County Juvenile Court Clinic
Baltimore County Therapy Clinic

Known facilities in district of Columbia currently not reporting   7 (est)   400
Freedmen's Hospital
Freedmen's Outpatient Clinic
George Washington Hospital, Psychiatric Ward
George Washington Hospital, Outpatient Clinic
D.C. General Hospital
Georgetown Adult Clinics (2)

Total known facilities currently not reporting .   13 (est)   800

* Does not include over 1,700 returns from long term leave which are considered as the beginning of a new episode of treatment.

in Maryland Psychiatric facilities are also processed in order to produce statistics used primarily for administrative and planning purposes. It is estimated that over 97 per cent. of the defined coverage has been achieved (Fig. 1).

When planning the establishment of the Register the major problems were recognized to be : (1) receiving complete and accurate reports of service for the defined population from all psychiatric facilities ; (2) processing of these reports ; (3) linkage of records that pertained to the same individual ; and (4) tabulation and analysis of longitudinal treatment histories for the patients.

Several methods were used to attain complete and accurate reporting. Safeguards for maintaining the confidentiality of reported information, continuing personal persuasion of administrators, feedback of data to the orginators, careful clerical scrutiny of report forms and prompt contact with the secretaries of the reporting facilities for late reporting and missing information were among these devices. We shall continue with these and other efforts in order to attain as nearly complete reporting as possible.

Considering the anticipated volume of data (Fig. 2) and the complexity of planned analysis, computer processing was deemed to be an absolute necessity. In fact, during the first five years, data for over 300,000 patient movement actions involving over 90,000 individuals and more than 160,000 episodes of service were collected.

In recent years there has been a rapid annual increase in the number of reported episodes of psychiatric service. The number of episodes (admission actions) reported to the Register annually has increased 41 per cent. during the first five years of operation (from 22,000 in the fiscal year 1962 to 31,000 in the fiscal year 1966). During the past two and a half years the number of known psychiatric clinics and hospitals in Maryland and the adjacent District of Columbia which service Maryland residents has increased 67 per cent. (from 90 to 150). These increases are due to changing concepts of the treatment of mental illnesses with a resulting increase in the number and type of psychiatric facilities and to increased public acceptance of psychiatric treatment.

An analysis of various methods of record linkage indicated the need to automate this process as much as possible. Digital computers and digital computer programmes used for record linkage (Newcombe et al., 1959 ; Acheson, 1964 ; Kennedy et al., 1965 ; Nitzberg, 1965) are probably more accurate, and certainly much faster than clerical methods. Other considerations in making this decision were lack of personnel, and lack of office space.

Automatic record linkage methods

The most common automated method of linking records is a matching of records by a unique identifying factor, usually a preassigned number. Examples of applications that use this method are as follows : (1) the use of stock item numbers for inventory control ; (2) the use of payroll numbers for payroll applications ; and (3) the use of a code derived from the name, address and other available data for linking magazine subscribers.

The unique factor matching method is the fastest, simplest, and most accurate (with proper verification of the match) of all automatic matching techniques. It has the disadvantage that one mistake in any part of the matching key will cause a linkage to be missed or, if proper verification techniques are not included, an incorrect linkage could be made.

A match strictly on name of a person has similar disadvantages. An error in any part of the name could cause a missed match, many persons have the same name which could cause incorrect linkage, and young women have the habit of getting married and changing their name and address which results in missing linkages.

Another method is one which I refer to as the ' grouping ' technique. In the ' grouping ' technique a common factor is derived from the identifying data contained in each record. All records which agree on the derived factor or ' key ' are matched to each record in the ' group ', and other reported identifying data are used to determine whether or not the reported events apply to the same person.

Any factors can be used as the grouping key. The general rules are : (1) the factors must be present in most records ; (2) they must divide the files into groups small enough to be handled by the computer, (3) they must create groups that are homogeneous, and (4) they must not be so restrictive that a minor error would exclude comparison of records for the same person.

Quality and quantity of identifying data

At the time of the inception of the Register (1961), the quality of patient identifying data in the central office of the Maryland State Department of Mental Hygiene was very poor and the quantity was very limited with serious gaps in the reporting of requested identity items. There were four types of report forms in use ; one for the State operated hospitals, one for the Veterans Administration hospital, one for other inpatient psychiatric facilities, and one for outpatient psychiatric clinics. The items of patient identifying information requested on these forms were name of patient (including maiden name), address, date of birth, age at admission, sex and race.

FIG. 2. *Summary statistics*

	On register 30/6/64		Under psychiatric care 30/6/61		First admitted in fiscal year 1962		First admitted in fiscal year 1963		First admitted in fiscal year 1964	
	Number	Per cent.	Number	Per cent.	Number	per cent.	Number	Per cent.	Number	Per cent.
All persons	66,006	100·0	21,505	100·0	15,422	100·0	14,391	100·0	14,688	100·0
Maryland residents	60,877	92·2	19,798	92·1	14,128	91·6	13,285	92·3	13,666	93·0
Baltimore City residents	23,933	36·3	9,271	43·1	5,177	33·6	4,760	33·1	4,725	32·2
Maryland County residents	36,944	55·9	10,527	49·0	8,951	58·0	8,525	59·2	8,941	60·8
Out of state residents	5,129	7·8	1,707	7·9	1,294	8·4	1,106	7·7	1,022	7·0
Status on 30/6/64—Maryland residents only										
On register	60,877	100·0	19,798	100·0	14,128	100·0	13,285	100·0	13,666	100·0
Not under care	34,480	56·6	6,505	32·9	10,445	73·9	9,648	72·6	7,882	57·7
Deceased	4,146	6·8	2,045	10·3	976	6·9	742	5·6	383	2·8
Receiving care	22,251	36·6	11,248	56·8	2,707	19·2	2,895	21·8	5,401	39·5
In state hospital*	11,018	18·1	7,593	38·4	992	7·1	930	7·1	1,503	11·0
Other inpatient*	1,501	2·5	664	1·4	222	1·6	192	1·4	423	3·1
Outpatient care*	7,567	12·4	2,238	11·3	1,163	8·2	1,355	10·2	2,811	20·5
Long term leave*	2,165	3·6	753	3·7	330	2·3	418	3·1	664	4·9
Receiving care	22,251	100·0	11,248	100·0	2,707	100·0	2,895	100·0	5,401	100·0
In state hospital	11,018	49·5	7,593	67·5	992	36·6	930	32·2	1,503	27·8
Other Inpatient	1,501	6·8	664	5·9	222	8·2	192	6·6	423	7·8
Outpatient care	7,567	34·0	2,238	19·9	1,163	43·0	1,355	46·8	2,811	52·1
Long term leave	2,165	9·7	753	6·7	330	12·2	418	14·4	664	12·3

FIG. 2a. *Patient movement actions recorded on the register*

Type of action	Total		State Hospitals		Other inpatient		Outpatient facilities	
	Number	Per cent.	Number	Per cent.	Number	Per cent.	Number	Per cent.
Total actions	190,998	100·0	84,776	44·4	33,861	17·7	72,361	37·9
Admissions	94,828	100·0	36,286	38·3	13,313	19·3	40,229	42·4
Transfers, discharges or death . .	69,609	100·0	21,929	31·5	15,548	22·3	32,132	46·2
Movements to and from long term leave and elopement	26,561	100·0	26,561	100·0				

125

There were major gaps even in this limited amount of identifying data. Maiden name was not requested from patients to the State operated hospitals and was reported in a haphazard fashion by other types of psychiatric treatment facilities. The complete date of birth was not reported for many cases.

The patient data report forms were revised to request the same items of identifying information from all facilities and a request for reporting of the social security number* was added to all forms. The only identifying information available in the central office for over half of the population under care on 1st July, 1961 was the name, sex, race, and year of birth. Contacts were made with reporting psychiatric facilities in an effort to collect as much identifying information as possible on people under care as of 1st July, 1961. These contacts were restricted and inadequate due to a lack of resources, particularly lack of personnel.

Social Security numbers were obtained for only 19 per cent. of the initial population. After the first three years of operation only 22 per cent. of the registrants had reported a social security account number at any time. This serious lack of complete accurate identifying information (Fig. 3) on patients under care at the inception of the Register and lack of adequate follow-up for missing information during the first years of operation has caused, and is causing, many difficulties in the linkage process and prevents many desirable refinements.

The quality and quantity of identifying information have improved steadily through the years. On 1st July, 1964 a uniform record report form was adopted and is being used for all reporting of patient service data. This report form has improved the quality of both the identifying information and the statistical information.

The details of the computer processing system (Fig. 4) have been described previously (Phillips *et al.*, 1962 ; Phillips & Bahn, 1966) ; and will not be repeated here since our primary concern is record linkage. However, some knowledge of the processing system is necessary to the understanding of the following text.

As usual in a processing system for maintaining a data bank, the first step is an intensive edit or validation of all data punch cards

---

* The social security number is a 9 digit number assigned to each person in covered employment for collection of the payroll tax and is used to maintain earnings records and to administer the payment of old-age and disability benefits under the Social Insurance System of the United States Government. Approximately 200,000,000 such numbers have been assigned to United States residents at the present time. Assignment of these numbers began in 1937. This number is now required on all Federal Income Tax Forms and is used in the processing of data from these forms.

FIG. 3. *Reporting of terms of identifying information requested at time of admission*[1]

Requested item	Number of admissions with item not reported				Percentage of admissions with item not reported			
	All Admissions	Fiscal year 1962 and prior Admissions	Fiscal year 1963 admissions	Fiscal year 1964 admissions	All admissions	Fiscal Year 1962 and prior admissions	Fiscal year 1963 admissions	Fiscal year 1964 admissions
Birth month *and* day	4,975	3,118	932	925	5·0	6·7	3·6	3·2
Birth month .	4,989	3,127	933	929	5·0	6·8	3·6	3·2
Birth day .	5,882	3,829	1,041	1,012	5·9	8·3	4·0	3·5
Social security number	77,066	38,390	18,592	19,584	77·1	83·6	72·2	69·1
Patient's name .	1,701	757	358	586	1·7	1·6	1·3	2·0
Address of patient .	625	593	15	17	0·6	1·2	0·015	0·017
Residence street name .	11,213	6,307	2,260	2,646	11·2	13·7	8·7	9·3
Residence street number[2] .	7,929	3,653	2,134	2,142	7·9	7·9	8·2	7·5
Street name *or* number	19,142	9,960	4,394	4,788	19·1	21·6	16·9	16·8

[1] Admissions include returns from long-term leave.

Fiscal year 1962 and prior — 45,883 admissions
Fiscal year 1963 — 25,722 admissions
Fiscal year 1964 — 28,309 admissions

Total — 99,914 admissions

[2] Those admissions with street name reported.

127

Fig. 4. *Systems chart*

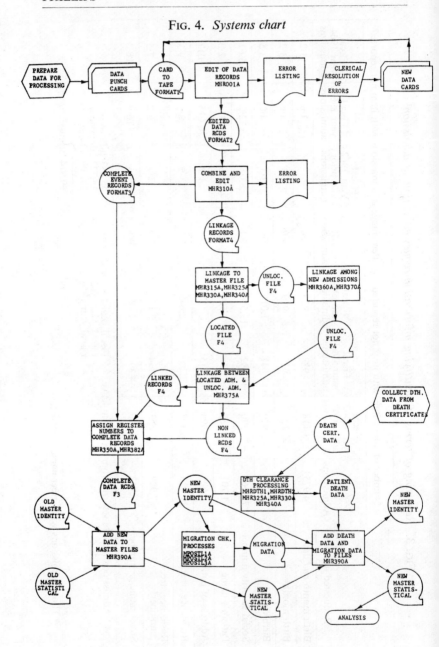

prepared for reported information and the correction of detected errors. The next step is the combining of all information for an episode of treatment and additional checks for possible errors made by the combination of data from several punch cards. During this process a unique temporary number referred to as a ' pseudo-register number ' is assigned for all actions having the same facility code and patient case number. This method of assignment of the ' pseudo-register number ' accomplishes a linkage of records of persons having multiple actions among the incoming data within hospitals or clinics, using a unit patient case number*.

A linkage record (Fig. 5) containing the identifying information of the patient for each episode is also created during this process. For each episode where a maiden or alias name is reported, a duplicate of the basic linkage record is produced with the phonetic code of the maiden or alias name instead of the surname. After being processed through the linkage programme, linkage records are collated with the complete data records during the updating phase by matching on the ' pseudo-register number ' and a permanent register number is assigned to the complete data records.

Linkage system

The record linkage system used in the Maryland Psychiatric Case Register is a ' computer assisted ' system rather than an ' automatic ' system. A majority of the computer linkages are automatic but a substantial percentage still require clerical review for verification. In some cases the computer programme is unable to make a decision and therefore produces a printout of all information from the compared records. These printouts are reviewed clerically and the proper decision is made by preparation of a punch card and a ' linkage correction ' programme.

The processing flow of all four programmes for linkage to the Master Register files is the same (Fig. 6) with the output file of unlinked records from one linkage programme becoming the input to the subsequent linkage programme. In the comparison of two records the computer arrives at one of three decisions—an acceptable or ' positive ' linkage, a ' possible ' linkage, or a rejection of the linkage. Listings are produced for all ' possible ' linkage decisions

---

* The unit patient case number assignment system involves a search of the facility files when a patient is admitted to see if the incoming patient has ever been serviced by the facility or hospital previously. If a prior record is found, the same patient case or history number is assigned to the admitted person and his medical history file is consolidated. Verification of the accuracy of this number assignment is made in the Register process of a comparison of names, date of birth, sex and race.

K

FIG. 5. *Records used by linkage programme*

Linkage record—admission type

Pseudo register number	Code	Located register number	Facility		Patient case number	Codes	Soundex code	Sex	Race	Admission			Name: last-first-middle	Street or box number
			Type	Code						Year	Month	Day		
1—8	1	1—7	1—2	1—3	1—8	1—3	1—4	1	1	1—	—	—6	1—21	1—5

Street name or Rt. & number	City or town	Zipcode		State	Maiden or alias name	Social Security number	Prev. care	Residence		Birth			Mar.	Ref. code	
		Area	Zone					Geo.	Tract or code	Year	Month	Day			
															bbb
1—13	1—13	1—3	1—2	1—3	1—8	1—9	1—2	1—	—5	1—	—	—6	1	1—2	1—3

Master register file identity record

Code	Register number	Facility		Patient case number	Codes	Soundex code	Sex	Race	Admission			Name: last-first-middle	Street or box number
		Type	Code						Year	Month	Day		
1	1—7	1—2	1—3	1—8	1—3	1—4	1	1	1—	—	—6	1—21	1—5

Street name or Rt. and number	City or town	Zipcode		State	Maiden or alias name	Social security number	Status	Residence		Birth			Marital	blanks
		Area	Zone					Geo.	Tract or code	Year	Month	Day		
1—13	1—13	1—3	1 2	1—3	1—8	1—9	1—2	1—	—5	1—	—	—6	1	1—5

FIG. 6. *Logic flow chart of programmes for linkage between two files*

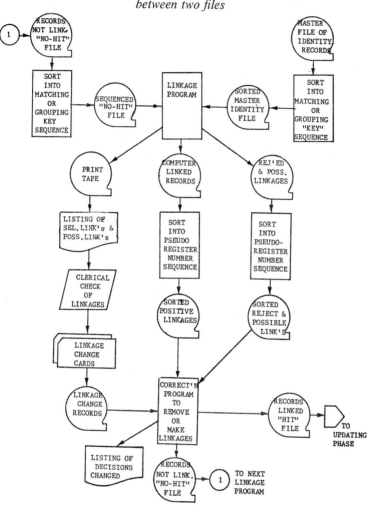

and a majority (60 per cent.) of the 'positive' linkage decisions* for clerical review.

Matching by a unique identifying factor, most commonly numerical, is the fastest, most economical and easiest method of

* Pridtouts are not produced for 'positive' decision Reference Codes A0000, A0100, A0110, A0200, and A0200 that also are in concordance on month and day of birth (see Figs. 11 – 13.)

arriving at an accurate, positive decision. Therefore, this method is the first one used in the linkage process. Two programmes of this type are used to link incoming additional data to the master Register files. The first of these programmes uses the hospital or clinic code and patient case number as the key matching factor. This programme accomplishes linkage for readmission episodes to those facilities which use a unit patient case number assignment system and also links other types of actions for incomplete episodes of service already recorded on the Register. The second programme uses the social security number as the matching key.

For both of these programmes verification of the linkage is made by comparison of other available identifying factors after detection of agreement on the matching key. The slight tolerance allowed in the comparison of additional factors of identification for verification is due to our knowledge of the poor quality of identifying data introduced into this system during the first year of operation.

The next two programmes in the linkage system use the group linkage technique to match new additions to the master Register files. The first of these two programmes is the most original, most valuable, and is becoming the most expensive programme in the system. The grouping factor used is a combination of the sex code of the patient and a phonetic code of the surname based on the Russell Soundex Coding System (Fig. 7). This phonetic coding system has been used for many years to minimize the effects of common errors in the spelling of names.

FIG. 7. *Phonetic coding of names* (*usual method based on Russell Soundex Coding System*)

The code used is as follows:

Code	Letters
1	b, f, p, v
2	c, g, j, k, q, s, x, z
3	d, t
4	l
5	m, n
6	r

Rule 1

The code for any name consists of the initial letter of the surname followed by three numbers or digits. It there are not sufficient coded letters in the name to give three digits, ciphers (zeros) should be added to complete the three digits, (*e.g.*, Lee : L000). If the name contains so many letters that coding all of them would give more than the required three digits, disregard all beyond the three-digit limit.

Rule 2

The letters a, e, i, o, u and y are called vowels and are not coded—also w, h.
Weinberg is coded: W 516 : W is the initial letter ; e and i are not coded n is 5 ; b is 1 ; e is not coded ; r is 6 ; the rest is disregarded according to rule 1.

Rule 3—A

If two or more consonants which have the same coded number come together ; they are coded as only one letter :

Williard is coded W 463 : W is the initial letter ; the i is not coded (rule 2) ; two together are coded as only one 4 ; the a is not coded ; the r is 6 ; and the d is 3.

Dickson is coded D 250 : D is the initial letter ; i is not coded ; c, k, and s all have the code value 2 and, ocurring together they are coded as one letter or only one 2, o is not coded ; n is 5 ; to make up the 3 digits required by rule 1, one cipher must be added.

Mac Cann is coded M 250 : M is the initial letter ; a is not coded ; the two c's are coded as one 2 ; the a is not coded ; the two n's are coded as one 5 ; one cipher is added to make the 3 digits required by rule 1.

Rule 3—B (deleted)

Rule 4

Consonants having the same code number but separated by one or more vowels are coded individually.

Diciccio is coded D 220 : D is the initial letter ; i is not coded ; the next c is followed by an i so it is coded 2 ; the i is not coded ; the next two c's are together so only one 2 is coded. One cipher is added to give the required 3 digits.

Wyman is coded W 550 : W is the initial letter ; the y is not coded ; the m a and n because they are separated by a vowel are coded 55 ; one cipher is added to give the required 3 digits.

Rule 5—(deleted)

Rule 6

All abbreviated names are coded as though they were fully written out:

St. John is coded S 532 : Ray—coded R 00 ; Wahl—W 400 ; Daye—D 000 Ehn—E 500 ; Danag—D 520 ; Danagor—D 526 ; Danacartosky—D 526.

Cards are filed alphabetically by the first name within each soundex code group.

A—Alma Allen

    Betty Allen

A variation (Fig. 8) of this system has been used for the Register

Fig. 8. *Phonetic code used in maintaining register*
(*July 1, 1961–June 30, 1964*)

The consonants of the surname are assigned numbers according to the following schedule and rules.

Code	Letters
1	B, F, P, V
2	C, G, J, K, Q, S, X, Z
3	D, T
4	L
5	M, N
6	R
Not coded	A, E, I, O, U, W, H, Y

133

Rule 1

The code for any name consists of 4 digits. If a name does not have sufficient coded consonants, zeros are added to complete the code. (*e. g.* Lee : 4000). If there are more than 4 coded consonants, the code is truncated. (*e.g.* Malinauskas : 5452).

Rule 2

If 2 or more consonants which have the same coded number come together, they are coded as only one letter.

Phillips is coded 1412 : P is coded 1, I is not coded, H and I are not coded, P is coded 1, LL is coded 4, S is coded 2.

Dickson is coded 3250 : D is coded 3, I is not coded, C K and S all have the same code value 2, and ocurring together they are coded as one letter, O is not coded, N is coded 5, and a zero is added to complete the code.

Rule 3

Consonants having the same code number but separated by one or more vowels (a, e, i, o, u, y) are coded individually.

Diciccio is coded 3220 Wyman is coded 5500

Rule 4

W and H do not separate consonants. If two consonants having the same code are separated by a W or H, they are coded as one consonant.

Sachs—2200

in the past. This variation was made primarily to reduce the probability of missing matches due to incorrectly reported first letter of the surname for names beginning with characters which sound alike such as c and k (*e.g.* Cramer—Kramer, Cane—Kane). A further variation (Fig. 9) was recently initiated in order to reduce further the

FIG. 9   *Soundex coding method*
fiscal year—1965

The consonants of the surname are assigned numbers according to the following schedule and rules.

Code	Letters
1	B, F, P, V
2	C, G, J, K, Q, S, X, Z
3	D, T
4	L
5	N, M
6	R
Not coded	A, E, I, O, U, W, H, Y

Rule 1

The code for any name consists of 4 digits. If a name does not have sufficient coded consonants, zeros are added to complete the code. (*e.g.* Lee : 4000). If there are more than 4 coded consonants, the code is truncated. (*e.g.* Malinauskas : 5452).

Rule 2

If 2 or more consonants which have the same coded number come together, they are coded as only one letter.

Phillips is coded 1412 : P is coded 1, I is not coded, H and I are not coded, P is coded 1, LL is coded 4, S is coded 2.

Dickson is coded 3250 : D is coded 3, I is not coded, C K and S all have the same code value 2, and occurring together they are coded as one letter, O is not coded, N is coded 5, and a zero is added to complete the code.

Rule 3

Consonants having the same code number but separated by one or more vowels (a, e, i, o, u, y) are coded individually.

Diciccio is coded 3220.

Wyman is coded 5500.

Rule 4

W and H do not separate consonants. If two consonants having the same code are separated by a W or H, they are coded as one consonant.

Sachs—2200

After Soundex Coding to 4 digits, make the following checks and changes.

1. If 1st position of code is ' 0 ', make no change.

2. If 1st position of code is 1, 3, 4, 5 or 6 check the second position of the code.

(*a*) If second position is ' 0 ' or ' 1 ', place zeros in the 3rd and 4th positions.

(*b*) If second position is ' 2 ', check first position for a ' 5 ' . If first two positions are ' 52 ', leave the 4 digit code as computed. If not ' 52 ', place a zero in the 4th position.

(*c*) If 2nd position is ' 3 ', and first position is ' 3 ' or ' 4 ' (*i.e.* positions 1 and 2 = ' 33 ' or ' 43 ') place zeros in the 3rd and 4th positions only.

(*d*) If 2nd position is ' 4 ', check 1st two positions for ' 14 ', ' 44 ', or ' 64 '. If ' 14 ', leave code as computed. If ' 44 ' or ' 64 ', place zeros in the 3rd and 4th positions. If '34 ' or ' 54 ', place a zero in the 4th position.

(*e*) If 2nd position is ' 5 ', place a zero in the 4th position.

(*f*) If 2nd position is a ' 6 ', check the first 2 positions. If ' 16 ', leave code as computed. If ' 46 ' or ' 66 ', place zeros in the 3rd and 4th positions. If ' 36 ' or ' 56 ', place a zero in the 4th position.

3. If first position is a ' 2 ', check the second position. If second position is ' 0 ', ' 3 ', ' 4 ' ' 5 ' or ' 6 ', leave code as computed. If 2nd position is ' 1 ' or ' 2 ', place a zero in the 4th position.

effect of misspelling. These variations create larger groups and groups that are not so homogeneous as might be desired. However, it also allows a larger tolerance of errors in the spelling of the surname. No analysis has yet been made of the value of these variations over the original Russell Soundex Coding System.

Decision tables are employed to explain the logic used in the computer programmes. The rules used for deciding concordance in the comparison of items of identifying information from two records accompany the decisions tables. The logic and rules for this programme have been modified several times but the general concepts remain the same as that planned and used at the start of the Register (Phillips *et al.*, 1962 ; Phillips & Bahn, 1963).

Because of the importance of obtaining all linkages, a fourth programme is run using the sex code of the patient with the month and day of birth as the grouping key. The number of linkages obtained by use of this programme has been small but of sufficient importance to justify its use. Several linkages of patients reported without name have been obtained with this programme.

There are several possible reasons why so few linkages have been obtained with this programme : (1) the decision table (Fig. 10) used may have been invalid, (2) the month and day of birth may not be a very reliably reported item of information, or (3) the preceding linkage programmes may have worked exceedingly well. Evidence indicates that the last reason is probably the most valid. However, an entirely new decision table (Figure 11) for use in programming the logic of this programme has recently been designed.

A number of items of data, generally about 50 per cent., are about persons who have not had previous psychiatric service recorded on the Register. These are referred to as 'new admissions'. Among these 'new admissions' there are persons who have been admitted to two different facilities or twice to the same facility during the period covered by the updating. Two group linkage type programmes are used to discover this duplication. The processing flow (Fig. 12) is slightly different from previous group matching programmes because there is only one input file and one output file. The internal logic of the programme makes it very difficult and there have been problems due to programmer errors.

The first of these two programmes uses the Soundex code of the surname and the sex code as the grouping key. The decision table (not shown) is very similar to that used by the Soundex group check to the Register files.

The second of these programmes uses the month and day of birth and the sex code of the patient as the grouping key. The decision table (Fig. 13) used for this programme is the same as that used for the month and day of birth group match to the Register files. Very few linkages have been detected with this programme but again by divorcing the surname from the programme logic we are able to link some records for facilities which do not report patients' names.

During the period of updating (generally one year's data), a person may have been admitted to two or more psychiatric facilities. In one of the admissions he may have a social security number reported or he may have been readmitted to a facility that used a unit case number assignment system and been linked to the master file by one of the first two linkage programmes. The other admission record may not have a social security number or not be linked for

136

FIG. 10. *Date of birth group check to master files, fiscal year 1964, to be applied to all 'rejects' and unaccepted 'possibles' from soundex group check*

Reference Code	Birth month and day; sex	Middle name	Birth year	Maiden name	First name	Address	Birth year range	Decision	Computer counts	Clerical rejects	Net linkages
B01	0	0	▨	▨	▨	▨	▨	Accept	2	2	0
B02	0	1	0	0	▨	▨	▨	Accept	33	8	25
B03	0	1	0	1	0	▨	▨	Possible	808	712	96
B04	0	1	0	1	1	0	▨	Possible	57	25	32
B05	0	1	1	1	1	1	▨	Reject			
B06	0	1	1	0	0	▨	▨	Accept	14	9	5
B07	0	1	1	0	1	▨	▨	Possible	872	872	0
B08	0	1	1	1	0	0	0	Accept	3	2	1
B09	0	1	1	1	0	0	1	Possible	3	3	0
B10	0	1	1	1	0	1	0	Reject			
B11	0	1	1	1	1	0	0	Possible	55	54	1
B12	0	1	1	1	1	0	1	Reject			
B13	0	1	1	1	1	1	▨	Reject			
								Total	1,847	1,687	160

NB: 0 indicates agreement; 1 indicates discrepancy between the records.

Tolerance rules for concordance

Middle name—agreement on initials or 3 letters if present.

Maiden name—complete agreement in either maiden names or in cross-check with surname

Birth year, first name, address, birth year range—same as in Figure 13

Computer running time

Sorting for linkage — 156 minutes
Linkage programme — 249 minutes
Linkage correction — 25 minutes

Total — 430 minutes
Clerical time — 40 hours (estimated).

137

FIG. 11. *Decision table month and day of birth linkage programmes*

	First check					Second Check			
Reference code	Birth month and day sex	Year of Birth	Address	Race	Decision	First name	Maiden name	Birth year range	Decision
B000	0	0	0	0	Accept	0	0	0	Accept
B100	0	0	0	1	Possible	0	1	0	Possible
B120						1	0	0	Accept
B140						1	1	0	Possible
B160						0	1	0	Accept
B200	0	0	1	0	Possible	0	0	0	Possible
B220						1	1	0	Accept
B240						1	0	0	Possible
B260						0	1	0	Accept
B300	0	0	1	1	Possible	0	0	0	Possible
B320						1	1	0	Possible
B340						0	0	0	Reject
B360						0	1	0	Accept
B400	0	1	0	0	Possible	0	0	1	Possible
B410						0	1	0	Possible
B420						1	0	1	Reject
B430						0	0	1	Possible
B440						1	1	0	Reject
B450						1	0	1	Reject
B460						1	1	0	Reject
B470						1	1	1	Reject
B500	0	1	0	1	Possible	0	0	0	Possible
B510						0	0	1	Possible
B520						0	1	0	Possible

FIG. 11. *Decision table month and day of birth linkage programmes*

					Result
	0	1	0	Possible	
	0	1	1	Reject	

Code				Result
B530	0	1	1	Reject
B540	1	0	0	Possible
B550	1	1	0	Possible
B560	1	1	0	Possible
B570	1	1	1	Reject
B600	0	0	0	Accept
B610	0	0	1	Possible
B620	0	1	0	Possible
B630	1	1	1	Reject
B640	1	0	0	Possible
B650	1	1	1	Possible
B660	1	1	0	Reject
B670	1	1	1	Reject
B700	1	1	1	Reject

0 indicates concordance 1 indicates discordance

Tolerance rules for concordance:

Address—Agreement on street number and first 8 letters of street name. If street number fields are blank check street name only. If street number is blank and street name is a rural route, agreement of city or town is required.

Birth Year Range—

If current age is ;	Range must be within
0–17	2 years
18–29	5 years
30–49	10 years
50 and over	15 years

Maiden name—One-to-one correspondence of the maiden names or cross-check with the surname with only one disagreement allowed and at least 4 equals required. Checking is limited by the longest name.

First name—In a one-to-one comparison only one disagreement is allowed. Checking is limited by the longest name.

Complete agreement is required for ; Month and day of birth, Sex, Race, and Year of Birth.

Discordance is assumed for missing information.

139

other reasons. To provide for this possibility, we initiated a programme that matches the records that linked to the records that did not link to the Register file. This programme was first used in 1964 with an additional 100 linkages being made to the Register file. The procedures and logic of the programme are the same as the Soundex sex group match of incoming data to the Register file.

FIG. 12. *Processing flow for group linkage among records of a single file*

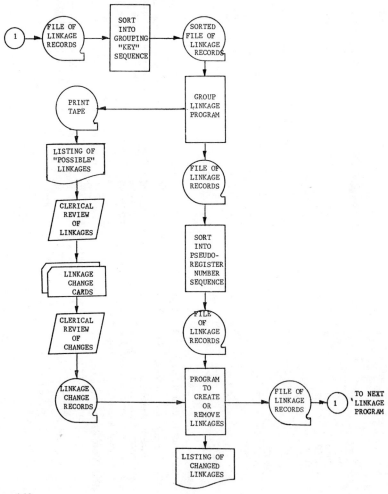

FIG. 13. *Date of birth group check among new admissions fiscal year 1964*

Reference code	Birth month and day; sex	Social security number	Birth year	Maiden name	First name	Address	Birth year range	Decision	Computer counts	Clerical rejects	Net linkages
B01	0	0	0	0				Accept	8	0	8
B02	0	1	0	1				Accept	9	5	4
B03	0	1	0	1	0			Possible	66	52	11 (3)
B04	0	1	0	1	1	0		Possible	59	17	26 (16)
B05	0	1	1	1	1	1		Reject			
B06	0	1	1	0	0			Accept	2	2	0
B07	0	1	1	0	1			Possible	161	161	0
B08	0	1	1	1	0	0	0	Accept	2	0	2
B09	0	1	1	1	0	0	1	Possible	1	1	0
B10	0	1	1	1	0	1		Reject			
B11	0	1	1	1	1	0	0	Possible	7	6	1
B12	0	1	1	1	1	0	1	Reject			
B13	0	1	1	1	1	1		Reject			
								Total	315	244	52 (19)

NB: 0 indicates agreement
1 indicates discrepancy between records

Tolerance rules for concordance

Social security number—complete agreement.
Maiden name—agreement in either maiden names or in cross-check with surname.
Birth year, first name, address, birth year range—same as in Figure 13.

Computer running time

Sorting for linkage — 33 minutes
Linkage programme — 60 minutes
Linkage correction — 17 minutes
——
Total 110 minutes
Clerical time —8 hours (estimated).

141

Death clearance operations

One of the most important aspects of any register designed to record the longitudinal medical history of individuals is the notification of the fact, date and cause of death. For a file the size of the Maryland Register this is a tremendous task. The number of persons recorded on the register who are at risk of dying is cumulative with 15,000 additions each year. After five years of processing, it will be necessary to check for deaths among 80,000 registrants. To perform this check against death records by clerical methods would be totally impossible.

For the death clearance operations covering the first three years (1st July, 1961–30th June, 1964) we collected identifying and statistical information from over 80,000 death certificates. Where possible we collected duplicate decks of punch cards from the vital statistics sections of the Health Departments.* From these cards we obtained the necessary statistical data but very little identifying information. It was necessary to collect additional identifying data for all deaths and to prepare punch cards to combine this data to that already punched by the various health departments.

Arrangements have been made with Baltimore City Health Department to have the Social Security number and the complete date of birth punched at the same time other death data is punched. Similar arrangements with the Maryland State Health Department have not as yet been possible.

The information from the various death data punch cards is converted to the format of linkage type records similar to that used in the regular register processing. Two of the regular linkage programmes, the Social Security number match and the Soundex-sex group match, were modified slightly and used to check for deaths among the registrants.

In the checks for death during the first three years, 696 deaths among persons on the register who were under psychiatric care at the time of death and 335 deaths among registered persons who were under outpatient care only were detected. In addition the cause of death and verification of the date of death for 2,756 persons reported as dying while they were inpatients of a psychiatric hospital were added to the Register. In addition, hospitals reported 598 deaths

---

* Maryland death certificates are filed in one of two health departments according to the place of death. If a person dies in Baltimore City, the certificate is filed in the Baltimore City Health Department. If the death occurs in any other part of Maryland, the certificate is filed in the Maryland State Health Department. Copies of death certificates for Maryland residents who die outside the State are forwarded to the health department of residence.

among their patients which were not linked during the computer matching process. Clerical checking located the certificates for 570 of these persons and the cause of death was added to the Register files. An investigation as to the reason for these missed linkages revealed that data for all deaths among Maryland residents occurring outside the State were not included in our death data cards.

This method of death clearance seems to be effective and will be used in the future. However, more careful checking will be made to insure inclusion of data from all death certificates. The major difficulty with the system is the necessity of preparing additional punch cards (17,000–20,000 annually) for over half of the recorded deaths.

Recently, an intensive review of all identity records (95,000) was made in an effort to discover missed and incorrect linkages. It was necessary to make 72 changes (33 incorrect and 39 missed) in our linkages. Almost all of these errors could be traced to the clerical review and correction of computer decisions. Although these figures suggest an accuracy rate of over 99·9 per cent., several factors are involved that reduce this : (1) there are some records on the file reported without the patient's name ; (2) many records of the first year's reports have other missing identity items ; (3) due to the nature of the reporting population, it can be assumed that a few patients successfully report alias names ; and (4) some patients have their name changed legally. Our best estimate is 99·7 per cent. accuracy of linkage.

Over 60 per cent. of the computer ' positive ' linkages are never reviewed clerically. This percentage will increase as we obtain the missing identifying data for earlier reports. Some of the deterrents to our attainment of completely automatic record linkage which we have learned empirically are : (1) reported family members with similar names (especially twins) ; (2) use of the same social security number by different members of the same family ; (3) reporting of different social security numbers by the same person ; and (4) the large number of persons with the same name and other similar characteristics. These are in addition to the inevitable reporting and data preparation errors and the omission and lack of reliability of some reported items.

Two aspects of the linkage system that cause the most concern are the amount of clerical review required to check ' possible ' linkages produced by the group linkage programmes, and the ever-increasing amount of computer time required for the Soundex-sex group matching between the Master Register file and other files. These factors reduce the efficiency of the linkage system by increasing

143

the cost. The solution of these problems has a high priority.

Changes have been made in the linkage process periodically. Not all of these changes were for the better and some experiments were rejected after a brief trial. A major revision of the Soundex-sex group matching programme is being planned. Although the types of revision are known, a more detailed analysis is required before these revisions are finalized. Primarily these changes involve the introduction of additional factors into the logic of the computer decision process to decrease the number of indefinite decisions (possible linkages) and a change in the sequence of checks to perform the checks that require the least amount of computer time and would allow for a definite computer decision prior to the expensive comparison of names.

DISCUSSION

The linkage system described was developed from necessity and modifications were made based primarily on empirical knowledge. It was developed for a specific purpose and the logic was determined by the types and quality of identifying data, the nature and size of the project, and the nature and size of the equipment available.

Some aspects of the system could be applied to other record linkage projects. The group matching technique, primarily the Soundex code-sex programmes, is the most valuable innovation produced by the system. A partial analysis of the first three years results of one of these programmes (Figs. 14–15) demonstrates its efficiency. The decision table currently being used in programming all Soundex-sex group linkage programmes is shown in Figure 16.

Automatic linkage among recorded events of a person's life must be based on identifying information that is readily available and known, and which the person reporting this information is willing to furnish. Means of verifying the reported information are also useful. Name and sex are two items which most nearly fulfil these requirements. Address, date of birth, a unique identifying number (such as social security number) and race fall into that category to a lesser degree. Maiden name, mother's maiden name and birthplace are also items which partially fulfil the requirements.

Completely automatic and accurate record linkage may never be attained. However, a great deal of improvement seems feasible and logical. The technology and methods of obtaining good linkage among records are within our grasp and better methods of achieving accurate record linkage will be developed in a very few years. The

FIG. 14. *Soundex-sex group check to register file positive linkage decision summary*

Reference code	Fiscal year 1962		Fiscal year 1963		Fiscal year 1964		Totals	
	Computer linkages	Net linkages	Computer counts	Net linkages	Computer counts	Net linkages	Computer counts	Net linkages
A0000	1187	1187	2193	2193	2469	2466	5849	5846
A0100			4	4	2	2	6	6
A0110	1	1	2	2	2	1	4	4
A0120	2	2	10	6	27	17	39	25
A0130	11	11					11	11
A0131			17	14	18	18	35	32
A0200	8	8	187	187	255	255	450	450
A0210	96	96	233	233	288	288	617	617
A0220	192	192	1111	1022	1209	1087	2512	2301
A0230	894	894	1086	1081	1271	1250	3251	3225
A0231	93	93	442	168	541	273	1076	534
A0234	17	17	11	11	8	8	36	36
A0300			4	4	2	2	6	6
A0310			6	6	7	7	13	13
A0331			20	9	27	12	47	21
A0400	2	2	9	9	10	10	21	21
A0410	3	3	10	10	25	25	38	38
A0420	2	2	15	13	18	14	35	29
A0430	45	45	25	25	57	57	127	127
A0431			14	4	32	11	46	15
A0500			0	0	0	0	0	0
A0510			0	0	0	0	0	0
A0520			3	0	7	0	10	0
A0600							0	0
A0610	5	5					5	5
A0620	27	12					27	12
A0630	77	63	124	116	132	114	333	293
A0800	23	23	36	34	57	57	116	114
A0900							0	0
A0910							0	0
A0920							0	0
A0930							0	0
A1200							0	0
A1210							0	0
A1220							0	0
A1230			8	8	27	26	35	34
A1231			13	5	21	11	34	16
Total	2685	2656	5583	5164	6511	6011	14779	13831

L

FIG. 15. *Soundex-sex group check to register file possible linkage decision summary*

Reference code	Fiscal year 1962		Fiscal year 1963		Fiscal year 1964		Totals	
	Computer counts	Net linkages	Computer counts	Net linkages	Computer counts	Net linkages	Computer counts	Net linkages
A0131	20	0					20	0
A0132								
A0133			14	0	19	0	33	0
A0135			1	0	0	0	1	0
A0137	227	192	111	13	135	10	473	215
A0232	690	68	1196	5	1733	3	3619	76
A0233			16	5	23	4	39	9
A0234-N	3	3	241	2	285	6	529	11
A0235			264	6	446	8	710	14
A0320			898	9	1337	0	2235	9
A0331-N			8	0	7	1	15	1
A0335			6	3	4	2	10	5
A0430-N	8	8	2	0	2	1	12	9
A0432			41	0	49	0	90	0
A0433			0	0	0	0	0	0
A0434			0	0	0	0	0	0
A0435	1	0					1	0
A0437								
A0530			32	0	44	5	76	5
A0531			0	0	0	0	0	0
A0532			0	0	6	0	6	0
A0535			776	12	1257	15	2033	27
A0630-N	95	3	166	5	243	16	504	24
A0631	2127	12					2127	12
A0632			16	2	12	1	28	3
A0634	44	0					44	0
A0635			7	0	9	0	16	0
A0900			0	0	0	0	0	0
A0932			58	32	96	50	154	82
A1030			27	5	59	14	86	19
A1031			2	1	1	0	3	1
A1034	2	2					2	2
A1230			0	0	0	0	0	0
A1231			1	0	3	0	4	0
A1232			1	0	0	0	1	0
A1234			2	0	4	1	6	1
A1235			284	1	447	1	731	2
A1300			1	1	0	0	1	1
Totals	3219	288	4168	102	6221	138	13608	528

main barrier to complete record linkage is not a technical one but is due to human factors.

People do not want various events of their life to be known or stored in a central file, regardless of the benefit to mankind in general. Many people like to feel that they can change their identity and make a fresh start in life at any time, discarding all of their past. The right of persons to conceal any fact or event regarding their life will be defended to the death by many individuals regardless of whether or not such knowledge would harm the individual or would be of benefit to mankind.

A good example of the latter is what is commonly referred to as the confidentiality of doctor–patient relationship. A large segment of the medical profession, possibly a majority, refuses or is reluctant to divulge any information about their patients. This is particularly true for patients in the higher socio-economic groups. In a free and independent society it will be extremely difficult to overcome this philosophy and achieve the ultimate goal of a data bank containing complete birth to death medical histories of individuals.

REFERENCES

ACHESON, E. D. (1964). Oxford record linkage study : a central file of morbidity and mortality records for a pilot population. *Br. J. prev. soc. Med.* **18**, 8.

BAHN, A. K. (1960). The development of an effective statistical system in mental illness. *Am. J. Psychiat.* **116**, 798–800.

BAHN, A. K. (1965). Experience and philosophy with regard to case registers in health and welfare. *Community ment. Hlth. J.* **3**, 245–250.

BAHN, A. K. (1966). Some research tools for community mental health planning and evaluation with particular reference to psychiatric case registers. In Proceedings of International Research Seminar on Community Mental Health Programs, May 1966.

GORWITZ, K., BAHN, A. H., CHANDLER, C. A. & MARTIN, W. (1963). Planned uses of a statewide psychiatric register for aiding mental health in the community. *Am. J. Orthopsychiat.* **33**, 494–500.

KENNEDY, J. M., NEWCOMBE, H. B., OHAZOKI, E. A. & SMITH, M. E. (1965). Computer methods for family linkage of vital and health records. Pamphlet AECL-2122, Atomic Energy of Canada.

NEWCOMBE, H. B., KENNEDY, J. M., AXFORD, S. J. & JAMES, A. P. (1959). Automatic linkage of vital records. *Science*, **130**, 954–959.

NITZBERG, M. (1965). The methodology of computer linkage of health and vital records. *Proc. Am. statist. Ass.*, Soc. Statist. Sect.

PHILLIPS, W. Jr., & BAHN, A. K. (1963). Experience with computer-matching of names. *Proc. Am. statist. Ass.*, Soc. Statist. Sect., pp. 26–37.

PHILLIPS, W. Jr. & BAHN, A. K. (1966). Computer processing in the Maryland psychiatric case register. Presented at the Public Health Records and Statistics Conference, Washington, D.C.

PHILLIPS, W. Jr., BAHN, A. K. & MIYASAKI, M. (1962). Person-matching by electronic methods. *Communs Ass. comput. Mach.* **5**, 404–407.

PHILLIPS, W. Jr. GORWITZ, K. & BAHN, A. K. (1962). Electronic maintenance of case registers. *Publ. Hlth. Rep.* **77**, 503–510.

Fig. 16. *Maryland psychiatric case register—decision table for soundex sex group linkage programmes July 1, 1964*

Reference code	First check						Second check			Third check				Fourth check	
	Soundex code and sex	Sur-name	First name	Add-ress	Birth year range	Decision	Maiden name	Middle name	Decision	Race	Birth month & day spec.	Birth year	Decision	Birth month & day	Decision
A0000	0	0	0	0	0	Accept									
A0100	0	0	0	0	1	Possible									
A0110							0	0	Accept						
A0120							0	1	Accept						
A0120-N							1	0	Possible						
A0131							1	1		0	0		Accept		
A0133										0	1	1	Possible		
A0135										1	0	1	Possible		
A0137										1	1	1	Possible		
A0200	0	0	0	1	0	Possible									
A0210							0	0	Accept						
A0220							0	1	Accept						
A0220-N							1	0	Possible						
A0230							1	1	Possible	0	0	0	Possible		
A0230-N										0	1	1	Possible	0	Accept
A0231										0	0		Possible	1	Possible
A0231-N										0	0		Possible		
A232															
A0233										0	1	1	Reject	0	Accept
A0234										0	0	0	Possible	1	Possible
A0234-N										1	1	0		0	Accept
A0235										1	0	1	Possible	1	Possible
A0235-R													Possible		
A0236										1	1	0	Reject	0	Reject
A0237										1	1	1	Reject	1	

A0300	0	0	0	Accept	0	0	Possible	Possible	▨	▨
A0310			1	Accept	1	0	Possible	Reject	▨	▨
A0320			0	Possible	0	1	Possible	Possible	▨	▨
A0320-R	0	0	1	Possible	1		Reject	0	1	Possible
A0331								1	▨	Reject
A0331-R	0	1			0	1	Reject	0	1	Possible
A0333					1	0	Possible			Reject
A0335									▨	▨
A0335-R									▨	▨
A0337									▨	▨
A0400	0	1	0	Accept	1	1	Reject	0	▨	▨
A0410	1	1	1	Accept	0	0	Possible	1	0	Accept
A0420			0	Accept				1	0	Possible
A0430	0	0	1	Possible	1	0	Possible	0	1	Accept
A0430-N									▨	Possible
A0431					0	0	Possible		▨	▨
A0431-N					1	1	Possible		▨	▨
A0432					0	0	Possible		▨	▨
A0433					1	1	Possible		▨	▨
A0434									▨	Possible
A0435								0	1	Possible
A0435-R								1	▨	Reject
A0436					0	1	Reject		▨	▨
A0437					1	1	Reject		▨	▨
A0500	0	0	1	Accept	1	0			▨	▨
A0510	0	0	0	Accept	1	1	Possible	1	0	Accept
A0520	1	1		Accept	0	0	Reject	1	0	Possible
A0531	1	1	1	Possible	1	1	Possible	0	1	Possible
A0533								1		Reject
A0535								1	0	Possible
A0537								0	1	Reject
A0630	0	0	0	Possible	0	0	Possible			Possible
A0630-N										Accept
A0631	(1)	(1)	0	Possible	1	0	Possible	1		Possible
A0631-R							0	1		Reject

FIG. 16. *Maryland psychiatric case register—decision table for soundex sex group linkage programmes July 1, 1964*
continued

Reference code	First check						Second check			Third check				Fourth check	
	Soundex code and sex	Sur- name	First name	Add- ress	Birth year range	Decision	Maiden name	Middle name	Decision	Race	Birth month & day spec.	Birth year	Decision	Birth month & day	Decision
A0632										0	1	0	Reject		
A0633										0	1	1	Reject		
A0634										1	0	0	Possible	0	Possible
A0634-R														1	Reject
A0635										1	0	1	Reject		
A0636										1	1	0	Reject		
A0637										1	1	1	Reject		
A0700	0	0	1	1	1	Reject									
A0800	0	1	0	0	0	Accept									
A0900	0	1	0	0	1	Possible									
A1030	0	1	0	1	0	Possible	(1)	(1)	Possible	0	0	0	Possible	0	Possible
A1030-R														1	Reject
A1031										0	0	1	Possible	0	Possible
A1031-R														1	Reject
A1032										0	1	0	Reject		
A1033										0	1	1	Reject		
A1034										1	0	0	Possible	0	Possible
A1034-R														1	Reject
A1035										1	1	0	Reject		
A1036										1	1	1	Reject		
A01037															
A1100	0	1	0	1	1	Reject	(1)	(1)	Possible						
A1230	0	1	1	0	0	Possible				0	0	0	Accept		

Code							Possible		Possible 0 1	Possible	Accept / Possible
A1231	0			1	0	1	Possible	0	0	Possible	▨
A1231-N	0			1	1	0	Reject	0	1	Reject	▨
A1232	0			1	1	1	Reject	1	1	Possible	▨
A1233								1	0	Possible	▨
A1234								1	1	Reject	▨
A1235								1	1	Reject	▨
A1236											▨
A1237											▨
A1300											▨
A1400											▨
A1500											▨

0 = Agreement ; 1 = Disagreement ; (1) = Assumed Disagreement.

SURNAME CHECK
In a one-to-one correspondence of each letter of each name, based on the longest of the two, only one disagreement allowed.

FIRST NAME CHECK
(Same as Surname).

ADDRESS CHECK
Agreement on street number and first 8 positions of street name. If street name blank, agreement on street number. If street name not blank, and it is RT, RF., or RD—agreement on first 5 positions of City/Town.

MAIDEN NAME CHECK
Agreement on 8 positions of maiden name.

MIDDLE NAME CHECK
Agreement on middle initials ; or middle initial/maiden name first letter crosscheck.

BIRTH YEAR RANGE

If current age is:	Range must be within :
0—17	2 years
18—29	5 years
30—49	10 years
50 and over	15 years

MONTH AND DAY OF BIRTH : SPECIAL
Agreement on either month and day of birth or in crosscheck or any of month and day of birth fields are blank.
Complete agreement required for Social Security Number, maiden name, sex, race, birth month and day, and birth year.

Discussion

Mr Fisher : I worked with Dr Acheson in 1963 and 1964 ; in fact I was responsible for devising the earliest match programmes for the Oxford Record Linkage Study. I can well remember the awe with which I regarded Dr Newcombe in Canada and Mr Phillips and Dr Bahn in Maryland ; and the respect we had in Oxford for the Maryland work has been amply justified by the paper we have just heard. For example, we heard Mr Phillips' modest disclaimer that although the figures appear to show accuracy of 99·9 per cent. this is misleading, for the accuracy is only 99·7 per cent. His achievement must be envied by any programmer in record linkage.

I have three technical points to raise, mainly suggested by the very interesting decision tables. Thus from these tables it is easy to see how very few 'possible' linkages were in fact shown, after clerical scrutiny, to be exact linkages. A possible saving would be to make the computer criteria more strict and less flexible, so as to reduce what is elsewhere referred to in the paper as the substantial percentage of linkages which required manual verification.

The second point concerns the extraordinarily high accuracy. The problem of costs mentioned elsewhere in the paper, in maintaining the Soundex programme, must be closely related to accuracy : the extra cost on going, say, 97·5 per cent. to 99·9 per cent. is considerable—is it worthwhile ?

The third point arising from the decision tables concerns the great (negative) power of birth range. The Maryland programmes, using birth range instead of full calendar date of birth, avoid the problems we face in the United Kingdom in overcoming these irritating but by no means uncommon discrepancies. You will see, from the decision tables, how very few cases indeed exist where a discrepancy in birth range on a 'possible' linkage was finally judged to be 'acceptable'.

Mr Phillips : I just want to say that in our Soundex coding the first letter also was one of my variations. We also tried another variation to the Soundex code which was to shorten it to only three numerical positions. We tried once when we took a sample file and in a timing study we found the programme was going to run one hundred computer hours so we discontinued this experiment and went to another modification. I thought if I shortened the number of digits I would get more commonly misspelled names, like my own, Phillips and Phillip which would never come together if I coded to four digits. So I decided to cut back to three, create larger groups and make more comparisons. We found that the computer programme would run one hundred hours and that was too much, at $170 an hour, for one programme.

Mr Healy : I have been a little puzzled by the extent to which the Soundex code, and fairly minor variants of it, is relied upon by a number of systems. Name coding is of immense importance in record linkage, as a means both of cutting down search time and of decreasing error rates. Soundex-coding is designed to be simple, and computer processing would allow far more sophisticated procedures to be used. Research in this area would be difficult and expensive, because it must be based on an empirical study of what errors are actually made in reporting names ; errors which defeat Soundex coding are simply not identified by systems such as Dr Acheson's. However, I suspect the scope for improving computer linkage systems is greatest in this direction.

Dr Nitzberg : I will be talking about just those points later this afternoon.

Professor Alwyn Smith : One of the most important defects, it seems to me, of the Russell Soundex code is the fact that it doesn't code the first letter. In fact errors in the first letter are important and we have in Glasgow developed a version of Soundex which in fact codes the first letter in order to minimize errors of this sort. Since the code is essentially Soundex with the initial numericized, and since it was devised by my colleague Esther Granick and myself it is called SINGS code and stands for Soundex Initial Numericized Granick Smith.

Mr Sunter : I would like to say something about this grouping programme. It is not by any means clear that Soundex is the best basis on which to group or block a file and it is not clear that any code based on the surname is the best characteristic on which to divide a file. We are trying to develop a theory to give some insight into the best way to group a file. It is not clear either, I might say, that the best course of action is to sequence a file in any one way. It may pay, as Dr Newcombe has pointed out, to have multiple sequences in the files and try and search for matches according to some other sequence. On this point, I think that it is as well to remember that this problem of dividing a file sets an upper limit on the sort of accuracy you can hope to get in record linkage. This will apply for third-generation computers or for fifth-generation computers because I think there is an upper limit to the internal speed of computers which is going to become significant when you try record linkage with a large population.

PART 4

METHODOLOGY II

Chairman : Mr M. J. R. HEALY (London)

A COMPUTER SYSTEM FOR MEDICAL
RECORD LINKAGE

M. R. HUBBARD and J. E. FISHER

THE Oxford Record Linkage Study has been collecting information about certain health events since the beginning of 1962. From 1st January, 1963, sufficient identifying information has been punched to permit record linkage to be performed by computer. The population studied has been expanded from 335,000 in 1962 to about 750,000 persons in 1966. The study area consists of the central part of the area served by the Oxford Regional Hospital Board.

Information is collected from birth and death certificates, hospital inpatient spells (including maternity), and from domiciliary maternity events. Information is abstracted and coded from the non-confidential portion of the vital certificates and from copies of the hospital or midwives' notes (Table I).

For the years 1962–64 a manual master index was maintained for all persons encountered. The incoming records were matched with the master index by clerks who then allocated a Hogben number (Hogben and Cross, 1948 ; Hogben, Johnstone and Cross, 1948) to be punched on machine cards. The successive records of an individual could then be collated mechanically. Computer matching and manual systems were maintained in parallel for the years 1963 and 1964, enabling the development stages of the computer programmes to be monitored closely, as well as providing a standard which the computer system should attain.

THE MATCH SYSTEM

Implementation

The match programme is written in IBM 1401 Autocoder language, for a maximum 1401 tape system. The machine used has six magnetic tape units, card input and output, line printer and 16,000 characters of core storage, as well as all advanced programming features.

Data

The coded data are punched into standard 80-column Hollerith cards. Two cards are prepared from each source document, one containing the identifying information (the ' names ' card) and the other the coded information required for statistical purposes (the ' stats '

157

Table I. *Number of records abstracted 1963–65 related to population size and source of information*

Year	Estimated population	Birth	General hospital	Maternity (hospital)	Maternity (home)	Death	Total records
1963	339,510	6,808	24,659	5,818	1,542	3,397	42,224
1964	347,980	6,875	26,221	5,928	1,686	3,144	43,854
1965	353,510*	15,267	27,206	13,313	5,430	3,250	64,466
Totals 1963–1965		28,950	78,086	25,059	8,658	9,791	150,544

* In 1965 the population studied was extended with respect to birth and maternity records to an estimated 751,230. Hospital and death records have also been processed for this population since 1966.

card). The two cards are linked together by a common number which is also the serial number by which the source document is filed.

The punched cards are read into the computer in pairs (each names card followed by its associated stats card) and the information edited. The cards are checked for correct punching, and the validity of the information verified. From the two cards a pair of records is formed, the names and stats records which are written out to separate magnetic tape files. During the editing run the Soundex* code of the surname is generated, and a further number (the computer number) allocated to the names and statistics records. This number is used in all subsequent operations within the computer where communication is required between names and statistics records.

The match

The function of the matching operation is to bring together information referring to the same individual derived from different sources. To achieve this, it is necessary to build up a master index consisting of records defining uniquely the identities of all persons known to the system. Each incoming record must contain corresponding information to that used in the master file, and the latter must be searched for any reference to the individual concerned. If no such reference is found, it can be assumed that the incoming record refers to a person not previously encountered and the identity is added to the master index. If a reference is found, then procedures may be invoked which will bring the incoming statistical information into the cumulative record maintained for that individual.

In order to bring the running time of the programme within reasonable limits the incoming and master files are broken down into compartments, and the search made only within corresponding sections of the files. The choice of the criteria by which this breakdown is achieved is critical to the effectiveness of the overall programme, since any such action results in a certain number of potential linkages being lost owing to incoming and master file records falling in different sections. In Table II the identifying items used in the Oxford system are displayed according to the frequency of omissions and discrepancies in either record of pairs derived from the same person. After a number of experiments the following items were chosen with which to subdivide the file :

Soundex code of surname

Sex

Initial of first forename

* For details of the Russell Soundex code, see Appendix II.

Potential linkages lost due to the use of these criteria are thought to amount to 2·5 per cent. approximately of all linkages. This is regarded as an acceptable figure.

Table II. *Proportions of omissions and discrepancies in a sample of 1137 pairs of records derived from the same person*

Item	Availability in both records per cent.	Percentage of discrepancies
Surname (Soundex code)	100	1·0
First forename initial	100	1·5
Second forename	49	1·0
Sex	100	0
Date of birth		
Day	96	4·0
Month	96	2·0
Year	99	5·0
Place of birth	60	7·0
General practitioner	86	16·0
Address (first 3 chs.)	100	21·0
N.H.S. Number	10	19·0

The method of processing an incoming and master file block pair is as follows :

1. One input record is read from magnetic tape.

2. Master file records from the corresponding block are read one at a time, each being matched against the input record. Each master file record read is kept in a list held in the core store of the computer. If this list exceeds the capacity of the core the entire list, with subsequent additions, is written out to magnetic tape.

3. During this procedure, a note is made of any linkages obtained with the input record, and at the end of the master file block the best (if any) is accepted, provided that it meets the minimum satisfactory level of probability.

4. If no acceptable linkage is obtained the input record is added to the master file list in core, since it may be regarded as referring to a person not previoulsy encountered by the system.

5. Further incoming records are read, one at a time, and matched against the entire master file list, which is either held in core, or must be read from magnetic tape each time. The same action of either accepting a linkage or adding the incoming record to the master file list is taken after each pass of the master list.

6. Whenever a linkage is accepted, a small record is written to a magnetic tape, containing information from which the position of the incoming statistics record associated with the matched incoming names record may be found, and also the position of the cumulative personal statistics record on the master statistics file. When these records are combined with the incoming statistics records the latter may be updated with this linkage information (which consists of a pair of computer numbers), and the incoming items may be merged eventually with the master file.

7. At the end of the incoming soundex/sex/initial block the entire master file (in core or from tape) is output to magnetic tape, forming the updated master file for the next run.

8. The process is repeated until the incoming file is exhausted. Any records remaining on the master file are copied onto the new master file.

The matching routines

The matching process itself is divided into two parts, primary and secondary. A large proportion of linkages is obtained using the primary match, which is a relatively simple and quick process, and the secondary match is invoked only where detailed evaluation of a doubtful linkage is required.

The primary match involves the comparison of five items of information. The comparison is made character by character, and the decision made is simply one of total agreement or disagreement without any attempt at evaluating the nature of discrepancies.

The items of information compared are :

> Surname (12 characters)
> 1st Forename (8 characters)
> 2nd Forename (3 characters)
> Day and month of birth
> Year of birth

If all five of these items agree, or if four agree and second forename is missing from one or both records being compared (except in the case of twins), a match is considered to have been made, and no further attempts at linkage of that incoming item are made.

If only one primary match item agrees, a failed linkage is recorded for this comparison. If two, three or four agreements are found, the secondary match is entered.

The secondary match repeats in detail the comparison of the information studied in the primary match, and also examines additional information, viz:

M

> Maiden surname
> Address (first three characters of street address)
> Place of birth (coded)
> General practitioner (coded)
> National Health Service number

Each pair of items is compared character by character, and a weight assigned for the agreement or disagreement, the value of which is dependent upon the discriminating power of the item in question (Newcombe & Kennedy, 1962 ; Newcombe & Rhynas, 1962). Missing items in one or both records result in a ' no comparison ' action, and no weight is assigned.

If the summed weights from the various comparisons add up to less than +4, a ' no linkage ' decision is made. If they add up to +4 or more, a linkage is recorded, which will be accepted unless a better one is encountered in later matchings of the incoming record.

Special procedures

In the course of the match special action is taken for particular types of record which otherwise might fail to link or be linked incorrectly. Amongst these are the following :

1. A woman previously known to the system under her maiden name may marry and yield subsequent records under her married surname. For this reason, where maiden and married surnames disagree on any incoming record, the editing run generates two records on the names file, one for each name. A sort of the records into soundex/sex/initial order will present to the master file records under both names, so that linkage may be obtained in either situation.

These records are subsequently discarded to avoid inflation of the master file, and when a linkage with the maiden name record is achieved a copy of this record is written out to be resoundexed, resorted and merged back into the new position under married surname at a later stage. By these means records encountered before marriage may be brought together with records occurring after marriage.

2. Multiple births also present particular problems. The fact that an individual is one of twins, triplets, etc., is known to the system if the birth took place since 1st January, 1963. Information from the obstetric record, which is manually linked with the birth certificate, is added to the record derived from the latter. This record is invariably the first for that person encountered by the system, so that at the first attempted linkage records derived from multiple births can be identified. Parents have a tendency to name

twin children of like sex with forenames having the same initial letter, *e.g.* Michael and Martin, Jean and Joan, etc. For this reason the matching of twins is treated with particular stringency, and no such records are permitted to be linked in the primary match. Where twins of the same sex who were born before the beginning of 1963, having similar forenames and living at the same address are encountered the system still finds some difficulty in achieving a satisfactory match.

Output

The following output is produced during the matching run :

1. The new master file, consisting of the old master file to which has been added the identities of all persons new to the system who were encountered during the run.

2. The file of short records defining the linkages obtained, for further processing, adding to the incoming statistical records, and eventually resulting in the merging of these statistical records with the master file.

3. A file of matched maiden name records, for processing and eventually merging with the master names file.

4. A printed report of linked pairs, and similar pairs which achieved weights greater than -20 during the matching process.

RESULTS

The results discussed in this paper derive from the matching of data for the whole of 1965 with the master names file resulting from the linkage of 1963 and 1964 data. The computer programme reports all linkages achieved, and all ' near ' linkages, *i.e.* all pairs of records which, when matched, produced a weight greater than -20. A random sample of these reported linkages was clerically checked back to the source documents. Use was also made of the 1963–64 manual index. Table III displays the results of these checks.

Table III. *Computer decisions in a sample of 1,564 linked pairs of records*

Correct Linkages (based on primary match)	1,250	85·0
Correct Linkages (based on secondary match)	185	12·6
Linkages missed by computer	36	2·4
Total linkages	1,471	100·0
Incorrect Linkages	1	

163

A further study of the types of discrepancy encountered by the system was made, which was based on the analysis of 400 discrepant pairs known to be derived from the same person, in which either or both of the records contained an omission or discrepancy in the primary match items, resulting in the secondary match procedure being invoked. It was thought that such a study might lead to a possible redefinition of the primary match criteria so that the secondary part might be entered less frequently. Tables IV and V summarize the results of this study, giving details of the distribution of the first discrepancy within each item of information.

Table IV. *Frequency of missing items in one or both records in a sample of 400 linked pairs discrepant in the primary match criteria*

Item	Total	Per cent.
Surname . .	0*	0
Forename (1st) .	0*	0
Forename (2nd) .	210	52·5
Date of birth		
Day . . .	53	13·3
Month . .	51	12·8
Year . . .	17	4·3

* The edit programme rejects any incoming records lacking either surname or a first forename. Percentages are calculated on a base of 400.

DISCUSSION

As may be seen from Table III, whilst false linkages are rare, the computer programme is missing 2·4 per cent. of the potential linkages. It is estimated that about a further 2·5 per cent. is lost owing to records being sorted into different parts of the file and never being matched together. (This occurs when they are discrepant in Soundex of surname, sex or initial of first forename.) Thus, some 95 per cent. of possible linkages are being achieved. Whilst this proportion is satisfactory for most statistical purposes, it must be remembered that the programme is working at present with rather small populations (some 100,000 individuals have been encountered by the system to date), and that as this population expands, so the number of closely similar identities will increase. It may be expected that the matching decisions will become the more difficult as the files become larger.

Table V. *Frequency of discrepancies of various types in a sample of 400 linked pairs of records discrepant in the primary match criteria*

Item	Total	Per cent.
Surname . .	55	13·8
1st character . .	0*	0
2nd . . .	2	0·5
3rd . . .	2	0·5
4th . . .	7	1·8
5th . . .	14	3·5
6th+ . . .	30	7·5
Forename (1st) .	93	23·3
1st character . .	0*	0
2nd . . .	18	4·5
3rd . . .	11	2·8
4th . . .	20	5
5th . . .	28	7
6th+ . . .	16	4
Forename (2nd) .	9	2·3
1st character . .	2	0·5
2nd . . .	2	0·5
3rd . . .	5	1·3
Date of birth		
Day . . .	120	30
Month . .	44	11
Year . . .	103	25·8
any† . .	229	57·3

* The method by which the sample is defined results in the omission of discrepancies in the first character.
† Includes multiple discrepancies.

It is interesting to note that only 12·6 per cent. of linkages are achieved in the secondary match. If the files were to be used for purely statistical purposes, a small reduction in the number of calls made upon this procedure would permit it to be discarded entirely. However, a considerable number of the uses to which the linked files are put operate at the level of the individual, where a 90 per cent. accuracy would not be acceptable. Further, as the proportion of the population known to the system increases so the number of calls made on the secondary match will increase. It seems probable that the criteria for a primary match linkage will have to be made more stringent, rather than less so, as had been hoped. Already two pairs of records have been encountered where surname, both forenames and day and month of birth agreed—in one of the pairs the discrepancy in year of birth was only by one year. The inclusion of another factor in the primary match seems to be inevitable.

Whilst the present performance of the programme is encouraging, the small proportion of the population encountered, and also the fact that all linkages have been achieved over a maximum period of only three years, indicate that the decisions which it will be called upon to make in the future will be altogether more subtle. For this reason, it will be necessary to study its performance in the next few years very carefully, and a policy of continuous modification and improvement will have to be adopted. Fortunately, it will be possible to make the programme self-monitoring to a certain degree, so that the amount of checking necessary may be kept to a manageable minimum (the output from the 1965 vs 1963–64 run consisted of well over 1,000 pages).

The existing programme is experimental, with all the inefficiencies inherent in a programme written for this purpose and repeatedly modified. It has been decided that a new version should be written at this point in the development of the technique, to remove the inelegancies of the experimental version, and to enable a computer other than the IBM 1401 to be used. Further, it is hoped to produce the new version in a high level language with a reasonable degree of machine independence.

At the same time the system in which the matching procedures operate may be redesigned to offer a considerable gain in overall efficiency. It is envisaged that the matching routines will be rewritten in a new language initially, without any major modifications, but that the file formats, twin and maiden name procedures, etc. will be revised completely. The programme will incorporate facilities for modification of the weighting of individual items of information in the light of future experience, and also include some self-monitoring features to indicate sources of possible errors.

Attention must also be given to the retrieval of information from the linked records. Standardization of the statistical records is being undertaken, and the use of list processing methods can make access to successive records efficient. Certain routine operations (*e.g.* the production of death, operations and diagnostic indices ; formation of cumulative personal morbidity records, etc.) require that the statistical records be both standardized and held in a convenient form.

SUMMARY AND CONCLUSIONS

1. A system for matching records based on comparisons between the following identifying data is described : surname, first and

second forenames, sex, place of birth, date of birth, general practitioner, address and National Health Service number.

2. The incoming data and master files are divided into blocks on the basis of Soundex, sex and initial of first forename, and the search for a match for each incoming record is limited to the appropriate block on the master file.

3. The matching procedure is divided into a primary and secondary match. The primary match compares surname, first and second forename and date of birth. If all agree (or if only second forename is missing), a linkage is held to have been achieved. If more than one of these criteria agree, the secondary match is invoked ; otherwise no linkage is scored.

4. The secondary match repeats the comparison of the items used in the primary match, and also compares all remaining items in the records. The comparison is more sophisticated, and the decision of linkage based upon the sum of weights applied to agreement or disagreement of each item. A sum of weights greater than $+3$ results in a linkage being accepted.

5. 64,466 records relating to events in 1965 have been matched with the master file, and a systematic clerical check of 1,564 decisions has been made. It was found that the computer was correctly linking 97·6 per cent. of all linkages possible under the constraints of the subdivision of the files, and 95 per cent. approximately of all possible linkages. Incorrect linkages accounted for some 0·2 per cent. of decisions made.

6. The frequency of various types of discrepancy and of omission in identifying factors is reported. It is concluded that in this area at least a match system depending upon complete agreement would result in an unacceptable proportion of missed linkages.

7. It is hoped that the system described, with a number of modifications, will be satisfactory for a population of at least 2,000,000, though a further factor will almost certainly be needed in the primary match to prevent an unacceptable number of false linkages being obtained in this part of the programme.

REFERENCES

HOGBEN, L. & CROSS, K. W. (1948). Statistical specificity of code personnel cypher sequence. *Br. J. soc. Med.* **2,** 148.

HOGBEN, L., JOHNSTONE, M. M. & CROSS, K. W. (1948). Identification of medical documents. *Br. med. J.* **1,** 632.

NEWCOMBE, H. B. & KENNEDY, J. M. (1962). Record linkage making maximum use of the discriminating power of identifying information. *Communs Ass. comput. Mach.* **5,** 563.

NEWCOMBE, H. B. & RHYNAS, P. O. W. (1962). Family Linkage of Population Records. The uses of vital and health statistics for genetic and radiation studies. New York: United Nations, 135.

APPENDIX I

Secondary match procedure

Weights assigned by match programme (with modifications made as a result of this study)

		AGREEMENT		DISAGREEMENT
Surname	Initial letter	BCHMSW +2 DGLPRT +3 IOQUVXYZ +6 AFJKNE +4		1 char. discr. −3 2 char. discr. −4 2 char. discr. −6

Forenames 1st	Initial letter	Female	Male
		CEGHJM +2	AFJKM
		ABDIKLPSV +3	BCEGHLPR
		FNORTWY +5	DNSTVW
		QUXZ +7	IOQUXYZ

−5 but

+2 { Bridget(itte), Diane(a), Isa(o)bel, Nora(h), Sara(h), T(e)resa }

Alan/Allen, Den(n)is, Edmo(u)nd, H(u)erbert, Jack/John, Phil(l)ip, Tom/Thomas, Ste(ph)ven

2nd — As 1st forename

(i) If either master or incoming forename is blank, match its 1st forename v. other 2nd forename. If identical, +4 (*e.g.* Mary May) *vs.* May. If different, +0

(ii) If both blank, +0

(iii) If neither blank, −5

N.B. Cross checks Donald Dav / David Don } = +5

* These weights are under continuous review

APPENDIX I (continued)

Secondary match procedure

Weights assigned by match programme (with modifications made as a result of this study)

Year of* birth	+3	>10 yrs. discrepant <10 yrs. discr. pre 1900 post 1940 1900–1940	−15 −3 −5 −4
Month/day*	+5	>1 digit discr. 1 digit discr. −3	−5 −4
Address*	<015 +4 >015 +7		
Maiden* name	As current surname	As current surname	
Place of* birth	Oxford City +2 Oxon +2 Other +6	Oxford City/Oxon Other	−2 −5
N.H.S.* G.P.*	+7 +4	−2 −1	

* For all these factors, if either master or incoming record is blank, no weight is attached.

APPENDIX II

Rules for the Russell Soundex coding of surnames, as used in the O.R.L.S. System.

1. The code consists of a single alphabetic character followed by three digits.
2. The initial letter of the surname forms the first character of the code.
3. Subsequent characters of the surname are coded according to the following table,

Letters	Code
B F P V	1
C G J K Q S X Z	2
D T	3
L	4
M N	5
R	6

until three digits of code have been obtained.

The letters A, E, I, O, U and Y are not coded, but may act as separators (see 4 below).

W and H are ignored.
Hyphens are ignored.

4. Letters which follow letters having the same code are not coded unless preceded by a separator.
5. 'TCH' is coded as 'C'.

This system, with the exception of 5 above, is that used by Drs H. Newcombe and J. Kennedy at A.E.C.L., Chalk River.

Discussion

Dr Adelstein : We who are interested in record linkage realize how much we owe to this Oxford study and the criticism which they have put to their own work is very valuable to us. Perhaps to try and come away a little bit from the points that have already been discussed this morning and the papers before us this afternoon, I would put one or two points on a different plane. What do they do with the data ? That is, after the link is made. How much data can they take ? What is the form of the data ? Do they have variable length records or must they use space for all possibilities ? That is one kind of question I should like to ask, and the second is, what do they think about the kind of language they write these programmes in ? Is there any advantage in using high-level languages for such enormous jobs, or shouldn't they be used ? And what kind of computers do they think are particularly suitable, that is, what kind of stores and so on do they prefer and do they think are particularly suitable ; particularly if, one day, we are going to make the enormous jump from a limited study of, say, this region to a national level.

Mr Hubbard : To take the points approximately in order : first of all, the statistical information associated with any particular names record is updated with linkage information. When a linkage is achieved a short record is output containing information that essentially defines the position of the associated statistical information on the input file, and also defines the position of the previously encountered records on the master file. The incoming statistical records may be updated by this, sorted to master-file order, and then simply merged into the master statistical file. We keep the identifying information and the statistical information on separate files and in separate orders. This was a result, first of the fact that we weren't quite sure in what order the identifying information would eventually be held and second, it was thought wise to keep the two files separate in the interests of security.

With reference to the length of items, every incoming record produces a standard 102-character statistical record which contains a linkage to the associated names item (and also in earlier cases a Hogben number) and the complete statistical information. These items are held merely as blocks of ten such records. There is no upper or lower limit to the number of items one can have for any one person. They follow each other in order of internal allocated reference number. It will, of course, be a multiple of 102 characters, in the same way as it is a multiple of a particular number of events.

Considering computers for this sort of programme, it is very pleasant to have a machine that operates comfortably in a character mode because so much of the information that is processed consists of characters. This means that in many cases scientific machines with long word length and a very fine repertoire, for example, of floating point instructions, without many shifts and character instructions, aren't perhaps quite as suitable. This is what made the 1401 such a very nice machine to experiment on although I think the programme has outgrown it now. The current version uses a maximum 1401 tape system with 16,000 characters of core. I think we have at the moment five characters to spare and they are not all in the same place, so we can't really get very much more into that computer.

The computer that one would like to use is a machine that has core storage large enough to contain a single Soundex sex-initial block of the incoming data. This is essential. You have to be able to hold either the incoming or the master file block in its entirety in core-store at one time. In normal circumstances the data block is smaller than the master block. The population that this sort of programme can serve is not really dependent on the size of the machine but more dependent on the number of times one is willing to process ; how many times one has to to process depends on the number of times the incoming data are going to fill up the available core-store. This in turn depends not only on the population one is serving but on the sort of information one is collecting. Of the purely medical records, we deal only with hospital inpatient events, but if we dealt with outpatient events obviously we would want either a very much bigger core-store or much more frequent processing.

Languages : high-level languages are very nice and very convenient and many of them, for example particularly COBOL and to a certain extent FORTRAN do provide the means to process character information with a certain amount of ease—COBOL of course much more so than FORTRAN. But at the same time even modern compilers are not as efficient as a machine-coded programme and one has to strike a balance between the speed of operation of the programme and the speed with which one is able to write and get it going. We in our rewrite are going to write very largely in FORTRAN because the two computers—ATLAS at Harwell and an English Electric KDF9 at the University Computing Laboratory—both happen to have pretty good FORTRAN compilers, and this is possibly the most suitable language to us for this reason. It is also quite a good language if one wants to publish the results. I think this is important, that one wants to have a language which is perhaps to a certain extent machine-independent, so that other people wanting to use your system can take over quite a lot of it without having to embark on expensive rewriting.

Dr Doll : You say you have 2·5 per cent. linkages which are missed through compartmentalizing in this way. Have you an idea what proportion of these would be missed by normally efficient clerical linking ? And, secondly, can you give us some idea of how much of the hospital discharge records you put into your data ?

Mr Hubbard : Firstly the clerical system : On the whole the computer seems to be doing slightly better than the clerks. We have maintained a clerical system to check the operation of our own programme and there has been a friendly war between the two factions to beat each other. In general we are bettering them slightly in achieving slightly more of the linkages that they missed, than they achieved of the ones that we missed !

The coded information concerning each hospital discharge really consists of the front summary sheet of the notes, including two diagnoses, operation, source, date of admission, date of discharge and result.

THE PERSONAL NUMBERING SYSTEM IN DENMARK

Henrik Nielsen

In the following pages I will give an account of the Personal Number System, which we are currently introducing in Denmark. First I will make a brief statement of the reasons which have brought about our introduction of a national personal numbering system. I will then describe the construction and assignment of the number itself, and finally I will give some examples of the fields in which the number is expected to be used in Denmark. Further, I will mention the analogous personal number systems, which at present are being created in Norway and Sweden.

As a consequence of the development of the administration—especially public administration—which has taken place during this century in Denmark, a wide range of registers for supporting the various branches of administration have come into use. The administrations maintaining such registers are very different ; they include the military authorities, the health insurance societies, the taxation authorities, insurance companies, registers of hospital patients, etcetera.

The registers may comprise a large or a small number of persons. However, certain information contained in these registers is to a great extent identical, especially such information as the persons' names, occupations, addresses, and birthdays. Add to this that most citizens in this country are listed in many of such registers, we find at the moment a widespread reduplication of effort takes place for keeping the aforementioned personal information up to date. Meantime, it is typical of these different registers or administrations that generally speaking they work isolated from each other and only with difficulty exchange information that they need mutually.

For a long time there has been a need for a system which could procure general information about persons, particularly information about addresses, but first we have lacked an administrative system which would pass on such information, and secondly—and this is of very great importance—we have lacked unique identification of the individual citizen, since a national system, undertaking such a project, would not with any degree of certainty correspond with other authorities using the present systems of identification.

For the moment, normally we use as identification the person's name and address, often also birthday and occupation. However

173

anybody working with registers will know that information such as name, address, and occupation is far from being reliable identification of the individual, as these data very often change. In other words, there is a need for a reliable and unamibiguous identification of the individual person and preferably also an identification which is as brief as possible. It should also be unchanging from the person's birth to his death.

It is the appearance of electronic data processing which has made it possible for us in Denmark to establish a central person register and in this connection to introduce a general personal system of numbers.

The Central Person Register, which we call CPR, will include all persons living in Denmark and it will be kept up to date by means of reports from the local administration, so that CPR will always be up to date. CPR will start around 1st January, 1968. The personal number will be introduced as an integral part of this central register to provide an unambiguous identification in relation with the administrations, which CPR will furnish with information. It has already been decided that a number of the most important registers in Denmark will accept the personal number as identification and the more widespread the number becomes, the greater advantage will be gained by using the number.

CPR will contain copious data, which will be at the disposal of all branches of the administration, the central public as well as the local municipal administration. However, CPR's principal task will be that of administrating the personal number system, *i.e.* to keep in order the assigned numbers, to assign new numbers to new-borns and immigrants and eventually to trace a previously assigned person number, if an immigrant has previously lived in Denmark.

As far as the construction of the number itself is concerned, it consists of 10 digits. The first six digits describe the person's date of birth, two digits for day, two digits for month, and two digits for birth-year. The next three digits are a serial number to distinguish between persons born on the same day. As in Denmark between two and three hundred persons are born daily, a three-digit serial number will suffice for many years. The tenth and last digit of the personal number is a check digit, the function of which is to disclose errors. The digit is a result of a mathematical calculation of the preceding nine digits and by repeating the calculation mechanically each time the number is processed in the EDP equipment possible errors will be disclosed. In the construction of the digit we have chosen a system called modulus 11, which is believed to be the system giving the greatest extent of certainty (see p. 182).

The personal numbers will be assigned so that odd numbers are assigned to men, while even numbers are assigned to women. In other words : A man born on 21st November, 1930, will be assigned a personal number starting with six digits 21.11.30 followed by four digits of which the last one is an odd number.

The construction of the personal number has been a problem and we considered as an alternative possibility the use of a straightforward serial number, *i.e.* a number without built-in information. This solution might have involved certain advantages over the solution we chose, in that the personal number could be less than 10 digits. As it is the insertion of date of birth involves a waste of digits because only numbers from one to thirty-one are used in the first two digits, and only numbers from one to twelve in the following two digits. Moreover, a random number might avoid uncertainty when assigning numbers in cases where a person's birthday is unknown or cannot be proved. However, the latter cases are growing more and more infrequent in Denmark, as we have a highly developed and reliable birth registration.

The following were our reasons for inserting date of birth in the personal number. Firstly, most registers will already contain information on this point so that the use of the personal number in such registers will only entail the recording of a further four digits. Registers already working with EDP will also be able to provide space more easily for the personal number in the system. Secondly, we believe that it will facilitate the spreading of the personal number among the population, if it contains the date of birth, as the number will thereby be easier for the individual to remember. And thirdly, a personal number containing the birthday can, to a certain extent, be used as identification for a register stored in sequence of date of birth, even if this register does not want to use the person number as identification.

As in Denmark there are not more than five million people, there are only a small number of persons born on the same day so that normally a register will contain only a few persons with the same birthday. Thus a register in birthday sequence will actually also be in personal number sequence. Both Norway and Sweden have chosen to insert the birthday in the personal number.

I shall briefly mention some of the principal fields in which the personal number will be used in Denmark. The conscription administration wants to replace the numbering system now in use with the personal numbers and CPR will furnish this administration with the relevant personal information. Furthermore, at this time a reorganization of all assessment and collection of taxes is being prepared in Denmark. This reorganization is expected to establish a central adminstration for the whole country. This is a very considerable task which can be solved only by means of the personal numbers as identification. The national pension scheme, in which all salaried and wage-earning employees participate, intends to use the personal number instead of the special identification number now in use.

I could name many other fields in which the numbers will be used ; in this audience it will presumably be of interest that to-day, in a certain big hospital, experiments with electronic data processing of hospital statistics are being based on information of each discharged patient. The experiment is being made with a view to a national health record system and when the personal number is introduced, it will be used as identification. In this way it will be possible via the personal number to combine the medical data with the general personal information which is contained in CPR. Taken overall, the spreading of the personal number in Denmark will open vast new possibilities for the preparation of statistics, as it will be possible to combine information from several different registers, when these work with the personal numbers.

In this connection it is important to mention a problem which arises each time it is desired to introduce the personal number into the existing registers. The most difficult question is how to link with certainty the correct personal number with the correct person in the register. There is no easy solution. I shall not go further into this but only mention that it is possible to perform the linkage mechanically, if the central register, CPR, and the register into which the personal numbers are to be entered both have certain data in common, *e.g.* the birthday and the name, However, as the nominal information is often unreliable a mechanical solution will not always be successful. As an emergency solution the individual persons in the register could state their own personal number, but this presupposes that the person can prove his number. Therefore, it has been decided, for this and other purposes, that CPR, a short time after its introduction, shall forward to all persons in Denmark a certificate stating the personal number assigned to them. At the same time some of the data content of the CPR will be checked.

Finally, I shall mention the personal numbers which are used in Norway and Sweden. These two personal numbers are in principle constructed in the same way as the Danish number, but there are small deviations. The Norwegian person number has 11 digits, *i.e.* one digit more than the Danish number. The six first digits contain birthday, month, and year. Thereupon follows a three digit serial number, and the last two digits are check digits, both following the system modulus 11, one digit according to the standard system and the other especially constructed. By having two check digits the greatest possible certainty is obtained for using the personal number, provided that the right person's number is used. In Denmark we have only one check digit because we fear that otherwise the number will be too long for practical use. As in Denmark the Norwegian number is assigned and controlled by a central authority.

The Swedish personal number is 10 digits like the Danish number. The first six digits stating the birthday are, however, in reverse order, *i.e.* year—month—day. Thereupon follows, as in Denmark, a three-digit serial number, and finally a check digit. Thus Denmark and Norway both have the date of birth in the order day—month—year. This solution has been chosen because it harmonizes with Danish and Norwegian usage and it is the order generally used when stating the birthday.

In spite of these small deviations we can, however, note that we are working with closely similar personal numbering system in Norway, Sweden and Denmark. In all three countries we expect that this system, in the course of time will have very great importance in the solution of many kinds of administrative problems especially those solved by means of EDP.

Discussion

Dr Cross : Dr Nielsen has given us a very clear account of a method of numbering records about people, although of course the number doesn't identify the individual. He has given several reasons for choosing a longer number, in order to incorporate the date of birth, than would otherwise be necessary. I know there are arguments against incorporating useful data in such a number, but on balance I would have thought his reasons were the more convincing.

It seems to me—and I don't think that Dr Nielsen went into this —that there will be some difficulty in constructing the central person register in the first case. There seem to be two possibilities ; either to use an existing file which contains every member of the population with names and addresses, or to carry out a complete census of the population at a given time as happened in this country in 1939 when, what is now the National Health Service Number was given.

The other point I would like to ask Dr Nielsen about is how the central person register, which will contain details other than date of birth, will be kept up to date. Presumably methods of collecting information about changes in names and addresses will have to be worked out. He will also need—and he has probably thought of this—a method for adjusting the central person register for immigrants and emigrants. Whereas he can easily pick up all the new entrants by birth and the deletions by death, immigration and emigration may present a problem in maintaining the central person register up to date.

He mentioned an interesting experiment that was taking place in a large Danish hospital, which intended to use the CPR number. Presumably people coming to this hospital and eventually to all hospitals in Denmark will be asked to bring along a document bearing their number, and if this is the case I wonder how Dr Nielsen believes that the Danish population will react to this. As he has already heard, there is very little success in this country in getting people to bring along their National Health Service Number at present.

Dr Nielsen : First I will deal with the question about how to start the system. I should explain that we already have the population registered in municipalities. In Denmark we have about one thousand municipalities and in each of these they have a file which includes all persons living in the area. Furthermore we have six punch-card centres in Denmark. These centres belong to the municipalities. In these centres we have a punch card for every person in the country and on this punch card we have name and address and birth date and other information. So starting the system will not pose a great problem for us. We can simply get a copy of those punch cards and then we can make our central register. I know that other possibilities exist ; for example in Norway they started with a general census.

You asked how to make the system work in cases, for instance, where a person gets a new name or he moves from one address to another. As I mentioned, we now have a system according to which the local administration gets a report every time something has to be reported to the central register. In case of death, for instance, they get a report ; in case of immigration or emigration also. The basic registrations that take place are not in the municipalities. For instance, births will be registered by the priest in the priest's books ; if a person dies he will record it and so on. In case of divorce it is the county office or the court. From all these places there will come reports to the municipalities' offices and they have to note it in the files and to report further to the central system.

About your third question, I told you that we intend to give a person proof of his personal number, a sort of identification card. We haven't had any reaction yet, but these are early days. You asked how the Danish population will react to this. Perhaps you fear that the cards will disappear. I don't know. I hope not. The personal number will be used in our income tax system and it will be absolutely necessary to have the number in this connection.

Mr Sunter : I don't know whether it is guaranteed in our Bill of Rights, but I think most Canadians would feel that it is the right of the individual to try and beat the system by giving an employer a false age and certainly one of the arguments encountered against the use of a birth number has been that the number contains the age of the person being identified and on these grounds many people prefer the Social Insurance number which contains no information about the person at all. I wonder if this has been a factor in discussions in Denmark ?

Mr Healy : Dr Acheson has made a similar point in his recent book.*

Miss Jones : My point was the same. I wondered to what extent the date of birth was disclosed to an employer.

Mr Healy : The question was whether a number containing date of birth is offensive to people who do not like their age to be disclosed in public.

Dr Nielsen : No, I don't think in Denmark we have this problem. The matter has been discussed in newspapers and we have had no reaction.

* Acheson, E. D. (1967). *Medical Record Linkage.* Published by the Oxford University Press for the Nuffield Provincial Hospitals Trust, London.

RECORD NUMBERING

M. SMYTHE

WHEN a numbering method is being designed there are several important factors which should be considered. One of the first should be to design the layout of the number in such a way that the likelihood of it being misquoted is reduced to the minimum. If for example a number is to contain two alpha characters and four numeric digits the error rate will depend on its presentation. All of the presentations shown in Figure 1 will attract different misquotation rates.

AB1234

12AB34

1234AB

A12 B34

12A 34B

etc.

FIG. 1. The error rates attracted by these presentations of a number will all differ.

As a basic rule it can be assumed that an alpha content in a number will increase the misquotation rate unless it is meaningful, *e.g.* BOW 1234 as opposed to XQJ 1234. Various tests have been made and show that an all-numeric number, presented in a fragmented form, is considerably less likely to be misquoted than the unbroken version whether it is being spoken or copied. Further the insertion of punctuation marks, boxes, etc. also helps to reduce the misquotation rate (Fig. 2). When numbers are printed, large simple typefaces produce the best results.

123456789

123 456 789

12 34 5 67 89

1234 56789

| 123 | 456 | 789 |

1234-56789

123/456/789

FIG. 2. The error rates attracted by these presentations of an all numeric number will all differ.

Patterns of errors

When a number is misquoted, the incorrect version usually bears a close resemblance to the correct version. For example if the number 1257 was misquoted it is much more likely that the wrong version would be 1267 than say 8971. A study has revealed that it is valid to classify errors into four types.

180

1. TRANSCRIPTIONS which are those cases where a single character is misquoted, *e.g.* 1274 instead of 1234.

2. SINGLE TRANSPOSITIONS which are those cases where two adjacent digits are reversed, *e.g.* 1324 instead of 1234.

3. DOUBLE TRANSPOSITIONS which are those cases where a group of three characters are reversed, *e.g.* 1432 instead of 1234.

4. RANDOM ERRORS which are any error not falling into one of the other three categories or a combination of two or more of those errors already described.

Error rates

Not only will the misquotation rate vary according to the layout of the number, but the pattern of errors will also be affected. As a rough rule of thumb, however, the following figures may be helpful if used in the broadest context : The total error rate will be of the order of one character in every 2,000 and the distribution of errors would be

Transcriptions	—	80 per cent.
Single transpositions	—	8 per cent.
Double transpositions	—	2 per cent.
Random errors	—	10 per cent.

Check digit systems

The basic concept of check digits is that by adding one or more characters to a basic number, a new number is formed with the property that, if quoted incorrectly, the chances of it matching a correct number are minimal. It has already been described how errors fall into fairly well defined categories and it is possible to design numbering systems in such a way that all the logical errors, transcriptions, etc. will be trapped.

The commonest method of creating a check digit is to split the basic number into its component characters. Each character is then multiplied by a fixed value termed a weight, which is determined by its position in the number. The check digit is the character which has to be added to the total of the products to make it exactly divisible by another number termed a modulus. Hence if a number is expressed in the form $ABCDEF$, etc. and the weights are m, n, o, p, q, r, etc., the check digit will be the number due to be added to the expression $Am+Bn+Co+Dp+Eq+Fr$, etc. so that the result is exactly divisible by the modulus.

An example of a weighted check digit is shown as Table II. The effectiveness of this system varies according to the choice of modulus

181

and, in some cases the weights. To trap all logical errors it is necessay to use a modulus which is a prime number of 11 or more, but this has the disadvantage that a check digit of 10 has to be accommodated, or those numbers requiring the check digit 10 (or more) have to be omitted. If a modulus of 10 is used the error detection rates depend on the choice of weights. This is shown in Table III.

A second method of selecting a subset of numbers from a complete range, so that they will not be error prone, is to use only those numbers which are exactly divisible by a prime number. In this case provided the prime number is greater than 10 all transcription and single transposition errors will be detected. If the divider is 13 all double transpositions will also be detected. If this method is used, the number range is reduced to one-eleventh or one-thirteenth of its full capacity. There is a third method of obtaining a check digit. This is to split the number into its component characters, or groups of characters, and to perform simple addition and or subtraction so that the result is a multiple of 10 or some other convenient number (Table I).

Table I. *An example of check digit calculation by addition and subtraction*

Regard each odd character position as positive.
Regard each even character position as negative.
Hence for the number 178234
The check digit is calculated as follows
$+1-7+8-2+3-4+$Check Digit $= 10x$
i.e. $12-13+$Check Digit $= 10x$
i.e. Check Digit $= 1$
The full number is therefore 1782341.

To conclude it is true to say that the check digits created using the weighting method and the division method can be made equally effective. The advantage of the weighted method, however, is that more numbers are available for issue. For example a modulus 10 system allows a tenth of the range to be issued whereas the best that can be obtained from the division method is an eleventh or a thirteenth.

Table II. *Example of a weighted check digit*

The basic number is 6 characters.
The modulus is 10.
The weights are 7, 6, 5, 4, 3, and 2 respectively.
Hence, for the number 543,345 the calculation is as follows :
$$\text{sum of products} = 5 \times 7 + 4 \times 6 + 3 \times 5 + 3 \times 4 + 4 \times 3 + 5 \times 2$$
$$= 35 + 24 + 15 + 12 + 12 + 10$$
$$= 108$$

It is necessary to add 2 to make the sum of the products 110 ; the next number divisible by 10. The full number, therefore, becomes 5433452.

Table III. *Statement of rates of error detection according to the weights used*

Modulus	Range of Weights	Weights Used	Percentages of errors detected			
			Trans-criptions	Single T'postns	Double T'postns	Random
10	1–9	1-2-1-2-1	94·4%	100%	Nil	90%
		1-3-1-3-1	100%	88·9%	Nil	90%
		7-6-5-4-3-2	87%	100%	88·9%	90%
		9-8-7-4-3-2	94·4%	100%	88·9%	90%
		1-2-7-1-3-7	100%	88·9%	88·9%	90%
11	1–10	Any	100%	100%	100%	90·9%
13	1–12	Any	100%	100%	100%	92·3%
17	1–16	Any	100%	100%	100%	94·1%
19	1–18	Any	100%	100%	100%	94·7%
27	1–26	Any	100%	100%	100%	96·3%
37	1–37	Any	100%	100%	100%	97·3%

DISCUSSION

Professor Armitage : My qualifications for speaking on this paper are solely the possession of a singularly inaccurate memory and a high propensity for making all sorts of errors of transcription. The sorts of errors that Mr Smythe has talked about fall into various categories. There are errors of memory, errors of transcription either from the spoken or the written record, errors of punching and no doubt others as well. The first question I would like to ask him is whether the overall error rate that he has quoted is applicable to each of these types of error. One might have thought that some sorts of error would be more likely in certain contexts than others. For example one might well confuse a 1 and a 7 in writing, or perhaps mistake a 4 and a 5 for a 1 and a 2 in punching on a keyboard. Memory errors might depend on the general context in which the numbering system was used, on the frequency with which an individual was called on to give it, the length of time we had been familiar with it and so on. I find, for example, that the number written on my identity card 28 years ago is more deeply embedded in my memory than my car registration number or my telephone number, presumably because I was at a more malleable stage of development when it was given to me.

As regards the check digits, I was very interested in Mr Smythe's reference to the General Post Office book (Post Office, 1962) because Dr Acheson refers to this in his book (Acheson, 1967) and I regretted before I came here not having come across it. I came across the other day a paper by Selmer from Norway (Selmer, 1967). This is a translation into English of a paper published in 1964 which has a number of points of interest and I wonder whether the people who work in this field who are not in full command of Norwegian are aware of all the points he made. Perhaps these points are already in the Post Office book. Selmer discusses the choice of a system of weights in the check digit system to detect the sort of errors that are likely to be most common. He is particularly interested in the Norwegian national system which Dr Nielsen has already described and so he is interested in detecting certain errors which are particularly likely with the date of birth form of number. He mentions also certain mechanical devices for handling check digits. Apparently it is possible to have key punches which automatically calculate and punch these at the time of punching. Also there are devices for checking these on verification of numbers. An interesting point, by the way, about the Norwegian system which I think Dr Nielsen didn't mention is that the two check digits use different systems of weighting and the second digit incorporates the first check digit as well as the informative numbers.

The final point I wanted to ask was whether the differing method which Mr Smythe mentioned at the end is just a particular case of the weighted sum, namely one in which the weights are plus and minus one alternately.

Mr Smythe : I think I have a note of most of the points that were raised. As regards error rates between memory, writing and punching, I haven't really got any information on this although I seem to recall that they are about the same in writing and in punching. The difference is, of course, that in punching one normally has a verification process which immediately follows it and this tends to reduce the number of errors that are made. But they tend still to be round about one in two thousand so far as we could ascertain back in 1964.

I regard the value of punches with automatic check digit calculation as somewhat suspect. Unless you want to find out that the number is wrong at the time it is punched, then there is no point in wasting the money and getting the device. The only reason that would really make it worthwhile, would be if you wanted to stop a wrong number going to the computer. If the computer received one it would certainly reject it because it would have no number on its file of the same value. But if the computer did have a number on the file of the same value it would have got through the checking device anyhow. So you are still going to get two sources of error. You are going to get valid numbers that in fact are wrong that have gone through the checking device but in fact are not on your computer files, so you are going to get your errors coming from two sources instead of one. The correction rate would be the same.

As regards these addition and subtraction check digit methods, the only real value of them is that these can be formed at an outstation. For example—I am sorry to keep referring to GPO—there are something around 20,000 post offices scattered all over the country and with savings bank work it would be most helpful if when the clerk is taking in the number he can find out whether or not it is wrong. It might in those conditions have been worthwhile having a slightly less effective system than a very good one if in fact you could have some device on the counter that would help detect wrong numbers.

Dr Acheson : I hope I won't give away any secrets if I say that Mr Smythe is the author of the GPO book. As it is published anonymously it took a bit of detective work to find out who in fact was the author, but in this I was helped by Dr Nielsen of Denmark. This work has already influenced Scandinavia to a considerable extent and I hope that when the warring factions in our own Government decide that we should have a number for health, education and welfare at least, they will remember Mr Smythe, and perhaps consult him. There is just one point of clarification I would like from Mr Smythe : Am I right in thinking that in fact the check digit does not reduce the number of occasions on which an incorrect number is recorded ? It simply makes it possible for the computer easily to recognize incorrect numbers and it leaves open the question of how one should deal with the incorrect numbers that the computer has recognized to be wrong.

Mr Healy : Since it produces an extra digit it must surely increase the number of occasions when a mistake is in fact made.

Mr Smythe : This is in fact quite true. If you add a check digit to your number you don't necessarily solve the problem. It lets you know where the wrong numbers are but it gives you rather more errors to cope with than you would have had if you didn't have the check digit. For this reason I would recommend that you don't rush into check digits. If you have got something else on your file that will track wrong numbers, for example a man's name or the number of his street or his date of birth, this could be a better check digit than any mathematical concoction.

Dr Bahn : I wonder to what extent there has been experimentation with the use of an embossed number of a plastic credit type of card, as a method of eliminating transcription errors. In one community in the United States, it is planned to equip every medical and social agency with a machine to use such cards for imprinting the individual's Social Security Number on his records. Theoretically, no service will be given to a person who does not come with a plastic card containing his Social Security Number. If he does not have a card he will be given one. I don't know whether the system has been started but it sounds like a very efficient one.

Mr Sunter : I am willing to be corrected on this but if you have an idea of the probability distribution of errors that arise in numbers I don't see any reason in principle why you couldn't use a check digit to detect the errors that have been made, or at least to make a probability assessment of the most likely error that has been made. A two-digit one would be better than a one-digit but in principle I think it could be done.

Dr Nielsen : In Sweden they have had a personal number for many years without check digits. They had to give it up because of the frequency of errors accumulated over many years. They have now adopted a check digit. I think it is very important to have one.

REFERENCES

ACHESON, E. D. (1967). *Medical Record Linkage*. Published by the Oxford University Press for the Nuffield Provincial Hospitals Trust, London.

Post Office (1962). Report No. 170. The Function and Mathematics of Check Digits.

SELMER, E. S. (1967). Registration numbers in Norway : some applied number theory and psychology. *Jl R. statist. Soc.*, A, **130**, 225–231.

RESULTS OF RESEARCH INTO THE METHODOLOGY OF RECORD LINKAGE*

DAVID M. NITZBERG

THIS paper deals with the main results of the author's research into the nature of record linkage from the viewpoint of methodology, with particular emphasis on computer methods. In the research, five linkage operations involving death clearance, *i.e.*, linkage between cohort and death certificate records, were performed during 1964 and 1965 (Nitzberg & Sardy, 1965). The area of death clearance was chosen for such an investigation because it is frequently performed in health research and is methodologically typical of most linkage operations. Deaths which occurred to members of the five cohorts were ascertained not only by the linkage operations but also by various means independent of the operations. In this way, data were gathered concerning what went wrong—and why—and what proved worthwhile in each of the operations, and the results of each operation could be generalized to all of a cohort's potential linkages, rather than be confined only to those linkages the operation itself actually found. The methodological framework of the study is depicted schematically by Figures 1 and 2 ; Appendix 1 is a glossary of the record linkage terms used.

* This paper is a modified version of the final chapter of a thesis submitted in 1966 by the author in partial fulfilment of the requirements for the degree of Doctor of Science in Biostatistics at Harvard University. The paper presents in broad terms only the main results of the research upon which the thesis is based ; for details and other results the reader is referred to the thesis itself (on file at Harvard University). The thesis has been submitted as a report to the National Center for Health Statistics (U.S. Public Health Service, Department of Health, Education and Welfare, Washington, D.C.) and may result in the Center's publishing an abbreviated version of it soon as part of Series 2 (Data Evaluation and Methods Research) of their Vital and Health Statistics Series 1000. The author wishes to acknowledge the cooperation and support given him during his research by Professor R. B. Reed of the Harvard School of Public Health, Dr P. M. Densen of the New York City Health Department, and Mr S. Binder of the National Center for Health Statistics.

187

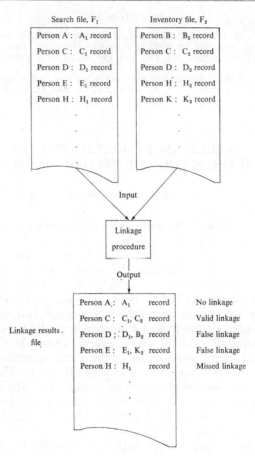

FIG. 1. A linkage operation.

Records of the following cohorts were used in the research, linking them to New York City death records for the period 1961–63 (a total of 281,208 death records).* Computer programmes written under a contract from the U.S. National Center for Health Statistics to the New York City Health Department, the former's IBM 7010 data processing computer, and certain clerical procedures needed to supplement the computer results were employed.

* Cohort and death records were all on magnetic computer tapes. Additional cohort records, not on tape, were used only during the operation for Cohort 1 to supplement the computer results.

		Number of F_1 Records Declared linked		Number of F_1 records Not linked
		Valid	False	
Event occurred to the F_1 person concerned	Recorded in F_2	V	e_1	m_1
	Not recorded in F_2	...	e_2	m_2
Event did not occur to the F_1 person concerned	Not recorded in F_2	...	e_3	b_1
	Recorded in in F_2	...	e_4	b_2

The total number of records in file $F_1 =$

$$N_1 = V+E+M+B,$$
$$\text{where } E = e_1+e_2+e_3+e_4$$
$$M = m_1+m_2$$
$$B = b_1+b_2$$

V represents the number of valid linkages which were found by the operation.
E represents the number of false linkages.
B represents the number of valid nonlinkages.
M represents the number of false nonlinkages.
$M+e_1+e_2$ equals the number of missed linkages.
$V+e_1+e_2+M$ equals the number of potential linkages.

FIG. 2. Results of a linkage operation.

COHORT 1. *The members of the medical groups participating in the Coronary Health Disease Study of the Health Insurance Plan of Greater New York (HIP)* (Shapiro *et al.*, 1963). This cohort was the largest studied (approximately 175,000 people). A purely computer operation was not possible because the information common to both the HIP and death computer tapes turned out to have insufficient discriminating power. The linkage operation in this case, therefore, involved a complex computer-manual (clerical) procedure.

COHORT 2. *The population of transit workers in the New York City Health Department's Respiratory Disease Study* (Densen *et al.*, 1963). This cohort consisted of 8,440 males for whom United States Social Security numbers were available ; death clearance was based on these numbers and was a computer operation.

COHORT 3. *The subjects involved in epidemiological studies being conducted by the Columbia University School of Public Health and Administrative Medicine.* This cohort was the smallest one used (635 subjects). The results of the computer linkage operation were

189

validated independently by telephone contact with the subjects' families.

COHORT 4. *The people interviewed as part of the Washington Heights Master Sample Survey conducted in 1960 by the Columbia School of Public Health* (Elinson & Lowenstein, 1963). Some 5,000 people made up this cohort. Addresses were available but since there was no computer programme for comparing addresses effectively death clearance could not be performed solely by computer. Therefore, a combination of computer and clerical methods was used.

COHORT 5. *A sample of deceased individuals for whom requests for copies of their death certificates were received by the New York City Health Department in 1965.* This cohort contained 816 deceased individuals, 706 of whom died between 1961 and 1963. The remaining 110 died outside the 1961–63 time period of the death records employed in the investigation, and thus provided a basis for studying false linkages. In addition to providing a study of record linkage, this sample also provided estimates of the frequency with which various identifying variables are missing from current death certificates (Table I).

The purpose of this paper is to summarize what was learned from the research, to point out areas which appear to merit further study and to comment on future possibilities. This will be done in the context of the major objectives of the research which, briefly stated, were to : (1) determine to what extent it is possible to link records ; (2) test and develop computer linkage procedures ; and (3) determine how much information is needed to link records successfully.

The extent to which it is possible to link records

The ability to link records depends primarily on the identifying variables which are common to the files to be linked. Insufficient discriminating power, noise, and missing data, in that order, are the major obstacles to the linking of records. Although fairly successful techniques exist to overcome the noise, and additional clerical follow-up can be used in an attempt to overcome the insufficient discriminating power and the missing data, the presence of a large number of variables common to the files (in addition) is the best way of overcoming all three sources of error. While this fact is extremely relevant when setting up files which are eventually to be linked, it is of only limited value when using already existing records, and it is this latter case which was thoroughly investigated by the research upon which this paper is based.

As the number of variables common to the records of the files being linked (F_1 and F_2) increases, more and more of the linkage operation can be handled solely by the computer ; clerical processing of the computer results can then do what could not be done automatically.

Table I. *Percentage of death certificates in the requests sample having missing identifying data (1960–63)*

Identifying data	Per cent.* with data missing
(1) Middle initial	82·4
(2) Date of birth	32·2
(3) Occupation	5·7
(4) Social security number	57·4
(5) Birthplace	4·7
(6) Father's name	13·4
(7) Mother's maiden name	34·9
All 7 identifying variables	2·4
(4) Social security number and (2) Date of birth	23·8
(4) Social security number and (5) Birthplace	3·8
(4) Social security number and (5) Birthplace and (2) Date of birth	3·2
(4) Social security number and (5) Birthplace and (7) Mother's maiden name . . . , .	2·8

* 100 per cent. = 807 certificates, the number of death certificates found by the NYC Health Department for the 816 requests received.

After problems which are associated with identifying variables, it is the geographical limitations of the file to which cohort records are to be linked (the F_2 file) which play a major role in preventing the linkage of records. For example, if the death records of a particular region are used, then deaths which occur to that region's inhabitants while they are outside the region will not be found. Consequently, the existence of a national centre to integrate the vital records of all the regions of a country would help to reduce the magnitude of this problem ; in the United States, in particular, a national death clearance centre appears to be a logical first step in establishing such an integrated system. In this context the results presented below are particularly relevant.

The above considerations make it clear that each linkage operation must be planned separately in the light of the particulars involved. The following statements summarizing the extent to which it was possible to link records in the five operations are offered as guidelines for such planning :

1. Using *surname, first name, and age*, the ratio of the number of matching F_1, F_2 pairs agreeing on these variables to the number of valid linkages is about 2·5 ; when Soundex name agreements and age ± 5 years are tolerated, the ratio increases to about 30. Using only surname and first name *initial*, the ratio is so large as to preclude a feasible linkage operation. Surname and *full* first name are also inadequate for linking records, these variables resulting in a ratio of approximately 50 pairs agreeing exactly on name for every valid linkage.

2. The use of *Social Security number, surname, and first name initial* produced a found linkage rate* of only 61 per cent. even though 100 per cent. of cohort 2 has Social Security numbers. The main reason for such a poor result is that the space for such numbers on death certificates is often left blank.

3. Using *surname, first name, age ± 5 years and address*, a found rate of 67 per cent. was attained for cohort 4.

4. Augmenting the computer matching operation based on *surname, first name, and age* by a complex clerical process in which such variables as *address, month and year of birth, spouse's name, occupation and marital status* were used in addition, a found rate of 81 per cent. was achieved for cohort 1.

5. An even higher found rate, 87 per cent. was attained when *borough and date of death* were used in conjunction with *surname, first name, and age*. The decision model in this operation (cohort 5) was not as conservative as in all the others and a false linkage rate† of 5 per cent. occurred.

It is evident, therefore, despite limited identifying data, that linkage can be successful if present computer methods are augmented by clerical processing. Furthermore, recommendations (see below) arising from this investigation should improve present methods sufficiently to raise the found rates from their present 60–80 per cent. range to the 75–95 per cent. range.

---

* Number of valid linkages found, divided by the total number of potential (valid) linkages.

† Number of false linkages, divided by the number of linkages declared.

Computer procedures for linking records

How a computer is to be used in a linkage operation depends on what identifying variables are available ; not only the order of the files and the matching rules, but the decision rules as well are dependent on them. For example, there is no reason to programme a decision model such as Newcombe's Binit Model (Newcombe *et al.*, 1959) when the variables used in the computer run do not contain sufficient discriminating power for making a final decision. The following discussion of computer procedures, therefore, is arranged by identifying variable.

1. *Name.* With rare exceptions, this variable appears on most records. Although other variables may be more discriminating (*e.g.*, Social Security number) or less subject to change (*e.g.*, date of birth), none is as nonchanging, available *and* discriminating, at present, as a person's name. Hence, its use in a linkage procedure is crucial and much effort was expended on computer methods for processing names. The following statements are based on analysis of the linkage operations performed :

(a) First name discrepancies were found to occur in 8·9 per cent. to 11·9 per cent. of potential linkages ; surname discrepancies in 3·8 per cent. to 6·4 per cent. First name and surname discrepancies were found to be correlated. Between 11·9 per cent. and 16·3 per cent. of potential linkages contained some sort of name discrepancy.

(b) The Russell Soundex code was able to overcome the name discrepancies in 60 per cent. of the potential linkages containing such errors, indicating that (at a name discrepancy rate of 15 per cent.) 6 per cent. of potential linkages can be expected to contain name discrepancies that cannot be overcome by Soundex. In terms of surnames only, Soundex overcame 65 per cent. of surname discrepancies, indicating that (at a surname discrepancy rate of 5 per cent.) 1·75 per cent. of potential linkages can be expected to contain surname discrepancies not overcome by Soundex. Appendix 2 displays the name discrepancies among the linkages from cohort 5 : Part I represents the discrepancies which were overcome by Soundex ; Part II, those not overcome.

(c) To improve the usefulness of Soundex, the following is recommended :

(1) Only the first three letters of first name should be used for the Soundex code, and a table of first name

Table II. *Distribution of age discrepancies among the linkages for Cohort 5*

Age Discrepancy (Years)	Linkages	
	Number	Per cent.
(Age on F_2—Age on F_1)		
−20 to −30	0	0·00
−16 to −19	2	0·50
−11 to −15	1	0·25
−10	1	0·25
−9	0	0·00
−8	1	0·25
−7	1	0·25
−6	4	0·99
−5	1	0·25
−4	8	1·98
−3	4	0·99
−2	16	3·96
−1	34	8·42
0	270	66·83
+1	28	6·93
+2	10	2·47
+3	7	1·73
+4	4	0·99
+5	3	0·74
+6	2	0·50
+7	2	0·50
+8	0	0·00
+9	0	0·00
+10	0	0·00
+11 to +15	2	0·50
+16 to +19	2	0·50
+20 to +30	1	0·25
	404	100·03
Unknown*	412	
	816	

* Four hundred and six requests (F_1) contained no age data and death records (F_2) for six requests could not be found.

derivatives (*i.e.* nicknames) should be part of any computer programme for comparing first names.

(2) Sex data should be used to narrow the field of matching pairs, by preventing the records of males and females with first names having the same Soundex codes from being brought together by the computer.

(3) Many different surnames share the same Soundex code, making it a gross noise filter. It can be refined by requiring that two surnames with the same code have, in addition, some minimum proportion of letters in common. This suggests a similarity statistic approach (Smith, 1964) for comparing surnames already agreeing on Soundex. Further research in this area is necessary, especially to determine optimal proportions.

(d) A name field of 20 character positions is adequate for recording first and last names. For efficient computer processing, surname should be recorded first, followed by a blank position and then first name. All blanks, apostrophes, hyphens, etc. which exist within a surname or first name should be suppressed so that only a consecutive string of alphabetic characters is recorded for any name.

(e) If the lengths of the name fields in the F_1 and F_2 files are not equal, names should be compared (and their Soundex codes based) on only as many positions as exist in the smaller of the two fields.

2. *Age.* This variable is more commonly available than date of birth, although the latter is much more discriminating and hence is a better linkage variable.

(a) When the records being compared both contain age data, the following results apply : between 67 per cent. and 73 per cent. can be expected to agree on age exactly ; between 91 per cent. and 94 per cent. on age within ± 3 years ; and 96 per cent. within ± 5 years. See, for example, Table II. (Care should be taken to prevent two blank age fields from being declared as agreeing on age by the computer.)

(b) No correlation was found between age and the magnitude of age discrepancy, although the existence of age discrepancies was positively correlated with age (see Tables III and IV).

3. *Address.* The results of the investigation indicate the value of address as a linkage variable : even though it is subject to change, address is generally recorded and has high discriminating ability. However, computer use of address data will depend on how successful future research is in the area of automatic address comparisons ; such research should be undertaken as soon as possible. In the meantime, computer results should be augmented by clerical processing of available address data (see, for example, Table V).

Table III. *The existence of age discrepancies by age among the known linkages* for Cohort 1*

		Age discrepancies		
		Exist	Do not exist	
Age †	≤49	76 (123·7)	424 (376·3)	500
	50–59	164 (207·4)	674 (630·6)	838
	60–69	246 (219·1)	639 (665·9)	885
	≥70	189 (124·8)	315 (379·2)	504
		675	2,052	2,727

$\chi^2 \gg 20$ (3 d.f.)
$P < 0·001$ (significant)
(Numbers in parentheses are expected values.)

* There were 2,779 known linkages of an estimated 3,125 potential linkages for Cohort 1 : 2,527 were found by the operation and 252 were known to have been missed (data on these 252 were ascertained independently of the operation) of an estimated 598 missed linkages. Since 52 linkages contained no age data on the F_1 records, the above table refers to the 2,727 linkages for which age data were available.

† As given on the death records (F_2).

Table IV. *The magnitude of the age discrepancies by age among the known linkages* having age discrepancies for Cohort 1*

		Absolute value of the age discrepancies		
		1 and 2 years	3–19 years	
Age †	≤49	65 (56·6)	11 (19·4)	76
	50–59	125 (122·2)	39 (41·8)	164
	60–69	176 (183·3)	70 (62·7)	246
	≥70	137 (140·8)	52 (48·2)	189
		503	172	675

$\chi^2 = 6·7$ (3 d.f.)
$0·05 < P < 0·10$ (not significant)
(Numbers in parentheses are expected values.)
* See footnote, Table III.
† As given on the death records (F_2).

Table V. *Distribution of Cohort 4's declared linkages by the variables on which they agree*

Exact Soundex of first and last names and age ±5	Name		Matching pairs	Declared linkages†	
	Exact first	Exact last		Number	Proportion of pairs
*	‡	‡	545	2	0·004
*	*	‡	745	8	0·011
*	‡	*	212	17	0·080
*	*	*	464	80	0·172
			1,966	107	(0·054)

Legend

* : Agreement

‡ : Disagreement

† Matching pairs were declared linkages if, based on a clerical check, they contained exact agreement on address and sex (surmised from first name) in addition to the computer found agreements on name and age. The 107 linkages thus declared represent 66·5 per cent. of the 161 expected number of deaths for this cohort.

Knowing how and to what extent to rely on computer processing in a linkage operation before clerical processing becomes necessary is essential. Even if the entire operation cannot be automated, it is desirable to do as much as possible by computer.

It does not appear likely that a linkage operation can be entirely automated successfully without a system of unique identity numbers such as Social Security numbers. Nevertheless, while such a system would alleviate many of the methodological problems existing today, automated linkage would still have to depend on such identifying variables as name and date of birth in addition. These additional variables would permit checking the validity of the linkages agreeing on Social Security numbers, and would also make possible more sophisticated approaches to linkage as well. For example, the linkages found using Social Security numbers could be supplemented by another run in which name (and/or date of birth) served as the major sorting variable(s); in this way, linkages for which Social Security numbers were missing or discrepant could also be located. Such an approach, of course, is not possible when only a limited amount of identifying information is available.

The amount of information needed to link records

The results of the study indicate that successful linkage depends on the existence of a large number of variables common to the files to be linked. This not only provides the necessary discriminating power, but also permits the overcoming of the noise and missing data bound to exist. But the existence of data, or information, by itself is not enough ; it must be processed and manipulated. As file sizes increase and the contents of each record expands, proper processing presupposes computer processing. *The merging of a large number of variables with effective computer processing techniques, therefore, is the key to successful linkage.*

The results of the investigation indicate that name and age alone are not enough information for linking records. It is posible to link records using only name, age and address, but the found rate is bound to be low (probably between 60 per cent. and 70 per cent.). Each additional variable that can be used will increase the found rate to more acceptable levels. If unique identity numbers, such as Social Security numbers in the United States, are available, these, in addition to name and date of birth, would probably be sufficient. Without such numbers, the *following set of identifying variables is recommended* : *surname, first and middle names, date of birth, sex, spouse's name, mother's maiden name, father's name, and address.*

CONCLUSION

Despite noise and limited amounts of identifying data, it is possible to link records by present computer techniques, but these techniques can and should be improved, as discussed earlier. An even bigger advance in the ability to link records, however, will occur when the recording of a large number of discriminating identifying variables—such as those listed above—can be achieved on the records eventually to be linked.

REFERENCES

DENSEN, P., BREUER, J., BASS, H. & JONES, E. (1963). New York City Health Department Chronic Disease Survey. Interim Report, unpublished.

ELINSON, J. & LOWENSTEIN, R. (1963). Community Fact Book for Washington Heights, New York City, 1960–1961. School of Public Health and Administrative Medicine.

NEWCOMBE, H. B., KENNEDY, J. M., AXFORD, S. J. & JAMES, A. P. (1959). Automatic linkage of vital records. *Science*, **130**, 954.

NITZBERG, D. M. & SARDY, H. (1965). The methodology of computer linkage of health and vital records. *Proc. Am. Statist. Ass.*, Soc. Statist. Sect., p. 100.

SHAPIRO, S., WEINBLATT, E., FRANK, C., SAGER, R. & DENSEN, P. (1963). The HIP study of incidence and prognosis of coronary heart disease : Methodology. *J. chron. Dis.* **16**, 1281.

SMITH, R. V. (1964). Similarity and Entropy. Research Paper RC-1169. Yorktown Heights, N.Y., I.B.M. Watson Research Center.

APPENDIX 1

Glossary of record linkage terms used in this paper

Decision model.—The matching and decision rules together.

Decision rules.—Linkage procedure rules which specify which record pairs are to be declared linkages and which nonlinkages, based on the results obtained by applying the matching rules.

Declared linkage.—A pair of records said to be a linkage according to the decision rules ; it, in fact, might be a valid or a false linkage.

Declared nonlinkage.—A record for which no declared linkage was found by the linkage procedure.

F_1 *file.*—The cohort file ; records of individuals for whom the linkage operation is being performed.

F_2 *file.*—The master file to which F_1 is being linked ; records of an event (or events) that occurred to a population during a certain time period.

False linkage.—A declared linkage whose records do *not* pertain to the same person ; a *false positive*.

False nonlinkage.—A declared nonlinkage for which a valid linkage exists ; a *false negative*.

Linkage.—A pair of records pertaining to the same person ; more commonly referred to as a *valid (or true) linkage*, to distinguish it from a declared linkage.

Linkage operation.—The entire linkage undertaking, including the files to be used as input to the linkage procedure, the linkage procedure itself, and the output (declared linkages and nonlinkages). This is meant to be an all-encompassing term including every aspect involved in linking the records of a cohort to another file of records.

Linkage procedure.—The process whereby records from the F_1 and F_2 files are brought together, compared, and declared linkages if they match sufficiently (according to the decision model).

Matching pair.—A record from the F_1 file and one from the F_2 file which agree (according to the matching rules) on at least a minimum number of identifying variables.

Matching rules.—Linkage procedure criteria which specify how much discrepancy, if any, will be tolerated for each identifying variable involved in the comparison of two records ; the comparison is made to determine how much *agreement* exists between the records of the pair in terms of the identifying information they contain.

Missed linkage.—A false nonlinkage or a false linkage for which a valid linkage exists.

Noise.—Discrepancies between the same information in different files ; also referred to as errors.

Nonlinkage.—A record for which a linkage does *not* exist ; also referred to as a record *validly not linked*.

Possible linkages.—All the valid linkages involving records from the F_1 and F_2 files.

Potential linkages.—The possible linkages plus all the other valid linkages for which the correct event records are not in the F_2 file.

Record linkage.—A process of bringing together separate records pertaining to the same person.

Valid linkage.—A pair of records pertaining to the same person.

Valid nonlinkage.—A declared nonlinkage for which *no* linkage exists.

APPENDIX 2. *Name discrepancies among the linkages from the sample of death certificate requests (Cohort 5)*

PART I. *Linkages with name discrepancies overcome by Soundex*

Name on sample (F_1) record	Same person's name on death (F_2) record
ADCOX JACK	ADCOCK JACK
ADDONISSIO SALVATORE	ADDONISIO SALVATORE
ALAIMO DIAGO	ALAIMO DIEGO
AMOROS ANTHONY	AMAROS ANTHONY
ANDUR DAVID	AMDUR DAVID
ANCONA MARIE	ANACONA MARIE
ANTONOPOULOS ROSE	ANTANOPULUS ROSE
BECK ISSAC	BECK ISAAC
BREGER ABRAHAM	BERGER ABRAHAM
BRITEL FANNY	BREITEL FANNIE
CAMIOLO ANTONIO	CAMIOLO ANTHONY
CARRIELLO JAMES	CARIELLO JAMES
CARRINGTON CORNELIA	CARRINGTON CORNEL
CHAMBER CLINTON	CHAMBERS CLINTON
CLARK WILLIAM	CLARKE WILLIAM
CLARKE SUSIE	CLARK SUSIE
CROCHFORD JAMES	CROCKFORD JAMES
DAN LYDIA	DAN LYDYEA
DAY JIMMIE	DAY JIMMY
DEBITETTO NICHOLA	DEBITETTO NICOLA
DIAZ DELORES	DIAZ DOLORES
DIGNAM ARTHUR	DIGNAN ARTHUR
ERVIN ELLIS	ERBIN ELLIS
ETTLEMAN IRVING	ETTELMAN IRVING
FEINBERG PHILIP	FEINBERG PHILLIP
FRANCES WILETHA	FRANCIS WILEATHA
FRYE MILDRED	FRY MILDRED
GANGI DOMENICK	GANGI DOMINICK
GINZLER ROBERT	GENZLER ROBERT
GLASS SARA	GLASS SARAH
GRASSO BERETHA	GRASSO BERTHA
GREEN SAMMY	GREEN SAM
GROSSMAN EMMA	GROSMAN EMMA
HENNESSY CHARLOTTE	HENNESSY CHAROLTT
HESSION MATHEWE	HESSION MATTHEW
JACKSON LUCILE	JACKSON LUCILLE
JONES BERNIECE	JONES BERNICE
KALMUSS GARY	KALMUSS GARRY
KIMBERLY ELIZABETH	KIMBERLY ELIZABET
KUHN PHILLIP	KUHN PHILIP
LESHINSKY LAWRENCE	LESHINSKY LAWRENC
LESLEY LILLIE	LESLIE LILLIE
LOEFFLER SIEGFRIED	LOEFFLER SIGFRIED
LUSTGARTEN PAULINE	LUSTGARTEN PAULIN
MASCELLARO ANTONIETTA	MASCELLARO ANTOIN
MCCLELLAND FRED	MCCLELLAN FRED
MCCLOSKY MARGARET	MCCLOSKEY MARGARE
MCKENZIE UNA	MCKENZE UNA
NICKLASSON HILMER	NIKLASSON HILMER
NOVICK GUSTAV	NOVICK GUSTAVE

Name on sample (F₁) record	Same person's name on death (F₂) record
OBERLANDER JUDIT	OBERLANDER JUDITH
PHOTINOS ELIZABETH	PHOTINOS ELIZABET
PRIEM ANTOON	PRIEN ANTON
QUAGLIA MADELINE	QUAGALIA MADELINE
RODRIGUEZ ELOISA	RODRIQUEZ ELOISA
ROLAND ERNEST	ROLLAND ERNEST
ROONEY FRANCIS	ROONEY FRANK
SANTAELLA JOSEFINA	SANTAELLA JOSEPHINE
SCHLESINGER MURRAY	SCHLESINGER MURRA
SOPERN LILLIAN	SAPPERN LILLIAN
SEGER ISABELLA	SEGER ISABELLE
STEIN ABRAM	STEIN ABRAHAM
SURACI DOMINIC	SURACI DOMINICK
TWEED NICHOLAS	TWEED NICOLAS
URMAN SALOMON	URMAN SOLOMON
VONDANNENBERG FRANCES	VONDANNENBERG FRANC
WECHSLER MOLLIE	WECHSLER MOLLY
WEIL ELLIS	WEIL ELIAS
WORRINGER MARGARETT	WORRINGER MARGARE

PART II. *Linkages with name discrepancies not overcome by Soundex*

Name on sample (F₁) record	Same person's name on death (F₂) record
ALEKSIEWICZ FLORENCE	ALEKSIEWICZ FLORE
ATAMANTASCHUK VOYTECH	ATAMANTASCHUK VOY
BARCHURSKY JACOB	BACHURSKY JACOB
BENTLEY W	BENTLEY WALLACE
BERKOVITS HARRY	BERGOVITZ MALE
BILYK WOLODYMYR	BILYK VLADMIR
BROADHURST WILLIAM	BROADHURST WILLIA
CARLO GIUSEPPE	CARLO JOSEPH
CARNEY COLUMBUS	CARNEY CHRIS
COOPER WILLIE	COOPER WILLIEMAE
DEPATTERSON CLARENCE	DEPATTERSON CLARE
ENGLER SONYA	ENGLER FEMALE
EUER DAVE	EUER DAVID
FISHBERG BENJAMIN	FISHBERG BENNY
FOLKS H	FOLKS HOMER
FAUNTICIN WILLIE	FOUNTAINE WILLADE
FRANCESCHINI GIUSEPPE	FRANCESCHINI JOSEPH
FRIEDMAN HYMAN	FRIEDMAN HERMAN
GAGLIARDI JOSEPH	GAGLIARDI GUISEPPI
GOVAS GEORGGIA	GOVA GEORGIA
GIETSAS CONSTANTINE	GRETSAS CONSTANTINE
GUZEWICZ STEPHEN	GUZEWICZ STANLEY
HACHMEYER CATHARINE	HACHMEYER CATHARI
HALATZIS ERNEST	HALATIORS ERNEST
HALLEY A	HALLEY A MCCLURE
HOGAN MAE	HOGAN MARY
JEFFERSON MARIE	CLARK MARIE
JOHNSON FREDERIC	JOHNSON FRED
JUBA HARRISON	DZIUBA CHARLES

Name on sample (F₁) record	Same person's name on death (F₂) record
KRYVANOS NELLIE	KRIVANOS PETRONEL
KUKLIKOWSKI ANTHONY	KULIKOWSKI ANTHON
LANAS JOE	LANAS JOSE
LOBODA MICHAEL	SLOBODA MICHAEL
LUCATUORTO PETER	LUCATUORTO PETE
MALDONADO MARGRO	MALDONADO MANGARO
MISKOWITZ JOHN	MISKIEWICZ JOHN
MANDEL KATHERINE	MANDELL KATE
MAYES TENNA	GRANT TENNA
MULERO RAYMOND	MULERO RAMON
NAYWOOD JOSEPH	HEYWARD JOSEPH
NORMAN KATHLEEN	NORMAN KATHERINE
OTTENHEIMER ISIDOR	OTTENHEIMER ISIDO
POLEN BEN	POLEN BENJAMIN
RATZERSDORFER EDMOND	RATZERSDORFER EDM
RIND MOISZER	RIND MOISHE
RIVERA REGINA	ROMAN REGENA
ROCCO COSIMO	DIROCCO COSIMO
RUCKLOS MARGARET	RUCKLOS SYLVIA
RUSSELL KAY	RUSSELL CATHRINE
SAMBERG LOUIS	SANDBERG LOUIS
SCHLEGEL GEORGE	SCHLEGEL JOSEPH
SCHOEN A	SCHOEN ARTHUR
SEEMANN CATHERINE	SEEMANN KATHERINE
SELNER ADOLPHE	ZELNER ADOLPH
SULLIVAN GRACE	SULLIVAN KATHERINE
SZRAYER NATHALIE	SZRAJER NATALALA
TAUBENBLATT MARGA	TAUBENBLATT MARGARE
VASQUEZ AMADO	VASQUEZ AMPARO
VILLANI KATERINA	VILLACCI CATHERINE
VONLUCCA SERNANDA	VONLUCCA FERNANDA
YOUNG BURT	YOUNG IVBERT
ZIEGLER PAULINE	ZIEGLER MARY
ZURAIN D	ZURIAN DAVID

DISCUSSION

Dr Spicer : The point I want to make arises from a contribution I made to a meeting which was held in Oxford about three years ago on the use of computers in Medicine. In that I said, as a result of the experience that we had at the General Register Office, where I was working at the time, that we were not at all convinced of the relative economy of computer matching compared with clerical matching. This is rather a Luddite thing to say and I feel on much stronger grounds for discussing it now that I have left the GRO and am actually running a computer unit. My remarks were reported in Computing Reviews (1966), which said that they called up a Dickensian picture of the General Register Office with clerks sitting on high stools with quill pens behind their ears. However, as a result of the criticisms I got after that meeting I did go into the matter quite thoroughly with the people at the General Register Office, which maintains a very large death clearance file—it is not by any means 100 per cent. efficient but it quite efficient—on the actual costing, and I do think that clerical procedures of the kind discussed by Dr Nitzberg compare, in the wage structure of the British economy, quite favourably with the computer. I think that where the computer wins on all this is not on the fact that it can match. I have never had any real doubt that it could match to a perfectly sufficient degree of approximation, and now people like Dr Nitzberg and Dr Acheson's group have shown it, but you don't just want a match. In keeping up a death clearance file at the GRO that is about all that was needed. We just wanted to keep it up-to-date, not to do anything complicated with it. But in all these record linking procedures the matching is merely the first stage in maintaining a file which you want to use for a great many other things, and those are the things which you have to do by computer and you can't do them in any other way than by computer. I don't think that matching itself is intrinsically, necessarily a very suitable computer problem at all.

Dr Nitzberg : The comments bring many thoughts to mind. Certainly the second-generation computers are not suitable for searching or matching of this type. They are somewhat inefficient. A good clerk who knows where to look, and who knows how to translate words like Wood to Holz (the German word for wood) when matching discrepant records, will be able to locate records that would never be found by a computer. The thing that struck me, however, as I did this work with the clerks in New York City, who are quite experienced, was that the computer was more reliable and it did the work faster. I think I would agree with you on cost and at this time I would not like to justify linkage on the basis that the computer would be cheaper. However, to have tried to match 175,000 members of a cohort to deaths for three years manually would have been staggering, and although I don't think I could justify the linkage in terms of cost, I think we did a piece of research that would simply not have been feasible at all without a computer. Furthermore, I think that the purpose for which the records are being linked is more important than the record linkage operation itself ; so if you can do linkage automatically and get timely results and then go on to the important part of the research, this then would become very cost-effective.

Dr Newcombe : I wish to make two points very briefly. The first one relates to the comparison of computers with clerks. We have evidence that it is hard to generalize in this matter. Putting the computer to match death records and handicap records back to the birth records, we have in fact found that the manual searchers were

203

often wrong, so it is quite possible that in a situation where the searcher arrives at a conclusion and is not checked up on by somebody else, the relative accuracies may lean the other way.

The other point is that it would be unfortunate if this session wound up after so many people saying, ' Let's do something about the Soundex code, make it less discriminating or make it more sophisticated ', without something being said about how to test the various modifications to see whether they really represent improvements. There is a simple mathematical way of carrying out such tests. The two qualities that are needed in information which is used to subdivide a file are discriminating power and freedom from errors or discrepancies when two records that ought to match are compared with each other. In fact what one looks for in any items of information that are used to sequence a file is a high ratio of discriminating power to errors, and there is a simple way of determining this ratio. If part of the Soundex code is inefficient in these terms and is thrown away, it then becomes necessary to pay for the additional searching in the resulting bigger pockets, or else to use some additional piece of sequencing information which has a superior ratio to subdivide the Soundex pockets. It is by this test that one would have to judge whether one has done a good thing or a bad thing to the Soundex code by modifying it.

Dr Nitzberg : Two points. First, I want to agree with you about Soundex. I hope I did not give the impression that I was downgrading Soundex. Second, in the fifth cohort, the death records were actually found by clerks. We then located them independently by computer and came out a little ahead. The clerks had found some incorrect death records which the computer had not. As I indicated before, I personally felt more comfortable with the computer results. I think I can state why. I knew that the rules I specified were being followed and that I therefore had control over what was being done. With the clerk I was never certain. For example, if they found a death record for a Mary Smith, aged 50, they might link it ; but because this was a common name I knew enough to have other rules that had to be pursued and I was certain they would be carried out before the computer came out with the linkage.

REFERENCES

Spicer, C. (1966), Computing Reviews, ACM **7** (1), 7.

PART 5

SESSION ON EPIDEMIOLOGY

Chairman : DR S. JABLON (Washington)

COHORT STUDIES IN ASSESSING ENVIRONMENTAL HAZARDS

R. A. M. Case

ALTHOUGH environmental hazards can often be identified by epidemiological methods other than those called 'prospective', 'longitudinal' or 'cohort', there are certain questions concerned with such hazards that are not readily answered by any other means.

In the case of diseases characterized by a long latent period between entry to an adverse environment and the first manifestations of illness—such as environmentally induced cancers of various types—early answers to these questions are of great importance because the continuation of a hazard, or the introduction of a new hazard, can have done irreparable harm to men exposed before the situation can be appreciated and remedied.

Apart from the primary and fundamental question of whether a hazard does in fact exist, the key questions that must be considered, are :—

1. How severe is the hazard ?

2. How soon after the introduction of the adverse environment can it be detected ?

3. How does it vary with the severity of the exposure, or the duration of the exposure, to the adverse environment in question?

None of these questions is simple, and all of them are made up of further questions such as ' What is the latent period in this instance and to what degree may it vary ? '

Since we must assume that any study of an environmental hazard is not being conducted solely as an academic exercise, it is perhaps pertinent to ask why we need to know the answers to these particular questions. Here are some of the reasons :—

1. How severe is the hazard ?

We need information about this for at least two cogent reasons. One is that we are always faced with the necessity of making a judgement about whether the benefits which may accrue to mankind from a particular situation do or do not outweigh the risk involved. The second is that it is necessary to establish a datum line from which we can later judge whether any measures that we may take to mitigate the risk are in fact effective. Obviously, because a failure in the effectiveness of our preventive methods could lead to irreversible harm to the men involved, we need to know this answer at the earliest possible moment. Doll and Hill (1964) succeeded in answering this question in relation to the fall in mortality from lung cancer in a

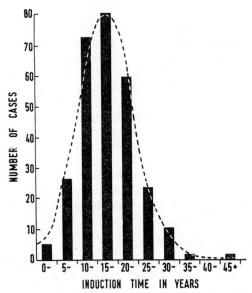

FIG. 1. To show how the induction times of occupational tumours of the urinary bladder in men employed in the British Chemical Industry varied from less than five years to over 40 years with a mode at 15–20 years. When dealing with a situation where the risk has remained fairly steady for several decades, as in this instance, the curve tends to normality.

group of men many of whom gave up the habit of smoking cigarettes, but I was unable to answer the question in relation to whether the abandonment of certain antioxidants in the rubber industry in 1949 has completely removed the risk of a man contracting an occupational tumour of the urinary tract in that industry. My failure was due to the fact that, because no cohort study was made, no datum line had been effectively established. However, investigations designed to clarify the position have now been set in motion.

2. How soon after the introduction of an adverse environment can the hazard be detected ?

208

Here we are in the position of needing to seek information about whole classes of risk as well as individual situations, for we may have to use our background knowledge to make analogies. For instance, tumours of the urinary tract which are due to carcinogenic aromatic amines develop in a population at risk as a cumulative normal curve, and, according to the severity of the risk, a well conducted survey might be able to identify the hazard within 5 to 10

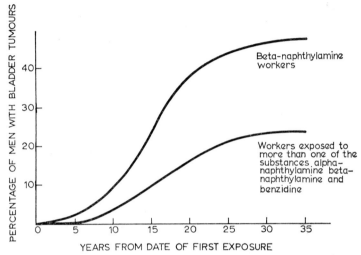

FIG. 2. To show how the incidence of occupational tumours of the urinary bladder builds up in workers exposed to certain carcinogenic aromatic amines. (Adopted from Case *et al.* 1954).

years of its introduction, for the average latent period for this class of carcinogens is, as we have seen, about 20 years. When we come to study mesotheliomata due to exposure to asbestos, it has been suggested that the mean latent period is perhaps nearer to 40 years, although new evidence puts it at rather less, so it may well be that the risk to a community could not be detected in the first 15–20 years, a time lag which could well induce a false sense of security.

3. How does the extent of the hazard vary with the severity of the exposure, or the length of the exposure, to the adverse environment in question ?

Plainly, we cannot answer the two previous questions unless we can standardize our calculations with respect to these variables, and we need the questions to be answered with considerable precision. Perhaps more important, however, is the need to answer the question

' Would it, in the long run, be better to expose a large number of men to the risk (minimized by good working conditions) by only allowing each man to work a particular type of process for a short time during his working life, or should a few highly trained men be asked to work such a process for as much of their working life as may be practicable ? ' The studies made in relation to certain dye-stuff intermediates in the British chemical industry enabled us to say that relatively short periods of exposure, say of about one year, were sufficiently dangerous to offset any possible advantage of a rapid labour turnover *in the conditions prevailing at that time*, but this is not necessarily the correct answer in other situations or even in the chemical industry now that special precautions are observed, and the manufacture of the most dangerous substance has been abandoned.

Now that we have seen why we need to answer the questions which make cohort analysis the method of choice, we must consider what information we need to conduct such studies, and whether such information is, or can be made, available. Firstly, we must be able to define with individual identification the ' population at risk '. Secondly, we must be able to follow the relevant events that befall these individuals subsequently to their initial definition, and obtain unambiguous records of their illnesses or death. Thirdly, we must have some standard of comparison with which to compare the sickness or mortality experience of the ' population at risk '. Often this will be derived from the morbidity or mortality rates of the country as a whole. This third requirement will not be discussed further here, since the considerations involved are not necessarily connected with record linkage.

We are at present a long way from being able to meet the first two requirements, and the cohort studies which I have chosen for discussion, all made in this country, were, although productive, hampered to a greater or lesser extent by lack of adequate sources of information.

Let us now consider the major cohort studies that I have in mind. Doll and Hill's (1956, 1964) classical study on the mortality of doctors in relation to their smoking habits took advantage of the fact that all doctors' names and addresses appear on a statutory list, making it possible to send out a questionary to which many replied. This defined the population. Furthermore, doctors would be so described on their death certificates when they die. With the co-operation of the Registrar General, it was possible to single out such certificates and provide the necessary facts in relation to mortality. In the case of the survey of dyestuff workers in the British chemical industry (Case *et al.*, 1954), the men at risk had to be defined by reference to old works' records, which of course had not been designed to provide such information in the best possible way. Obviously, since the entries on death certificates would not define such workers in an unambiguous manner, no total mortality study was possible. However, the investigation had been undertaken with reference to tumours of the urinary bladder, and because of the earlier interest of the late Sir Ernest Kennaway and the late Dr Sydney Henry in the matter, copies of all the death certificates relating to tumours of the urinary bladder in males in England and Wales since 1921 had been kept as separate bundles. These death certificates, extending over a period of 30 years, had to be sorted into alphabetical order by hand, and then all the names of chemical workers which had been listed checked against them. All possible matches had to be further investigated by a variety of other means.

Because the available register of death certificates related only to this one form of neoplasm, we are today in ignorance as to whether the action of the carcinogenic aromatic amines is in fact confined to the urinary tract or not. There is certainly some clinical suspicion that benzidine may be able to cause tumours of the gastro-intestinal tract and of the liver in man.

Another survey (Case & Lea, 1955), made to study the suggestion that mustard-gas poisoning due to enemy action in the 1914–18 World War might have resulted in the development of lung cancer in some of the men affected, utilized the records of war pensioners who were awarded a pension because of mustard-gas poisoning. Death records of these men were of course kept by the Ministry concerned, if only for the purpose of knowing when the pension ceased to be payable. Here it was possible, with the co-operation of this Ministry, to proceed from the record in relation to the pension to the final mortality picture in the group of veterans concerned, but because pensions were granted for only a small number of well-defined conditions, the situations where the Ministry could provide the material for similar studies are limited in number.

A further survey, which has been under periodic review since 1949, was set up to investigate the relationship between work in the bichromate-producing industry and the development of lung cancer (Bidstrup & Case, 1956). Initially, this population at risk was obtained from the records of an X-ray survey carried out in the factories concerned, but since about 1954 the Medical Adviser to the factories has kept systematic records of the men entering employment and their subsequent medical history whilst remaining in employment there or receiving retirement pensions from there. As far as possible track is kept of men who leave to work elsewhere,

211

but naturally this is incomplete. The operation of a system like this offers a ' built-in ' check on possible industrial hazards, and should be applied much more widely, for in a constantly evolving technological society it is almost inevitable that from time to time new health hazards will inadvertently be introduced, and it is essential that they are detected at the earliest possible moment.

Other cohort studies in progress are Dr Newhouse's study of asbestos workers (Newhouse & Williams, 1967), with special reference to mesotheliomata ; Miss Davies's study (1964) of malignant disease in a group of wartime munition workers ; and Miss Harley's study (1966), in collaboration with Professor Backett's Department in Aberdeen, of the mortality amongst Aberdeen trawl-fishers. These three studies share some common factors in that they are based on employers' old records, not designed to serve this purpose, that they exploit, *inter alia*, the technique of searching electoral registers to help to trace individuals in the defined population, and that help may be forthcoming from the Ministry of Social Security to try to complete the follow-up.

Two very important national surveys have recently been set up, one by the Ministry of Labour and the other by the Rubber Manufacturing Employers' Association. Both are concerned with the effects of the use of carcinogenic aromatic amines in rubber processing, one seeking to establish what the position is amongst men currently employed in the rubber and cable industries, and the other trying to determine whether the antioxidants which were withdrawn in 1949 were in fact the only carcinogenic ones which had been used. The investigations have been designed to be complementary to each other, and both will rely on information from employers and on the co-operation of the General Register Office and of some of the Ministries who have access to relevant records.

I have, I hope, now said enough to show that cohort studies form a very important part of a continuing programme of the investigation of the interaction of man and his environment, and I have indicated how such studies have been, in the past, dependent on *ad hoc* improvization to define and trace populations at risk ; I have also indicated that it appears that the concept of more systematic aid from national sources and official bodies is slowly taking root.

Now it is not my function to go into details of what forms of record-linkage could be introduced and what difficulties are going to be encountered in doing so, or what threats any such system might be thought to offer to personal liberty. What I would point out is that, in some place or other, we already have records of where a man is employed, which could be extended, in the future, to say what he does. We have also, elsewhere, records of a man's illnesses, and, at yet another place, records of the dead and what they were thought to have died from.

It should surely not be beyond our capacity to make it possible to bring this information together in a way that poses little threat to the individual. Surely the personal liberty to be free from unnecessary disease should rank at least as highly in our scale of values as the personal liberty to evade income tax, an activity which I have heard a Ministry official say was regarded as one of the reasons why record-linkage would be unacceptable to the British public.

REFERENCES

BIDSTRUP, P. L. & CASE, R. A. M. (1956). Carcinoma of lung in workmen in bichromates-producing industry in Great Britain. *Br. J. ind. Med.*, **13**, 260.

CASE, R. A. M., HOSKER, M. E., MCDONALD, D. B. & PEARSON, J. T. (1954). Tumours of urinary bladder in workmen engaged in manufacture and use of certain dyestuff intermediaries in British chemical industry. *Br. J. ind. Med.* **11,** 705.

CASE, R. A. M. & LEA, A. J. (1955). Mustard gas poisoning, chronic bronchitis, and lung cancer. *Br. J. prev. soc. Med.*, **9,** 62.

DAVIES, J. M. (1964). *Br. Emp. canc. Camp. for 1963.* 41st Ann. Rep., p. 170.

DOLL, R. & HILL, A. B. (1956). Lung cancer and other causes of death in relation to smoking. *Br. med. J.*, **2,** 1071.

DOLL, R. & HILL, A. B. (1964). Mortality in relation to smoking. *Br. med. J.*, **1**, 1399, 1460 ; **2**, 1071.

HARLEY, J. L. (1966). *Br. Emp. canc. Camp. for 1965.* 43rd Ann. Rep., p. 90.

NEWHOUSE, M. L. & WILLIAMS, J. M. (1967). Techniques for tracing past employees. *Br. J. prev. soc. Med.* **21**, 35.

DISCUSSION

Dr M. Newhouse : I think there is little I can add to what Professor Case has said about the methods of cohort study.

In my own work, linkage between records of pathological specimens and autopsies and death certificates would be extremely helpful. I have been making a mortality study of 5,000 past asbestos workers, and one of the conditions we are particularly interested in is mesothelioma, both pleural and peritoneal. A particular difficulty here is that it was not widely recognized as a pathological entity till about 1959. However, among the 430 death certificates which we have obtained on these 5,000 men the diagnosis of mesothelioma occurs five times on the death certificate : once in 1938, once in 1943 and after 1958 in the other three patients. In 17 other cases we have revised the diagnosis on the death certificate either by identifying published cases or by reviewing histological material. In five, the certified cause of death was cancer of lung, in two, carcinomatosis ;

213

in three, cancer of pancreas and in seven, neoplasm of the gastro-intestinal tract. This is an important little group because the average latent period is 22 years, not 40 years, and ranges from 40 to nine years.

Eleven of these patients started work before the regulations which were passed in 1933 and which form a watershed in asbestos history, 11 after the regulations. In the latter period five times as many men were exposed. This might be interpreted as suggesting that the risk has been reduced since 1933 but many of these men may not yet have developed a tumour. Another point against this interpretation is that my records are very incomplete and likely to remain so. A third of the 430 deaths occurred at home and we can find nothing further out about them. Of those who died in hospital less than half had an autopsy. Records of all autopsies have not been kept. I hoped that the records of coroners' inquests, where an autopsy is mandatory, would be a fruitful field. I found besides the industrial deaths from asbestosis, where there is a complete file of autopsies, 118 more who had been recorded as having had a coroner's inquest. Although two-thirds of these 118 were in 1950 or later we have only succeeded in obtaining the autopsy report in about half. Coroners don't treat their records with very much respect. They bundle them up together with bits of string and in one court at least, as I know to my cost, they sling them in the loft up a perpendicular and very rickety ladder.

Professor R. Schilling : I was interested in Professor Case's paper because we have had similar experience in getting the sort of data that he got so successfully in the chemical industry. This is an example of the need for record linkage. Frequently in a defined population in an industry, it is necessary to trace individuals who have left the industry and whose fate is unknown. If such people had a National Health Service number on their industrial records, they could be traced relatively easily through the National Health Register at Southport. We have been tracing an industrial population living in an easily defined area and with the help of the National Health Register, we have information on 95 per cent. of this population. This task would have been much easier if they had had National Health Service numbers on their industrial records.

COMPARISON OF DIAGNOSIS ON SUCCESSIVE HOSPITAL ADMISSIONS

A. S. FAIRBAIRN

THE Oxford Record Linkage Study brings together the records of different medical events in the same individual. Each of these events may be a hospital admission. Acheson and Barr (1965) studied hospital readmissions in 1962 in the Oxford Record Linkage area. This study relates to the two-year period 1963–64. The number of patients either admitted from home or transferred from other hospitals, found by Acheson and Barr for 1962 and in this study for 1963 and 1964 are shown in Table I. Both series relate to the same

Table I. *Frequency of admission to hospital*

Number of patients discharged from hospital, Oxford Record Linkage Study area, 1962 and 1963–64, according to number of completed spells

No. of completed spells	1962 (Acheson & Barr 1965)	1963–64
1	15381 (84 per cent.)	29266 (77·3 per cent.)
2	2183 (12 per cent.)	5923 (15·7 per cent.)
3	573 (3·1 per cent.)	1606 (4·2 per cent.)
4	158 (0·9 per cent.)	604 (1·6 per cent.)
5		253 ⎫
6		109 ⎪
7		36 ⎪
8		25 ⎪
9	71 (0·4 per cent.)	18 ⎬ 459 (1·2 per cent.)
10		5 ⎪
11		6 ⎪
12		2 ⎪
13		3 ⎪
15		2 ⎭
Total	18366 (100 per cent.)	37858 (100 per cent.)

geographical area with a population of about 325,000. The patients are classified according to the number of spells ending in the defined period, whether these spells ended in death, discharge home or transfer to other hospitals. The proportion of patients with more than one spell is, as would be expected somewhat greater in the two-year period 1963–64 (22·7 per cent.) than in the single year 1962

215

(16·0 per cent.). All the 37,858 patients leaving hospital in 1963–64 incurred 51,088 spells of inpatient admission. 21,822 spells (43 per cent. of the total) were incurred by patients with two or more spells.

In the two-year period 1963–64 the highest number of spells was 15, incurred by two patients. One of these patients, a woman of 70 with aplastic anaemia, was repeatedly admitted for blood transfusion. All her admissions were booked beforehand except for the last admission, which began as an emergency and ended with her death. The other patient, a man of 42, was diagnosed on 10 occasions as suffering from Other Disorders of Heart Rhythm (433·1) and on the other five occasions as Diseases of the Mitral Valve (410) or Other Heart Diseases specified as Rheumatic (416). All his admissions, except one, were emergencies. Other causes of frequent admission, more than 12 in two years, were leukaemia, malignant disease, asthma and urethral stricture. Of the seven patients who were admitted 12 or more times, four died during their last admission.

The reasons for readmission to hospital are very varied and the study of the relationship between successive diagnoses is therefore complex. Some readmissions are the result of new illnesses which may be expected on grounds of chance. Others, particularly short-term readmissions and transfers, may occur during the same illness and may be dictated by administrative needs such as transfer from teaching to long-stay hospitals, or by planned therapeutic procedures. In such cases the diagnosis may be exactly repeated, or be at least consistent with the diagnosis on first admission. To get a preliminary classification of the diagnostic relationships to be expected, I examined, with the help of Dr Leo Kinlen, one pair of diagnoses from each of 1,746 patients admitted to hospital *from home* and discharged more than once in 1962.* We looked for some obvious explanation for the succession of two diagnoses and classified the relationship between them in a rough and ready manner, as shown in Table II. In only 17 per cent. of pairs could no ostensible connection be found. In 41 per cent of pairs, the diagnostic code was exactly repeated. In the remaining 42 per cent. of pairs the code was different but probably related in some way. For instance, one diagnosis was specific while the other was stated in symptomatic or indefinite terms, or the two codes indicated conditions which are known to occur together or to cause diagnostic confusion. Some of the associations found in group II may be of clinical interest and illustrate differing diagnostic habits

---

* The number of patients is less than the 2,985 patients with two or more spells in 1962, shown in column 1, Table I, because transfers to other hospitals were excluded. The choice of patients was convenient since they were already listed in a special index. The diagnoses could be rapidly inspected.

Table II. *Apparent relationship between 2 successive hospital diagnoses*

I *Repeated:* The 3-figure code is identical.	716	(41 per cent.)
II *Explicable:*		
(a) One or both diagnoses may be indefinite or symptomatic : .	390	(22 per cent.)
e.g. 784 Symptoms referable to upper gastro-intestinal tract 540 Ulcer of stomach		
818 Fracture of radius and ulna Y10 After-care		
(b) Illnesses known to be associated :	230	(13 per cent.)
e.g. 002 Pulmonary tuberculosis 519 Pleurisy		
(c) Probable diagnostic confusion : *e.g.* 361 Trigeminal neuralgia 535 Other diseases of teeth and supporting structures	116	(7 per cent.)
III *Fortuitous.* There is no apparent connexion between the 2 diagnoses. . .	294	(17 per cent.)
Total	1,746	(100 per cent.)

or fields of diagnostic uncertainty. The epidemiological interest is, however, likely to be greatest in group III, where superficially unconnected diseases might be shown to occur together with unusual frequency, thus pointing to a common aetiology.

The objective of this study has been to develop a computer programme to cross-tabulate one diagnosis against another diagnosis in a subsequent admission to hospital of the same patient. It is hoped that inspection of the resultant tables will show clusters of diagnostic pairs occurring with striking frequency and which could provide the starting-point of more rigorous clinical or epidemiological investigation. The approach has thus been exploratory and the simple intention has been to show what diagnoses can coexist in the same patient. Berkson (1946) has explained the pitfalls in trying to prove disease associations from hospital data. No attempt will be made to show that the number of occurrences of any combination is statistically significant, or to quantify the results further by computing readmission rates.

The study has been carried out wholly by computer without the agency of punch-cards. The tables have been derived by programme from a special multiple admission magnetic tape file obtained from the Oxford Record Linkage Study Master File. The programme was written in CHLF3, one of the extensions of Mercury Autocode, and was run on the Science Research Council's Atlas computer at Chilton. The contents of one section of the multiple admission file is shown diagrammatically in Figure 1. The records of two patients are shown. The personal characteristics of each patient

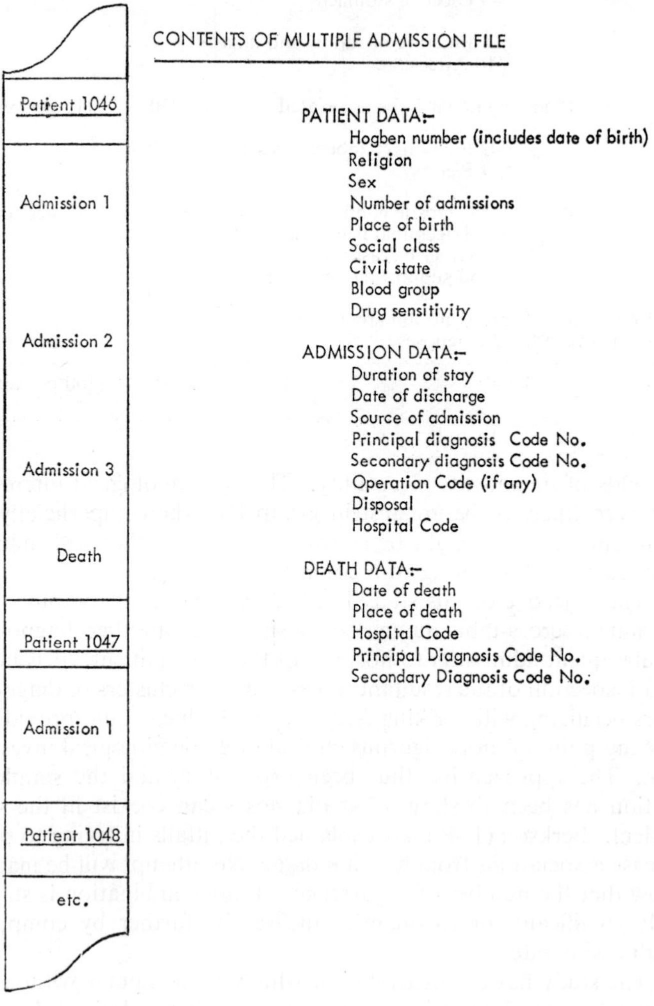
CONTENTS OF MULTIPLE ADMISSION FILE
Patient 1046
Admission 1
Admission 2
Admission 3
Death
Patient 1047
Admission 1
Patient 1048
etc.
PATIENT DATA:-
Hogben number (includes date of birth)
Religion
Sex
Number of admissions
Place of birth
Social class
Civil state
Blood group
Drug sensitivity
ADMISSION DATA:-
Duration of stay
Date of discharge
Source of admission
Principal diagnosis Code No.
Secondary diagnosis Code No.
Operation Code (if any)
Disposal
Hospital Code
DEATH DATA:-
Date of death
Place of death
Hospital Code
Principal Diagnosis Code No.
Secondary Diagnosis Code No.

FIG. 1.

are followed by the details of each successive admission. The particulars of death, if recorded on the master file, follow those of the last admission. All patients with at least one spell of inpatient admission, including single admissions, were included on the file. The variables recorded in respect of each patient, admission or death are listed on the right-hand side of Figure 1. Two personal numbers are recorded for each patient. The computer number is allocated serially to each patient at the time of assembly of the matched data. The Hogben number is a 10-digit identification code dependent on surname, given name and date of birth. The computer programme can print out the whole record from the multiple admission file of patients with any specified characteristics. In this way, it is possible to get back to the examination of the patient's hospital inpatient summary sheet, since these sheets are filed in Hogben number order (see p. 157). Each diagnosis in the admission and death data is recorded on the file in the 4-digit international code. For tabulation, only the first three digits of the principal diagnosis on admission are used, but by printing out the complete record the full code for every diagnosis can be ascertained.

Figure 2 is a flow-chart of the tabulation programme. The programme scans the multiple admission file and finds, in the example shown, a patient's record with 12 admissions. Had there been only one admission, the principal diagnosis could not have been cross-tabulated and the programme would have returned to scan the tape for the next record. Among the 12 admissions, several codes are exactly repeated and it is unnecessary to tabulate the same combination of codes twice for the same patient. The programme therefore produces a reduced string of three unique diagnoses, but meanwhile records the repetitions in a special ' repetitions ' table. Each column of this table corresponds to a diagnosis and each row to the number of repetitions found. In this patient, the code 171 was repeated eight times and 176 was repeated twice, so that one would be added into each of the following cells : column 171, row 8 and column 172, row 2.

The programme then generates all three possible combinations of two codes from the three unique diagnoses. Every pair of codes thus generated is retained in its original order within the string of three codes. Each pair in turn is tested for entry to a series of tables to be described below. If an appropriate table is found, the table is updated. The pair is not entered in more than one table and the programme returns to process another pair in the same way. If no appropriate table is found, the pair is allocated to a residual table before the programme returns for another pair. When every pair

DIAGNOSTIC TABULATION PROGRAM

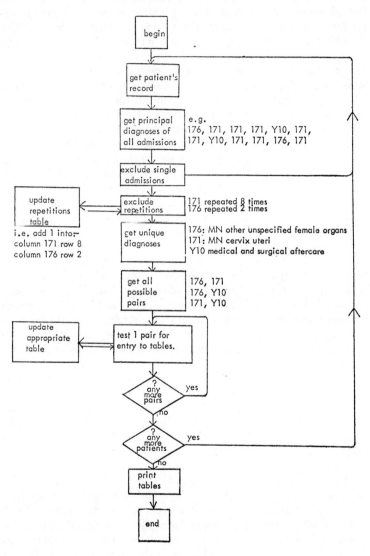

Fig. 2.

from one patient has been processed the programme repeats the operation for each patient until the end of the file is reached. The tables have initially been held within the store of the computer in skeleton form and are held there during updating. When the end of the file is reached, they are printed out.

The nature of the tables and the system by which each pair of diagnoses is allocated to them is shown in more detail in Figure 3.

TESTING AND UPDATING TABLES

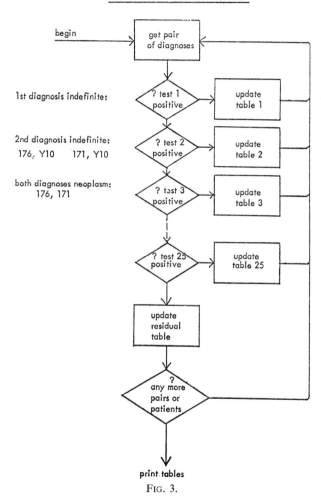

FIG. 3.

After the 'repetitions' table there are 25 other computer tables followed by the residual table. The purpose of the 25 tables is to show separately the ' explicable ' combinations of diagnoses. In the first two of these 25 tables the pair is tabulated if the first, or the second, diagnosis falls into certain symptomatic or indefinite categories (group II (a), Table II).

If two medical conditions are related clinically, the diagnostic codes often fall within the same one of the main 17 divisions of the International List. Computer tables 3–25 have therefore been made to correspond broadly to these divisions, the condition for entry of a pair to a table being that both codes shall lie within the same division. By enlarging these diagnostic groups to include other conditions coded elsewhere in the International List it is possible to include in the same table other clinically related conditions. For instance, Respiratory Tuberculosis (001–008) can be added to Diseases of the Respiratory System (470–527) so that the appropriate table would demonstrate the common sequence of pulmonary tuberculosis followed by pleurisy. In this way it is hoped that tables 3–25 should show most of the combinations which on visual inspection would have been allocated to groups II (b) and II (c), Table II. To allow for group III, the ' fortuitious ' group of combinations, there is a final large residual table for all pairs which have failed to qualify for entry to the preceding tables. The specification for the tables is punched on paper tape after the programme proper. Their number and type can be altered as desired.

Of the three pairs generated in the example given in Figure 2, the second and third would both have been allocated to computer table 2 since the second diagnosis Y10 (medical and surgical aftercare) is indefinite. In the first pair, both codes indicate a malignant neoplasm. One of the tables 3–25 provides for this combination and it happens coincidentally to be table 3.

This study is in its initial stages and the first complete run on the computer occurred only one week before the Symposium on 10th July, 1967. There has been little time to digest the results. Many of the tables are large and unwieldy. The residual table, which might otherwise have outrun the store of the computer has been drastically reduced in size by combining the 1000 diagnoses into 95 groupings, the rows and columns corresponding to groupings and not individual codes. It has already become apparent that the specification of the tables could be greatly improved. It is not proposed to describe in detail the specification of the tables or to show many of the results. in order, however, to illustrate the form of the computer output, two small tabulations are shown in Tables III and IV.

Table III illustrates how different diagnoses can be applied to mental disorders on different hospital admissions. It shows the

222

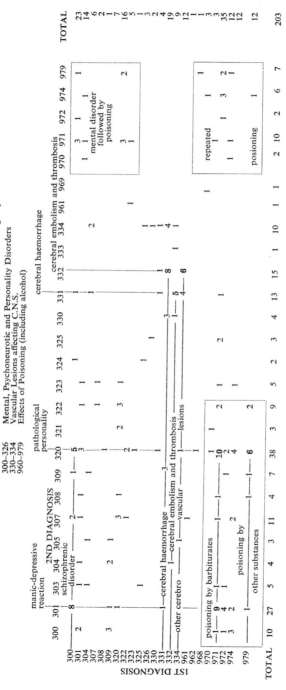

TABLE III. *Mental disorder, alcoholism, vascular diseases of C.N.S., poisoning*

Both 1st Diagnosis (row) and 2nd Diagnosis (column) lie within code groups :—

300–326   Mental, Psychoneurotic and Personality Disorders
330–334   Vascular Lesions affecting C.N.S.
960–979   Effects of Poisoning (including alcohol)

223

diagnostic overlap which exists in the field of cerebrovascular accidents. It also shows how frequently mental disorder of different types is followed by poisoning, or is diagnosed where poisoning has previously occurred. In cases of repeated poisoning, the order in which different types are used can be seen.

Table IV shows a small group of patients who underwent successive hospital admissions for eye complaints. The main feature of this table is the frequency with which a diagnosis of cataract is followed by that of detachment of the retina, glaucoma and other diseases of the eye.

TABLE IV. *Eye diseases*

Both 1st diagnosis (row) and 2nd Diagnosis (column) lie within code groups :—

192	Malignant Neoplasm of Eye
370–389	Inflammatory and Other Diseases and Conditions of Eye

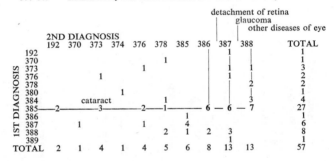

detachment of retina — 387
glaucoma / other diseases of eye — 388

1ST DIAGNOSIS \ 2ND DIAGNOSIS	192	370	373	374	376	378	385	386	387	388	TOTAL
192									1		1
370						1					1
373				1					1	1	3
376			1						1		2
378										2	2
380				1							1
384					1					3	4
385	2		3		2	1		6	6	7	27
386							1				1
387		1			1	4					6
388					2	1	2	3			8
389									1		1
TOTAL	2	1	4	1	4	5	6	8	13	13	57

(cataract)

Essentially the problem of such a study is to design the tables so that features of interest are more clearly brought out. So far, the clusters of diagnostic pairs that have been found appear to confirm clinical experience. Probably, important new associations could only be demonstrated by accumulating data, with more careful design of the tables, over a much longer period of time.

ACKNOWLEDGMENTS : This Study owes deeply to the encouragement of Dr E. D. Acheson, Director of the Oxford Record Linkage Study. I would like to thank my colleagues, Dr. Leo Kinlen who gave clinical advice, Mr Martin Hubbard who helped with several aspects of computer technique, and Mrs Sheelagh Watts for her efficient preparation of the multiple admission magnetic tape file.

We are indebted in this and other studies to Dr Jack Howlett, Director of the Atlas Computer Laboratory, Chilton, for a generous allocation of computer time.

REFERENCES

ACHESON, E. D. & BARR, A. (1965). Multiple spells of inpatient treatment in a calendar year. *Br. J. prev. soc. Med.* **19,** 182.
BERKSON, J. (1946). Limitations of the application of fourtold table analysis by hospital data. *Biometr. Bull.* **2,** 47.

DISCUSSION

Professor R. Schilling:* It is interesting to speculate on the many possible uses that may be made of comparisons between diagnoses in successive hospital admissions. First they offer an opportunity of studying the natural history of disease and even more unusual of expressing the natural history of disease in quantitative terms. For example, there were 19 patients who on second or subsequent admissions were diagnosed as suffering from carcinoma of the bronchus who on first admission had been diagnosed as suffering from bronchitis. The tables provide pointers to conditions that clinicians should look at in more detail because they may be the prelude to a more serious disease. There were 23 patients who were diagnosed on first admission as suffering from schizophrenia and eight were re-admitted with manic-depressive reactions. Five of the 23 patients were subsequently admitted suffering from the effects of self-inflicted poisons.

The second use which hospital doctors could make of these data is to measure the effectiveness of treatment. It should be possible also to compare the effectiveness of the follow-up procedures. For example, Dr Fairbairn's tables show that of 22 patients who were first admitted with malignant neoplasms of the bladder, 20 were readmitted at a later stage. This shows a good follow-up.

Thirdly, this type of analysis of hospital records can be of value in studies of organization, *e.g.* the extent to which efficient use is made of hospital beds in various areas and for particular types of disease.

Dr Anita K. Bahn : Dr Fairbairn mentioned that he tabulated information on all patients including those who did not come back a second time. I think this is particularly important where one is dealing with diagnoses that refer to the same specialty. For example, I think in studying psychiatric readmissions it is important to consider the frequency of the diagnosis in the population and whether the pattern of readmissions differs from what would be expected by chance. We found the index of predictive association one way of tackling this problem.

* Professor Schilling has had an opportunity to study the complete tabulations. These are too voluminous to publish in this volume.

Dr F. Brimblecombe : I should like to ask Dr Fairbairn if in the study he took account of patients in hospitals outside the Oxford linkage area ?

Dr Fairbairn : I am afraid the answer to that question is that we were unable to take any account of hospital admissions outside the area. These were admissions of which we were aware because they took place in hospitals within the Study area. Perhaps I may also make one point in commenting upon what Professor Schilling said : Unfortunately the data as they stand are no use for assessing the chances of readmission to hospital for the simple reason that we have not distinguished in the data between admissions from hospital and hospital transfers. This I think can be done but it would need a further extension of the programme. The meaning of an entry in one of these tables is that the diagnosis A can occur with the diagnosis B, but we have no idea at the moment of the time-relationships or whether in fact it was a different episode of the disease or merely a transfer from one hospital to another in the course of the same illness.

Professor Dr med. Wagner : I would like to ask Dr Fairbairn if this technique was also used to get an impression of the reliability of the coded diagnosis. For instance, if in the first admission the patient had a coded diagnosis 764 and the second time it was 746 ; this would suggest a coding error due to inversion of digits.

Dr Fairbairn : I think this is an extremely pertinent question. If any interesting associations are found one of the first steps will be to get back to the recorded data. This we are able to do because on a subsequent run of the computer we can print out the patient's complete record and from the identification code which appears at the beginning of the patient's record we can then get back to the hospital inpatient summary and if necessary back to the hospital notes. We have not done any systematic checks along the lines suggested.

LONGITUDINAL STUDIES USING PSYCHIATRIC CASE REGISTERS

ANITA K. BAHN, IRVING D. GOLDBERG, and KURT GORWITZ

THE psychiatric case register, a recently developed tool for epidemiological research related to mental illnesses, provides some excellent illustrations of the value of linked medical records. The source of data for a psychiatric case register is a statistical abstract or report on

226

each admission to and release from a defined set of psychiatric facilities serving residents of a delineated area. The statistical reports contain name and other identifying information and therefore can be linked to provide a longitudinal person-record of psychiatric experiences. Earlier in the Conference (p. 120) Mr Phillips has described the techniques of record linkage used in the Maryland register. This paper will describe some uses and studies related to the registers in Maryland and Monroe County, New York.

To place the psychiatric case register in proper perspective, brief comment should be made about the nature of mental illness and the changes which have taken place during the last decade in the care of the psychiatric patient. Certain forms of mental illness are characterized by alternating periods of active disease and remission, and in this sense such disorders may be considered as chronic diseases not unlike rheumatoid arthritis. With respect to patterns of care during the past decade, the major innovations include the rapid treatment of patients in their acute phase, the use of ataractic drugs, and the development of a broad spectrum of new kinds of psychiatric resources to meet the needs of patients. Concomitantly there has been a gradual and continuing decline in the length of hospitalization of newly admitted patients, a rapid increase in the cohort of former hospital patients functioning as community members, and increased patient flow between psychiatric facilities.

Because of the nature of the illness and the change in delivery of services, statistics based on a single episode of care or of a single hospital or clinic are of limited epidemiological value. Epidemiological observation, like a jig-saw puzzle, requires the piecing together of reports from the many psychiatric agencies which may treat an individual over a period of time. Registers can serve such a purpose by accumulating reports from various psychiatric facilities for each patient. Such a data bank amassed over an extended period is valuable for planning, administrative research and epidemiology.

Several techniques can be applied to the exploitation of such data for research. First, there is the analysis of the basic systematic information on psychiatric patients and services contained within the data bank itself. Secondly, registers constitute a sampling frame for the unbiased selection of patients with specified characteristics in order to carry out intensive studies through record search and field investigation. Such sample studies can be a powerful tool for testing hypotheses generated by the basic register data. Thirdly, the psychiatric data bank can be matched against other data banks for a variety of purposes.

This paper will illustrate how such methods are being used for the

227

epidemiological study and control of mental illnesses. The topics discussed will be (1) readmission for care and chronicity, (2) diagnosis and the ' natural ' history of mental diseases, (3) incidence and prevalence, (4) mortality, (5) evaluation of mental health programmes and (6) some other areas of interest.

Before describing these studies, however, it is important to emphasize several points. To assure confidentiality required by law (Maryland State Legislature, 1963) and by the participating facilities, the register can be used only for research purposes. Secondly, the potential uses of the register increase as it matures by accumulating information on individuals over a long period of time. The third major point is that only clinics or agencies directed by psychiatrists report to the register. While the Maryland register at present excludes data on patients treated by psychiatrists in private practice, such patients are included in the Monroe County register. Both registers contain no information on mentally ill persons seen exclusively by social and other nonpsychiatric agencies, as well as the large group who receive no professional services for their illness. Thus the source of the reports to the register imparts to it both the epidemiologic strengths and weaknesses found in other medical research based on records.

EXAMPLES OF STUDIES BASED ON THE REGISTER

Readmission for care and chronicity. Systematic follow-up information on all subsequent psychiatric episodes experienced by released patients is a primary objective of the register. A variety of methods have been developed for tabulating and presenting such sequential data in a useful way.

At the simplest level, annual ' follow-up ' tables are prepared for each clinic and hospital (Maryland Psychiatric Case Register). These tables indicate the proportion of patients discharged during the preceding year who were readmitted to any facility within a year after release. Data such as these can aid the hospital or clinic in evaluating the success of its programme against established goals, particularly when taking into account such factors as the interval between discharge and readmission and the characteristics of patients and services.

In the research field recurrence rates have been determined for cohorts of patients using life table methods developed by Bahn for variable-length observation periods (Bahn & Bodian, 1964). For example, Figures 1 and 2 show the patterns of first release and first return rates over an 18-month period to the same or another hospital

228

for three diagnostic cohorts (Gorwitz *et al.*, 1966). Demographic and diagnostic characteristics associated with both low and high retention and return rates were determined. The data showed that, in many instances, early release was followed by early readmission. The total number of hospitalizations and total number of bed days required during the same 18-month interval were also tabulated.

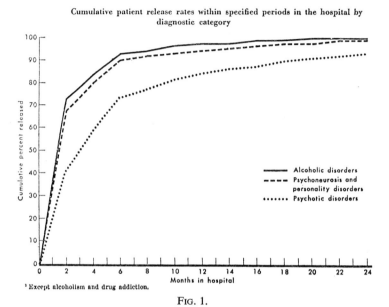

Cumulative patient release rates within specified periods in the hospital by diagnostic category

FIG. 1.

Source: Maryland Psychiatric Case Register—data for patients admitted to three State mental hospitals, July 1, 1961—December 31, 1962.

Data such as these can aid the hospital administrator in evaluating his release policies and in estimating the number of future bed days required for patients seen in his hospital.

A potentially useful analytic approach is to classify patients according to various operational criteria of chronicity such as being continuously or repeatedly hospitalized for specified time periods. Samples of patients from such groupings may be selected for further study ; data from records or from field investigations may reveal those symptomatic patterns which will help to identify the potentially chronic patients. Factors or conditions contributing to chronicity, such as mobility, or familial or household composition, could

229

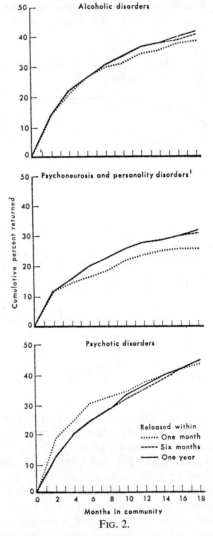

Cumulative percentages of patients rehospitalized after specified periods in the community, by length of initial hospitalization and diagnostic category

Alcoholic disorders

Psychoneurosis and personality disorders[1]

Psychotic disorders

Released within
...... One month
----- Six months
—— One year

Months in community

FIG. 2.

[1] Except alcoholism and drug addiction.

Source: Maryland Psychiatric Case Register—data for patients admitted to three State mental hospitals, July 1, 1961—December 31, 1962.

230

possibly be delineated. Utilizing the Maryland register, a start in this direction has been made in following a cohort of new admissions for schizophrenia (Warthen *et al.*, 1967).

Studies of diagnosis and the ' natural ' history of mental disorders. It is generally recognized that difficulties in diagnosis are especially pronounced in the area of mental illness. We hope that registers can improve the reliability of nosology and diagnostic practice and provide new information on patterns of progression or exacerbation of mental illness over long periods of time.

The register can aid diagnostic studies in several ways. It provides a means of readily identifying patients with similar diagnostic labels from different institutions. The following questions could then be studied. For a given diagnosis is there a common constellation of symptoms, or is there a significant variation in symptoms suggestive of differences in diagnostic practices ? How much similarity is there in the symptomatology of patients with different diagnostic labels ?

The consistency of the patient's diagnosis in successive admissions to the same or different hospitals within relatively brief periods of time has been partially explored. In Monroe County the diagnostic concordance on repeated admissions was relatively high for patients initially diagnosed with syndromes due to chronic brain damage or with schizophrenia but low for affective disorders because of marked disagreement in distinguishing between the psychotic and non-psychotic states (Babigian *et al.*, 1965). In Maryland diagnoses of adolescent patients were most consistent for chronic brain syndromes and mental retardation and were least consistent for personality disorders and psychoneuroses (Bahn & Oleinick, 1966). While studies on diagnostic consistency are not new, the register is a logical vehicle for further exploration of this problem.

Using the register as a diagnostic index, various other epidemiological studies have been carried out with focus on disorders such as alcoholism (Cooper, Bahn & Gorwitz) and schizophrenia (Warthen *et al.*, 1967). Studies on admission and prevalence rates, sequences of psychiatric episodes and degrees of current disability have been developed based on the register's longitudinal psychiatric record supplemented where necessary by data collected in the field.

The sensitivity and specificity of interview protocols can be tested with samples of former patients and appropriate controls. For example, Hetznecker *et al.*, (1966) interviewed a sample of schizophrenic men drawn from the Monroe County Register to develop and validate checklists of symptoms as a means of obtaining over-all ratings of mental illness. Predictions made in such surveys of the

231

need for psychiatric care can be checked against subsequent register evidence as to psychiatric care received.

Of great value to the epidemiologist concerned with the problems of mental illness are data on change in diagnosis and mental status over a long period of time, from childhood through adulthood. This might be called the ' natural ' history of mental disorders. Due to the infancy of these registers, no studies can be cited, but some examples of questions requiring long-term data can be indicated. Is a maladjusted child aged 10 more or less likely than an apparently healthy youngster of similar characteristics to be classified as psychotic at age 20 ? What is the probability that the young adult male with a personality disorder will be classified 15 years later as psychotic or alcoholic rather than as an adult with a satisfactory adjustment to life. Information on such long-range prognosis is not only of epidemiological value but also of administrative value of a cost-benefit nature.

Estimates of diagnosed incidence and prevalence. In addition to using the register to go ' forward ' with respect to the status of the patient, it is possible to go ' backward ' to the date of the first reported episode of treatment and thus obtain information on the previous psychiatric history. In the absence of a register it is difficult to obtain reliable data on past psychiatric experience.

A recently established register can be of little value in distinguishing new and old cases. As the register matures, however, new records will reflect more accurately true accretions to the ' ever ' psychiatric patient population or ' lifetime ' prevalence. Of course, account must be taken of the prior psychiatric experience of immigrants to the register area. The Maryland register identifies new residents so that specified studies of their previous psychiatric history can be undertaken. In time, therefore, the register should provide a firmer source of data on first diagnosed psychiatric illness. Eventually, from such qualified incidence data, reliable lifetime estimates of the risk of becoming a psychiatric patient should be possible.

As with other register data, caution must be exercised in interpreting first diagnosed incidence as true incidence. Changes with calendar time in the availability and delivery of psychiatric services affect the number and kinds of persons with psychiatric illness who come under care. It is known, for example, that new patients today tend to be seen at earlier stages of their illness than was true of new patients 10 or more years ago. Trends in diagnosed and treated incidence therefore are a composite function of changes in psychiatric resources, changes in public attitude regarding the use of these resources, as well as of changes in the mental health of the population.

Better estimates of psychiatric prevalence are also possible through the register. The register automatically provides unduplicated counts and rates of persons receiving psychiatric care during a specified time period, that is, treated prevalence (Table I) (Bahn

Table I. *One-year prevalence ratios of psychiatric patients of Maryland by sex, age, and geographic area, per 1,000 population,[1] Maryland psychiatric case register, fiscal 1962*

Sex and age group	1-day (point) prevalence[2]	Entering care during year[3]	Total 1-year (interval) prevalence
	Maryland		
All patients . . .	6·37	4·43	10·80
Males	6·74	4·91	11·64
0–14 years . . .	3·17	3·68	6·85
15–44 years . . .	7·08	5·73	12·81
45–64 years . . .	9·69	5·24	14·93
65 and over . . .	14·14	5·02	19·16
Females	6·01	3·97	9·97
0–14 years . . .	1·63	1·96	3·59
15–44 years . . .	6·36	5·26	11·62
45–64 years . . .	9·00	4·30	13·29
65 and over . . .	14·11	4·52	18·62

[1] Based on population estimates as of July 1, 1962.
[2] Persons on psychiatric rolls, July 1, 1961.
[3] Not on rolls July 1, 1961.

et al., 1965). To such rates can be added estimates of untreated illness among former patients no longer under care. This would include patients whose treatment was completed as well as those whose treatment was interrupted. Such estimates can be based upon observed rates of recurrent episodes for specified groups of patients and upon their latest reported condition. However, in order, to establish proper criteria for estimating the current prevalence of mental illness, follow-up studies in the community of samples of former patients undoubtedly are essential. It should be recognized that those estimates would still be minimal since they do not take into account the mentally ill who have never been treated.

Mortality. A fourth type of epidemiologic study relates to the association between various mental illnesses and death. Since the entire register is routinely ' cleared ' against files of death certificates,

233

deaths while under psychiatric care as well as deaths after release from care can be readily determined.

A general mortality study under way will compare the death rates for the Maryland psychiatric and general populations. Patients will be classified by diagnostic variables and by extent and type of care. Comparisons with the death rates of the general population will take into account socioeconomic and demographic characteristics.

In another study (Gorwitz *et al.*, 1966), relatively high death rates have been observed for selected cohorts of patients—namely alcoholics, psychotics and those with psychoneurotic and other personality disorders (Table II). While one might expect that suicides

Table II. *Comparison of cohort death rates during 18-month followup period with death rates for the Maryland population, by age and sex*

Age and sex	Total Maryland[1]	Alcoholic disorders	Psychotic disorders	Psycho-neuroses and personality disorders[2]
Total 25–54 years . .	0·6	4·9	2·0	1·9
25–34 years . .	0·2	1·7	0·5	1·1
35–44 years . .	0·5	4·1	1·6	2·6
45–54 years . .	1·2	7·5	4·6	2·4
Male 25–54 years .	0·8	5·2	2·3	1·7
25–34 years . .	0·3	1·7	0·3	0·8
35–44 years . .	0·6	4·6	1·8	4·0
45–54 years . .	1·5	7·7	6·8	...
Female 25–54 years .	0·4	3·6	1·8	2·1
25–34 years . .	0·2	1·6	0·9	1·4
35–44 years . .	0·4	2·3	1·5	1·5
45–54 years . .	0·9	6·8	3·5	4·5

[1] The Maryland Department of Health supplied the rates for the Maryland population for the comparable 18-month period.

[2] Except alcoholism and drug addiction.

NOTE : Rates are per 100 population.

SOURCE : Maryland Psychiatric Case Register—data for patients admitted to three State mental hospitals, July 1, 1961–December 31, 1962.

and accidents would be the major factor contributing to these death rates, excess mortality was found in fact to be widely distributed among the various causes of death.

One research goal is the development of reliable guidelines to assist the psychiatrist in predicting the probability of suicide in various types of individuals. From psychiatric register follow-up data it is possible to begin to delineate groups with increasing risks of suicide. Compared with the suicide rate for the general population of Monroe County, New York, the suicide rate for all persons registering as a psychiatric patient for the first time was 16 times as great ; that for new patients with depression 23 times, and for persons known to have attempted suicide within the previous two years 90 times as great (Table III) (Gardner *et al.*, 1964). Of the County residents who committed suicide almost two-fifths were known either to the psychiatric register or to a mental hospital prior to the establishment of the register (Fig. 3).

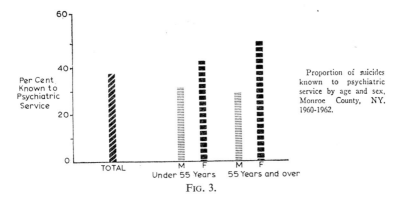

Proportion of suicides known to psychiatric service by age and sex, Monroe County, NY, 1960-1962.

Fig. 3.

The register can be used readily for investigations based on clinical impressions. For example, it has been noted that a significant number of patients transferred from general hospitals to State mental hospitals die shortly thereafter. In a test of the hypothesis that such transfers may not always be beneficial the time lapse between transfer and death and the cause of death is being determined.

The full potential of a register for analyses of mortality is still to be realized. For example, as the length of observation of registrants increases life table analyses will be possible and measures of their expectation of life computed.

Mental health programme evaluation. The register's built-in potential for operational research results from its accumulation over time of information relating to episodes of care received by all residents of an area admitted to any of the reporting psychiatric facilities serving that area. Thus, it is a reservoir of data for conducting ' before ' and ' after ' comparisons for the evaluation of new

235

service programmes introduced at any point along the time conti-
nuum. The baseline ' before ' information is readily available in the
register for such evaluation studies. Furthermore, since the data
were prospectively gathered the potential biases of retrospectively
collected data have been largely avoided.

For example, the register has documented the specific changes in
use of State mental hospitals and other psychiatric facilities following
the establishment of a psychiatric ward in a Maryland county-
operated general hospital (Locke, Duvall, & Newborough, not
published). It has been used in Monroe County both to make predictions about the utilization of new facilities and to test these predictions (Gardner, 1967).

Comprehensive community mental health centres, designed to
facilitate the free-flow of patients between service units and to maintain continuity of care, represent a new treatment modality in the
United States. The impact of this new programme on services provided and the outcome of these services must be assessed scienti-
fically. Psychiatric registers can help uniquely in this evaluation.

A comprehensive centre serving one section of Baltimore City
was recently opened. Prior to its establishment an ecological study
(Klee *et al.*, 1967) was conducted of diagnosed mental illness for the
entire city. Tracts were ranked in quartiles according to psychiatric
morbidity rates obtained from the register as well as by various socio-
economic indices, indices of social disorganization and health
indices. The analysis illustrated the marked ' nesting ' of crime, other
social, economic and public health problems, and mental illness
within the same tracts. Data such as these were of considerable
value in early planning of this centre's activities.

The routine register reporting programme is accumulating data
on all episodes of psychiatric treatment experienced by residents
of the catchment area whether seen in the centre or other treatment
facilities. ' Before ' and ' after ' comparisons will be made of rates
of admission and readmission to the various components of the
centre, sequence and duration of care, use of other psychiatric services within and outside the catchment area, and other information
on the extent to which the centre is serving its intended population.

It is anticipated that additional evaluations will be made in relation to other comprehensive centres throughout the State. Such
analyses would not be feasible without a central record-linked system
for all psychiatric facilities serving a geographical area.

Other epidemiological studies. The possible relations of the
psychiatric register to other research programmes should be noted
briefly. The mortality study previously described illustrates the

Table III. *Average annual suicide rate, by selected population groups at risk, Monroe County, NY, 1960–62*

Group at Risk	Population at Risk, No.		Suicides, 1960–62, No.		Average Annual Suicide Rate Per 100,000 Persons at Risk		
	Under 55 Yr	55 Yr and Over	Under 55 Yr	55 Yr and Over	Under 55 Yr	55 Yr and Over	All Ages*
Monroe County population	467,733	118,654	105	75	7·5	21·1	9·7
All admissions to Psychiatric Service, 1960	3,891	1,112	14	7	143·9	251·8	163·2
All admissions to Psychiatric Service, 1960, with a diagnosis of psychotic or neurotic depression	752	363	3	5	(159·6)†	551·0	229·7
Attempted suicides, 1960	154	27	3	1	(779·2)	(1,481·5)	(905·1)

* Age adjusted to United States population by 1960 census.
† Parentheses are to emphasize those rates based on a small *n*.

237

linkage of the register with a vital records system. Another type of record matching under way involves the collation of register data on treatment episodes with data about earnings accumulated in Social Security records for the same individuals. From such interrelated data some measures of the cost-benefit of psychiatric treatment will be derived.

In one study (Oleinick & Bahn, 1966) records of children seen in the Division of Special Services of Baltimore City Schools were matched against the Maryland register. Children who received only school mental health services were compared with children who received both school services and outside psychiatric care. These two groups were further subsampled to obtain detailed information on the children's problems and their family background. Certain factors relating to the family, such as parental mental illness or inadequacy, and paternal and fraternal criminal behaviour, were more prevalent among children receiving outside psychiatric care (Table IV).

In a pilot project two family service agencies in Maryland are reporting all family members identified with emotional problems. These records will be matched against the psychiatric case register to determine whether visits by such individuals to a family service agency are in any way related to previous or subsequent psychiatric care.

In studies in Maryland and Monroe County samples of the case-load of general practitioners (Locke, *et al.*, 1967), internists, medical clinics in general hospitals, and industrial clinics have been matched against the registers. Such studies are providing insight as to the ability of the nonpsychiatric physician to detect mental illness, the extent of emotional disorders in these patient groups, the level of efficiency of nonpsychiatric treatment, and the pattern of psychiatric referral practices.

Interest has been expressed in studies linking the psychiatric register with various lists of persons with deviant behaviour, such as those with police records of arrests or with records of the abuse of drugs. While these psychosocial investigations have not been explored to an appreciable degree, they are pertinent to the identification and prevention of psychopathology in its broadest sociocultural aspects.

General interest in the study of fertility and reproductive rates among the mentally ill has been heightened by the increasing numbers of mentally ill kept close to home, and by suggested evidence of a possible genetic component in the etiology of some of the more common forms of mental diseases including schizophrenia. It is planned to use the register as a frame to identify schizophrenic women on whom detailed information relating to reproductive history will be obtained from case records and possibly birth certificates. Comparisons will be made with the general population with regard to fertility, survivorship of children, and other factors.

Table IV. *Family data*

Selective disruptive familial factors

Category	DSS† psychiatric cases	DSS† controls
Percent with :		
Number of disruptive factors : (P = ·01)		
None	25	27
One	20	29
Two	17	23
Three	19	8
Four or more	19	13
Selected disruptive factors :*		
Poverty	17	22
Physical illness—Mother . .	7	9
Father . . .	3	4
Mental illness —Mother (P = ·01)	11	3
Father (P = ·04)	7	2
Alcoholism —Mother . .	4	2
Father . .	11	6
Crime —Mother . .	0·7	0·6
Father (P = ·01)	9	3
Sibling (P = ·05)	9	4
Neglect —Mother . .	9	6
Father . .	9	6
Conflict —General . .	8	5
Regarding child .	4	5
Physical abuse	6	5
Rejection	12	10
Parent inadequate, etc. (P = ·003)	8	1

* Does not add to 100 per cent., since more than one disruptive factor may be present.

† DSS = Division of Special Services of Baltimore City Schools.

SOURCE : Division of special services of Baltimore City Schools February 1, 1963–March 31, 1964 and Maryland psychiatric case register July 1, 1961–June 30, 1964.

Methods are being worked out whereby routine postal enquiries will be made by computer as to the current address of all patients on the register. Registered persons found not to be living in the State will be excluded from the population at risk in respect of re-admission. Records of changes of address will aid in the conduct of follow-up studies on former psychiatric patients and also provide information on their mobility. The frequency and type of changes of residence will be determined. Such information on the geographic stability of its catchment population should aid the community mental health centre in shaping realistic objectives as regards treatment.

COMMENT

A variety of applications of a system of linked records for furthering the epidemiology of mental illness have been described. It is anticipated that further development and maturation of these registers will provide greater opportunities for research.

It is appropriate at this important International Symposium on medical record linkage to end on a note which stresses the value of cross-cultural register studies using uniform definitions. This was illustrated in a recent analysis in three register areas in the United States—Maryland, Monroe County, New York and Tricounty, North Carolina (Bahn *et al.*, 1966). The strong association of poverty, overcrowding, ghetto living and other aspects of the central city syndrome with high rates of admission, for both white and non-whites, was striking in each area. At the same time, differences between areas pointed to possible deficiencies in mental health services for certain groups of persons (Figs. 4–10). Further, complementary data from private practising psychiatrists in Monroe County (Fig. 11) provided some parameters on patients not covered by the other registers.

A comparison of psychiatric case registers is under way for the areas of Camberwell in England, Aberdeen in Scotland, and Maryland in the United States. An international study on schizophrenia based partially on register data is being conducted by the World Health Organization.

Comparative and complementary studies based upon well-maintained disease registers both in similar and dissimilar geographic areas supplemented by field investigations, will multiply manyfold the benefit of each register for epidemiology.

Comparative psychiatric register prevalence and admission age adjusted rates :
by place of residence

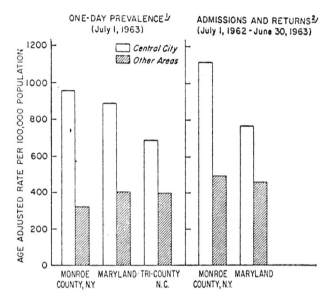

FIG. 4.

[1] Includes residents and long-term leave patients of State and County Mental Hospitals and Psychiatric Clinic Outpatients. Data for Tricounty as of July 1, 1964.

[2] Includes all psychiatric inpatient and outpatient facilities except mental retardation institutions.

Comparative psychiatric register prevalence and admission rates : by sex and age

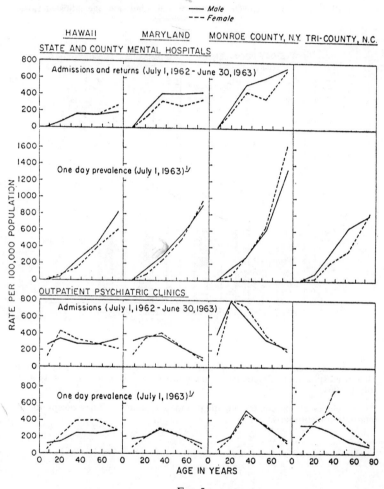

FIG. 5.

[1] Data for Tricounty as of July 1, 1964.

242

**Comparative psychiatric register prevalence and admission age adjusted rates :
by race and sex**

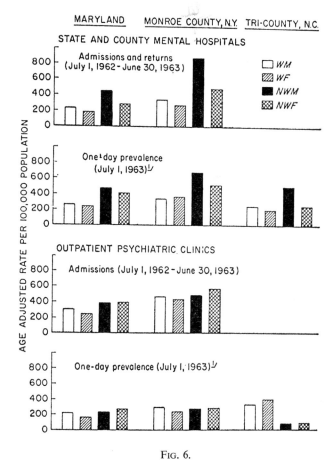

FIG. 6.

[1] Data for Tricounty as of July 1, 1964.

Comparative psychiatric register prevalence and admission rates by place of residence and age

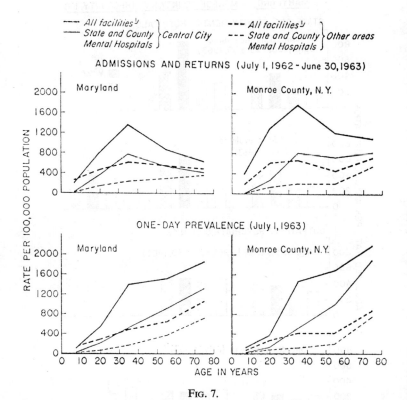

FIG. 7.

[1] Includes all psychiatric inpatient and outpatient facilities except mental retardation institutions.

Comparative psychiatric register prevalence and admission rates : for outpatient psychiatric clinics, by race

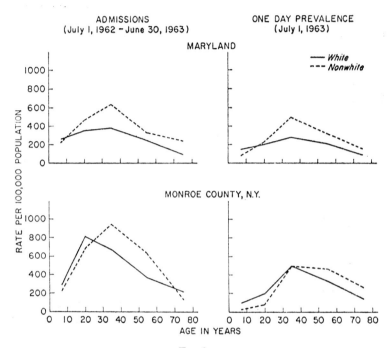

FIG. 8.

Comparative psychiatric register one-year prevalence age adjusted rates : by place of residence, race, sex, and age (July 1, 1962–June 30, 1963)

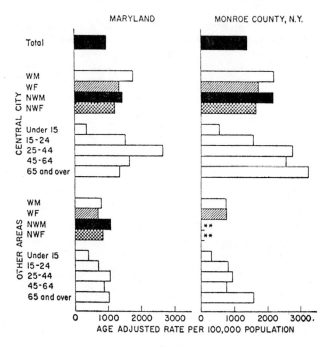

FIG. 9.

[1] Includes all psychiatric inpatient and outpatient facilities except mental retardation institutions.

** Fewer than 25 cases.

Comparative psychiatric register admission rates to state and county mental hospitals : by sex, race, place of residence, and age, Maryland and Monroe County, N.Y. (July 1, 1962–June 30, 1963)

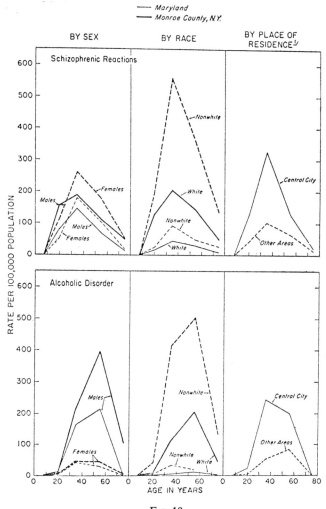

FIG. 10.

Some data based on less than 25 cases.

[1] Data not available for Monroe County, N.Y.

Admission rates to private psychiatric outpatient practice : by sex and age, Monroe County, N.Y. (July 1, 1962–June 30, 1963)

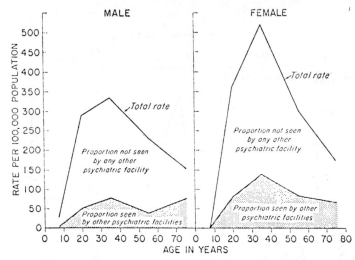

FIG. 11.

REFERENCES

BABIGIAN, H. M., GARDNER, E. A., MILES, H. C. & ROMANO, J. (1965). Diagnostic consistency and change in a follow-up study of 1,215 patients. *Am. J. Psychiat.* **121**, 895–901.

BAHN, A. K. & BODIAN, C. (1964). A life table method for studying recurrent episodes of illness or care. *J. chron. Dis.* **17**, 1019–1031.

BAHN, A. K., GARDNER, E. A., ALLTOP, L., KNATTERUD, G. L. & SOLOMON, M. (1966). Admission and prevalence rates for psychiatric facilities in four register areas. *Am. J. publ. Hlth*, **56**, 2033–2051.

BAHN, A. K., GORWITZ, K., KLEE, G. D., KRAMER, M. & TUERK, I. (1965). Services received by Maryland residents in facilities directed by a psychiatrist (first year of a state case register). *Publ. Hlth Rep.* **80**, 405–416.

BAHN, A. K. & OLEINICK, M. S. (1966). Recurrent episodes of psychiatric service in an adolescent population. Presented at the Sixth International Congress of Child Psychiatry, Edinburgh, Scotland.

COOPER, M., BAHN, A. K. & GORWITZ, K. Some epidemiology of alcoholism in Maryland. (Mimeographed.)

GARDNER, E. A. (1967). The use of a psychiatric case register in the planning and evaluation of a mental health program. In *Psychiatric Epidemiology and Mental Health Planning*, ed. MONRO, R. R., KLEE, G. D. & BRODY, E. B. American Psychiatric Association Psychiatric Research Report 22, Washington, D.C.

GARDNER, E. A., BAHN, A. K. & MACK, M. (1964). Suicide and psychiatric care in the aging. *Archs gen. Psychiat.* **10**, 547–553.

GORWITZ, K., BAHN, A. K., KLEE, G. & SOLOMON, M. (1966). Release and return rates for patients in state mental hospitals of Maryland. *Publ. Hlth Rep.* **81**, 1095–1108.

HETZNECKER, W., GARDNER, E. A., ODOROFF, C. L. & TURNER, R. J. (1966). Field survey methods in psychiatry. *Archs gen. Psychiat.* **15**, 427–438.

KLEE, G. D., SPIRO, E. S., BAHN, A. F. & GORWITZ, K. (1967). An ecological analysis of diagnosed mental illness in Baltimore. In *Psychiatric Epidemiology and Mental Health Planning*, ed. MONRO, R. R., KLEE, G. D. & BRODY, E. B. American Psychiatric Association Psychiatric Research Report 22, Washington, D.C.

LOCKE, B. Z., DUVALL, H. J. & NEWBROUGH, J. R. Evaluation of Prince Georges County General Hospital psychiatric wing. (Not published.)

LOCKE, B. Z., FINUCANE, D. L. & HASSLER, F. (1967). Emotionally disturbed patients under care of private nonpsychiatric physicians. In *Psychiatric Epidemiology and Mental Health Planning*, ed. MONROE, R. R., KLEE, G. D., & BRODY, E. B. American Psychiatric Association Psychiatric Research Report 22, Washington, D.C.

Maryland State Legislature, House Bill No. 61. Effective June 1, 1963.

OLEINICK, M. S. & BAHN, A. K. (1966). Characteristics of adolescent cases receiving psychiatric services and/or school facility services (a preliminary paper in the study of interrelationships of psychiatric facilities and school facilities adolescents). Presented at the Sixth International Congress of Child Psychiatry, Edinburgh, Scotland.

WARTHEN, F. J., KLEE, G. D., BAHN, A. K. & GORWITZ, K. (1967). Diagnosed schizophrenia in Maryland. In *Psychiatric Epidemiology and Mental Health Planning*, ed. MONRO, R. R., KLEE, G. D., & BRODY, E. B. American Psychiatric Association Psychiatric Research Report 22, Washington, D.C.

DISCUSSION

Dr G. Innes : I want to congratulate Dr Bahn on presenting such an interesting paper. The work of herself and her colleagues has acted as the model on which other case registers throughout the world have been based. Because so much psychiatric illness is chronic and recurrent in character, the case register approach in psychiatric research is essential, and the range of the research studies which Dr Bahn described this morning showed that there can be no doubt about the value of the register. I would agree with all Dr Bahn has said about the epidemiological uses of the register, its use in comparative studies, its use in the analysis of the data to isolate and identify the high-risk groups and its use as a sampling basis to pick out groups for more detailed studies. In fact similar studies to those which she has described this morning are either in planning stages or in progress in our own case register.

I was particularly interested in the excess mortality which she found in psychiatric patients. I have just finished a five-year follow-up of 2,000 patients in the north-east of Scotland and found that there is a marked excess mortality in all groups of patients, especially in the under 65 age group ; an excess mortality which cannot be accounted for by the suicides. This is something in addition to suicides.

Dr Bahn stressed that the main advantage of the register in

249

studying the natural history of psychiatric illness will not become apparent and obvious for 10–20 years. A great deal was said yesterday, however, about the need and the value of immediate dividends being available to the clinicians who were contributing towards this data store. In Aberdeen the case register is an integral part of the regional medical records system. Clinicians are encouraged to ask questions of the register and to use it as a basis for their research. I wonder whether Dr Bahn could tell us whether there is any such system in force for the Maryland register or whether it is just routine data from the research point of view. The only other point that I would like to make is that Dr Bahn has spoken about the use of life table methods in studying psychiatric populations. This method seems very suitable for dealing with large groups of patients. I wonder whether the statistical techniques that are available are sufficient to deal with smaller groups, for example dealing with units with 100 admissions annually.

Dr A. Bahn : With regard to feedback to agencies, I think it is highly important, because of the long time before register data become useful, that the cooperating facilities participate at every stage. A research committee helped to design the standard forms now in use in all facilities and to plan the routine register tables. We attempt to involve the clinicians in the research. There is a great deal of variation among clinicians ; some are more research-oriented than others. Whenever there is any show of interest we attempt to provide statistical advice and help to write up research projects. It is quite expensive to write computer programmes for data analysis and this is one reason why it is important that we be concerned with standardization of computer input and hardware.

I was interested in your suggestion that suicide is not the only cause of excess mortality. We too found that neither suicides nor accidents accounted for the excess mortality in certain cohorts.

With respect to the use of life table methods for analysis of data recurrence, good studies, particularly where individuals are not followed for the same length of time unfortunately require very large numbers. If one starts with 5,000 there is not very much left by the time one classifies by important variables. This is of course another reason why it is desirable to have cooperative studies so that you can pool data. This has been done in the United States with tumour registries in 100 cooperating hospitals.

Incidentally, our longitudinal data have not yet been used to test some stochastic models of psychiatric recurrence. I have been trying to interest mathematicians in using this valuable data bank for such purposes.

250

Dr Pearson : I would like to ask Dr Bahn if she has the Cornell Medical Index or other similar data about all these patients for cross-reference to the diagnoses that she is collecting.

Dr Bahn : Unfortunately we do not have symptomatic information as in the Cornell Medical Index. We do obtain some routine symptomatic data because, in addition to the primary diagnosis, we ask whether the person is dependent on alcohol or drugs and whether he has made a suicidal threat or statement, or a suicidal attempt or gesture. Earlier, an outpatient advisory committee helped to develop a check list of 20 symptoms and problems, like aggressive behaviour. This check list is used on a voluntary basis by about 12 of the Maryland facilities, but we do not obtain such data routinely. This is a great deficiency.

Dr Baldwin : I wonder if Dr Bahn has been able to assemble any family linkages within the Maryland register ?

Dr Bahn : We have not attempted any family linkage on a routine basis. There are many problems in maintaining a family register. I know that Newcombe has devised a method for linking families but we have not been able to do this in a routine way or even on a special study basis because we do not obtain the information needed for such linkage. It is possible, given a set of families and their members, to search the register to determine how many of the persons at risk of a secondary attack within the family have been reported to the register as a case. Also it may be possible to study families by selecting individuals with the same address. On a pilot basis a family service agency reports to the register all members in the family who have problems but these data have not been studied.

THE USE OF RECORD LINKAGE IN LONG-TERM PROSPECTIVE STUDIES

M. A. HEASMAN

In Scotland, apart from the linkage, for statistical purposes, of some of the records held by the General Register Office, we hope soon to be able to enter upon a programe involving the linkage of Hospital Inpatient data and death records, provided that we successfully negotiate the early experimental phase. Thus in a specifically Scottish context, this paper deals with matters which concern the future. Nevertheless I believe that the points that I wish to make, are ones which need to be considered by research workers who intend to use record linkage organizations, and by the organizations themselves, or at least those that operate on a large scale.

The Scottish position

Before entering upon the specific topic of my paper I will outline the Scottish position vis-à-vis record linkage now and in the near future. At the moment we are collecting data on all discharges from hospital in a form that could be used for record linkage. We propose to achieve this primarily by using sex, surname, initials, and date of birth with such other secondary identification as can be incorporated economically *e.g.* area of residence, occupation, marital status, etc. In Scotland with but 270 births per day I calculate that this will provide us with separate identification without duplication of over 99 per cent. of individuals. There will thus be a small amount of duplication and, in addition a loss of unknown proportions (at the moment) because of inacurracy or incompleteness. Neverthless our target is to obtain matches in more than 95 per cent. of all possible cases. Because we believe it is necessary to validate the scheme, and to build up slowly, our first linkage will be of intra-hospital records followed very closely by the record of death. We believe that linkage of these two items will be of the greatest benefit and the records are available in suitable form now, but we shall be looking to a wider extension to other records in the not too distant future.

Long-term prospective studies

One of the criticisms of record linkage has been that while the schemes are excellent in theory, they will be very little used in practice. Some of the uses certainly require considerable development. Our thinking has been so conditioned by 130 years of single-event statistics that the full uses of longitudinal data still require to be explored and popularized. This will undoubtedly take time, and although studies such as those described at this conference are doing most valuable work the users of linked data are still confined to a small though growing number of workers. It seems to me that the best way to prove the great usefulness of record linkage is to make it available to clinical and epidemiological research workers who are interested in follow-up of their own cases. Here is an immediate and important use, not because follow-up is impossible, but because with normal methods it is such a time-consuming procedure. With a linked file the procedure should become simplicity itself for those events which are held on the file.

An investigator who wants to follow up a series of cases has simply to provide the linkage organization with a list of identifying details which are then run against the up to date file and the names of those patients who appear on it after a certain date can be printed out with such other relevant material as may be required. This is the problem in its simplest terms, I would like to go into the procedure in rather more detail.

I think it will be essential for those workers wanting to use the service to agree to the use of standard forms of presentation of the request to the central oganization. I am speaking here of the identifying details of the individuals concerned. Because there may well be more than one ' central organization ' concerned either in different areas or for differing and possibly overlapping purposes, and also because there may be changes in the linkage procedure, I believe that, at this stage, the identifying details should be as full as possible and possibly rather fuller than any particular scheme might require. In addition to the identifying details a record will also be required of the date that the individual concerned entered the investigation. This material can be fed to the central organization either on a standard printed form, or in a form compatible with the organization's computer, *e.g.* punched card, paper tape, magnetic tape etc. with all details inserted in their correct field. To achieve this it will be necessary for the linkage organizations to get together and agree upon the standard fields which will be acceptable to them, and to make this agreement as widely known as possible.

I think it would be advisable for any worker who proposes such a study to get in touch with the record linkage organization at an early stage in his work so that he can be brought up to date with any recent changes in procedure. He should be quite explicit in his requirements. If this use of record linkage develops, as I believe it will, the central load could become quite considerable and it may be necessary for the print-out to be one of a set of standard packages, which might be for example,

(a) Notification of death, with a copy of the death entry.

(b) Notification of a hospital discharge with the name of consultant.

(c) Full print-out of history subsequent to entry date, etc.

Because the total file size will soon become very large it will be most economical if matching runs are carried out at regular intervals, with such runs containing requests from several workers. The data will be ordered according to the needs of the linkage organization and the matches will be held on file until the completion of the matching run, when a print-out will be prepared for each worker.

Limitations

The first and most obvious limitation of a scheme of this sort is that it will relate only to the data held on the central linkage files. In Scotland, for example, it will be limited to hospital and death records in the first instance. Possible extension into other systems will no doubt come in due course. We already plan to bring in our cancer registration and mental hospital statistics just as soon as we can. Other vital records may be fed in, as might local authority and general practitioner data. At the moment I think it is unlikely that a national population register will be available for record linkage purposes although it is just possible that in due course we might be able to provide reference to a patient's general practitioner via a computerized N.H.S. Central Register.

The second limitation depends upon the quality of the data. It is readily appreciated that when a scheme reaches national proportions the overall quality of the data is liable to suffer, and this is particularly so with matters of identification where data may be transcribed wrongly, let alone the variations in initials, forenames, surnames and dates of birth which can be given by the patients themselves. It is important to realize nevertheless that matching can not improve the quality of the original data although the various scoring routines described do allow for some variations. Nevertheless, care will need to be taken by research workers to understand that mismatches and failures to match will occur.

A third set of limitations depends on the sophistication of the matching routines. It is obvious that with increasing sophistication the law of diminishing returns very soon sets in. I am neither prepared nor qualified to say where this is, but as I said earlier I would hope that we might achieve correct matching in 95 per cent. of possibles, although a lower figure of, say 85 per cent., would not mean that we have failed. This means however that possibly one match in 20 will be incorrect, and I believe it must be recognized by all concerned that this is likely to be the case.

Ethical problems

One of the difficulties of a procedure of the sort described in this paper is that it raises questions of medical confidentiality. We have undertaken not to disclose the names of individuals held on our central files without the consent of the consultant concerned (in the case of hospital records) and not to permit any approach to an individual except via his family doctor. This means that the use of a record linkage system to indicate subsequent events during the life of a patient (death is not a confidential event) can be used only if the consultant agrees. However, I believe there is a way round this difficulty to which it would be difficult to raise objection. This is to ask each patient entering a prospective trial to sign a consent form agreeing that the investigator be informed of any subsequent hospital admissions, say, during the next x years. This would seem to me to absolve the Department from obtaining the permission of the consultant, who is, after all, looking after the interests of the patient. Of course, if reference needs to be made to the clinical notes, this can be done only with the permission of the consultant in the usual way. I presume permission for approaches to the patient could also be given in the same way by the use of a consent form, but if such access is necessary then it will be essential to keep the patient's general practitioner informed. At the same time, circumstances can be visualized when a procedure such as this would be unwise, and not in the interest of the patient.

A procedure such as that set out above will need to be discussed with the Central Ethical Committee of the British Medical Association and I should stress that we have, as yet, made no approach to them on this matter.

Thus, in order to make full use of the potentialities of record linkage for assessing prospective studies there should be :

1. Prior consultation with the record linkage organizations.

2. A standard form of presentation of identifying data to the organization, preferably in the form of punched cards or other acceptable computer input.

3. A consent form agreeing to the disclosure of the subsequent medical history signed by all persons entering such a study. (As it is possible that no written material relating to individual patients will be transmitted to the central organization, a declaration signed by the investigator will be sufficient. This will state that all persons on the list for matching have consented to disclosure.)

It is this third condition which has led me to relate this paper specifically to prospective studies. However, there is no reason why the same methods should not be used for retrospective studies, but in this event we should have to revert to the rather cumbersome procedure referred to earlier of obtaining the consultant's consent before disclosure, unless some other acceptable procedure can be found.

The suggestion to standardize the procedure for presenting data to the linkage organization can be important to the research workers themselves for without it additional work may be caused by his having to prepare a different set of data for each organization.

Such standardization might be reached first at a national and then at international level (in order to allow, for example, for migration studies). This suggestion for standardization relates only to the form of the data. The methods used for achieving linkage and the data required for this will differ considerably, but I believe that all linkage organizations ought to arrive at agreement on the form and position of the specific details on the input document.

I hope that what I have said does not make the procedure appear to be too cumbersome. I have said it now because I believe that unless we begin to get our ideas straight, anarchy may prevail and the resultant load on the system become too great for it to be efficient.

I started with a statement of the Scottish position which made it clear that much of the remainder of my paper would be of necessity unrelated to actual practice—although I hope the points I have made are practical ones.

May I end by reverting to the Scottish position and saying that while we are awaiting the development of our record linkage programmes we are prepared to offer a rather limited service which may nevertheless still be of value in this field. Provided that the search required can be a reasonably limited one (say to a diagnosis, or group of diagnoses or to a restricted age group, etc.) we would be prepared to have an alphabetical listing of hospital admissions made in the appropriate group and to link manually with lists provided by research workers.

Secondly, because we want to operate the scheme on real data as soon as possible we would welcome requests from research workers for details of hospital discharges and deaths occurring during 1967 or later. In other words even though the service is not working yet, prospective studies can be planned now, with record linkage in mind, provided the worker is prepared to risk failure on our part. My present hope is to have programmes working in early 1969, and for the data then to be retrospectively available from 1st January, 1967.

DISCUSSION

Dr T. Meade : I wonder if I could raise the problem of the quality of the material that is linked, which Dr Heasman touched on just now in connection with the question of matching. The quality of this material depends largely on the accuracy with which doctors complete various documents. Dr Heasman has himself done a great deal of work in this field.

With Dr Acheson's permission, Dr Alderson and I were able to assess the accuracy of recording on Death Certificates and Hospital Inpatient Summary Sheets in the Oxford Record Linkage Study Area. We found, in a sample of patients dying in hospital in 1962, that there were errors in the recording of the Principal Condition Treated in Hospital in 13 per cent. of cases. We really did lean over backwards to be as lenient as possible in deciding whether or not an error had been made. Thus we excluded all cases in which there was any possible doubt, and only attributed the term ' error ' to those cases in which, for example, obvious underlying causes had been omitted or in which unequivocal mistakes had been made for some reason that was not apparent.

The situation for Death Certificates was rather worse—there were errors in the recording of the Underlying Cause of Death in 22 per cent. of cases—and we have every reason to believe, as I am sure everyone here will agree, that the level of accuracy of recording in the Oxford Record Linkage Study area is probably as high as anywhere in the country. As might be expected we found that accuracy varied a great deal according to the condition involved. Errors were very much less frequent in cases of malignant disease than they were in cases of cardiovascular disease, for example. We were hearing yesterday about the effects in genetic studies of a relatively low percentage of miss-matches in terms of follow-up over three or four generations, and I wonder if Dr Heasman could say something about the effect that these rather high levels of error might have on the use that could be made of linked data from medical records.

Dr M. Heasman : I think the first point which I would like to make here is that I am only too well aware that the quality of the data of these national schemes is not good, but I don't think it is going to improve until we get a feed-back which is seen to be useful to the consultants who basically are responsible for producing it in the first place. The sooner we can get that, the sooner the quality of the data will improve. But for the sort of thing that I was considering this morning, I think the primary use that I see here will be to inform workers in the field that ' Mr. Smith has been in hospital again '. They may get a clue as to the diagnosis but if they really want accurate data they will have to go back to the clinical notes. I don't think you can expect too much from this, using the national data only. Nevertheless I hope that it will provide sufficient clues in some instances to avoid having to go back to clinical notes.

Miss Jones : May I say how interested I have been in Dr Heasman's description of what he is going to do in Scotland, precisely because he is not linking on a number. But I should like if I may just to say a word or two about the common number and its relation to epidemiology in general.

My Ministry is sympathetic towards this question of a common number but each of the numbers now in use has a function to perform. It is impossible for any Ministry to surrender the number it uses and adopt another one designed for a different purpose if that number will not fulfil the function for which its own number is designed. The National Insurance number is designed to allow an enormous volume of claims to benefit to be handled speedily. We receive about 10 million claims for sickness benefit, for example, in the course of a year. We may have half a million, in an influenza epidemic, in one week. It is essential that our National Insurance number shall be a number which allows us to allocate that half million claims to 100 ledger sections without letting any one of the ledger sections be overwhelmed.

The other function, obviously, is to allow us to do longitudinal studies—they are not longitudinal studies of health, they are longitudinal studies of a person's earnings over their lifetime, and the resultant pension entitlement which they have built up. This means that we must be able to use the number to match one year's record against the next, to match records essentially prepared for income tax to records which are designed for insurance.

I don't think it is generally realized that in this country there is a common number system between the Ministry of Social Security and the Inland Revenue. The Inland Revenue adopted the National Insurance number for their records because we are collecting contributions on the same form. This means that it lessens the freedom to alter the number. It means that any change has to be a matter of slow negotiation.

In a sense the wider the interest in common numbers, the more difficult it becomes to arrive at a common number because each of these numbers is functional, each one has to be designed for the purpose it has got to serve. That is, I think, the main difficulty, but if I could end on a rather more cheerful note, again more directly perhaps from the point of view of epidemiology, Professor Case talked about prospective longitudinal studies related to the use of dangerous materials. It is precisely this linking of records between ourselves and Inland Revenue which has meant that the names of employees become available to us in a different form from the way in which they came to us up to 1961. Since 1961 we have had a record on microfilm of an employer's employees, in batches, coming in each year. This opens up possibilities of helping with the sort of research described by Professor Case and Dr Newcombe over a wider area.

258

At the present time if any doctor who is doing research into the effects of particular chemicals needs help in establishing a cohort for a longitudinal study, I think it would be very much easier for us to give it now than it was a few years ago.

PART 6

SESSION ON GENETICS

Chairman : Dr J. A. FRASER ROBERTS (London)

GENEALOGICAL LINKAGE OF RECORDS IN TWO ISOLATE POPULATIONS*

VICTOR A. MCKUSICK and HAROLD E. CROSS

RECORDS linked genealogically have been collected in two Old Order Amish communities which represent about one-third of all members of this inbred sect, living in the United States and Ontario. Collection of data on all Amish, numbering about 50,000, is now under way.

The records have had two areas of use : demographic and genetic. The initial step has been collection of a complete census by family units, recording for all individuals date of birth (and death) and date of marriage. For living individuals all offspring living or dead are recorded as well as deceased spouses. These data for one community, that of Holmes County, Ohio, have been subjected to intensive demographic analysis (Cross, 1967). Age at marriage, number of children, sex ratio, birth interval and rate of twinning are some of the factors examined. A comparison with other Amish demes will be undertaken when the data have been assembled in the form used in Holmes County.

A second step has been assemblage of a total genealogy. By total genealogy is meant a tracing of ancestors, as completely as possible and as far back as possible, for each member of a defined population. In the case of closed populations, to which almost no new blood has been added since the founding (the American Old Order Amish answer this description), the total genealogy aims for completeness back to the immigrants. Since the Amish began arriving in America about 1725, such a total genealogy must consist of at least 10 generations.

The two populations for which total genealogies have thus far been assembled are the Lancaster County (Pennsylvania) Amish and the Holmes County (Ohio) Amish. Evidence that these represent separate demes is provided by their history, difference in the frequency of rare recessives, differences in family names and blood group differences.

* David R. Bolling, who directs the computer activities in the Division of Medical Genetics, deserves much credit for implementation of the computer applications described here. The work referred to here was supported in part by a training grant (GM 795) and in part by a research programme grant (GM 10189) from the National Institute of General Medical Sciences.

The genealogic file begins with the complete census. The information on each person constitutes a unit record which contains the name, birth, death and marriage dates, and unique serial numbers of the individual as well as those of the spouse and parents. Although computer usage of this file is restricted to the serial numbers, the addition of full names and dates is useful for reference and accuracy checks with published genealogical sources. This file has proved useful for both hand and computer construction of pedigrees. We have a programme for example, which will list ancestors as follows :

    1 father
    2 mother
    11 paternal grandfather
    12 paternal grandmother

    121111 father of father of father of father
        of mother of father of proband.

The uses to which the total genealogies are being put include the following :

1. Calculation of coefficients of consanguinity ;

2. Determination of the common ancestors of parents of persons with rare recessive disorders ;

3. *A priori* estimation of the contribution of each founder to the present gene pool ;

4. Estimation of the minimal degree of identity by descent of the Ohio and Pennsylvania gene pools.

Mange's programme for estimation of the coefficient of consanguinity (Mange, 1964 *a*, *b*) has been modified to remove the limitation of six generations. Our programme is presently capable of constructing pedigrees up to 12 generations using a genealogical file limited to a maximum of 9999 persons. The latter restriction will soon be removed, since the complete genealogical file now being constructed on all Amish in North America will consist of at least 60,000 individuals. The programme uses as input the parental serial numbers of each individual to construct the appropriate pedigrees of any number of probands and determines their consanguinity by searching for identical serial numbers among the ancestors in both the mother's and father's sides. Output consists of the printed pedigree (containing the serial numbers of the ancestors), the cumulative percentage completeness of the pedigree for each generation, the cumulative coefficient of consanguinity in each generation, the

264

common ancestors together with their contribution to the total consanguinity, and if desired, the sex-linked coefficient of consanguinity. By using the appropriate probands, it is possible to estimate mean coefficients of relationship for the entire deme, for separate church districts and for the whole deme (*i.e.* how closely related, on the average, is each person to all other persons ?). This can be separately calculated for males and females.

In a closed population such as the Amish with a limited number of founders, when an ordinarily rare recessive is found it is likely that only one of the founding fathers carried the given gene. This being the case, both parents of all homozygotes should trace their ancestry to one founder couple. (Of course, the tendency for sibs and other close relatives to migrate together increases the likelihood that more than one founder was heterozygous.) A programme was written to find the common ancestors of parents of recessive homozygotes. This programme also uses the parental numbers in the genealogical file as input and provides us not only with a list of all ancestors related to each parent, but summarizes the number of genealogical paths to each ancestor and the number of parents related to each ancestor. The hypothesis of recessive inheritance is strengthened when a single common ancestor is demonstrable.

Although originally done by hand, the demonstrations that all parents of persons with pyruvate kinase deficiency haemolytic anaemia (Bowman, McKusick & Dronamraju, 1965) trace their descent from ' Strong Jacob ' Yoder and his wife (imm. 1744) (Fig. 1), and that all parents of persons with the Ellis-van Creveld syndrome (Mckusick, Egeland *et al.*, 1964) (Fig. 2) trace their descent from Samuel King (imm. 1742) but that all parents of cases of cartilage-hair hypoplasia (Mckusick, Eldridge *et al.*, 1965) cannot be traced to a single ancestral couple, illustrate the use of the method. Once the common ancestral couple has been identified, the computer provides the information for drawing complicated pedigrees such as the one which has been published for the Ellis-van Creveld syndrome (McKusick, Egeland *et al.*, 1964). We are currently examining what founder couples are shared in common by persons with diabetes mellitus and the parents of such persons in the Lancaster community. Efforts are being made to adapt the existing genealogy programmes to print entire pedigrees without manual intervention.

About one-fourth of the Lancaster County Amish carry the name Stoltzfus (McKusick, Hostetler & Eldridge, 1964). Only one man of this surname was among the founders, Nikolas Stoltzfus, who immigrated in 1766. Obviously he contributed disproportionately

265

to the present gene pool. One can ask, calculating on the basis that either parent contributes 50 per cent. of the autosomal genes of the offspring, what is the contribution of each founder to the genes of each individual in the present population? Averaging these

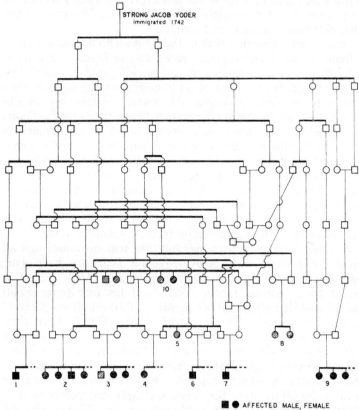

FIG. 1. Pedigree of Amish pyruvate kinase deficient haemolytic anaemia cases. The hypothesis of recessive inheritance is strengthened by the fact that all parents of homozygotes can be traced to the same ancestral couple, 'Strong' Jacob Yoder and his wife. Although complicated, the pedigree relates to only 26 of the 33 affected sibships.

values we arrive at stochastic estimates of the origins of the present gene pool.

How do the contributions of the several founders so calculated compare with the name count? How does the contribution estimated

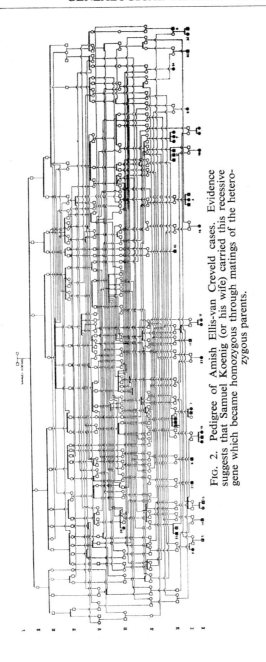

FIG. 2. Pedigree of Amish Ellis-van Creveld cases. Evidence suggests that Samuel Koenig (or his wife) carried this recessive gene which became homozygous through matings of the heterozygous parents.

for Samuel King and his wife compare with the present frequency of the Ellis-van Creveld gene (about 0·07) which is thought to have been introduced by one of them ? These calculations can be made for both Amish demes. The two demes which have been under most intensive study thus far (Lancaster Co., Pa. and Holmes Co., O.), although largely distinct, have some low-frequency names in common and some of these derive from single founders. The computer can provide a minimal estimate of the proportion of the two gene pools identical by descent.

It will be necessary in these calculations to define carefully the present gene pool. It may prove most useful to consider five or 10 year cohorts according to date of birth. Once the total genealogy has been assembled and the programmes written, the contribution of each founder to each cohort's gene pool over the last two centuries can be determined.

When we find that all parents of persons with a given presumed recessive trace back to a given founder couple, we, of course, like to know the probability that this would be found for randomly selected persons in the population. This we can determine from the computerized genealogy.

We plan a third file in which medical, blood group, sociological and other data will be kept in connection with the unique number of each individual.

In summary, we have a file with complete census and vital statistic data on about 18,000 Old Order Amish. A second file contains the total genealogy of these individuals which extends back 10 to 12 generations to the immigrants. These two files have been useful for demographic and genetic studies and we plan to extend them to include all living Old Order Amish. Future plans call for the construction of a third file with medical and other data.

REFERENCES

Bowman, H. S., McKusick, V. A. & Dronamraju, K. R. (1965). Pyruvate kinase deficient hemolytic anemia in an Amish isolate. *Am. J. hum. Genet.* **17**, 1–8.

Cross, H. E. (1967). Genetic Studies in an Amish Isolate. Ph.D. Thesis. Johns Hopkins University.

McKusick, V. A., Egeland, J. A., Eldridge, R. & Krusen, D. E. (1964). Dwarfism in the Amish. I. The Ellis-van Creveld Syndrome. *Bull. Johns Hopkins Hosp.* **115**, 306.

McKusick, V. A., Eldridge, R., Hostetler, J. A., Ruangwit, U. & Egeland, J. A. (1965). Dwarfism in the Amish II. Cartilage-hair hypoplasia. *Bull. Johns Hopkins Hosp.* **116**, 285.

McKusick, V. A., Hostetler, J. A. & Eldridge, R. (1964). The distribution of certain genes in the Old Order Amish. Cold Spring Harbor Symp. *Quant. Biol.* **29**, 99.

MANGE, A. P. (1964 a). Growth and inbreeding of a human isolate. *Hum. Biol.* **36**, 104.

MANGE, A. P. (1964 b). Fortran programs for computing Wright's coefficient of inbreeding in human and non-human pedigrees. *Am. J. hum. Genet.* **16**, 484.

DISCUSSION

Dr Stevenson : This is a remarkable example of a splendid opportunity splendidly accepted : a splendid opportunity because there is this community, who are unique in that they are an isolate in the genetic sense to all intents and purposes, yet are educated people and although peculiar accept modern medical care and modern diagnostic facilities. As we have heard not one but two populations have already been investigated.

I don't think there is very much really to be said about the findings in the study. They have been published and most geneticists are familiar with them and full of admiration for the work that has been done. The genetic findings on the whole are as expected, but nature only yields answers to properly posed questions and here the questions have been properly posed, giving a unique opportunity for developing a methodology of multi-generation linkage on a relatively simple basis.

Dr Fraser Roberts : I am sure there must be some questions for discussion, though I must say that the whole thing has been so beautifully done that many of the questions are answered already.

Dr Carter : Could I ask Dr Cross what in fact was the probability that he would have got a random group of half a dozen men back to a common ancestor. Has he worked that out ?

Dr H. Cross : I wish I could answer your question because I am curious about this myself, but the genealogy was completed only about three months ago and a lot of things remain to be done. We don't have the answer to your question at this time.

Mr Carpenter : I am very interested in this study. I was wondering the other day whether it is possible to trace in these records the percentage of names that had died out, because it is a nice example of a branching process. About 200 people come in and some of the names will die out, depending on the proportion of births per head. In theory the sizes of the other families will be normally distributed. I wonder if it would be possible to investigate this from these data.

Dr H. Cross : I think it would be rather difficult to do this, the reason being that the genealogical sources which are available now are primarily those of the majority of the descendants of a few immigrants rather than the complete composition of a single community as it existed at sometime in the past. The only data we have on this concerns the Holmes county Amish community which was previously studied in 1956. A complete tabulation of all surnames in the community at that time was compared with the frequency of surnames in 1965. Unfortunately this involves only a 10-year span so that relatively little change can be expected. Two names disappeared completely, but these represented only 0·26 per cent. of the population in 1956. Seven new names were added, representing migrants from other Amish groups. I should add that new names are always Amish since the Amish do not proselytize. No good census data are available for any Amish community prior to 1956.

Dr Edwards : There are two questions I would like to ask. One is this, has it been possible to find any case of familial infertility, that is brothers or sisters who were married but childless without adequate cause ? Secondly, could I question the statement that you would expect one individual to bring in all these recessives? I wonder if you have formally considered whether you would expect that. From the way boat-loads were likely to have been selected I would expect *a priori* either several heterozygotes or none, and that one heterozygote per boat would not be the modal number.

Dr H. Cross : With regard to your first question, again this is something we are studying at present. We do have fertility data on all couples but we haven't yet looked at familial aspects of sterility. With regard to the immigrant pattern, there are several instances in the Holmes county community where we found several immigrant couples who were common to all the parents of homozygotes. These couples always involve sibs or closely related individuals. As I mentioned, there is an expected tendency for related families to migrate as a unit. Immigration records are too inadequate to determine how frequently this occurred.

FURTHER STUDIES ON RECORD LINKAGE FROM PARISH BOOKS

I. Barrai, A. Moroni and L. L. Cavalli-Sforza

Our project for record linking is aimed at building the pedigree of an entire human population. As human geneticists, we feel acutely that the knowledge of the level of inbreeding is a necessary condition for testing hypotheses about gene and genotype frequencies. It would be idle to discuss if inbreeding is a consequence of isolation, or if isolation follows inbreeding. Of course, one may well visualize situations in which geographical isolation is the direct cause of inbreeding ; but in our species geographical isolation is only a factor in the complex interplay of variables which determine the level of consanguinity in a population. Caste systems produce in some cultures an almost complete isolation between groups which live in the same area.

When, several years ago, we undertook the project of building the pedigree of the population living in the high Parma Valley, we were confident that the task might be performed within a reasonable number of years. As far as the present is concerned, our confidence is supported by the results we have obtained in the first phases of the project. These results are of interest in so far as they give information on the reproductive performance of a rather stable human group for a period of more than 300 years, more than 10 generations. However, we have not yet reached our main goal, which is the construction of the pedigree of the population. At present we have the data in sibship groups each covering only one generation ; the next step is to link the records of the individual to his mother and father. Then the actual building of the pedigree of any individual will be a matter of computer time and computer size.

The data from which we started are the records contained in the parish books of 26 parishes of the high Parma Valley, in northern Italy. From 1545 (in some cases from earlier times), the parish priests register in three separate books the births, the marriages and the deaths of the people living in their parishes. Details of the type of records and discussion on their reliability was given in a previous report (Barrai *et al.*, 1965).

The records were transcribed on cards of standard format, whose alphabetical parts were coded numerically, and the whole numerical record was punched on cards. The cards were translated into magnetic tape, which is the standard input medium for the programmes.

The birth/deaths linkage

Our first step was the linkage of death records with baptism records. This process should generate the life span for every individual represented in the file of the deaths, since there is an excess of birth registrations over death registrations, so that one would expect that most, if not all, of the deaths should be linked to the corresponding birth. The death records which have not been identified are expected to result in individuals immigrated into the area. However, the identification rate between deaths and births depends on migration

271

between the area and the outside region, as well as of the completeness of the records which are tested for linkage.

We processed about 70,000 births and 35,000 deaths ; the number of birth records being almost exactly double the number of death records on which age at death was recorded. Of course, the births include people living now, and deaths include individuals born before the beginning of the registrations ; so that the excess is in part justified ; but the living population of the area under observation was not larger than 10,526 at the 1951 census. Considering that we did not use for linkage a group of 3,800 deaths cards on which the age at death was not declared, we are still confronted with 20,000 births inside the area for which only emigration or lack of death registration can account. This would make an emigration rate of 29 per cent. as an average for the whole period.

The identification rate may be examined as a function of the age of the records. The linkage is assigned to a period according to the date of birth. It may be observed that the identification rate is very low, only 25 per cent. of the death records, for individuals born before 1600. However, it increases rapidly in the successive periods, and it reaches a maximum in the period between 1851 and 1900 ; 80 per cent. of the dead individuals presumed to be born within that interval were linked with a registered birth. The average identification rate for the whole period for which records exist is just below 70 per cent., namely 69·7 per cent. (Fig. 1).

The reasons for an increase in the rate of linkage with time are to be sought in the quality of the records on the actual books. The books are handwritten in Latin by the priests, and some are more than 350 years old. Their legibility depends on their age, and on the handwriting style of a particular period. It is not surprising that the rate of identification increases with the more recent books.

Linkage into sibships of birth and death records

After the linkage between births and deaths, we generated a master file with essentially three types of records. The first type is made of the unlinked births, for which no corresponding death was found in the file of deaths. The second type is made of the birth–death linkages, and the third type is constituted by the unlinked deaths. The distribution of the three types of records in the master file is as follows :

Unlinked births	45,297
Linkages	24,397
Unlinked deaths	10,626

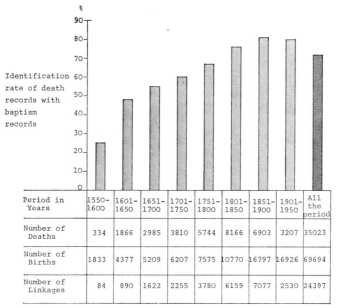

Identification rate of death records with baptism records

Period in Years	1550-1600	1601-1650	1651-1700	1701-1750	1751-1800	1801-1850	1851-1900	1901-1950	All the period
Number of Deaths	334	1866	2985	3810	5744	8166	6903	3207	35023
Number of Births	1833	4377	5209	6207	7575	10770	16797	16926	69694
Number of Linkages	84	890	1622	2255	3780	6159	7077	2530	24397

FIG. 1.

– Deaths–Baptisms Linkage –
The Linkages are assigned to the period according to
the date of birth in the baptism record

The file was printed for reference, and resulted in 13 volumes of about 400 pages each. In the master file the records are sorted for family and year of birth. All the individuals belonging to one family should be represented in the sequence characterized by the name of the family. The master file was used for the sib-sib linkage, namely for the creation of sibships belonging to one family. The criteria used for inclusion in the sibship of an individual under processing were the agreement on family name, on father's name, and on mother's names. The criteria for exclusion were the absence of agreement on the said items, and the date of birth removed by more than 30 years from the birth of the first sib.

The results of the linkage between sibs is more satisfactory than the birth–death linkage. The rate of identification is 87 per cent. over all the period ; it has a minimum of 78 per cent. in the years before 1600, and a maximum of about 96 per cent. in the period between 1851 and 1900. Since 1900, the rate of linkage has decreased to only 70 per cent. (Fig. 2). The explanation we offer for the high rate of

T

273

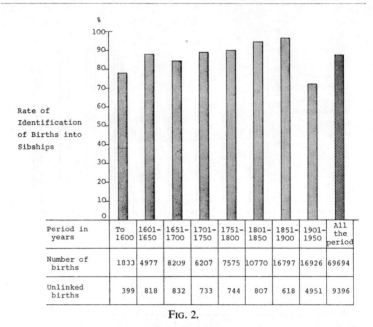

Fig. 2.

– Sib sib Linkage –
The sibships are assigned to a period according to the
year of birth of the first born.

linkage between sibs in the period to 1900, is that for each period the birth records are very similar in information content to each other. Contrary to what happens in the death records, the name of the mother is always present, and very often after 1700 her family name is also given ; it is not surprising then that the identification rate should be so superior if compared to the death–birth linkage rate. The decrease observed in the period 1901–50 is most probably due to the increase of families with single births, or to incomplete families, since living individuals are included in the sample.

If we assume that all sibs were linked together, the unlinked births in the periods before 1900 should represent the sibships of size one ; however, it is possible because of false linkages, that some individuals belonging to multiple sibship were included in the single births. The average sibship size (Fig. 3) was computed for each of the eight periods of 50 years in which the data are subdivided. Intervals of time of this length were used to minimize random sampling errors.

We may observe that the average sibship size increased up to 1900, with an exception in the period 1651–1700 in which a slight

Mean and variance

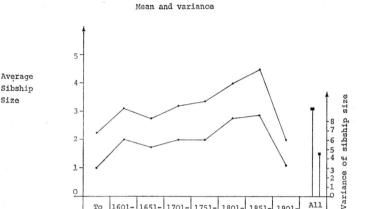

Average
Sibship
Size

FIG. 3.

Variation of Sibship Size in 8 Periods
of Fifty Years

decrease was observed. In the second half of the 19th century the sibship size reached a maximum average of 4·44 sibs per family ; the variances of sibship size increase proportionally as the means increase, so that the square of the variation coefficient, which is indicated by Crow (1958) as a measure of the selection differential due to fertility, shows little variation. In the first half of the present century, a sudden decrease is observed, and the average sibship size falls down to 2·06 sibs per family, with a decrease in the variance. The decrease in variance is smaller than the decrease in the mean, since the coefficient of variation of sibship size is highest in this period. This is what could be expected if a fraction of the married couples started planning the size of the family in the first half of this century ; in such cases, there would be an excess of families with a small size, which would skew the distribution of family size increasing its variance as compared to the mean.

Further, the effect would be inflated by the fact that some of the families have not reached their full size at this moment. It would thus be risky to assume that at the present time the opportunities for selection due to fertility differentials are in fact increased. Part at least of the increase in variance would be the consequence of social stratification, therefore not heritable, and invalid for evolutionary considerations. Actually, if the hypothesis of effective planning of family size will hold, one is to expect that the selection differential

275

due to fertility will decrease, leaving differential mortality as the most effective agent of selection. In the extreme instance, if all families were of the same size in terms of children born, differential mortality and nuptiality would be the only selective agents left.

Variation of birth interval

From the birth records, linked into sibships it was possible to compute the average birth interval in completed families. For each period of 50 years, the average birth interval was computed ; no great variation with time was observed. There is a tendency for the birth interval to decrease in the more recent periods ; still, the trend is not significant. All the sibships were then pooled together, and the resulting variation is given in Figure 4, where the overall mean of

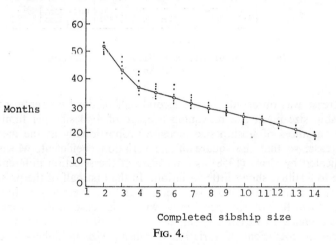

Completed sibship size

Fig. 4.

Average Interval Between Births
Each point is an average over a period of 50 years
1551 — 1950

the period is plotted together with the means for the single periods. As expected, there is an inverse relationship between sibship size and average birth interval ; families with two children have an average interval of 52 months, and families of 14 have an average interval of 19·1 months. The decrease is faster between the second and the third birth, and between the third and the fourth ; after the fourth birth, the decrease of birth interval is practically linear. It is not impossible that the deviation from linearity of the two first intervals may be due to spurious linkages. In fact, Kuchemann, Boyce and Harrison (1967)

276

found an average birth interval between first and second child of about 41 months, as compared to 52 months in our families ; and, since after the fourth birth our data can almost be superimposed on those of Kuchemann, Boyce and Harrison, it may well be that we have an excess of spurious linkages in the families of small size, unless the difference is due to a real difference in the reproductive performances of the populations being compared.

The average birth interval depends not only on the size of the completed sibship, but also on birth rank. In Figure 5, we have

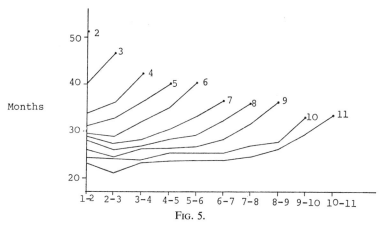

FIG. 5.

Average Birth Interval Between Successive Births
in Families of Different Size

plotted the average birth intervals between successive births in families of constant size ; it may be seen that there is a trend for birth interval to increase with birth rank. One feature of the variation of average birth interval as a function of birth rank, is that, starting from families with six children the interval between the second and the third-born is the minimum interval.

The dependence of birth interval on birth rank and sibship size may be studied, as far as the linear components are concerned, with a multiple regression. We regressed birth interval, I, on birth rank, B, and sibship size, S. The regression obtained is the following, in days :

$$I = 1514 \cdot 8 + 60 \cdot 4 \, B - 117 \cdot 7 \, S$$

Namely, an increase of one unit in birth rank increases the birth interval by 60·4 days, and an increase of one unit in sibship size decreases birth interval by 117·7 days.

277

Seasonal variation of births and marriages

One interesting product of the processing of the records is the marked seasonal pattern of some events. In the graphs of Figure 6, the monthly variation of marriages and births, in periods of one century, is given. It may be seen that before 1800 most marriages took place

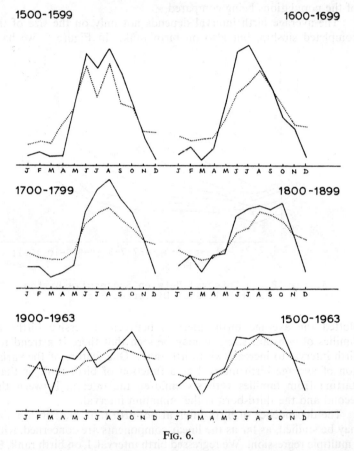

FIG. 6.

in the period May–October, with a maximum nuptiality in the summer months ; after 1800, the rate of nuptiality still maintains the same features, but a sizable fraction of marriages takes place in the period November–April. After 1900, the distribution of nuptiality rates shows four relative maxima, in February, April, June, and October. However, the distribution shows a tendency to become

278

rectangular which could be explained by the disappearance of the factors which possibly determined the low winter rate and the high summer rate. Since the high Parma Valley is cold in winter, environmental factors could have adversely affected the rate of marriages in this period when defence from cold was difficult ; further, winter and early spring are periods in which religious tradition dissuades from marriages ; the Lent period is an example of such an affect. During 1800, the influences of the French revolution begin to be felt even in this secluded area, and there is the appearance of marriages in periods which traditionally were unfavourable ; and the protection against cold afforded by technical progress in the present century, together with the abandonment of tradition, disrupts the seasonality observed in the previous centuries.

In Figure 6, the seasonal birth rate is superimposed on the nuptiality rate. The births are plotted eight months before their actual happening, presumably around the conception time. There is a strict correlation between the rates of birth plotted in this way, and the nuptiality rates. One hypothesis that could be entertained to explain such a finding, would be that the first birth is correlated with the time of marriage, and since our average family size is 3·01, about one-third of the births are first-born ; but, to entertain this hypothesis on a more firm basis, we still lack the average interval between date of marriage and date of the first birth, which will be available after the linkage between marriages and births. Were this interval of the same order of length as a pregnancy, the hypothesis could be accepted *pro tempore*. Otherwise the clustering of conceptions during the summer months may be due to other causes.

In the present century, the distribution of seasonal birth rate is almost rectangular, and births—as well as marriages—tend to become independent of seasonality.

SUMMARY

The product of record linkage from parish books may give relevant information for demographic and genetic studies. Baptism records were linked into sibships, and permitted the study of the variation in sibship size in a period of time covering about four centuries in the population of the high Parma Valley, in northern Italy. The average birth interval was also studied ; it was found that average birth interval tends to decrease with sibship size and to increase with birth rank. It was also found that there has been, in the past centuries, a very high seasonality of marriages and of births ;

279

such seasonality, which follows the same patterns until the end of 1800, is completely disrupted in the first half of the present century.

ACKNOWLEDGMENT : This work was carried out at the International Laboratory of Genetics and Biophysics (Pavia Section) under the Association Euratom-C.N.R.-C.N.E.N. Contract 012-61-12 BIAI and U.S.A.E.C. Contract AT (30-1)-2280.

REFERENCES

BARRAI, I., CAVALLI-SFORZA, L. L. & MORONI, A. (1965). Record linkage from parish books. *Mathematics and Computer Science in Biology and Medicine*, pp. 51–60. Medical Research Council.

CROW, J. F. (1958). Some possibilities for measuring selection intensities in man. *Hum. Biol.* **30**, 1–13.

KUCHEMANN, C. F., BOYCE, A. J. & HARRISON, G. A. (1967). A demographic and genetic study of a group of Oxfordshire villages. *Hum. Biol.*, **39**, 251–276.

DISCUSSION

Dr Nevin : Professor Barrai and his colleagues are most fortunate in having records of such quality. Although retrospective studies are thwarted by many difficulties and are usually viewed with some scepticism, the experience of this group in applying computer techniques to construct a pedigree for the whole population of those living in the Valley of Parma by linking records of births, marriages and deaths, though not completed, has already been extremely profitable. Their results provide data of interest to demographers and human geneticists concerned with family patterns, fertility, consanguinity and the structure of populations.

Of particular interest is the change in family size, increasing to a maximum of 4·44 sibs per family in the latter part of the nineteenth century, followed by a dramatic decrease in family size to 2·06 sibs in the early 1900's. The explanation for this, as has already been suggested, may be the increasing practice at that period of family limitation. In this country the spread of family limitation resulting in a two-child norm occurred about this period in the late 1920's and the early 1930's. Also of particular interest is the relationship of average birth interval with sibship size. Looking at the graph, after the fourth birth the relationship is almost a linear one and the deviation from this linear relationship for the earlier births is possibly the result of false linkages.

I should like to raise one or two questions. In your introduction you mention that one of the prime motivations for this work was the estimate of the rate and coefficient of inbreeding within this population. In testing hypotheses about a population it is essential to know the coefficient of inbreeding of the individuals and the accuracy of this depends on the number of generations in a pedigree. When you take into account the more remote generations, is there any difference from the coefficient of inbreeding already estimated for the recent ones, and secondly, as might be expected, does the rate of consanguinity differ in the 26 parishes ? One would expect it to be possibly greater in the more remote parishes. Somewhat related to this question is the problem of fertility in marriages. Is there any differences in marriages between individuals within a parish and those in which the mate comes from outside that particular parish ?

Professor Barrai : We are trying to build the pedigree of the population isolated in the mountains of the Parma River Valley, in order to estimate the contribution of remote consanguinity to the inbreeding coefficient. At present we have no data on the problem because we need the complete pedigree to assess what is the relative importance of remote consanguinity and of recent consanguinity on the determination of the true level of inbreeding. As far as the variation of the consanguinity level between parishes goes, we only know about the recent consanguinity and the variation is not high. This, however, refers to the recent component of inbreeding. I think that we shall only be able to answer all these questions if we are able to build the pedigree of the whole population.

Dr Carter : The average family size of about two in recent years of course is to be expected, but I was fascinated to see average family size back in the sixteenth century was also about two, and I wondered what caused this. Was this due to family planning or was it that the mothers were dying about the age of 30, by which time they only had about two children.

Professor Barrai : A family size of about two is just the minimum one would have expected to maintain a population of constant size. It is a growing population so that the family size of two in the earlier period is probably due to false linkages or to the possibility of the presence of half-sibs that are given only as single families because of the death of either of the parents and successive remarriage. A family size of two in the 1600's is too small for this population which is in fact growing.

Dr H. Cross : I was particularly interested in the plots of birth order versus birth interval. The Amish curves are quite different from those which Professor Barrai has shown ; in fact they are almost exponential and can be straightened on a log graph. Similarly plotted graphs for the Hutterites, another inbred group who similarly forbid contraception, do not resemble those of either the Amish or

281

the Italians. I am wondering how much of this may be due to family planning and how much may be due to biological variation. Groups with different ethnic backgrounds differ in their genotype and perhaps some variation in birth intervals is due to genetic causes. Social causes must be ruled out, but as the data accumulate it may be possible to pinpoint the relative contribution of these factors.

Professor Barrai : Of course it is very difficult to interpret birth intervals correctly from a genetical viewpoint and so I think there is plenty of work to be done on this particular aspect.

Dr Brimblecombe : Could I ask if there is any information about changes in custom over distinctions between perinatal deaths ? Any changes in ways of deciding between stillbirths or babies who might possibly have lived a day or so and then died ? Is there any information on the customs in say the sixteenth century or of changes up to the present time ?

Professor Barrai : There is not much variation until present times. There is a decrease which is very dramatic in this last 50 years but the perinatal death rate stays fairly constant through the first 300 years.

THE INTERPRETATION OF PEDIGREE DATA

J. H. EDWARDS

' YOU try to see the tree as a whole, I try to examine it leaf by leaf. The general run of historians try to take the tree branch by branch : and you and I agree that this last approach, at any rate, is an unpromising one.'

Namier to Toynbee (Toynbee, 1967)

Record linking allows the connecting together of events recorded at different times relating to one individual, and extends the field of research from associations between the observations of one observer at one time to those of many observers at many times. This is a fundamental advance in approach and comparable to the advance from the hunter to the farmer, or from the hook to the net.

Some events, such as marriage and birth, relate pairs or trios of individuals and may be used as connecting links, or branching points, between records of individuals. This requires linking not only across

FIG. 1. *Basic data for medical research*

FIG. 1. Representation of types of data available for numerical inference, with a sibship defined by parental identity.

	Civic Data				Medical Data				
Propositus Iden. B.D.	Mother Iden. B.D.	Father Iden. B.D.	Date	Markers I J K L	Variates A B C D	States P Q R S	Events p q r s	Environment w x y z	
XXX XXX	XXX XXX	XXX XXX	XXX XXX XXX	0 1 1 + +	107 55	1	+ (q)	A 6	112
XXX XXX	" "	" "	XXX XXX XXX	0 2 2 + +	213 73			B 7	12
XXX XXX	" "	" "	XXX XXX XXX	1 + +	112 11	2	+ (s)		
XXX XXX	XXX XXX	XXX XXX	XXX XXX XXX	2 2 − +	170 28	3 1 1 2	+ (p)	19	67
XXX XXX	XXX XXX	XXX XXX	XXX XXX XXX	+	171 57 48	C 3	+ (r)	C	

283

time but across administrative boundaries with their defensive mists of untested legislation.

We may consider the basic records of both civic and medical data (Fig. 1) and some analyses which may be made from them (Figs. 2, 3). The civic data consist of birth with parental identity and are

FIG. 2. *Studies of unrelated individuals*

Observation I		Observation II				
		Markers I J K L	Variates A B C D	States P Q R S	Events p q r s	Environment w x y z
Markers	I J K L	Association	Association	Association. blood groups and disease	Association	Interaction. Isoagglutinins
Variates	A B C D		Correlations Cholesterol/ blood pressure	Cholesterol/ diabetes	Cholesterol/ coronary thrombosis	Cholesterol/ diet
States	P Q R S			Associations of disease Gastric and duodenal ulcers	Predisposition to disease Value of cervical smears	Bio assay Ca. and smoking Trials (T)
Events	p q r s					Bio assay Accidents Trials (P)
Environment	w x y z					
		Gene frequency	Population values	Incidence	Epidemics Registered data	

Some examples of inference found on pairs of observations
on individuals. T and P refer to therapeutic and prophylactic trials.

shown sorted under parentage (sibs are shown in the top three records). After birth various events may be recorded, relating to both the internal and external environment, some of which are suitable for coding. Those relating the internal environment naturally fall into the categories of markers (sex, blood groups, and other invariant characters capable of accurate definition) ; variates (height, birth weight, blood cholestorol etc., which may or may not show appreciable variation with time) ; states (conditions of appreciable duration, such as absence of evident neoplasia, presence of carcinoma of some organ, having had three children, etc.) and events (times of change of state, *e.g.* childbirth, haematemesis, apoplexy etc). Environmental data (place, work, calory intake, atmospheric

FIG. 3. *Studies of related individuals*

		Markers I J K L	Variates A B C D	States P Q R S	Events p q r s	Environment w x y z
Markers	I J K L	Linkage	Coherence	Association in families	Association in families	
Variates	A B C D		Heritability	Predisposition within families	Predisposition within families	
States	P Q R S			(Heritability)	(Heritability)	
Events	p q r s				(Heritability)	
Environment	w x y z					

Types of inference available from pedigrees formed from linked data.

pollution etc) may be categorized similarly. This distinction between states and events has been considered in detail in the context of cervical cytology by Knox (1966). Markers are particular types of states, but are conveniently considered separately in view of their simple genetical basis. The environment may also be experimentally defined as in the therapeutic trial. These data cover the whole of that subset of medical enquiry amenable to communication by coding or measuring ; that is, the whole subset available for numerical inference, which takes the form of cross comparisons of values in these categories at different times in the same individual, in different individuals, and in different individuals who are related.

This is not however the total numeric data available, for coded observations involve a time, and, if analogies are to be used for linkable documents, the frame of a cine film would seem closer than the pages of a book. The whole data should be seen as analogous to tracings on a smoked drum showing variables, states, and events drawn against time: the investigator just has odd fragments of this available and has to infer the sequence between the observations.

The important implication of this is that for n sets of observations there are $n(n-1)/2$ comparisons if the records are linked, but far fewer if analysis is limited to clusters of data within which investigations are limited. This carries the implication that both in genetical and other studies (and in complex disorders independent genetical and environmental enquiry is prodigal of both talent and money), the patrons of research must encourage the uneven distribution of such research as is suitable for coding, including surveys and trials. The massive documentation of limited populations exposed to linking procedures will provide economies of the order of $1/n$ where n is the number of factors available for accurate coding, a number now increasing exponentially.

Unfortunately, in this field of massive linked data relating to families our ability to generate data, through linking records, considerably exceeds our ability to analyse these records or to give informed advice on economic strategy in its collection.

There are two large fields of enquiry in which only record linking can make any contribution. Firstly that of population structure ; that is, the breeding habits of our ancestors as far back as records are available, perhaps as far as six generations in some communities, as Iceland, and further in some small and curious groups, such as religious sects and royal houses. This will give us the genetical background. Secondly we have the interpretation of disease patterns at the family level. Simply inherited disorders are adequately catalogued by casual methods, but more complex conditions, which include all the commoner disorders, require large numbers of propositi and their first and second degree relatives. The disruption of any complex of unlinked genetic factors at reproduction makes relatives separated by more than one or two meiotic events of little value, although cousinships are of value in conditions in which the uterine environment deserves serious consideration.

These studies on what we may term the physiology and the pathology of heredity are quite distinct, although operating upon the same basic data, and will be considered separately. The former

286

requires a few very large families, preferable one : the latter numerous family modules or units of, for example, parents and children, or, at most, of the descendants of great grandparents.

Although the principles involved in building up massive pedigrees from civic data are very simple, the optimal strategy for the storage of pedigrees involves serious problems, since in sexually reproducing organisms a pedigree can only be expressed in three dimensions, and the reduction of the data into a form suited to the one-dimensional nature of the computer's memory is particularly difficult, as may be seen in trying to describe a complex pedigree in words. One approach is by the use of modules of pedigrees which can be linked to one another. The larger the module the greater the storage requirement, a handicap compensated for by faster processing. In the study of simple trait segregation a sibship may be an adequate module. For genetic linkage the module should consist of four grandparents, two parents, and their children, although when linkage is close the grandparents are relatively uninformative. For studies of inbreeding the minimum operational module is at the great-grandparent level. No general solution is possible due to the dependence of optimal strategy on the computer used.

Although the whole pedigree cannot be represented in a direct way within the computer, the ability to reconstruct the whole pedigree by inference from the limited data necessary, the specification of parents, makes it possible to regard the entire pedigree of a region as taking the form of a vast crystal in which the events of birth are linked by the bonds of parentage. The analogy may be considered further.

In a population each birth may be represented as a point in three-dimensional space, the dimensions representing latitude, longitude and time (Fig. 4) ; further, if each point is connected to the two points which represent the parents, a structure consisting of points connected to two or more other points will be formed. This structure represents the population, and, although irregular, it can be specified to some extent by a few parameters.

Density parameters will define the population of births (number of points) in various volumes bounded by planes defined by places and times, or in various strata defining seasons. These are the traditional raw material of demography and will not be considered further.

Parameters defining structure are more difficult ; the structure has some crystalline properties defined by the constraints of generation times and numbers of parents and children, and, although very irregular, volumes including a million points or so may appear

287

similar in the same way as volumes of the universe containing a few million stars may appear to be similar.

As with the universe, the fundamental problem is to know if a stable and steady state exists, or whether the whole machine is running down, or otherwise set on a destructive course.

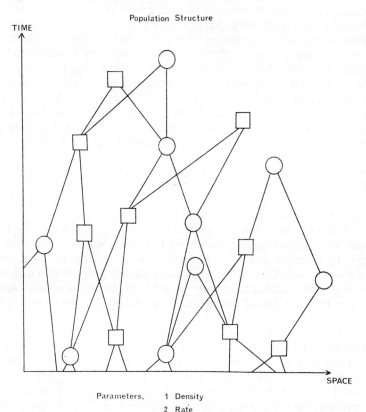

Population Structure

TIME

SPACE

Parameters, 1 Density
2 Rate
3 Valency correlation
4 Closeness

FIG. 4. Representation of a population as a molecular structure bonded by birth data.

This model also has the useful property that it can be inverted, in that we can consider the lines as the essential organisms and the nodes (that is, us) as mere places of meeting and reassortment. This gamete's eye view has many advantages, particularly in the mathematics of genetic linkage.

The simplest structural parameters, those relating only to the nodes and their immediate connections, are the generation time and the valency distribution, which, since the number of parents is fixed, is two plus a distribution representing the number of children. These parameters are not difficult to estimate, and may be obtained from data normally acquired at censuses.

The most important structural parameters in relation to gene flow are those relating the nodes to their neighbours ; firstly the distribution of valencies will probably be positively correlated between related nodes, relating to local clusters surrounded by less dense areas due to a positive correlation of the fertility of relatives. Little is known of these correlations, which are of great importance as, with increasing correlation, higher rates of change of gene frequencies will occur, as also will bigger fluctuations. These parameters may be regarded as those defining the branch structure of the crystal. A simple approximate procedure for estimating this correlation is to consider only one sex ; single sex pedigrees have a simpler branching structure and may be represented in two dimensions.

As well as a ' branch ' structure, such a crystal has a ' root ' strucure, and the extent to which the roots diverge before merging again in the common ancestral population determines the inbreeding. Although all roots are branches, not all branches are effective roots, due to not all births leading to births. The root structure determines the common pathways between any two points, and may be defined in terms of the inbreeding coefficient, which is a measure of the extent to which the roots merge to form a net.

The estimation of the degree of merging is most simply undertaken by either simple ancestor counting, and expressing the results in the form approximating to the binary series 2, 4, 8, which gives the ancestral number in an infinitive population with random mating, or by a Monte-Carlo approach in which a ' messenger ' is sent down the roots of a family tree, choosing a path at random and is then reflected up again from a stratum defining some earlier generation, again any choice being made at random. This procedure has some analogies to the exhibition of pattern by the exposure of complex molecules to photons, as in X-ray crystallography. In both cases the interpretation of the underlying structure from the pattern is far from simple. As in crystallography, analysis is likely to follow, rather than lead, the collection of suitable data.

In addition to providing data on the normal channels of flow of genes, the incorporation into such a population crystal of data relating to morbidity, mortality, and, genetic markers will allow estimates of :

1. The fertility of persons of differing genotype or probable genotype, and, indirectly, ' fitness ' in relation to specific alleles.

2. The elucidation of new genetic entities, including those causing sterility, by the detection of unusual families.

3. The estimation of associated segregation between markers, or, between traits and markers, from which genetic linkage may be estimated.

4. Evidence on the ' block ' inheritance of complex characters.

5. The estimation of the genetic contribution to diseases, allowing a quantitative study of diathesis.

The first three procedures are fairly obvious, although it is perhaps worth pointing out that, now that the automated analysis of blood and other tissues is practical, the systematic storing of blood, which is readily available from the ante-natal clinics, from the umbilical cord at birth, from donors, and from autopsies, will become the most economical procedure for mapping the human chromosomes. Although the precision of record linking procedures is probably inadequate for the study of disturbed segregation at single loci, this does not seriously disturb the estimation of dependent segregation of pairs of loci.

Although trait-trait linkage is probably valueless, I can see no formal objection to the study of linkage between defined markers and some variate such as intelligence, or hair colour, which might be predominantly related to loci on short chromosome segments.

One of the fundamental difficulties in the study of human disease is the difficulty in distinguishing unifactorial and multifactorial inheritance, and in estimating any tendency for a number of determining factors to segregate together. Where data are already available, as for example in school results, routine medical examination, etc. linking procedures may bring together relatives on a very large scale. Recent examples include linking blood pressures and haemoglobin levels to the civic records in Iceland, and obtaining school exam results on all children living in the same house, under the same name, with compatible ages and birth ranks, during five years in Birmingham.

A trait or character is said to segregate when several forms are recognized ; however, it is important to distinguish between purely semantic segregation, as in the definition of a minority by reference to some arbitrary threshold, such as is implied in tallness, mental deficiency, prematurity, or hyperglycaemia, and a true segregation in which the division into two or more classes is not dependent on any arbitary threshold, but due to a biological discontinuity in the distribution.

In the former case we may, to a first approximation, regard the determinants of the trait, or some metameter of it, to be normally distributed and the liability to be classified into the minority group as changing abruptly from zero to 100 per cent. at some threshold. In this case the distribution of the trait for all pairs of relatives defined by any specified relationship may be regarded as having a density distribution conforming to a bivariate normal surface, and the segregation ratios expected may be obtained by numerical integration of the tetrachoric functions, or by the use of tables. The functions are of some complexity, as is to be expected, since the distribution of any variate which is distributed normally in the population will not be distributed normally in the relatives of affected persons, a fact which has been overlooked in some solutions which have been proposed.

Various approximations are available, and, in the case of first degree relatives the approximation $s = p^{\frac{1}{2}}$ (Edwards, 1960) when s is the incidence in first degree relatives of those affected and p is the population incidence, is close, and may be used to provide the approximate estimate of hereditability, in the sense used by Falconer (1965) where the minority trait is not unduly rare (greater than 5 per cent.). Morton (1967) has compared these approaches by Falconer and myself ; as the former has a small systematic error, and the latter is only an approximation, such a comparison is difficult.

However, neither model covers the case in which the liability to manifestation increases smoothly, rather than suddenly, as might be expected in the manifestation of predispositions to most diseases or to such morphological variations as absence of a tooth or fusion-defects.

Since the iterative aptitudes of computers impose no serious restraints on analytical intransigence, we may consider some very simple parameters which, to a first approximation, appear to give meaningful measures of strength of inheritance.

Provided the liability to manifestation increases logarithmically with the underlying variant, the distribution of liability in the subgroup in which disease is manifest has a distribution which, if normal in the population, is also normal in the diseased subgroup.

Consider the simple case of a characteristic x, distributed normally with unit variance, and let the predisposition to manifestation be as^{bx}, then the proportion affected at any value of x will be

$$ae^{bx} . k\, e^{-\frac{1}{2}x^2} \text{ where } k = (\pi\, 2)^{-\frac{1}{2}}$$
$$= \; kae^{-\frac{1}{2}((x-b)^2 - b^2)}$$
$$= \; kae^{-\frac{1}{2}(x-b)^2} \quad e^{\frac{1}{2}b^2}$$

291

and this distribution will be normal, of unit variance, and its area, compared to the area of the population curve, will be $ae^{\frac{1}{2}b^2}$, which will be the population incidence of manifestation.

Since the distribution of x is normally distributed, its distribution in relatives, defined by their having a correlation coefficient r, will also be normally distributed, with unit variance, about the mean and mode, rb and, since this distribution will be exposed to the same liability ae^{bx} the distribution of affected relatives of affected individuals will be defined by

$$k \cdot e^{-\frac{1}{2}(x-br)^2} \cdot ae^{bx}$$
$$= ak\, e^{-\frac{1}{2}(x^2-2brx+b^2r^2-2bx)}$$
$$= ak\, e^{-\frac{1}{2}((x-b(r+1))^2-b^2(r+1)^2\,+\,b^2r^2)}$$
$$= ak\, e^{-\frac{1}{2}(x-b(r+1))^2} \cdot e^{rb^2} \cdot e^{\frac{1}{2}b^2}$$

and, as the incidence in the general population is $e^{\frac{1}{2}b^2}$, and the area of these curves is proportioned to the height of their modes, the relative incidence in relatives, compared to the general population, is e^{rb^2} which is Penrose's k (Penrose, 1953).

REFERENCES

EDWARDS, J. H. (1960). The simulation of Mendelism. *Acta genet. statist. med.* **10,** 63–70.

FALCONER, D. S. (1965). The inheritance of liability to certain diseases, estimated from the incidence among relatives. *Ann. hum. Genet.* **29,** 51–76.

KNOX, E. G. (1966). Cervical cytology : a scrutiny of the evidence. In *Problems and Progress in Medical Care*, second series. ed. McLachlan, G., p. 277. London : Oxford University Press.

MORTON, N. E. (1967). The detection of major genes under additive continuous variations. *Am. J. hum. Gen.* **19,** 23–34.

PENROSE, L. S. (1953). The genetical basis of common disease. *Acta genet. statist. med.* **4,** 257.

TOYNBEE, A. J. (1967). *Acquaintances.* London : Oxford University Press.

DISCUSSION

Dr Carter : It is always a pleasure to listen to John Edward's illustrations. He has a wonderful capacity for looking at things upside down in the most revealing way, taking the germ's-eye view as well as the diploid view and it really is very stimulating. He hasn't given us any results, but one is interested in the dividend of what they have been doing in Birmingham . I know in fact he has some results, for example relating events in pregnancy to intelligence of children at 11-plus,* and I wonder if he has a moment to tell us something about that.

Dr Edwards : I should mention firstly that it involves various co-authors and secondly that it doesn't involve any novel problems. The difficulty with record linkage, as in most of medicine, is that the most useful tends to be the most boring, but it did seem useful to put on a substantial basis what was happening to premature babies and in particular what was happening to children who had experienced difficult or untimely births. I think all that we have been able to demonstrate in Birmingham in 45,000 births linked to the 11-plus, and using sibs as controls whenever possible, is that, as various pathologists have repeatedly pointed out, there appears to be no such thing as a minor birth injury which is common and impairs intellect. If they get into school at all they really do remarkably well even if they have been through a precipitous labour or a breech delivery or some such apparently harrowing procedure— at least it is harrowing to those of us who are not obstetricians who see such events. We wondered if a first-class citizen can really emerge feet-first. But they do. The feet-first children in Birmingham are as bright as their sibs and those removed by Caesarean section are, if anything, slightly brighter.

A few other fairly obvious things came out. Those who were born in ambulances didn't do too well, nor did their sibs ; presumably children who are born in ambulances do not have the brightest of parents. Otherwise all our results were negative and perhaps very reassuring to any obstetrician who needed reassurance that there was virtually no such thing as damage which was commonly picked up by the school master and missed by the paediatrician. We did find, as has been demonstrated before indirectly, that the I.Q. of twins is half a standard deviation down. We are looking at this further.

We also found a steady deterioration of I.Q. with numbers of children using their sibs as controls. The first-born was the best and it dropped one point almost exactly for each further child. I assume this is partly because the I.Q. test is set by adults and the adult concept is more adequately thought of by a first-born who copies his parents than by the tenth-born who copies the ninth who copies the eighth and so on. This is really a very big factor : a ten-point span of I.Q. specifically from this cause alone in ten-child families.

Dr Bahn : Have you looked at the I.Q. by birth order within families, for example the eighth compared with the seventh child within the same family, to avoid bias ?

* A formal test of intelligence required of children in state schools in Britain about age 11.

293

Dr. Edwards : Yes. It would obviously be impracticable, particularly with limited coding of obstetrical details to make anything of the individuals, but they were linked under the address of the school with various restraints on age, parity and so on. Children in whom parity, the name, the address, and the mother's age at birth all were reasonable, who lived at the same address, were assumed to be sibs. Obviously we had the odd adopted cousin and so on, and no check was made of that.

Dr Fraser : What about the ones who didn't get to school ?

Dr Edwards : The Birmingham Education Authority doesn't do the 11-plus on these cases. The fate of children with major birth injury is fairly well known, of course, They get into mental defective colonies or, more likely, onto their waiting lists, into special schools, and into autopsy rooms. These have got a big subset of obstetric catastrophes but brain injury is a major factor. Obstetric catastrophes leading to minor cerebral damage do obviously exist but they appear too infrequent, or too mild, to show up in a series of this size. Exchange transfusion and conditions requiring it seem to have no demonstrable effect. Very small babies don't do too well but the combined analysis of birthweight and gestation is exceedingly treacherous, and data on this will be published shortly.

Mr Rowe : I wonder if I could raise a smallish point on the theoretical side. One of the things that has come out of the theoretical studies of social anthropology within the last fifty years has been the fact that there are two different aspects to kinship. One is the biological aspect and the other is the legal aspect. This comes out most clearly obviously in the father–child relationship and this is expressed in the terminology of the pater who is the social father and the genitor who is the biological father, but all other kinship relationships can have a social aspect and societies which maintain elaborate genealogical information may keep it because on the whole it seems to reflect and support the social structure. There is a beautiful paper by, I think, the Bohannans (1952) in which they actually observed a gathering of elders in an African community and in this community the social structure and kinship structure has got out of phase and in the course of the meeting they gradually adjusted the genealogy so that it then would reflect the lineage structure once more in the way the society expressed itself on the ground. I wonder if it would be possible to assess how far this two-edged aspect of kinship affects the genetic dynamics. Most of these studies are based, of course, on legal records and not on biological records, and whether it is possible to build into one's model some adjustment for this factor ?

Dr Edwards : I think it is really intrinsically impossible to study this sort of thing in populations which don't have a tradition of literacy and a storage of records extending over several generations. I agree this could be a problem but I think that this probably isn't a major problem within those societies which have records. Obviously adoption is an extremely hazardous situation from which to draw any inference unless the children are kidnapped and adopted at random. I think all one can do is leave it out ; it is just too complicated. As I said automated linking can only deal with that subset of medical enquiry which is suitable for the coding of records and there are vast areas of research, including most laboratory and clinical work in medicine and most, I presume, of social anthropology, which is too complicated to be specified by a hole in a punch card, and could only be damaged by attempts to convert words into numbers. I would have thought this type of enquiry could hardly impinge on such a problem.

REFERENCE

BOHANNAN, LAURA (1952). A genealogical charter. *J. int. Afr. Inst.* **22,** 301.

MULTIGENERATION PEDIGREES FROM LINKED RECORDS

HOWARD B. NEWCOMBE

FOR most of the participants at this meeting record linkage will be of interest chiefly as a means for deriving histories of events in the lives of individual people. The geneticists, however, will be more concerned with the extraction of family histories, and the more generations which these family histories, or pedigrees, include the more use they will be. I propose to describe briefly the ways in which family information from the routine records may be stored as multigeneration pedigrees, in retrievable form, and in particular the manner in which we are attempting to build such pedigrees by linkage of the British Columbia vital records.

In case it may seem that I am talking only to the geneticists it should be mentioned that family histories spanning a single generation have recognized uses in *demography* for studies of fertility, in *epidemiology* for studies of the effects of differences in family environments, in *administration* for the running of schemes of welfare assistance and family allowances, and there are *legal* applications in connection with inheritance. Similar uses for multigeneration pedigrees are not difficult to foresee and it is probably just a matter of time before access to the information becomes convenient enough for these to begin to be taken seriously.

Linear storage of pedigree information

Conventionally, geneticists have represented family groups by means of pedigree charts which fan out either in a forward direction to show the descendants of an individual or married couple, or backward to show the ancestors. This device works well only if a large proportion of the relatives are left out, and it becomes quite cumbersome if one tries to put into the same two-dimensional diagram the maternal and paternal uncles and aunts, the nephews and nieces, and the cousins and inlaws. It is even less suitable for one-dimensional or linear representation on a magnetic tape.

For any sort of linear storage the family must be broken up into units of convenient size and these cross-referenced to each other. The sibship group has been chosen as the unit of storage for our own studies. This may seem arbitrary, but it is difficult to design a workable system using larger family groups as the units, and to use the individual as the unit of storage would complicate the retrieval of pedigrees from the array and would increase the amount of cross-referencing needed to identify the relationships of individuals whose records are stored in different parts of the file.

Compactness of storage

The most compact storage of pedigree information for a population is possible where everybody is numbered from one onward and the linkage into family groupings have already been carried out and are unambiguous. In this circumstance the individual histories will contain in addition to the personal identity numbers those of the *parents*, the *spouse* or spouses, and the *offspring*. A so-called ' total genealogy ' of this kind for the American Old Order Amish of Pennsylvania and Ohio has been developed recently by McKusick (1967) and is described earlier in this volume (p. 263).

Essentially similar storage of pedigree information, in a form that is almost as compact, is possible for countries that assign a personal identity number at birth, at which time the identity numbers of the parents can readily be linked to it. Such a numbering system for Denmark has been discussed by Mr H. Nielsen (p. 173). A sibship history in this instance would be equivalent to a female reproductive history and would start with the mother's *personal identity number*, cross-referenced with the corresponding numbers for her *parents*, *husband* or husbands, and *children*, and containing the dates of her own birth, her marriage, the births of the children, and her eventual death, plus the dates of divorce and remarriage where these have occurred. The corresponding male histories could be much shorter as they would not need to contain information about the offspring, this being readily available from the female histories. It is a technically simple matter to compile such pedigree information from a central person register that takes cognizance of the individual identity numbers at the times of birth, marriage, parenthood, divorce and death.

Where the family linkages must be carried out by the computer, however, as in the studies in Iceland and British Columbia, the names and other identifying information required for the linkage operation necessarily increase the size of the main pedigree file. The reason for mentioning this is not to indicate any inherent disadvantage, since the pedigrees can readily be summarized later in compact form after the linkages have been completed. Rather, the purpose is to indicate that the larger size of the records when they carry the identifying information needed for linkage does not imply cumbersomeness or inefficiency, but merely that additional work has been left for the computers to do.

Multigeneration pedigrees from vital records

The particular system for compiling multigeneration pedigrees which I shall describe is one that we are developing at Chalk River using the British Columbia vital records.

The distinguishing feature of the system is that a sibship history starts with a marriage record wherever the appropriate one is present in the files. The choice of this particular form of organization may at first sight appear arbitrary since the histories could, instead, be arranged to start with the maternal birth records. This alternative form of organization is in fact being used in Iceland, so that there is already some experience with it (Edwards, 1967 and personal communication : Magnusson, M. p. 62). The reason for not starting with the maternal birth records in the case of the British Columbia study has to do with the limited period covered by the files currently being linked. These include records of marriage, births, and child deaths over the 20 years from 1946 through 1965.

With such a limited time span, the sibship groupings that could be built up by linkages solely with the maternal birth records would be few in number and would be restricted to the very early parts of the reproductive histories. On the other hand, the sibship histories that start with marriages in 1946 would be nearly completed by 1965 and would cover the whole of the reproductive lives of a substantial fraction of the 1946 brides.

Information about three generations of sibships may, in fact, be derived from the 20-year file. First, the marriage records themselves serve to identify members of brother–sister groups in the parental generation who married during the 20-year period, and the ages as stated at the times of the marriages permit the members of these groups to be arranged in approximate birth rank sequence. Secondly, the birth records for children out of the marriages provide relatively complete information about the current generation of sibships. And, finally, a few of the children born early in the 20-year period will be married and have started to raise families before the end of the 20 years. Thus the family information obtained in this manner greatly exceeds that which could be derived purely from the histories that start with the registrations of the maternal births.

Structure of the multigeneration file

Where a marriage record is present in the file it serves as a link between the generations. This means that information from the record will appear in three places in the file, at the head of a group of records representing the births of children out of that marriage, as a record of an event to a male child in the father's sibship, and as a record of an event to a female child in the mother's sibship. In each of these three positions it is cross-referenced to the other two. We use as cross-referencing information the parental surname (in phonetically coded form) plus the marriage registration number. Three such pairs of surnames are present on a marriage record, relating respectively to the new pair of potential parents, to the father and mother of the groom and to the father and mother of the bride. The file as a whole is arrayed in order of the surname pairs of fathers and mothers of the sibship groups of births.

This kind of organization of the files is suprisingly simple. Programmes that we are now using to link births and deaths of children to the parental marriages can be employed also to link into a sibship history the events of marriage into which members of the sibship have entered. Marriages and deaths are treated in the same manner, both being events to the offspring and both sorts of records containing essentially similar identifying information.

The form of the resulting sibship histories, complete with their cross-referencing information backward, forward, and sideways to the inlaw sibships, is shown in Figure 1.

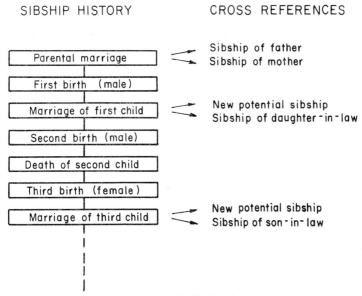

FIG. 1. Form of the sibship histories.

The process of searching such a file to draw out family information is also simple, and is particularly efficient when carried out for a large number of family groups all at the same time. A single scan extracts for each of the sibships under study cross-referencing information to six different kinds of closely related sibships, and starting from these a second scan draws out cross-referencing information to all of the sibships that are one step more distantly related, and so on in an ever widening circle (Fig. 2).

Current work on multigeneration pedigrees

In practice, the most laborious part of the operation of compiling the multigeneration pedigrees for British Columbia is that of converting the punchcard records into the appropriate formats on magnetic tape. Three punchcards are produced routinely for each marriage, a groom's index card, a bride's index card, and a statistics card. In addition to these we have had especially punched two cards containing the identifying particulars of the parents of the groom and the parents of the bride respectively.

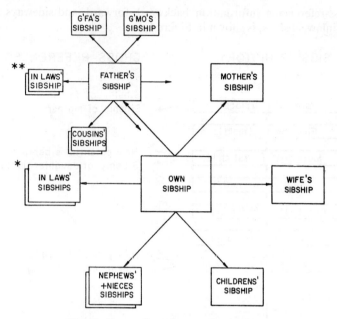

FIG. 2. Cross referencing to related groups.

Currently we are in the process of deriving from these five kinds of punchcards, as images on magnetic tape, the three kinds of marriage records needed for linkage into pedigrees (*i.e.* the ' head-of-family ' record, the groom's sibship record and the bride's sibship record). About a million punchcard images are involved, and it is expected that the conversion may take two years to carry out ; about a quarter of the work is finished at the present time.

By comparison, the actual linkage operations are relatively undemanding, and computers tend to be much faster at linking records than at changing the formats around.

The labour of converting from punchcards to the appropriate marriage record formats on magnetic tape will be less with the newer computers, and the work will be greatly reduced when punchcards are bypassed altogether so that information from a marriage registration is entered from the start into a single record on magnetic tape. This latter development is probably not far away.

Whether or not the information identifying the parents of grooms and brides will get entered routinely into such a machine readable record is less certain, and will depend upon the importance of the
300

possible administrative and statistical uses of the resulting multi-generation pedigrees.

Administrative and statistical uses of pedigree information

About 10 years ago there appeared to be little practical value in grouping vital records, even by sibships, but as the process of grouping or linking became simpler the possible administrative, statistical, and demographic uses have become more widely recognized. I would suggest that the same thing will happen over the next decade for the multigeneration pedigree.

The matter has been discussed in detail elsewhere but two examples are perhaps in order. The Canadian family allowance administration might actually find it easier not to drop from their files all girls reaching age 19, but to keep their names and other particulars rather than to have to re-enter these a few years later when they become mothers. Similarly, the demographers, who are just beginning to get seriously interested in the patterns of family building, may become curious about the similarities of these patterns throughout the wider family group. The costs are currently not great and will undoubtedly decline steadily over the next decade at least.

REFERENCES

EDWARDS, J. H. (1967). Linkage studies of whole populations. In *Proc. Third int. Congr. hum. Genet.*, pp. 479–482. Baltimore: Johns Hopkins Press.
McKUSICK, V. A. (1967). Genetic and bibliographic applications of computers in human genetics. In *Proc. Third int. Congr. hum. Genet.*, pp. 483–488. Baltimore: Johns Hopkins Press.

DISCUSSION

Mr Healy : I have two unrelated questions. Technically, your procedure amounts to generalizing the usual representation of a pedigree as a *tree*, to one by a *graph* in the top logical sense. Are you aware of the very interesting work being done on representing graphs inside a computer and on following paths through them ?

Secondly, you stressed that yours was a 20-year study. Is your system useful for maintaining, as well as creating, a file of this kind, or will it be liable to break down after, say 40 years ?

Dr Newcombe : In answer to the first question, I am familiar with the use of computers for plotting but not with this particular application. Figure 2 throws more light on the question of retrieval of pedigree information. It shows that by scanning the file once one

301

pulls out relatives of six different kinds. The arrows in the figure point to all the related sibships, so one scan will serve to extract six different kinds of relatives from as many different families as are regarded as of interest. Using a second scan the search fans out in all directions still further and so on.

The second question was whether this file will come to a sticky end when it gets too large ? I hope that if it works well for 20 years it will be worth pouring in another 10 years of data. But it does get bigger and there are two ways out that I can see : one is that the sibships that have reached the ends of their reproductive periods may be edited out and put in another file. This would help to keep the main working file small. The other hope that I have, and my computer friends throw a little cold water on my enthusiasm every now and then, is that more compact forms of storage will become available within the next decade. There are at least two centres in operation now which use photographic storage of digital information. We have calculated that, of the actual photographic material, it takes only about a cubic foot to hold 10^{12} bits. This would be about sufficient for all the major health records for Canada for 20 years. Perhaps 10 years from now such methods of storage will be more readily available and more convenient than they are now.

Dr Edwards : I wonder if I could ask Dr Newcombe to comment on this fanning in or out. It seems very interesting if in fact families die out or breed : of course they do this by definition but that they do it to such a spectacular extent has never really been documented I believe.

Dr Newcombe : For the next few years we would not be in a position to investigate this because of the problem of migration out of a province. This represents sheer loss from the files. The Family Allowance Administration does of course have all the changes of address, in and out of each province, and recently they have stopped throwing the address change forms away, but it would cost something to enter the information into punch cards. Eventually, the Family Allowance files will be mechanized, at which time there would be a better chance to do such studies.

Mr Carpenter : What do you do with half-sibships, which must be becoming increasingly common ?

Dr. Newcombe : I worry about it at night.

Dr Bahn : It has been some time since I read your material on family records. One reason I hesitated to develop family psychiatric registers is the complexity of their maintenance. For example, there is the problem of assigning family numbers. Apparently you do not assign a number for family of orientation and one for family procreation, but depend on association of the records each time to 'put the family together'.

Dr Newcombe : I am glad you mentioned this because you raised a similar point earlier. I think you would be relieved of concern if you tried such matching by families. They come naturally where use is made of the maiden name of the mother to get a breakdown of the file by two surnames. The discriminating power of the double surname pair is very much greater than that of either one alone. People have asked, what do you do with the Smiths because they are in a large pocket in the file. But the Smiths who married Browns represent only 16 marriages out of 100,000. The double breakdown, even with two names that are very prevalent, gives a very fine subdivision, and once a file is arranged into double Soundex pockets family groups tend to stand out like a sore thumb. This doesn't mean that the family groupings are 100 per cent. accurate. We do miss some of the family linkages because the mother's maiden name wasn't reported correctly, but false linkages are very rare indeed.

THE RECONSTRUCTION OF HISTORICAL MOVEMENT PATTERNS

A. J. Boyce, C. F. Küchemann and G. A. Harrison

It is being increasingly recognized that knowledge of the genetic structure of human populations is of considerable relevance to many aspects of medical genetics. An important component of genetic structure, of special interest not only to medical genetics but also to epidemiology, is the pattern of human movement. From the genetic point of view, movement determines the magnitude and distribution of the gene pool and is therefore the major factor delimiting a Mendelian population. In most circumstances only the contemporary movement situation can be examined but the genetic structure of a population at any one time has, of course, been influenced by the pattern of movement throughout the history of the population. Occasionally, as when parish register and other historical records are available, it is possible to gain insight into the history of the population and therefore make an analysis of the influence of changing movement patterns on genetic structure.

There are many components of human movement but the only one of consequence to the geneticist is that in which people move from one area to another, removing their genes from one gene pool and contributing, especially through their descendants, to a new one. This type of movement can be classified into two main categories. The first arises as a result of mate selection, in which, particularly through marriage, a partner is removed from one population and introduced into another. In this country it has been customary for the man to be married in the parish of the woman who then takes up residence in her husband's parish. Incidentally, it may be mentioned that this type of behaviour unfortunately complicates the reconstruction of genealogies for demographic and genetic purposes.

The second type of movement has socio-economic causes but also has genetic effects. It can be divided into movement prior to marriage which, though it may involve either one or both marriage partners, may still be regarded as singleton movement as there is no necessary connection between the movement of the marriage partners; and post-marriage movement of husband and wife, with or without their children, in which there is such a connection and, when children are involved, leads to a genetic correlation between the migrants.

During the last two years we have been carrying out a detailed reconstruction of the genetic and demographic history of a group of Oxfordshire parishes using parish register and census material. The purpose of this contribution is to consider the information provided by this material about the changing patterns of movement in an area consisting of the parish of Charlton-on-Otmoor and its adjacent parishes (Fig. 1). From the parish registers one can determine the historical changes in spatial exogamy and the distances over which marriage partners are obtained. These two parameters provide information about the population structure and the magnitude of the gene pool. From the census records one can establish overall movement patterns of genetic consequence and, for particular periods at least, determine any directional tendencies in these migrations.

Exogamy

Spatial exogamy, in which an individual chooses a mate from a population other than his own, is an important component of the movement pattern. In this study it is measured, for any particular parish, by comparing the number of marriages in which one partner was, at the time of marriage, resident outside that parish with the number of marriages in which both partners were resident within the parish. Figure 2 shows for the parishes in the area studied the

304

FIG. 1. Map of the arrangement of parishes and the distribution of villages in the Otmoor area.

individual and combined percentages of exogamy for 50-year periods since 1601 (in calculating the latter percentages, marriages between parishes in the area are still scored as exogamous). It is evident that there has been a gradual rise in the amount of exogamy with the result that in the present day populations the majority of marriages involve partners from different parishes. Even in the earliest period, however, there were quite high rates of exogamy (of up to 37 per cent.) and this clearly suggests that in this particular area the demographic units of parishes and villages have long been genetically open.

Marriage distances

Whilst the extent of exogamy determines the gene flow into parishes through marriage, the distances over which movement occurs are

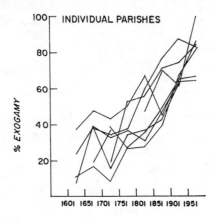

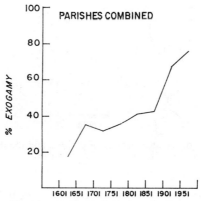

Fig. 2. Changing patterns of exogamy in 50-year periods.

important in the delineation of the gene pool and, so far as this is influenced by movement due to marriage, it can be examined in terms of the mean distance over which exogamous marriages are contracted and the distribution of the distances.

Figure 3 shows the changing pattern of mean marriage distance since 1601 plotted in the form of a 25-year moving average. This graph is based on the combined data of eight parishes and since this involves large numbers of marriages the occurrence of occasional marriages contracted over very large distances has only a slight effect upon the mean distance. It is clear, as has already been shown for the parish of Charlton itself (Küchemann, Boyce & Harrison,

306

FIG. 3. Mean marriage distance in the Otmoor area plotted as a
25-year moving average.

1967), that the mean marriage distance is remarkably constant in the
early part of the period and until 1850 remains in the region of 4–8
miles. After 1850, however, there is a marked and fairly continuous
rise until among present day populations the average distance is
between 24 and 32 miles. The period in which this rise occurs
corresponds closely with that in which mechanized forms of transport
were introduced into the area.

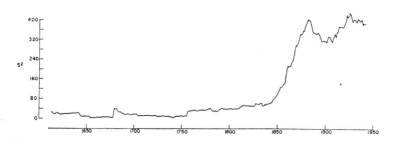

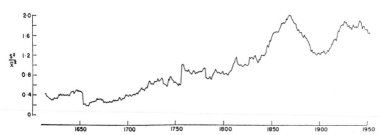

FIG. 4. Upper graph : variance of marriage distance plotted as a
25-year moving average.

Lower graph : corrected variance (square of coefficient of variation)
of marriage distance plotted as a 25-year moving average.

Not only is there a change in mean marriage distance but the variability of marriage distances also changes. This variability is shown in Figure 4 in the form of a 25-year moving average. The upper graph shows the change in variance of marriage distances while in the lower graph a correction for changes in the magnitude of the mean has been made. The pattern of changes in the corrected variance is somewhat surprising since although the mean marriage distance remains constant during the early part of the period there is a consistent rise in the corrected variance. Such a pattern could arise if a widening in the marriage circle were accompanied by a corresponding increase in the frequency with which marriages are contracted over very short distances. This is the type of situation which would occur if a central village increased exceptionally in size and provided many potential mates for villages within its immediate vicinity. Unfortunately, there is at the moment insufficient information about the relative sizes of the villages before 1801 to allow this possibility to be investigated further but this is a point on which additional work is planned.

It is clear that the increase in mean marriage distance has been accompanied by an increase in the variance of marriage distances and that this increase is particularly marked around 1850. Because of this division of the pattern of marriage distances into pre- and post-1850 periods, it seemed worthwhile to examine in detail the distributions of marriage distances in these two periods and these are shown in Figure 5. A comparison of these two distributions shows that the change in the mean and variance of marriage distances is largely due to an increased frequency of marriages beyond a 30-mile radius. The pattern within this radius remains remarkably constant throughout the whole period as can be more clearly seen in Figure 6 in which the proportions are based only on marriage distances of less than 30 miles.

With distributions of the form shown in Figures 5 and 6 which are highly positively skewed, the mean and variance are an inadequate description of the distribution and a somewhat different and more informative way of looking at the phenomenon of changing marriage distance is to plot the distances within which various percentages of exogamous marriages were contracted during 50-year periods. This has been done in Figure 7 which shows that there is almost a complete absence of temporal change when as many as 70 per cent. of marriages are included. Only when 95 per cent of the marriages within any particular period are included is there a marked change in the distance.

It may be concluded, therefore, that while the facilities for wider

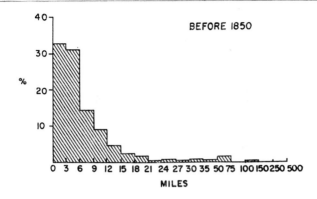

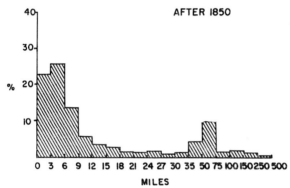

FIG. 5. Distribution of marriage distances.

travel provided by mechanized transport have increased the proportion of marriages contracted over 30 miles, in the local area within this radius they have had little or no effect on the general pattern of marriage distance distribution which has remained remarkably constant throughout the whole of the period studied.

It is apparent from Figure 5 that, both before and after 1850, although the overall distributions are highly skewed there is little change in the overall contributions made by villages within the limits 0–3 and 3–6 miles. The situation within this limited distance can be examined further by considering the distribution within a six-mile radius of one village, such as the central village of Charlton. This distribution is affected by two factors—the number of villages at particular distances and the individual contributions, in terms of

309

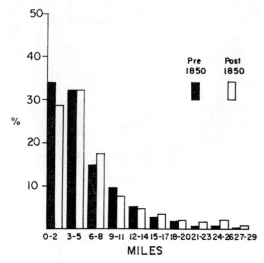

FIG. 6. Distribution of marriage distances of less than 30 miles.

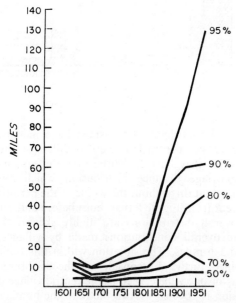

FIG. 7. Maximum marriage distances within various percentage limits.

marriage partners, of these villages. It has been shown previously, on the basis of the 1861 census returns for Charlton, that the contributions of individual villages within a 6-mile radius to the breeding population of Charlton are inversely proportional to their distance from Charlton. This relationship has been interpreted in terms of a model of neighbourhood knowledge (Boyce, Küchemann & Harrison, 1967). Analysis of marriage records over the whole period indicates a similar inverse relationship, of the form ar^{-b}, with exponent, b, close to 1. (In the previous analysis, based on the census returns, the derived exponent was 1·98.) Since the number of villages increases approximately linearly with distance, *i.e.* $N \simeq kr$, the total contributions will be of the form $T \simeq ar^{-1} \times kr \simeq ak$; a more or less constant relationship with distance therefore arises within this limited area because the decreasing likelihood of marriage with increasing distance is balanced by the increasing number of villages. It does appear that the factors which effect marriage movement within about a six-mile radius differ from those operating at greater distances and it is interesting to note that the neighbourhood knowledge model is expected to apply only within a radius of about six miles.

Direction of gene flow

In the preceding analysis of the degree of exogamy and marriage distance no attention was given to the actual geographical pattern of gene flow. Any attempt to represent the direction of such flow presents interesting methodological problems. When an individual village is considered it is possible to measure the comparative contributions that different villages within its immediate vicinity have made to its exogamous marriages. If, for instance, one takes the village of Charlton itself and considers the villages within a radius of, for example, six miles, one can represent the percentage contributions made by these to the total number of exogamous marriages which have taken place over the 350-year period. These contributions are plotted in Figure 8 where the number attached to each village represents its percentage contribution to the total of Charlton exogamous marriages. To aid interpretation, a series of ' contour lines ' has been drawn and these highlight the geographical variations in contributions to Charlton.

If there were no geographical orientation of the gene flow and a more or less constant relationship between distance and total contributions by villages, one would expect a series of concentric circles in which the distance between contour lines of constant decrement in percentage contribution increased exponentially. In principle, the

311

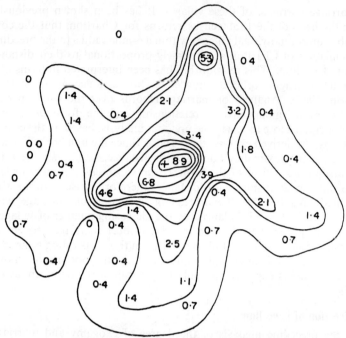

FIG. 8. Contributions (per cent.) to Charlton exogamous marriages of villages within six miles of Charlton.

deviation of the observed distribution from this expectation could
be measured by the departures from concentricity of individual contour lines and the deviation from inverse proportionality determined
by examining sections through the contour map. In the present case,
however, the number of points is small and the error attached to
each correspondingly large and such a sophisticated analysis
would probably be misleading. One can gain some insight, however,
from a visual inspection of the map which shows fairly obvious
deviations, at least from concentricity. There are clearly two main
factors associated with these deviations from expectation. The
first is the presence of unusually large villages in particular localities
(the above null expectation assumes villages populations to be
identical and the villages to be evenly distributed). The second
factor is the non-random orientation of roadways, the effects of which
can be seen more clearly in Figure 9, in which the variations in
village size have been partially eliminated by expressing the contribution of each village in terms of its 1851 population size. The

312

Fig. 9. Village contributions to Charlton exogamous marriages in terms of 1851 village sizes (given as contributions per 1000 inhabitants resident in 1851).

unpopulated region of the Ot Moor clearly acts as a somewhat impassable area and there is also a NE/SW elongation of the central contours which corresponds to the general orientation of roads connecting the villages.

While such maps provide information about the general orientation of movement, they do not in themselves indicate the direction of movement. Evidence for direction may be obtained by comparing the extent to which there is reciprocal exchange between each village and all its neighbours. As far as marriage movement is concerned, there is, as one would expect, little or no directional component but such a component does become apparent when total movement is estimated from those census returns which include data on the birthplaces of the inhabitants of villages. By relating, for any given village, the number of people born in it, but at the time of the census contributing to the breeding populations of neighbouring villages, to the number who at the time of the census were contributing to the breeding population of that village, but were born in neighbouring

313

villages, one has a measure of the extent to which different villages on average give to and receive from their neighbours. This ratio is independent of the total amount of emigration and immigration occuring in the villages. If the direction of movement were entirely random one would expect the ratio to be close to unity and one can see if deviations from unity are related to such factors as population size or geographical position.

There is evidence, at least from the 1851 census, that there is a relationship between this ratio (here abbreviated as ' g/r ') and population size such that the larger villages tend to receive from their smaller neighbours more than they give. This relationship is particularly clear when the natural logarithm of the above ratio is considered as is shown in Figure 10. This transformation makes the

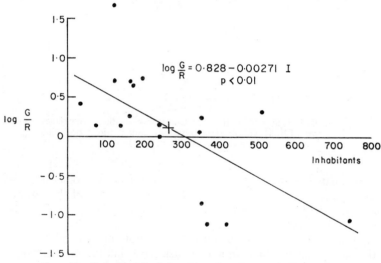

Fig. 10. Relationship between comparative emigration/immigration (g/r) and village population sizes in 1851.

relationship with population size appreciably more linear and the calculated regression is significant at the 1 per cent. level. There is also some evidence of a directional flow within the area from the NE to the SW in that the parishes in the NE tend to have ratios greater than unity and those in the SW ratios less than unity as is shown in Figure 11. As has been mentioned, this direction corresponds to the overall orientation of the roads in the area and the direction of flow is probably related to the further attraction of the large urbanized

314

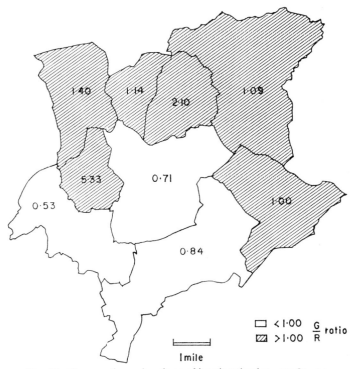

Fig. 11. Comparative emigration and immigration between Otmoor parishes.

area of Oxford, which lies on the south-western extension of the NE/SW axis.

The relationship between exogamy, marriage distance and direction

The three aspects of movement which this study has considered—exogamy, marriage distance and direction determine the pattern of gene flow within the area. Assuming no differential fertility on the part of exogamous as compared with endogamous marriages, the pattern of exogamy determines the total amount of gene flow arising from marriage movements. We have considered here the overall exogamy rates in the area and have classified unions between different villages in the Otmoor area as exogamous but whether one treats each village separately, takes an average value for the combined villages or treats the Otmoor area as a single unit, the general pattern of exogamy is the same (although treating the area as a single unit and

315

classifying marriages between villages inside the area as endogamous reduces the level of exogamy by about 10 per cent. in each period). Whereas exogamy determines the total amount of gene flow, mean marriage distance determines the area over which gene flow, through marriage, occurs in any particular generation and it is worth noting that the changing patterns of exogamy and mean marriage distance strongly reinforce one another as is shown, by their product, in Figure 12. This product is an index of the potential genetic disturbance that could occur through gene flow. Whether or not such

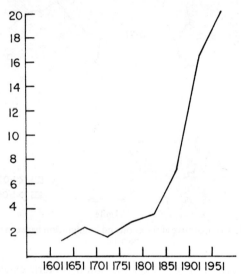

Fig. 12. Mean marriage distance x proportion of exogamous marriages.

disturbance does occur, if it does, its magnitude depends, of course, upon the pattern of genetic variation in any particular system within the area defined by marriage distance, and upon directional movement in relation to this pattern. As yet we have no information on gene marker frequencies within the area but if it should turn out, as a result of further work planned, that there is genetic diversity within the area one would expect from the above analysis some general NE/SW clinal variation extending over a considerable area.

CONCLUSION

This analysis illustrates some of the problems of defining population units in human societies particularly those in advanced rural

316

areas where there are no major cultural or geographical barriers to movement. It has widely been supposed that an area such as Otmoor, with its own unique history, has formed not only a distinct socio-economic unit but also a comparatively isolated one. The results of this study show how misleading such beliefs can be and that here, as no doubt in comparable areas of Western Europe, one has now and has had for many centuries an extremely open gene pool. It is evident that no precise limits can be given which define the overall population of the area. It is true that in the demographic sense fairly discrete units of villages can be recognized and to these one could apply Wright's island model of population structure (Wright, 1943) but it is clear from this analysis of movement patterns that genetic exchange between villages and with the outside area is and has been so high that the area is probably better regarded as a component of a much more diffuse system.

It may be noted that Alström (1958) and Alström & Lindelius (1966), working on agricultural parishes in Sweden, reached broadly similar conclusions and it seems likely that the situation is comparable in most advanced agricultural societies.

ACKNOWLEDGMENTS : Grateful acknowledgment is made to the Nuffield Foundation, the Eugenics Society and the Wenner-Gren Foundation for Anthropological Research for grants which enabled this research to be carried out.

REFERENCES

ALSTRÖM, C. H. (1958). 1st cousin marriages in Sweden 1750–1844 and a study of the population movement in some Swedish sub-populations from the genetic-statistical veiwpoint. *Acta genet. statist. med.* **8**, 295–369.

ALSTRÖM, C. H. & LINDELIUS, R. (1966). A study of the population movement in nine Swedish sub-populations from the genetic-statistical viewpoint. *Acta genet. statist. med.* **16** (Suppl.), 1–42.

BOYCE, A. J., KÜCHEMANN, C. H. & HARRISON, G. A. (1967). Neighbourhood knowledge and the distribution of marriage distances. *Ann. hum. Genet.* **30**, 335–338.

KÜCHEMANN, C. H., BOYCE, A. J. & HARRISON, G. A. (1967). A demographic and genetic study of a group of Oxfordshire villages. *Hum. Biol.*, **39**, 251–276.

WRIGHT, S. (1943). Isolation by distance. *Genetics*, **28**, 114–138.

DISCUSSION

Dr Fraser : This is a very ingenious approach and I congratulate Dr Boyce on all the work he has done though I share his confusion about the standard approach of population genetics to this sort of problem. I would like to ask him what he has found out about consanguinity, and whether he would say something about the markers he will be using.

Dr Boyce : With regard to consanguinity—as part of our general study we were concerned to make use, as Professor Barrai has done, of the records of baptisms, marriages and burials in the area, which go back to 1539 in this country with varying degrees of completeness. We have built up very complete pictures of family units and have looked in other work at various demographic parameters. Unfortunately we have not yet been able, and perhaps never will be, to build up a very complete picture of the genealogical relationships among people in this area. As you can see, movement in this area has been quite considerable and although traditionally Charlton-on-Otmoor and the Otmoor area have been regarded as an isolated, inward-looking part of Oxfordshire, when one makes a detailed analysis it is quite clear that this kind of belief is not really true. I think it is unlikely that we shall be able to build up sufficiently complete pictures of pedigrees to say very much about levels of consanguinity in the area. This is rather unfortunate but we feel that the other results which are emerging from our work are of considerable interest in themselves. We shall, however, be initiating a study of genetic markers in the area and will attempt to make this as comprehensive as we can. We are already in the process of considering taking samples from almost the entire adult population, and analysing the variation in the various systems as a result of this.

Dr Bahn : I noticed in your first slide a dip in the twentieth-century, somewhere around 1920. How do wars affect this pattern? There must be more going on than just the mechanized movement of cars.

Dr Boyce : I am not certain that I can really answer your question in detail. I think the dip, as shown by the graph, is in fact a little late to be attributed to the First World War and perhaps is more concerned with the lowering of economic conditions in the area towards the end of the 1920's. This might have brought about a reduction in the area over which people tended to move and choose their marriage partners, but short of actually finding out in more detail the causes in that particular group of people I don't think that I can say more than that at the moment.

Professor Barrai : In our material, we observed that after the First World War and the Second World War there is an increase in consanguineous marriages and we didn't find a good explanation for this phenomenon, which was also observed in France by Sutter. There are probably psychological reasons entering into a decision

318

of a person to marry a consanguineous partner, especially if he is a male who has missed his opportunities for marriage outside his kinship. But it is a fact that there is a sudden increase in consanguineous marriages after the last two wars.

Dr Barrett : I'd like to ask whether you were able to discover whether men tended to migrate more than women prior to marriage, or whether they migrated further.

Dr Boyce : As far as exogamous marriages are concerned it is the custom in this country for the man to be married in the parish of his future bride, and so most of our exogamous marriages are in fact due to movement by males, but after marriage very often the couple takes up residence in the parish of the male. At the moment we don't have any information on the differential movements of males as against females. It would be possible to extract it from the data that we have, but I have nothing I can say at the moment. Perhaps I could just take this opportunity to mention the work of Dr Wrigley and Mr Laslett who have a unit in Cambridge for the study of the history of population structure. They are not in fact at this meeting and some of you might not be aware of the detailed work which they are carrying out. They are primarily sociologists and historians, but they are gathering together in Cambridge an extensive collection of data based on parish registers and early census material, and are carrying out very extensive linkages—they call it family reconstitution—of parish register material. Although as I say they are primarily interested in sociological or historical changes they are amassing a very large amount of data which is of considerable interest to geneticists and biologists in general.

Going back to a point which was mentioned earlier in connection with family limitation, Dr Wrigley has found from an extensive study he has made of a small village called Colyton in South-East Devon, that there is considerable evidence of family limitation in the middle part of the seventeenth century, which is rather earlier than one tends to think of family limitation being employed in this country. I don't think I can go into the evidence now for this but I think it is a fairly strong conclusion which emerges from this family reconstitution work.

PART 7

SYMPOSIUM ON CONFIDENTIALITY OF MEDICAL RECORDS AND RELATED PROBLEMS

Chairman : PROFESSOR R. F. S. SCHILLING (London)

Y

MEDICAL CONFIDENCES, RESEARCH AND THE LAW

P. R. Glazebrook

An article in the *New Statesman* of 3rd March, 1967 carried the title : ' To Hell with Medical Secrecy ! ', and that will, I imagine, be the theme of our symposium within a symposium. My task, as a lawyer, I take to be this : to attempt to answer two questions :

1. In what circumstances might a patient successfully bring legal proceedings against a practitioner or against the governing body of a hospital, as a result of the practitioner or any hospital employee having communicated to a medical research worker information relating to that patient gained by interviewing or examining him ?

2. Is a practitioner, the governing body of a hospital, or a government department, ever justified in refusing a medical research worker access to the medical or social records in their possession, on the ground that they would be acting unlawfully if they did so ?

In attempting to answer these two questions I must, on the one hand, of necessity confine myself to a statement of what seems to me to be the law of England[1]—nothing that I say must be assumed to be true of the law of any other country, for law, unlike medicine, knows national boundaries ; and, on the other, readily admit that these questions, and particularly the first, cannot be answered with complete assurance—for the simple and sufficient reason that they have not in this country been litigated. And while the General Medical Council envisages that improperly disclosing information obtained in confidence from a patient might well be held to be ' infamous conduct in a professional respect '[2] no such case has ever come before the Council, and it has never had occasion to issue a statement on the subject.[3] I cannot, therefore, tell you what answers the judges have given : I can only prophesy as to what they would say if, in the future, these questions came before them for judicial determination. A lawyer must regret that the publication of Lord Moran's detailed account of the illnesses of his distinguished patient did not lead to litigation : had it done so, I should now be treading on firmer ground.

I know of only two reported cases, both in jurisdictions outside England, in which a medical practitioner has been sued for disclosing a medical confidence,[4] and in each the circumstances were so unusual that they provide little guidance in answering the questions which

323

confront us now. Whether this paucity of reported cases demonstrates that medical men are extremely scrupulous and extremely careful in not disclosing to others what they have learnt whilst caring for their patients (as medical men themselves would like us to believe) or whether it results from patients who believed they had suffered from a breach of medical confidence having nevertheless been advised that litigation was unlikely to show a profit (as a cynic might suggest), I do not know, but such a politically sensitive issue as medical record linkage might well provoke a test case, sponsored, perhaps, by some such association as that formed to oppose clinical experiments on hospital patients. It is, therefore, to the task of prophesying the result of such a test case that I address myself.

Turning to my first question : in what circumstances might a patient successfully bring legal proceedings against a practitioner, or against a hospital, on the ground that they had communicated to a medical research worker information relating to that patient gained by interviewing him ?—there are two different types of proceedings to consider. The patient might sue for damages to compensate him for the injury he claims he has suffered as a result of the disclosure, or he might seek an injunction, that is, a court order, forbidding the practitioner or hospital from communicating their records of him to anyone else, on the ground that to do so would constitute a breach of confidence—the information, it would be said, having been made available to the practitioner or hospital for one purpose, and one purpose only : to facilitate the patient's own treatment. If the court granted the injunction, that is, made the order, disobedience would constitute, and be punished as, contempt of court.

If a patient sued for damages, much might depend on whether he was a National Health Service or a private patient. The distinction is important because whilst the private patient is in a contractual relationship with his practitioner or hospital, the N.H.S. patient is not, and his rights and remedies fall to be determined solely by the principles of the tort, or legal wrong, of negligence—that is, by those principles familiar in cases of ' medical negligence ', where a patient seeks monetary compensation on the ground that the treatment he has received has been not just unsuccessful or mistaken, but such as displayed a failure by practitioner or hospital to care for him in the way that any ordinary and reasonably careful practitioner or hospital would have done, and that, as a consequence, he is in a worse state than he would have been if he had been treated with reasonable care. The standard is thus not an absolute one, but is fixed by reference to the level of care displayed by reasonably competent and careful practitioners and hospitals. The private patient having what the N.H.S. patient has not, the benefit of a contract between himself on the one side, and the practitioner, and/or the hospital, on the other, his legal rights and remedies will be determined not simply by the principles of the tort of negligence, but also in accordance with the terms, both expressed and implied, of that contract.[5] In so far as the terms of such a contract have been expressed, either orally or in writing, its effect will be determined by those terms : for the rest, the court will read into, imply into, the contract such terms, not being inconsistent with its expressed terms, as it considers to be customary, that is, to be understood as the basis of all contracts between medical practitioners or hospitals and their private patients. There undoubtedly is, among these implied terms, a promise by the practitioner or hospital which can broadly be said to be one to treat as confidential the information which is gained by interviewing or examining the patient. The real problem is, of course, to determine, in the absence of decided cases, the precise scope of this promise to treat such information as ' confidential '.

All that the N.H.S. patient, who is without the benefit of any such legally enforceable promise, can claim is that medical and social information acquired by practitioner or hospital while treating, or in order to treat, him, should be handled by them with the care that any reasonably efficient practitioner or hospital would handle it so as to prevent disclosure either to third persons, or to the patient himself,[6] in such a way that any reasonably thoughtful practitioner or hospital would realize that either financial or physical harm would result to the patient. Financial harm if, for instance, he lost his job and was only able to secure a less well paid one ; physical harm if, for example, he suffered a nervous breakdown on hearing the truth about his own condition, or on learning that someone else knew the truth about him. The N.H.S. patient's right to recover damages because his medical record has been disclosed to a third person is thus subject to several limitation : he must first of all show not merely that there has been a disclosure to some person not concerned in his treatment, but also that disclosure occurred not just by accident, but as the result of a failure to observe the precautions that are customary among reasonably competent practitioners, and in reasonably well-run hospitals (about which Professor Witts will doubtless have something to say), and then, secondly, that as a result of such disclosure he had not merely been annoyed or suffered embarrassment at someone else knowing what he would rather they did not know, but also had —as any ordinary percipient practitioner or administrator would have foreseen—suffered economic injury or actual physical injury or ill-health. It will not be enough simply to show that he has

325

suffered in either of these ways, for that may be something that no one could have anticipated.

And so it is, I think, tolerably clear that only in the most extraordinarily exceptional cases will there be any possibility of a N.H.S. patient recovering damages for what may loosely be termed a breach of medical confidence, and that such exceptional cases are, if anything, less likely to occur in the course of research work than they are in daily practice or in the ordinary work of a hospital. Doubtless practitioners and hospitals must take care to satisfy themselves that the research workers will be following procedures carefully designed to prevent the risk of a disclosure which might cause actionable harm before granting them access to their records— but they are not obliged to do more. As for the research workers themselves, they too will be liable to the patient in respect of any disclosure by them of his medical record only if they were careless, and only if financial or physical harm was caused.[7]

It is also, I think, reasonably clear that whether the N.H.S. patient has or has not consented to his medical record being made available to research workers is (at any rate as far as an action for damages is concerned) neither here nor there. Whatever a court may regard a patient as having consented to when he consented to his medical record being disclosed to such persons, it is unlikely (except in the face of a written provision to this effect) to hold that he has consented to being carelessly caused financial or physical harm, and it is only in such a case that legal liability could arise.

Granted, then, that the N.H.S. patient's rights and remedies are thus restricted, in what way may the private patient—albeit that his is nowadays the minority case—be in any better position? Since patient, practitioner and hospital are each likely to have assumed, rather than expressly agreed, that the medical and social information gained from the patient should be 'treated as confidential', the problem is to decide how precisely the courts would, if called upon to do so, spell out their assumption. In determining the precise scope of this contractual term the judges would be guided, though not bound, by the custom and usage of the profession, as revealed in such documents as the B.M.A.'s code of ethics[8]—the more so if, as appears to be the case, the practice of disclosing medical records varies from hospital to hospital, and from disease to disease. At this point the difficulty for the research worker is that the B.M.A. states the principle of medical confidence in absolute and unambiguous terms, without any exception in favour of disclosure for the purpose of scientific research—'It is a practitioner's obligation to observe the rule of professional secrecy by refraining from disclosing voluntarily without the consent of the patient (save with statutory sanction) to any third party information which he has learnt in his professional relationship with the patient.' The B.M.A. does not define what it means by ' a third party ', but we may, I think, safely assume that there is meant anyone who, unlike the nurse, pharmacist, medical secretary, or close relation, does not need to know about the patient in order to treat, or care for, him.

Some may think it ironical that the profession has, in its anxiety to protest against being compelled to disclose medical confidences in the witness box, and the increasing practice of government departments seeking medical information about claimants for welfare benefits, expressed the practitioner's obligation in terms which may hinder medical research.

It is, of course, possible that the courts would, in construing the contract entered into by the private patient, define the practitioner's obligation less rigorously, and hold that the patient may be assumed to have agreed that his medical record could be used for the purposes of properly conducted medical research—but it must be remembered that the matter will only be being debated if the patient is vigorously denying that he had consented to any such thing, and that it may easily be retorted that no difficulty arises if the patient is willing to consent, as an authoritative organ of the profession itself envisages.

If, then, we assume that the courts would read into the contract made between private patient and practitioner or hospital, the B.M.A.'s rule, two questions arise :

1. When will that contractual promise be broken ? and

2. For what sorts of harm will the patient be able to recover damages ?

Clearly, the promise will be broken if the information is disclosed to a research worker (or anyone else) without the patient's consent, and even if the patient does consent, if it is made available without the practitioner or hospital taking care to see that the research procedures incorporate precautions against disclosures to other persons. Nominal damages will be recoverable on the patient simply establishing that the contractual promise has been broken, and, in a test case, a plaintiff might be content with this. Substantial damages will be recoverable not only when, as in the case of a N.H.S. patient, he has suffered financial loss or physical harm, but also, and this is, of course, crucial, if he has suffered irritation, annoyance or embarrassment as a result of the disclosure. It would nevertheless seem that the attitude adopted by, for instance, the Medical Defence Union, is excessively, if understandably, cautious. The Union has viewed with grave disquiet a general practitioner making available to research workers on a pilot study for a community health survey the bare list of his patients.[10] Not even the B.M.A.'s statement of the practitioner's obligation extends as far as concealing the mere existence of the professional relationship, and it is difficult to see to what legally actionable harm the general practitioner's conduct could possible give rise.

Before leaving the subject of actions for damages, it is perhaps worth noticing that the ' healthy ' volunteer who participates as a subject in a research project will, in the absence of any express and detailed contract between him and the research worker, be in a position similar to that of a private patient who has consented to his medical records being available to researchers : he will be able to recover damages for irritation, annoyance or embarrassment as well as for financial loss or ill-health, if, and only if, this is caused by a careless disclosure to a third person. The courts are likely to hold that he has, by volunteering, agreed to take the risk of harm resulting from an accidental, but not from a careless, disclosure.

The possibility of a patient seeking from the courts an injunction to restrain a practitioner or hospital from disclosing to a research worker his medical record on the ground that this would constitute a breach of confidence can be more briefly considered, for here it is unnecessary to distinguish between the N.H.S. and the private patient, the judges having on several occasions stressed that their jurisdiction is based on the confidence given, and is not dependent on there being a contract or any other property right. That medical as well as professional,[11] business,[12] and marital confidences[13] are protected by this jurisdiction has been settled since at least 1820 when Lord Eldon, the then Lord Chancellor, is recorded as saying— ' If one of the late King's physicians had kept a diary of what he heard and saw, the court would not, in the King's lifetime, have permitted him to print and publish it.'[14] But once again, the absence of reported cases on the exercise of what is necessarily a discretionary jurisdiction allows no more than speculation on the outcome of a test case. The patient's contention would be that he had given the information and consented to clinical examination for one purpose, and one purpose only, namely, his own treatment, so that to use the information thereby gained for any other purpose would be a breach of confidence. The reported cases have concerned very different circumstances, but from them two broad principles emerge : (1) that the breach of confidence must be such as can be stigmatized as ' improper ', and (2) that the person seeking the injunction must be threatened, as a result of the breach of confidence, with harm sufficiently serious to justify the intervention of the court. It is doubtful whether our patient would be able to satisfy either of these requirements. The ' improper ' breaches of confidence that have so far been enjoined by the courts have all been in cases where the defendant would have gained, directly or indirectly, some undeserved financial advantage from the disclosure, and thus stand in marked contrast with one where the disclosure would have been made in the honest belief that it might contribute to medical progress. Even if a judge held that such a disclosure was ' mistaken ', it is unlikely that he would go as far as saying that it was ' improper '—for all of us, even judges, are in favour of medical research, and the practice of disclosure appears to be common in the most respected professional circles. Then again, the court would certainly decline to intervene by granting an injunction simply in order to vindicate some individualist's desire to assert his own privacy, unless he could also show that disclosure would be likely to cause him substantial harm—though here the court would regard serious annoyance or embarrassment as sufficiently serious[15] and would not require the patient to show that he was threatened with financial or physical harm. And since it is, of course, against such annoyance or embarrassment that modern research procedures are expressly designed to guard, there is, I think, here too little cause for the prudent practitioner, hospital or research worker, to fear the intervention of the courts.

My second question—Is a practitioner, the governing body of a hospital, or a government department ever justified in refusing a medical research worker access to medical or social records in their possession, on the ground that they would be acting unlawfully if they did so ?—permits of a more precise answer than my first. In no case, of course, can a research worker claim any legal right of access to the records, not even if the patient expressly requests that the researcher should be given access, for the records are in no sense the property of the patient. The general practitioner's records of a N.H.S. patient, made in accordance with the requirements of his terms of service, are the property of the Ministry of Health, the local Executive Council being the Minister's agent. Hospital records of N.H.S. patients are the property of the governing body of the hospital which in this, as in all other matters, will be guided by, but is not bound by, the advice given by the Minister. A general practitioner owns the records he makes about his private patients, and also any he makes about his N.H.S. patients over and above those that are required by his terms of service with his Executive Council. The ownership of records made by a consultant on the private patients he treats in hospital will depend on the terms of his contract with the hospital. It therefore follows that a hospital is free to make available to research workers its records on its N.H.S. patients so long as it takes care to assure itself that the research procedures are designed to prevent any careless disclosures, but that the general practitioner is not, because they do not belong to him. He will need the consent of his Executive Council, acting on behalf of the Minister of Health. The records of private patients may, as we have already seen, probably be disclosed by either practitioner or hospital only with the patient's consent.

Mention of the general practitioner's records of his N.H.S. patients, which belong to the Minister of Health, anticipates what has to be said about the records of government departments. The broad principle to be deduced from s.2 of the Official Secrets Act, 1911, is that disclosure to persons not themselves government employees is not itself unlawful, but becomes so only when the document is handed to a civil servant ' in confidence ', and whether or not the document is treated as confidential is, therefore, not a matter of law, but of departmental practice. That such legal consequences as are provided by the Official Secrets Acts should follow from a decision as to departmental practice may seem surprising, but this is probably the only feasible legislative technique. Whether, therefore, the records of the Ministers of Health and Social Security are made available to medical research workers is purely a matter for the Minister's discretion : the law leaves him free to say yea or nay, provided only that he too takes care to assure himself that the re-search procedures are designed to prevent careless disclosures. A Minister reluctant to accord access might well be reminded that he is empowered by statute to assist ' by grant or otherwise ' research into the causes, incidence, and prevention of disease. In practice, I am told, the Minister of Health exercises his discretion after consulting the Central Ethical Committee of the B.M.A., as to the conditions upon which permission should be granted. To this broad principle there appear, so far as the Ministries of Health and Social Security are concerned, to be only one exception : records of patients attending V.D. clinics. These are specially protected by a Statutory Instrument[17] (which has the force of statute) providing that they shall be treated as confidential. It must be an open question whether this legal rule would be complied with by coding of the sort that Professor Alwyn Smith will describe.

The records accumulated by the Registrar General under the powers conferred on him by the Births and Deaths Registration Act 1953, the Marriage Act 1949, the Census Act 1910, and the Population (Statistics) Acts 1938–60, are, however, in another category.

There have always been, and there still are, those who view the functions and powers of the Registrar General with suspicion, and in order to allay their suspicions, Parliament by statute, the Minister of Health by Statutory Instrument, and the Registrar General himself by departmental practice, have rendered confidential the returns made to him, so that it is clearly not now open to the Registrar General, even were he so willing, to make available to research workers anything more detailed than the bare registers of births, marriages and deaths, and statistical abstracts derived from the other records in his possession. An examination of the legal basis of this state of affairs may, however, reveal what rules would have to be changed if the information collected by him in the future was to be accessible to research workers.

Perhaps the most potentially useful information for the medical research worker is that obtained under the Population (Statistics) Acts 1938–60 from the informant on the registration of every birth, stillbirth and death. However, s.4(2) of the 1938 Act provides—' No information obtained by virtue of this Act *with respect to any particular person* shall be disclosed except so far as may be necessary ' to enable the Registrar-General to collect and publish any available statistical information with respect to the number and condition of the population. Clearly, nothing short of an Act of Parliament will suffice to change that.

There is no similar provision in the Census Act 1920, governing information obtained at a Census, but the Statutory Instrument made by the Minister of Health for the purposes of the last census included the regulation :

' No person shall use, publish or communicate to any other person any information given under [these] provisions . . .'[18] and there was nothing else in the regulations allowing information to be made available to research workers. Further, all the census forms which were prescribed by this same Statutory Instrument bore such rubrics as :

' Strictly Confidential '
' The contents of the schedule are strictly confidential '
' CONFIDENTIALITY. No information about any individual
    person, family or dwelling, will be given to anyone not employed on the Census. "[19]

These clearly prevent researchers having access to the detailed information acquired in the 1961 (or any earlier) Census. Since, however, there is nothing in the Census Act itself requiring the Minister to make regulations in precisely these terms, it may be that representations should be made to him before the regulations for the 1971 Census are drafted, in order that some exception shall then be expressed in favour of research workers.

Finally, there is the information contained in the Register of Births, Marriages and Deaths. With the exception of the registers and books kept by the Registrar General for the purpose of connecting entries in the Adopted Children's Register with the original entries in the Registers of Births[20] there is no statutory provision or regulation preventing the Registrar General allowing research workers access to them, though this may be done only ' with the express authority of the Registrar General.'[21]

Any national system of record linkage will undoubtedly require enabling legislation. If and when this comes to be drafted it will be necessary carefully to consider the desirability of amending the statutes under which the Registrar General at present works. And once a national system of medical record linkage is established the day will not be far distant when a hospital's or practitioner's failure to utilize it while treating a patient will be held by the courts to be evidence of negligence entitling that patient to damages for any maltreatment that he has, as a result, suffered.

NOTES

[1] For a useful survey of the U.S. position see a Note, *Medical Practice and the Right to Privacy.* (1959) 43. Minnesota Law Review, 943–963.

[2] General Medical Council, *Functions, Procedure and Disciplinary Jurisdiction,* The Council, London, 1967, p. 7.

[3] Letter from the Council's Deputy Registrar to the writer, 26th July, 1967.

[4] *A.B. v. C.D.* (1851) 14 Dunlop 177 (Scotland), and *Furniss v. Fitchett* [1958] N.Z.L.R. 398 (New Zealand.)

[5] Edwards v. Mallon [1908] 1 K.B. 1002.

[6] As in *Furniss v. Fitchett,* supra.

[7] For discussions of research procedures designed to guard against disclosure see, in addition to Professor Alwyn Smith's paper,

    Butler, R.N. *Privileged Communications and Research* (1963) 8 Arch. Gen. Psychiatry, 139–141.

    Whittier, John R. *Research on Huntington's Chorea : Problems of Privilege and Confidentiality* (1963) 8 Jo. Forensic Sciences, 568–575.

[8] Cf. *Furniss v. Fitchett,* supra, per Barrowclough, C. J. at p. 404.

[9] British Medical Association, *Members Handbook,* London, 1965, p. 60.

[10] Information from Dr. N. G. Pearson, University of Exeter.

[11] *Rakusen v. Ellis* [1912] 1 Ch. 831 (Solicitor).

[12] *Saltman Engineering Co. v. Campbell Engineering Co.* (1948) 65 R.P.C. 203.

[13] *Argyll (Duchess) v. Argyll (Duke)* (1965) 1 All E.R. 611.

[14] *Wyatt v. Wilson* (1820) (unreported).

[15] *Prince Albert v. Strange* (1849) 1 Mac. & G. 25 ; *Pollard v. Photographic Co.* (1889) 40 Ch. D. 355.

[16] Minister of Health : National Health Service Act, 1946, s. 16(1) ; Minister of Social Security : National Insurance (Industrial Injuries) Act, 1946, s. 73(1).

[17] National Health Service (Venereal Diseases) Regulations, 1948. S.I. 1948. No. 2517, Reg. 3. It is just possible that this S.I. would support an action for damages for breach of statutory duty, as has happened in the United States : *Munzer v. Blaisdell*, 183 Misc. 773, 49 N.Y.S. 2d 915 (Sup. Ct. 1944).

[18] Census Regulations, 1960, S.I. 1960. No. 1175. Reg. 16(2).

[19] See the forms printed at pp. 489–503, *Statutory Instruments 1960, Part 1*, London, H.M.S.O. 1961.

[20] See Adoption Act, 1958, s. 20(5).

[21] Registration (Births, Stillbirths, Deaths and Marriages) Consolidated Regulations, 1954. S.I. 1954, No. 1596, Reg. 10(2).

PEOPLE IN CONFIDENCE. THE EXPANDING CIRCLE

L. J. WITTS

It is a truism that medicine has undergone great changes during this century but it is rarely appreciated how widespread the effects have been. The difference between Luke Fildes's picture, painted in 1891, of the doctor sitting at the bedside of a sick child and the situation of a child today being treated for acute leukaemia in a specialized unit under near-sterile conditions is obvious and dramatic but it is less generally realized that concepts such as the doctor–patient relationship and the confidentiality of records have changed with equal pace. Most serious illnesses and many minor ones are now investigated and treated in hospital and many hospitals now work on a unit record system which means that the records of the patient on the first and subsequent admissions are brought together in a single file. The confidential relationship is now between the patient and the hospital as a whole and it is not confined to a single doctor.

Few people who have not themselves recently been patients in a large hospital, particularly a teaching hospital, realize how many people may come in contact with a patient and learn about his affairs. There are the initial procedures of inscription on the waiting list, the completion of the admission form with its identifying details and the registration of the patient so that previous admissions can be checked and he can be given a hospital number. This work is done by clerical workers and is similar to that of receptionists and secretaries in private practice. In the ward the patient becomes known to a large number of doctors, nurses, medical students, secretaries, technicians, radiographers, physiotherapists and so on. His illness may be discussed not only in small classes on or near the ward but at a case demonstration in a lecture theatre.

If an illness is likely to be protracted or to affect the patient's capacity for work or if there are environmental or emotional problems, the patient is interviewed by a medical social worker who not only sees his case history but supplements it with an intimate enquiry into his private life. Social information is one of the sensitive areas in case taking and most medical social workers do not file their notes in the unit case record but merely note the fact of referral, *e.g.* ' There was a complex matrimonial situation, a full record of which is available in the Medical Social Department'. There is at present a dichotomy between medical information which is regarded as neutral and therefore employable for statistical purposes, and social information which is confidential and not so employed. This is appreciated to be unsatisfactory by medical social workers and by doctors interested in the relation of psychological and social factors to somatic and psychosomatic disease. We can expect that before long social information will be coded so that a transcript giving the appropriate details in stenographic form can be incorporated in the unit case record.

Most professorial clinical departments and many others hold a weekly meeting at which the ward sister, medical social workers, house officers, registrars, research assistants and senior medical staff are present, anything up to a dozen people or more. The list of patients in the ward is gone through in relation to progress, treatment and research investigations, discharges are discussed with special references to social problems, after-care and follow-up, and deaths are analysed with particular reference to possible mistakes in diagnosis and treatment. This is a simplified form of the Medical Audit which is now widely used in the United States. On discharge a summary of the case record is made by the registrar and a copy of this, usually with a covering letter from the consultant in charge of the ward, is sent to the patient's general practitioner and often to other consultants or practitioners who may have seen the patient or be interested in the outcome of the case.

The completion of the case record after the discharge of the patient from hospital is a complicated process and the patient's dossier passes through the hands of many people, each with a specified task, before it is finally coded, stapled and filed in the hospital records department. Details are extracted for the Hospital Inpatient Enquiry, Hospital Activity Analysis or other procedures by which a statistical analysis of the hospital's work can be prepared. In the Oxford area this is closely linked with the Oxford Record Linkage Study. The preliminary work is done at the hospital itself and the final work at the offices of the Regional Hospital Board.

In most regions there is a Cancer Registry which usually attempts to register all cases of cancer in the area under study and therefore searches the hospital notes for cases of cancer. The work is nearly always done by record clerks who work under the general supervision of the director of the Cancer Registry and complete a detailed registration form for each patient diagnosed as suffering from cancer. Although registration of cancer is carried out at the same time and place as the other procedures mentioned above, once the information about cancer has been abstracted it is usually handled as an entity and arrangements are made to keep it up to date by enquiries from practitioners and consultants and by obtaining notifications of deaths from cancer from the medical officers of health.

The maintenance and use of the case records in mental hospitals deserve special mention. There has been a surprising change from the atmosphere of secrecy in which people with mental illnesses were once treated. Restriction of communication with the patient to a single doctor is rare outside the practice of psychoanalysis and even there the analysis may, with the patient's permission, be overheard and overlooked by students through a one-way screen. Mental nurses usually work in shifts and maintain detailed case histories to keep their co-workers informed about the patients and their progress. The difficulty is faced that patients will sometimes read their own notes and even those of other patients. Therapy is often carried out in groups and these are sometimes large. The patient consents to the procedure beforehand and complaints that information filters out beyond the group are unusual. Indeed, the only trouble is occasional embarrassment at the revelations made or the language used by some other member of the group. On discharge a summary of the patient's notes including his name is sent to the Ministry of Health, which has kept statistics on mental illness for a number of years, and a copy may also be sent to the local medical officer of health, as he is in charge of the mental welfare officers who work in association with the psychiatrists in following up the patient and his treatment, which is increasingly carried out within the community rather than the hospital.

In hospitals using the unit record system the notes on any subsequent re-admission are filed together with the old under the same number. No one is likely to complain louder than the patient if previous information about him is not available. Follow-up studies are accepted as part and parcel of the unit record system and in Oxford it has been shown that nearly 100 per cent. of patients can be followed up without objection (Edwards and Truelove, 1963 ; Beveridge et al., 1965). These studies normally involve only one or

335

two doctors, a medical social worker and a secretary, but in a recent study of the need for terminal care in cancer a relatively large number of people were involved—hospital doctors, general practitioners, health visitors, medical social workers and secretaries. There had been fears that the patients might be alarmed or the relatives critical but this did not happen.

Records circulate freely within a hospital or group of hospitals covered by a unit record system. If the patient gives a history of previous medical treatment it is assumed that this implies consent to any necessary enquiries from the practitioners or hospitals concerned. It is interesting to find that psychiatric hospitals have advanced farther than general hospitals in this field. Every effort is made to secure continuity in the documentation of mental illnesses, including records of admission to other hospitals. This is done to discover the duration of remissions, the frequency of relapse, the difference in the diagnostic label which may be attached to the patient at different times or by different psychiatrists, and the effect of particular psychotropic drugs on the presentation of symptoms.

In spite of the large number of people with access to information about patients it is surprising how rarely leakage occurs or complaints about the system are received. I have been unable to find evidence of any medico-legal actions. Hospital staff are warned that if they divulge information about patients to unauthorized people they will be subject to instant dismissal. Record clerks sign a declaration of confidentiality. When there are leakages, they are likely to come from those in direct contact with the patient and to be the result of careless talk. There are special difficulties in a relatively small area like Oxford and on two occasions over the last few years office cleaners have gossiped about patients whose notes had not been locked up and whose names they had recognized. The Senior Records Officer deals personally with notes of staff and with notes of people she recognizes as relations of members of the staff, particularly that of the Records Department. Special care is necessary in cases such as abortion and attempted suicide. The sooner the notes can be abstracted and an identification number can be used instead of the patient's name, the simpler for all concerned. As a general rule, the further the notes move from the patient, the more anonymous they become and the smaller the risk of leakage.

The system I have been describing has grown up spontaneously in response to the complexities of medical treatment today, the large number of people involved and the necessity for maintaining the efficiency of the hospitals in the face of a rapidly increasing load of work. Indeed, most people would feel that management committees

336

and boards of governors were failing in their duty if they did not use modern methods of processing data and retrieving information about their work, and that this implies that case records can be used as required for statistical purposes. The handling of the notes by records clerks is quite compatible with the confidentiality of the individual case record which is the responsibility of the hospital authorities. Enquiries from self-styled friends, solicitors, journalists, institutions like insurance companies and others are not answered without the patient's consent. Solicitors sometimes go to considerable lengths to obtain information which may be used in divorce or similar proceedings, and journalists have been known to disguise themselves as medical students or house officers to obtain information.

Some check must therefore be maintained before the unit case record is allowed to pass beyond the ambit of the hospital or hospital group, but a hospital will normally provide access to its records for bona fide research workers and statisticians. Once the notes have been abstracted and coded, as for record linkage, the data are depersonalized and the issue of confidentiality hardly arises in work with coded material. The medical defence societies appear to have no record of complaints from doctors or patients because of the use of records for statistical purposes, and they appear not to expect any.

So far I have been discussing the confidentiality of medical records as seen by a professor of medicine at the head of an active department of clinical research and this is really all that the title of my paper requires. I might, however, add a coda on the subject of medical ethics which has been at the back of my mind in writing this paper. In discussing record linkage we must not think only of the legal ownership of medical records and of the furtherance of medical progress. Indeed, the latter is a dangerous obsession for anyone who works with patients. We must think also of medical ethics while admitting that they are constantly changing. Medical ethics are concerned not only with the welfare of the patient but with the relation between doctors and with the discouragement of anything which might produce friction between patients and doctors.

Doctors desire confidentiality of medical records to save themselves from possible personal embarrassment as well as to protect the interests of their patients. The problem and its solution can be illustrated from the work of the Committee on Safety of Drugs. The Committee operates an early warning system under which doctors are asked to report adverse reactions to drugs suffered by their patients. The original reports are identified by means of the name of the patient and the reporting doctor to avoid duplication

z

of reports on the same case. Doctors were originally afraid that by reporting adverse reactions they might expose themselves to the risk of legal proceedings but their anxieties were allayed when it was explained that the information would be coded and transferred to punch cards or magnetic tape. The Ministry of Health has done a good deal of work on prescriptions under the National Health Service to obtain statistics on drug usage and these statistics can sometimes be compared with those for adverse reactions. There is no ethical conflict when work of this kind is done in a statistical frame of reference. Problems only arise if one wishes to work back from the statistic to the patient, as, for example, when one wishes to find out what has happened to people for whom a particular drug has been prescribed. This is only possible with the agreement and co-operation of the prescribing doctor. In so far as it concerns record linkage this point about the direction of flow of information will be discussed by Professor Alwyn Smith to whom I must now give place.

REFERENCES

BEVERIDGE, B. R., BANNERMANN, R. M., EVANSON, J. M. & WITTS, L. J. (1965). Hypochromic anaemia : a retrospective study and follow-up of 378 in-patients. *Q. Jl. Med.* **34,** 145.
EDWARDS, F. C. & TRUELOVE, S. C. (1963). The course and prognosis of ulcerative colitis. *Gut,* **4,** 299.

PRESERVATION OF CONFIDENCE AT THE CENTRAL LEVEL

ALWYN SMITH

THE term ' Medical Record Linkage ' has been used in two different, although related senses. The first use denotes either the process of so arranging a series of records that where more than one record exists for each of several individuals the records relating to each individual are brought together ; or the process of bringing together the records of individuals who may be related to each other familially or in some similar way. The second use of the term denotes the maintenance of a centralized permanent file which assembles the various records relating to individuals into a series of personal dossiers.

The first use of the term describes a common procedure in many different contexts where the necessity arises to assemble in respect of a series of individuals a set of multiple records which may refer to events separated by time or may arise from different sources. A well established application occurs in epidemiological or genetic surveys using multiple sources of ascertainment and where multiple inclusion of individuals would be undesirable. A more complex example arises in the assembly of pedigrees when families may gain inclusion through more than one member being a propositus. The procedures generally involve arranging the records in such a way that multiple records relating to an individual may readily be identified. The principal technical requirements for such record linkage are an adequate identification of the individuals represented by each record. The adequacy of identification depends on the context ; application of suitable procedures based on estimating the probability of identity of two slightly differently identified individuals can effect linkages adequate for many purposes even in the face of errors or anomalies in recording. Such procedures may be programmed for computer application and thus facilitate faster working and larger files than may be practicable using clerical records procedures.

In the context of this first use of the term the issue of confidentiality arises when the necessary scale of an enquiry involves the scrutiny of identified records which would not normally be available to the investigator in the course of his own practice. The problem arises, of course, whenever such a scale is involved and identified records must be used, whether or not linkage is a part of the exercise. But in other applications it is usually possible, if desired, to make unidentified records available for the work. Where linkage is involved some identification is essential.

In a very large number of cases the use of conventional personal identification will give rise to no ethical problems. In these cases no linkage problem need arise. However, in some cases it may be desirable to ensure that the personal anonymity of the individuals whose records are involved is safeguarded. This may particularly arise in relation to records where legal confidentiality is involved or where the records are the responsibility of a government agency. In such cases it may yet be possible to effect appropriate linkages.

Most linkage systems that have been developed for computer use make use of coded versions of individual's names. It is generally a feature of these name codes that they may be uniquely constructed from the names but that the names cannot be re-constructed uniquely from the codes. The identification of persons by these codes together with such information as date of birth, sex, etc., usually

339

permits positive linkages to be made, especially where more than one name is available to identify an individual. If records which need to be kept anonymous but which might be needed in linkage studies, were simply identified by name codes, the records would be safeguarded against casual access but remain inherently linkable.

A simple example of such a name code is used in the Office of the Registrar General for Scotland. For all registrations of births, stillbirths, marriages and deaths, at least two surnames are requested for each individual ; these are the person's own surname and his mother's maiden surname. For married women the woman's own maiden surname is also requested. In the enormous majority of cases all the requested surnames are, in fact, recorded. On the punched cards which contain the statistical data handled by the Registrar General these names are each represented by a surname code. This (Fig. 1) is a two digit code which distributes surnames alphabetically and in approximately their proportionate frequencies of occurrence. Two surnames thus define a four-digit, paired-name sequence which divides a population into 10,000 approximately equal groups, within each of which, sex and date of birth will usually uniquely define an individual, without identifying him in the conventional sense. Even so common a name as Smith occurs in less than 1 in 50 individuals ; therefore, individuals for whom two names are Smith occur less often than once in 2,500. Since in Scotland, there are only about 150 births a day of each sex and even in England only about 1,500, identification is usually simple, positive and yet anonymous.

Familial linkage can equally easily be achieved since birth records contain the date of the parents marriage, and birth and death records contain date of birth. A simple assembly of familial occurrence of stillbirth was achieved by sorting stillbirth records into a sequence comprising paired parental names and date of parents' marriage. Records relating to siblings then lay adjacently. This was verified by tracing the conventional records *via* the register entry number but such verification is not necessary for most research purposes.

It is not difficult to devise even more discriminating codes. Soundex is such a code although it is also subject to the defect that errors in spelling a name are quite likely to affect the code since its first digit is the initial of the surname where errors are particularly common. An improvement in this respect is the code devised by the present author and a colleague for use in Glasgow and which consists essentially of Soundex code with an appropriately numericized first letter (Fig. 2). This code is currently referred to as SINGS (Soundex, Initial Numericised ; Granick, Smith). It has been tried

Fig. 1. *Two-digit surname code for Scotland*
(Alphabetic code listing)

AA-AK	01	HAE-HAZ	36	N	71
AL-AM	02	HB-HH	37		
AN-AZ	03	HI-HOL	38	O	72
		HOM-HT	39		
BAA-BAQ	04	HU-HZ	40	PA-PD	73
BAR-BD	05			PE-PN	74
BE	06	I	98	PO-PZ	75
BF-BN	07				
-BQ	08	JA-JN	41	Q	98
BROWN	09	JO-JZ	42		
BR (Ex 09)	10			RA-RD	76
BS-BZ	11	KA-KEL	43	RE	77
		KEM-KEZ	44	RF-ROB (Ex 79)	78
CAA-CAM (Ex 13)	12	KF-KZ	45	ROBERTSON	79
CAMPBELL	13			ROC-RZ	80
CAB-CG	14	LA-LD	46		
CH-CN	15	LE-LH	47	SA-SC	81
COA-CON	16	LI-LN	48	SD-SH	82
COO-COZ	17	LO-LZ	49	SI-SL	83
CP-CR	18			SMITH	84
CS-CZ	19	MAC/McA, B	50	SM-SS (Ex 84)	85
		CA-CL	51	STEWART	86
DA-DD	20	CM-CZ	52	ST (Ex 86)	87
DE-DN	21	D	53	SU-SZ	88
DOA-DON	22	E, F	54		
DOO-DT	23	G	55	TA-TG	89
DU-SZ	24	H-J	56	TH	90
		KA-KE	57	TI-TZ	91
E	25	KF-KZ	58		
		LA	59	U, V	99
FA-FH	26	LB-LZ	60		
FI-FL	27	M, N	61	WAA-WAQ	92
FM-FO	28	O-Z	62	WAR-WAZ	93
FP-FZ	29			WB-WH	94
		MAA-MAQ	63	WILSON	95
GA-GH	30	MAR-MAZ	64	WI (Ex 95)	96
GI	31	MB-MH	65	WJ-WZ	97
GJ-GQ	32	MI-MN	66		
GRA	33	MOA-MOO	67	X-Z	99
GRB-GZ	34	MOP-MT	68		
		MUA-MUN	69	NONE	00
HAA-HAQ	35	MUO-MZ	70		

on 12,999 representative Scottish persons whose 3,239 different surnames fell into 839 different codes. The code with the greatest frequency included the name Smith together with eight other names and accounted for 1·8 per cent. of the persons. Thus the largest paired surname code block would contain only 0·03 per cent. of the file. Many of the codes will more or less uniquely identify an individual while still preserving conventional anonymity.

A problem which may arise in the use of governmental data in this way is that the linkage and analysis may have to be carried out within the government agency involved but to the specification of the investigator requiring the analyses. This raises no problems beyond that of availability of the appropriate resources but experience suggests that this problem may often be troublesome and

FIG. 2. *SINGS* code for surnames*

Letters	Code
b, f, p, v	1
c, g, j, k, q, s, x, z, tch	2
d, t	3
l	4
m, n	5
r, w†	6
a, e, i, o, u, h, y	7*
Mc, M', Mac	8*

†*only coded if the first letter of a name ;
two adjacent consonants of the same group are coded only once ;
two consonants of the same group are coded twice if separated by a vowel or by h, y, w, ', or -.

If a name has insufficient letters to give four digits the requisite number of zeros is added to give four digits.

*SINGS is an acronym for Soundex, Initial Numericized ;
Granick, Smith.

A programme which encodes names and sorts into code sequence is available in IBM 360 Assembly Language.

occasionally insuperable. Usually, however, duplicate punched cards containing the required data and an adequate identification code may be made available to investigators.

Although this first use of the term ' Medical Record Linkage ' denotes a set of procedures which will satisfactorily meet most research needs for linked records, the maintenance of permanent linked record files is frequently useful in the context of management studies and for improving the accessibility of comprehensive data on individuals. This second use of the term involves a different problem of confidence.

The existence of a permanent comprehensive file of linked records might possibly be held to be undesirable for two rather different reasons. The first is that casual access to personal dossiers may be simplified and that this may be contrary to the individuals' interests. The second raises a more difficult problem in that such permanent centralized files of dossiers greatly facilitate organized access by government or other central agencies and this also may be deemed undesirable. For example, declarations about health on applications for driving licences might be checked from regionally held personal medical history files. Whether this is in principle desirable or not is a question which might well be debated on some other occasion. What seems quite certain is that many medical men and their patients would regard it as undesirable. It is therefore important that records should not only be preserved from such access but should also clearly be seen to be so preserved.

In order to examine the possibility of such preservation it will be useful to distinguish two different applications of the permanent linked record file. These are : first, statistical analysis of longitudinal or familial data ; secondly, rapid retrieval of personal medical histories involving multiple records from possibly many different sources or contacts with the health and medical services.

Statistical analysis of linked records is unlikely to require that the records should be identified although the linkage procedure may well require such identification. Fortunately, a circumstance of current file-handling techniques is helpful. Many records in a linked record file may be of variable length and the personal dossiers will usually be variable in respect of the number of records they contain. This variability would complicate the linkage procedures to an unacceptable extent if linkage were carried out on the complete linked records.

In practice, therefore, it is usual to maintain two files. One contains the data required for statistical analysis while the other consists mainly of identification data and a suitable reference to each individual's entry in the statistical file. Linkage is carried out by first matching each new record to the corresponding entry in the identification file and then re-sorting the new records for convenient updating of the statistical file. In adopting this procedure in a linked child health record system in Glasgow, my colleagues and I arranged to order the statistical file in an identifying number sequence with the identification file holding the key to the identity of each numbered person and the statistical file holding only the data and the number. Thus the data and the individuals' identities are separated into distinct files. Some such procedure is common and quite convenient. It provides a degree of safeguard to the anonymity of the statistical records. The safeguard may be enhanced if special security arrangements are made with respect to the identification file and where this would be desirable it may be arranged that this file is kept by a different agency from that involved in maintaining the statistical file. For example, responsibility for identification files could be assigned to a suitable ' ombudsman ' department. For most purposes, the existence of the barrier afforded by separation of the identification and statistical files together with the necessity for

SMITH

writing a programme to produce any printout of data for an identified person, would be regarded as adequate safeguards.

But another potential application of the permanent linked record
file involves the storage and rapid retrieval of medical records in the
form of personal medical histories. Such an application might fill
the need to be able to look up a patient's medical history or an episode
from it, despite the constituent records having been made in many
different units of the health or medical services. For example, it
might often be helpful to be able to consult the record of a surgical
operation performed many years previously in a different hospital
from the one in which a new operation is currently contemplated.
Such retrieval of records is at present usually a cumbersome and un-
certain process ; the existence of a central file of linked records would
probably improve it. On the other hand it may not always be desirable for such records to be readily available ; the patient's interest
is not necessarily always best served by total disclosure of his past
history to his current medical attendant. It would not be an adequate
safeguard to require the patient's consent to a search of his medical
history file ; the patient may not be in a position to grant or withhold
such consent and in any case, withholding of consent is often not a
real option for the patient who might fear the consequences of such
withholding in terms of his relationship with his current doctor. At
present no consent is usually required to retrieve earlier records made
and stored in the institution with which a patient is currently involved.
However, it would normally be considered courteous to seek permission from the previous attendant or institution to consult records
made elsewhere. Current practice, as it often does, here suggests
a possible solution to the problem. If the linked file consisted of an
identification file containing reference to the location of records in an
associated information file, the former might be used to discover the
existence of the latter and access to the latter might involve a procedure designed to justify such access. Since, technically, the development and maintenance of computer-stored, linked plain language
records is likely to involve just such a two-stage indexed file procedure, the system need involve few, if any, unnecessary complications. Most practical developments in computerized medical record
procedures involve the development of a file of record abstracts
which summarize record content and provide a multiple access
index to the full records. When these latter are also stored for
computer access it is likely that convenience will dictate that they
remain separate from the abstract or index file.

Hitherto in this discussion it has been assumed that the development of Medical Record Linkage will inevitably involve linked or
344

linkable records being centrally stored and that governmental or closely related agencies will be the appropriate bodies to accept responsibility for their maintenance and protection. However, it may sometimes be important to interpose some degree of barrier between these records and the central government considered as a political agency. In many of the countries of Europe which were occupied by Nazi Germany before and during the war, local citizens felt it to be their duty to destroy as many personal records as possible so as to protect such files from possible misuse. The memory of these events is still fresh for many people to whom, in consequence, the existence of comprehensive files in the hands of political governments constitutes an unacceptable threat. It may be possible to devise acceptable barriers by vesting responsibility for maintenance of records in agencies which are to some extent independent. However, it is probable that we shall have to accept that the potential power of governments to control individual lives will necessarily increase with every technical advance ; the remedy against misuse of such power will have to lie largely elsewhere than in the development of the techniques themselves.

Meanwhile, it seems important to assert that identifiable medical records may only be used to illuminate issues of medical care in relation to the patients they concern or as observations whose study may contribute to a better understanding of medicine. It should be an established principle that their use in any other context must be subject to the consent of their authors or their subjects or in many cases of both. In particular, their use for governmental purposes in relation to the individuals whose medical history they contain must be regarded as absolutely proscribed.

DISCUSSION ON PAPERS OF MR GLAZEBROOK, PROFESSOR WITTS AND PROFESSOR ALWYN SMITH

Dr Bahn : I feel it may be helpful to give very briefly some of our experience with the problems of confidentiality as they affect the Maryland psychiatric case register because psychiatry is probably the most sensitive of all clinical areas. When we set up the psychiatric case register in Maryland we found that whereas there had been no previous objection to our collecting information about the names of the patients, once we announced that we were going to link the information there were many objections. In the end we found it necessary to take the radical action of getting a statute placed before the State Legislature. This was passed.

We had already obtained administrative action but this was not deemed to be sufficient. The Director of the National Institute of Mental Health which is one of the co-operating agencies, had issued, under the powers of his office, a regulation protecting the privacy of the case records. This regulation included an important provision which will interest Professor Alwyn Smith (p. 339) namely, that no other Government agency could have access to the records. However, this did not satisfy the medical profession. The primary reason for this dissatisfaction, as was hinted by Professor Witts (p. 338) was not concern for the privacy of the patient but concern that the records might be used in litigation against doctors. Therefore the Statute which we worked out with the lawyers and which was passed has provided that the data may not be used in litigation and, furthermore, that the courts may not sub poena the records. Another important point is that the Statute is concerned with health data in general and is not limited to psychiatric data. Any data reported for research purposes to the State Mental Health Department may only be used for research purposes, and may not be divulged. Further, the identity of any person in this file may not be disclosed to anybody. A penalty was instituted for wilful disclosure. It was a wonderful thing to be able to get this Statute passed and to save the day.

Dr Doll : I should like to give my own experience of the co-operation I have had from hospitals and doctors in trying to collect material about people on a fairly extensive scale over the last 20 years. I have whenever possible avoided including private patients in any study, for reasons which were made obvious by Mr Glaze-brook's presentation, but from time to time private patients have been included and I have in fact only once had a consultant refuse to give me information subsequently about a private patient who was included in a study, and that was 15 years ago.

When obtaining information from hospitals about groups of employed persons or about patients, I have been struck by the frequency with which information is now provided by a records officer. It has always been my practice whenever possible to approach the consultant, but one doesn't always know his name, and I have been somewhat surprised that in so many hospitals the records officer writes back directly and provides the information. I wonder how far records officers have been authorized to do this by the consultants ; but it seems to be something that is fairly generally established and has presumably been approved.

I have had one objection from one of the 15,000 spondylitic patients we have been following. One person wrote on behalf of his wife and asked what I was doing making enquiries about her. I had no right to know anything about her illness and he refused to give me any information. I once also had an objection from one of the 11,000 gas workers who were being followed ; he also wished me to cease making enquiries about his future health.

I would like to ask Miss Jones a question relating to research into occupational health problems. In my view it is unnecessary and undesirable to obtain the written consent of members of a population before you start following them to study occupational diseases which may develop, and I am sorry that she suggested that we may have to do this before making use of her records. I would have thought that the ordinary procedure would be to obtain the approval of the representatives of the men, namely their trade union representatives, and that this would have been adequate. This has always been my practice and as far as I know the practice of people especially concerned with occupational medicine ; and I should be interested to hear what Professor Schilling thinks about it. Would Miss Jones accept that it was adequate if consent had been given by the elected representatives of the men one was studying ?

Miss Jones : I am not responsible for disclosure policy within the Ministry. If the consent of the people concerned has been obtained you are on absolutely safe ground. If there were a question of following up a population in respect of whom it was possible to obtain the consent of their representative, that is the trade union and perhaps the employer's organization, it would certainly be considered but I wouldn't commit myself in advance. I think it is a possibility.

Professor Case : I had wanted to comment before Miss Jones replied to the last question. If we are going to use her records to follow up a population group, in some circumstances it could be most undesirable that the members of this group should know this, lest they become unnecessarily frightened. We might be checking an occupational group to see whether a new process that had been introduced was in fact harmless and it would be quite wrong to subject these people to any worry until we knew that there were grounds for anxiety.

The other point I wanted to make was that I do not think my views conflict at all with Professor Alwyn Smith's views about freedom. I had to outline in a very brief time that there are more than one type of freedom. But I think we might run into some difficulties if we proscribe absolutely the access of other Government departments. For instance, one extremely valuable investigation in public health is being carried out at the moment by the Ministry of Labour into occupational disease. If the Ministry, because it is a government department, were to be denied access to other records it would make it extremely difficult to carry out such a survey.

347

Mr Healy : Hitherto, it has been fair to assume that magnetic tape as a storage medium is somewhat more confidential than a conventional paper file. With the new multi-access systems, this may no longer be so. Anyone who knows a few code-words will be able to sit at his own typewriter or display screen and scan as much of the information in the system as he chooses to call up. To some extent it is possible to build elaborate security checks into this kind of system but they are expensive both to design and to operate. What duty has the systems-designer to guard against malicious misuse of this kind?

Mr Glazebrook : The short answer to that is that courts wouldn't hold computer manufacturers or computer owners liable for the acts of a very clever and malicious person but they would expect the best precautions known at the time to be used, provided that this did not make the system too expensive. They would take the point that you cannot be expected to spend thousands and thousands of pounds to guard against a very remote possibility.

Professor Alwyn Smith : It seems to me that anyone who is prepared to devote energy and ingenuity on the scale that would be required to crack a code that Michael Healy had designed, for example, might get into practically any type of record system, and might even in fact steal the Crown jewels !

Mr Reed : I only want to make one very brief comment about the Registrar General's position. Mr Glazebrook is of course right about the Population Statistics Act material, and about the ordinary registration material which we not only can but do make available quite freely to research workers. As far as the Census is concerned he said that the Minister of Health could quite easily alter the situation by framing the regulations differently. He could, I am convinced, do so only at the cost of wrecking the Census. We ourselves have very little doubt that if there were any question of Census data being handed over to anybody, however bona fide, the whole thing would break down and we should cease to have the public co-operation which we do at present get.

PART 8

GENERAL SESSION III

Chairman : Dr A. LINDGREN (Stockholm)

RECORD LINKAGE IN EDUCATION

A. A. Croxford

This paper is concerned with the official statistics of students in the various fields of education which are available after finishing compulsory schooling, as produced by the Department of Education and Science (formerly the Ministry of Education). Until now record linkage has played little part in the production of these statistics, and as a consequence certain areas of investigation which are becoming of increasing importance to educational planners have been almost entirely unexplored. The second part of this paper will explain how record linkage is expected to make good these deficiences while the first part will explain what these deficiences are and how they have been inevitable under their traditional method of collection.

Present methods of data collection

There are two possible methods of collection of the basic information —it may be collected for groups of ' similar ' students or alternatively for individuals. The definition of the word ' similar ' will vary according to the analysis required, and since few groups of people are exactly alike in all respects the first method tends in the limit to become the second method.

In some sectors of education information is now collected about individual students, which enables a wide range of analyses to be undertaken. We are at present, however, in a transitional period, and for ease of presentation the sectors which collect individual information are treated by this paper as if they were in the future. For this reason the paper tends to underplay the developments already achieved.

The degree of detail in which data are collected and the complexity of the ways in which they are analysed depend on two distinct factors. These are what might be termed the strength of the demand for the information and the availability of resources (both of people and machines) to produce the analyses required. For many years the major purpose of official statistics was that they should form part of an annual report by the Ministry of Education. The tables which were published in this report showed the numbers of students in each part of the educational system. The tables were not varied greatly from year to year and thus enabled a very simple

351

system of data collection to be employed. It consisted in essence of sending blank copies of the tables to be published to each educational establishment, which inserted its own students in the tables and returned them to the Ministry. There the individual tables were added up in order to form national totals. The staff which was required by the Ministry to do this work was of the order of 20 in number and these were supported by various card machines. Although the scheme may seem extremely simple when described in one or two sentences in this way it did in fact involve an enormous amount of work, of coding the original returns, punching the data on to cards and then processing the cards themselves. Over the last six or seven years the demands for analyses have been increasing, and to a great extent the traditional methods have managed to keep pace with these demands, although this would not have been the case had the Department not bought a computer which took over much of the work which was done by the Hollerith machinery. However, not only has there been a demand for further analyses of the traditional type, that is, showing the number of students undergoing particular forms of education, but there has been a growing demand for a completely different type of analysis.

The system which has been described so far produces a series of snapshot pictures of the educational system at different times, which shows how the stock of students and their deployment have been changing over the course of time. What the figures do not do however is to enable one to estimate the number of different students that have been catered for by the system, or what one might term the annual turnover of students. That is to say, the figures do not give any accurate idea of the extent to which the students reported in one year are the same ones as were reported in the previous year. Far more important however than the gross turnover figure is the study of the many different ways in which students may progress through the educational system. After leaving school they may for instance go to university and perhaps then to teacher training college, or they may enrol upon a vocational course at a technical college, where the number of combinations of courses which may be followed consecutively is for all practical purposes limitless. A study of the various paths traced by individuals through the system will yield benefits in two distinct fields. The pure educationalists will be extremely interested in evaluating the effects which previous academic experience and qualification has upon performance on the current course. It is already well known that on certain courses where there are two streams of entry to the course, students who enter by one stream are much more likely to succeed than those who enter by the other, but very little is known about the effect upon success rates of academic experience in the less recent past. When the facts have been established it may prove to be worthwhile varying the entry regulations or perhaps the syllabuses of certain courses.

A major problem is that of wastage. It is known that the proportion of students who fall by the wayside before reaching their final examination is fairly high, although it is some years since figures were collected. This wastage means that a fairly large proportion of resources in higher education is being devoted to students who do not continue with their study. It might be argued that this does not represent a complete waste of resources because these students have undoubtedly learnt something which would be of use to them in later life, yet on the other hand few employers would attach much significance to a partially completed course of education which did not result in some form of certificate, and thus for practical purposes this education has been wasted. If means could be found to recognize and also deter the students who were not likely to continue their course to the end there is no doubt that a great saving of resources would be achieved.

The second major use to which figures of the flow of students can be put is in the estimation of future numbers in education. Without a knowledge of the flow of students an estimation of future numbers is a very crude process. One can only observe the numbers over a period of years and in many cases simply extrapolate them, either by extrapolating the numbers themselves or by extrapolating the percentage which these numbers represent of the population. If, however, it proves possible to document the flows of students throughout the entire field of education a far more elegant way presents itself. If one knew the origins of all the students in a particular year one could so to speak work backwards and reassemble these students as they were in the previous year. The number of those who had wasted during the year would be found by deducting the assembled numbers from the known total. By examining any single course for this previous year one could establish what proportion of its students had flowed in the many different directions available. It is our hope that by repeating this exercise over a series of years one could then establish with a certain amount of assurance the probability that students now on any course will in fact flow in any particular direction. It is then simply a matter of multiplication to calculate the expected numbers on each course in the following year. By repeating this multiplication until the expected numbers for all courses have been established one can arrive at a complete picture of the expected numbers in the following year. It is then theoretically possible to take these expected numbers and multiply them once again by the same probabilities and thus arrive at the expected numbers in the second year ; and so on. The number of multiplications involved would be enormous, since the students on any one course would need to be divided into many sections in order to arrive at an answer which was logically sound. There would need to be separate transitional probabilities for every year of the course, for each sex separately, and probably also for various groupings of the students by age. Almost certainly these transitional probabilities will change from year to year and trends will have to be recognized in these, rather than in the numbers themselves as in the past. The total number of groups of students, N, will certainly be very large and the total number of transitional probabilities for any one year would approach N^2. This is because, with certain obvious exceptions, a student on any course can theoretically proceed to any other course. The obvious exceptions are for instance that a student in a group of 17-year-olds must proceed to a group of 18-year-olds in the following year, a group for any other age being impossible. When all the basic data has been assembled it is certainly going to need the services of the large computer to perform this calculation (referred to within the Department as the Model project) upon which a statistician has been working for the last two years.

Provision of the basic data required

There are three methods open for the acquisition of the data required. The educational establishment could be asked to continue to submit returns on the present basis, these returns having been made far more complicated by the sub-division of individual courses into the many groups of students required for the Model project. It soon becomes clear however that such a system of collection would place an intolerable burden upon all concerned since, as was stated earlier, the number of possible paths which may be followed in order to arrive at a particular point in the educational system is practically limitless. A course containing 30 students might well have to be entered on a return which had to allow for say 3,000 different combinations of past paths and present details, and it is obvious that this is not an economical proposition. In fact it becomes plain that the only satisfactory method is for the collection of the details of individual students. Having decided that this must be done, the choice of the best method of doing so is less clear-cut. One method of obtaining the past histories of students would be to send out each year a questionnaire addressed either to a sample of students or to all students, in which they or their colleges would be required to give details of their present course of study, their past educational experience, and the qualifications they had achieved. If this were done on a sample basis, it might omit details of important yet small groups of students, whilst if it were done on a 100 per cent. basis it would require an enormous administrative effort. In either case it would be galling to a college if on a course which lasted say five years, details of the history of a particular student had to be submitted five times before he finally completed the course. To avoid this repetition of work it has been decided to establish a central computer-held record of students, which will be updated each year by the additional information for that year, and this will naturally require some means of record linkage.

It will therefore be seen that in education, record linkage is not the only possible solution of our particular problems but merely the most economical one in our estimation.

It is not intended at the outset to include school pupils in the central record. Instead of collecting information on school pupils year by year, use will be made of an existing annual survey of school leavers, which asks for details of the educational achievements, and expected destination on leaving school, of a 10 per cent. sample of pupils who have left school during the past year. The schools themselves perform the ' record linking ', *i.e.* the assembly of the required facts, which is necessary in this case. Plans are being prepared at present for using this survey as a basis of the central record, to which will be added details of university students, trainee teachers and students in further education establishments.

Whenever sampling is employed it will be by date of birth, *e.g.* a 10 per cent. sample will be those students born on the 5th, 15th, or 25th day of any month. By using the same days in different surveys we can be sure that students shown in any sample will already be contained in the original sample of school leavers, irrespective of the year in which they left school.

Method of record linking

There are no apparent reasons why the linking of educational records should be any more difficult or less difficult than the linking of medical records, with the possible exception that there exists a national health number but not a national educational number. Although we are hopeful that in the future there will exist a national numbering scheme we have had to make plans for linking without such a number in the meantime. So far these plans have been on a purely theoretical basis, for no experiments have yet been tried on a group of students having no numbering system. Even where a

355

numbering scheme exists, as in the case of teachers, there is naturally a failure to link in some cases. It seems feasible to link records using as keys the usual personal details, surname, initials, sex, date of birth, plus the powerful key provided by ' college attended '. This would provide a linked record for students who stay in the same college from one year to the next, but would be quite inadequate for those who change colleges. In order to link these latter, further keys will be required, and, with a view to the possibility that linking may eventually be attempted with records other than in education, these keys should be items which are in universal use rather than educationally based.

DISCUSSION

Professor Cheeseman : Mr Croxford has shown us that medicine hasn't the exclusive right to disorganized records. There has been, as I know, a great deal of hard work done in this field in the Department of Education and Science recently ; possibly this was prompted by the Robbins Report (1964) but there is an attempt now to get data which will enable us to at least try to forecast the numbers of students whom we will expect to get in the different faculties in universities. Some of us might like to go further and try to forecast the numbers we shall get in the so-called subject groups, but I think this will have to wait until a record linkage system is established.

There is a suggestion that record linkage of the educational data might be done by means of a sample and this makes me apprehensive. Apart from the objections which we have heard over the last few days, it would be impossible to do genetic studies in education—which might be of interest—and it would be difficult to link educational records to medical records—which again would be most certainly of interest. There is always the very great danger that if we only have a sample of records linked then the sampling ratio used might well prove to be quite inefficient for hypotheses which we might want to test at some future date. These are hypotheses which are as yet unformulated. Perhaps I could close by asking Mr Croxford if he could just say a little bit about the proposal concerning samples.

Mr Croxford : The proposal is in fact that eventually we should collect 100 per cent. of students but because at present we don't know the computer time that would be involved in the process of linking, the present proposal is to attempt to link 10 per cent. These 10 per cent. will be selected by a date of birth method, in other words those born on the 5th, 15th and 25th of any month, the beauty of this system being that you can draw the same sample next year and the

356

year after and know that you should still link the same people. It also accords with various samples which are already made by the Department of Education on a 10 per cent. basis by this method, and so the theory is that you would be able to draw them all into the same system. It doesn't, however, prevent us from attempting to link 100 per cent. of the students at some future date if the need arises.

Dr Newcombe : Everyone seems worried about the time it takes for the computer to carry out the linkages. However, assuming that the identifying information is pretty uniform from year to year, and presumably it would be in a school system, the computer times ought to be trivial. We put in 2,300 records per minute, linking them into a master file of several hundred thousand. A more important point may relate to the cost of keypunching the information in the first place. If it cost between 4d. and 8d. per student to punch an appropriate card, how would this compare with the cost of the 30 clerks who look after the preparation of these tables at present ?

Mr Croxford : One disadvantage that the collection of educational statistics has is that they are of no benefit to the colleges which supply them. It is an additional job for them in the present form. If, however, we were to collect individual information on a punched card, the object of the system, to put it that way, is to encourage colleges also to operate punch card systems for other benefits so that the statistics will then be a by-product of an existing record system rather than as at present a completely separate job. Not only the 30 clerks in the Ministry of Education are involved, but the 700-odd people—more than that—throughout the country who have to work on various types of records. Six man-weeks per college is one estimate I have had.

Mr Sunter : I don't think there is any particular problem about sampling in this context. We have a 10 per cent. continuous work history sample in Canada and, speaking for myself, I would rather have a good 10 per cent. sample than a lousy Census. I would like to ask a question, not so much of Mr Croxford but of the whole audience. It is not hard, I think, to think of reasons which are not entirely frivolous for linking an educational system to a medical system. Has anybody got any particular requirements for doing this ; in particular is it one of your considerations in the linkage systems which are being set out ?

Mr Croxford : In fact this hasn't been a consideration. It has been touched upon as a remote possibility but no work has been done on this. The only reference, perhaps, that we have made to it is the thought that in linking keys we shouldn't place too much reliance, as we might be tempted to do, upon say the college which is now attended, because this wouldn't have any use outside education. We would have to choose keys which would be of use, say, in health as well.

REFERENCE

The report of the Committee appointed by the Prime Minister under the Chairmanship of Lord Robbins, 1961–63. HMSO 1964.

A STUDY OF BIRTHWEIGHT AND OTHER FACTORS IN SIBSHIPS

M. S. T. Hobbs

OBSTETRIC information has been collected in the Oxford Record Linkage Study area since 1st January 1962, and it has therefore been possible for us to start assembling information about successive pregnancies of mothers who have had more than one baby. In the four years 1962–65 approximately 22,000 women had babies, of whom 3,439 have had two or more.

In this paper the following topics will be examined :

1. The correlation of birthweight in sib pairs.

2. The correlation of the period of gestation in successive pregnancies.

3. The relationship of birth interval to reproductive performance.

For convenience the study has been limited to women who have had two singleton babies during the time of the study.

All sib pairs are included regardless of the birth order of the first sib recorded by the study. No exclusions have been made of pairs in which one or both pregnancies resulted in stillbirth or neo-natal death. It is important to point out that as our study has operated over a short period of time women with the shortest birth intervals will be over-presented in the sample, as will be social class groups who have the largest families. As an example of the effect that this selection has, the proportion of women from Social Classes I and II included in this study was 15·6 per cent. compared with 18·2 per cent. for all women. However, the perinatal mortality among the cases included—23 per 1,000—is identical to that for all births in the period 1962–65.

358

On the other hand, the material is drawn from the whole population and does not have disadvantages of material drawn from hospital records as for example was the case of a previous study among sib pairs prepared by Karn and Penrose (1951), which will be referred to later. For the benefit of overseas guests approximately 55 per cent. of babies in this country are delivered in fully equipped maternity units, while the remainder are delivered either at home or in G.P. Units. The hospital deliveries, as one might expect, tend to be highly selected in terms of obstetric complications and in terms of survival in the perinatal period.

Basic information including age, parity, and social class of the mother, interval between deliveries, period of gestation in approximately half of the pairs, sex, birthweight and survival in the perinatal period, have been transferred from our original data cards to summary cards for machine analysis.

CORRELATION OF BIRTHWEIGHT IN SIBSHIPS

Several workers have studied the relation of birthweight within sibships and have found a correlation coefficient close to 0·50 (Table I). In our material the correlation coefficient of 0·47 is in close agreement.

Table I. *Studies of the correlation of birthweight in sibships*

	Correlation Coefficient
Donald (1939) . .	0·54
Karn & Penrose (1951)	0·47
Robson (1955) . .	0·50
Present Study . .	0·47

Figure 1 shows the linear regression of birthweight of earlier born sibs on that of later born sibs, calculated from all sib pairs. The points indicate the regression of mean birthweight of the later born sibs on that of the earlier born sibs. These fit the linear regression line closely except where the earlier born sibs weighed $3\frac{1}{2}$ lb. or less. This may be due to small numbers in this birthweight group, or it may be due to the effects of obstetric complications associated with low birthweight which may not necessarily recur in successive pregnancies.

359

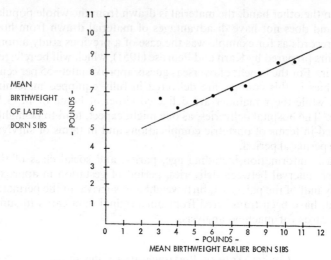

FIG. 1. Regression of birthweight of later born sibs on
birthweight of earlier born sibs.

CORRELATION OF GESTATION IN SUCCESSIVE PREGNANCIES

There are several problems in studies involving period of gestation. Firstly this can only be approximated by calculation from the
date of the last menstrual period which does not correspond with
date of conception. Secondly, the date of the last menstrual period
is often difficult to obtain ; in our material it is missing in 13 per cent.
of cases. A third difficulty lies in the fact that pregnancy may be
deliberately curtailed for various obstetric reasons.

Correlation of period of gestation

The correlation of period of gestation in successive pregnancies was
examined in a series of 1,400 sib pairs by Karn and Penrose (1951),
who found a correlation coefficient of only 0·15. In our material the
gestation period was readily accessible for analysis in only 1,200 sib
pairs but the correlation coefficient, 0·26, was higher than in Karn's
series. A possible explanation for this difference is that Karn's
material was selected from hospital cases in which there would
have undoubtedly been a higher incidence of obstetric abnormalities
than in our material.

In Figure 2 the linear regression line, calculated for all sib pairs,
is shown of gestation time of the later born sibs on the gestation time

360

of the earlier born sibs. The points represent the regression of mean gestation time of the later born sibs on that of the earlier born sibs.

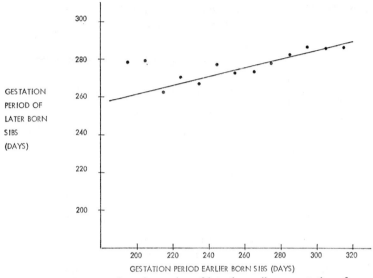

FIG. 2. The regression of gestation of later born sibs on gestation of the earlier born sibs.

The fit is seen to be less exact for lower gestation times of the earlier born sibs. As in the case of low birthweight this may be due to relatively small numbers of sib pairs where the earlier born sib was of short gestation, or it may be due to the effects on gestation of complications of pregnancy which may not necessarily be repeated in successive pregnancies.

Correlation of period of gestation and sex combination of sib pairs

A question examined by Karn was whether the sex combination of sib pairs affected the relationship between gestation in the successive pregnancies. Table II shows the correlation for the four possible sex combinations found by Karn and the same for our own material. In the latter there is no significant variation in the correlation of gestation within the sex sub-group except for female/male pairings which have a correlation coefficient of 0·37 compared with 0·26 for all pairs. This difference is technically highly significant, but for lack of any rational hypothesis to explain this finding it is assumed to be due to chance. Despite this finding it will be noticed that there

361

is more consistency between the groups in the present study than in that of Karn which was based on hospital data.

Table II. *Correlation between gestation periods in sibships according to sex composition*

		O.R.L.S. Study			Karn & Penrose	
Sex combination of sib pairs		Number of pairs	Correlation coefficient	P	Number of pairs	Correlation coefficient
Earlier	Later					
Male	Male	354	0·21	<·001	396	0·113
Male	Female	317	0·24	<·001	358	0·227
Female	Male	295	0·37	<·001	344	0·183
Female	Female	296	0·25	<·001	355	0·085
All pairs		1262	0·26	<·001	1433	0·156

THE RISK OF REPEATED PREMATURITY IN SIBSHIPS

A practical point of importance to obstetricians and paediatricians is the risk of a mother having a premature baby if her previous baby has been premature. In Table III this is examined firstly

Table III. *The proportion of babies weighing up to 5½ lb and over 5½ lb in sib pairs*

Earlier born	Later born		
Birthweight	Birthweight		
	−5½lb.	>5½lb.	All
−5½lb.	44 (21·2 per cent.)	163 (78·8 per cent.)	207 (100 per cent.)
>5½lb.	105 (3·7 per cent.)	2767 (96·3 per cent.)	2872 (100 per cent.)
All	149 (4·8 per cent.)	2930 (95·2 per cent.)	3079 (100 per cent.)

accepting the conventional definition of prematurity of birthweight of 5½ lb. (2·5 kg.) or less. It is seen that 21·5 per cent. of the mothers who have had one premature baby are likely to do so again in their next pregnancy. Expressing this slightly differently, 30 per cent of mothers who have a later born child premature will have had a previous premature baby. In other words if all who have had one premature baby are booked for delivery in fully equipped hospitals, one could at least be sure that one-third of those who have premature babies in later pregnancies would be booked for the most appropriate place of delivery.

In Table IV the question is re-examined, defining prematurity as a gestation time of less than 260 days (37 weeks or less) : 13·6 per cent. of mothers who had a short pregnancy for the earlier born sib

Table IV. *Gestation time in sib pairs*

Earlier born	Later born <260	260 & over	All
<260	9 (13·6 per cent.)	57 (86·4 per cent.)	66 (100 per cent.)
260 & over	45 (4·2 per cent.)	1028 (95·8 per cent.)	1073 (100 per cent.)
All	54 (4·7 per cent.)	1085 (95·3 per cent.)	1139 (100 per cent.)

had a reduced gestation period in the subsequent pregnancy, compared with 4·2 per cent. of mothers in whom the earlier pregnancy was of normal gestation. Mothers who have had one premature baby, as measured by gestation period, thus have a threefold risk of a prematurity in the succeeding pregnancy, whereas the risk of prematurity in the succeeding pregnancy defined in terms of birthweight was four and a half times as great. Thus birthweight of earlier born children appears to have more value in defining women who are likely to have babies requiring special care than does period of gestation.

These criteria of prematurity are of course very arbitrary, and in the light of recent studies it would be meaningful to examine this question from the point of view of dysmaturity, *i.e.* small babies of normal gestation and those that are truly premature by dates.

BIRTH INTERVAL AND REPRODUCTIVE PERFORMANCE

From the studies of Yerushalmy (1938) it has been shown that stillbirth and neonatal mortality rates are high following very short and very long birth intervals. Conversely, Newcombe and Rhynas

(1962) have shown that women who have a stillbirth are likely to have a further baby sooner than women who do not, and this also applies to women who lose a child in the neonatal period. An interesting question raised by these findings is whether reproductive efficiency is directly related in some biological sense to birth interval or whether the two are simply associated with some other factor such as social class. If the latter alternative is true then one would expect to find similar patterns of reproductive performance for earlier and later born sibs when the pairs are classified by birth interval. Two indices of reproductive performance which can be used to test this are perinatal mortality and birthweight.

Figure 3 shows perinatal mortality rates per 1,000 for earlier born and later born sibs classified according to birth interval. It is clear that there is no association between the two : whereas perinatal mortality is very high in earlier born sibs of pairs with short and, to a lesser extent, long birth intervals, there is no important variation in perinatal mortality in the later born sibs with variation in birth

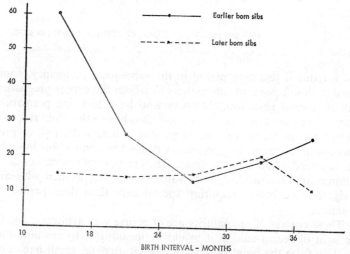

FIG. 3. Perinatal mortality in earlier and later born sibs according to the interval between births.

interval. This difference in the pattern of perinatal mortality may be partly due to the fact that 54·8 per cent. of the earlier born sibs occur from first pregnancies in which the complications likely to cause perinatal death are not necessarily repeated. This is supported by

364

Karn's finding that there was no correlation of stillbirth or neonatal mortality within sib pairs when the earlier born sib was also the first born in the sibship, whereas there was a significant correlation for both when the earlier born was of a higher birth order. Another possible explanation is that couples who lose a child in the perinatal period may deliberately compensate for their loss by having a further child in a relatively short time. In view of this possibility, birthweight, which can hardly be influenced by the intentions of the parents, may be a more satisfactory index than perinatal mortality by which to measure the relationship between birth interval and reproductive performance.

Figure 4 shows the mean birthweight of earlier and later born sibs classified by birth interval in months. The mean birthweight for both earlier and later born sibs is lowest for birth intervals of less than 12 months, and shows a tendency to rise with increasing

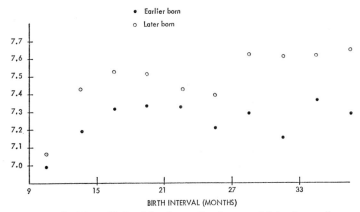

FIG. 4. Mean birthweight for earlier born and later born sibs according to the interval between births.

birth interval. However this is obviously not a simple linear relationship. Nevertheless, it appears that for birth intervals up to 27 months at least, there is some form of association between birthweight of earlier and later born sibs classified according to birth interval, which suggests that variation in birthweight among the later born sibs with birth interval may be dependent on factors other than the birth interval itself. One such factor may be Social Class.

In Figure 5 the cumulative frequency distributions by birth interval in months are shown for Social Classes I and II combined and Social Class V. Overall there is remarkably little difference

365

between the two, but it must be remembered that these distributions are probably biased because of the restricted period of the study. Thus the proportion of mothers from Social Classes I and II included in the Study was 15·6 per cent. compared with 18·2 per cent. in all

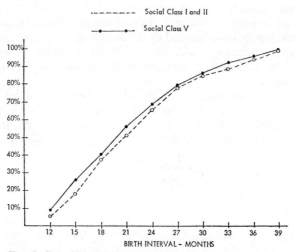

FIG. 5. Cumulative birth interval distribution by social class.

births which occurred in the area during the period of the study, while the proportion of mothers from Social Class V included in the Study was 11·5 per cent. compared with 9·2 per cent. in all mothers. There is thus over-representation of Social Class V mothers and under representation of Social Class I and II mothers which can only be partly accounted for by differences in family size. It is thus likely that there are greater differences between the two groups in birth interval than is apparent from Figure 5. Despite this, it will never-theless be noticed that for birth intervals up to 15 months 26 per cent. of Social Class V women have had a further pregnancy com-pared with 18 per cent. of women from Social Class I and II. Thus social class differences may account for the more marked deviations in perinatal mortality and birthweight which occur with short birth intervals as shown in Figures 3 and 4. However the evidence, within the limits of the present study, is not conclusive.

CONCLUSIONS

1. The correlation of birthweight within sib pairs was found to be 0·47 while that for gestation time in successive pregnancies was 0·26.

2. The relationship of duration of gestation in successive pregnancies does not appear to be affected by the sex of the offspring.

3. The risk of prematurity defined as birthweight of 5½ lb. or less, is four and a half times as great for mothers who had a premature baby in the previous pregnancy than in mothers who had a baby of birthweight greater than 5½ lb. When prematurity is defined as a gestation time of less than 37 weeks, the risk is three times as great in women who had a premature baby in the previous pregnancy.

4. When the sib pairs were classified according to their birth interval it was found that in earlier born sibs, perinatal mortality was high with short, and to a lesser extent, with long birth intervals. No such variation in perinatal mortality with birth interval was observed in the later born sibs. On the other hand mean birthweight was low in both earlier and later born sibs in the pairs with very short birth intervals and tended to increase with increasing birth interval.

When the mothers included in the study were classified by birth interval and social class it was found that a higher proportion of mothers from Social Class V (26 per cent.) had a birth interval of less than 15 months compared with 18 per cent. from Social Class I and II. This could at least partly explain the tendency for perinatal mortality to be high and birthweight to be low in sib pairs with the shortest birth intervals.

REFERENCES

DONALD, H. P. (1939). Sources of variation in human birth weights. *Proc. R. Soc. Edinb.* **59**, 91.

KARN, M. N. & PENROSE, L. S. (1951). Birthweight and gestation period. *Ann. hum. Eugen.* **16**, 147.

NEWCOMBE, H. B. & RHYNAS, P. O. (1962). Child spacing following stillbirth and infant death. *Eugen. Q.* **9**, 25.

ROBSON, E. B. (1955) Birthweight in cousins. *Ann. hum. Genet.* **19**, 262.

YERUSHALMY, J. (1938). Neonatal mortality by order of birth and age of parents. *Am. J. Hyg.* **28**, 244.

DISCUSSION

Mr Miller : Dr Hobbs has left us very little to discuss in this paper, having dealt with it so completely and I can't do very much more than underline some of the points that he has already made. I think it is perhaps worth saying that some of you may not realize how unusual this type of data is. It would seem obvious in considering better care and obstetric organization that we ought to take into account the patient's previous performance in pregnancy and labour. Certainly a number of attempts have been made to do this but they are based on a statistical method, if it even can justify that name, which is suspect. What has happened in the past is that all of this, as Dr Hobbs said, has been based on hospital statistics and one suspects that if in a given pregnancy a patient has a serious complication she will, or certainly ought to be, delivered in hospital next time. Since the ascertainment of all complications, certainly in our material, is better in hospital than it is in home confinements, it would be surprising I think if we couldn't show that most conditions or complications tended to recur in successive pregnancies.

Even despite this, one of Dr Hobbs' main conclusions, that low birthweight from any cause tends to recur in about 25 per cent. of pregnancies, was shown many years ago quite convincingly by Penrose but it hasn't, certainly nationally, been acted upon. Many places don't regard a history of a previous premature of low birthweight infant as being an indication to have that patient delivered in hospital, and of course this is quite wrong because low birthweight is associated with very high neonatal mortality rates, and perinatal mortality rates, and it is partly preventable, the mortality at any rate, by delivery in the proper place.

To go on a bit, yesterday several speakers mentioned the difficulty in convincing authorities of the need for record linkage and for the likely rewards : they wanted to demonstrate something fairly quickly and something fairly dramatically. I suggest, as Dr Hobbs has shown today and Dr Acheson mentioned yesterday, that there really isn't a better field to do this than obstetrics. It certainly perhaps won't affect the immediate clinical care of the individual patient, but it should improve the decision-making on place of hospital confinement, the complications and so on that are to be expected. An area so disorganized as the obstetric service certainly needs some feedback and help in management. I think that I can say this being an obstetrician myself.

There are two other points that I want to make here because it is not often that I have an opportunity of talking and putting my point of view to an audience containing a number of statisticians. The first is that I think we must avoid the term ' premature '. Dr Hobbs used it but qualified it and I think it is much better if we dropped it altogether and called infants weighting 5½ lb. or less ' low birthweight infants '. In fact in our material we find that of low birthweight infants more are born after a normal gestation period than are delivered after a short gestation period. Conversely, of the infants delivered after a short gestation period, say 37 weeks or less, more of them weighed more than 5½ lb. than weighed less than 5½ lb. One here has two variables that are related of course in the majority of pregnancies, namely gestation period and birthweight, but when the nutrition of the infant is adversely affected then the normal relationship doesn't hold and in these pregnancies at least we must regard the two variables as separate.

The second and final point I want to make, is that we must take much more account of gestation period. It is open to all the difficulties that Dr Hobbs mentioned and to some others and I think intuitively we are inclined to ignore it or downgrade it, but it remains much the best estimate of gestation age and this is very highly correlated with perinatal mortality, the relationship being rather better than for birthweight. I think we must try and find good estimates of gestation age and for the time being use the menstrual history as the best that is available.

Mr Sunter : I think the difficulty over the length of gestation period is more apparent than real. It is just a case of variation in which both the variables are subject to error. In any event it doesn't bias the correlation coefficient although it would certainly bias the slope of the regression line.

Dr Edwards : This is a very small point but I suspect that the familial low birthweight is a much more benign condition than unexpected early gestation, and one would have to go into this very carefully as an administration procedure for selecting women who ought to get hospitalization. This is a biological variant as opposed to the pathological variant of ejection which is somewhat distinct I think.

Dr Hobbs : We have not examined this closely in our material, but I think Dr Miller has and I think that he can give an authoritative statement on this.

Mr Miller : I suspect that this familial low birthweight is perhaps less severe and less important than the occasional low birthweight, but I am certainly sure that it would be wrong to ignore low birthweight at the present time. It is an important determinant of how the infant is going to do and until we have better evidence I think that one should regard it seriously always.

AN INTEGRATED MEDICAL RECORDS SERVICE AT THAMESMEAD

M. E. ABRAMS

THE planning of an integrated automated medical records service for a new community health service such as at Thamesmead presents both a challenge and an opportunity. A challenge in that as yet no group has been able to develop a computerized service that will not only provide book-keeping facilities such as making clinic appointments, immunization schedules, inventories, costings of treatment and so forth but will also handle the complete personal medical record. At Thamesmead we are in an almost ideal position to attempt to meet this challenge. For here, we have a new health centre which is to provide a service for a completely new population. The centre is to be designed for our needs ; similarly we can design our records system to suit our ideas of record keeping and of record storage. We are indeed fortunate that when the service starts there will be no backlog of records ; nothing will need transcribing for a new system. We thus start with a clean sheet. Before turning to the main point of my talk I would just like to outline briefly the major aspects of the services we hope to supply :

1. A complete community health record system for general medical and dental practitioners and the local Health Authority.

2. Links with the local hospital service.

3. An appointment system for the patients using the health centres.

4. Immunization scheduling.

5. Organization of screening and other clinics.

6. Facilities for epidemiological and other clinical research.

7. Facilities for cost benefit analysis of the health services.

Rather than dwell on the advantages we would gain from such a system, I will now turn and consider what we feel to be the kernel of our problem : how to deal with the personal medical record as obtained at the interview between physician and patient. Straightaway, I should like to say that all our thinking is aimed at providing a system that will allow the physician or other professional or ancillary worker (in his office or clinic) both to enter data directly into the

370

computer record and to interrogate the computer's memory. To us this means that we have to provide visual display units—as these would seem to provide the only way of displaying formatted information rapidly and clearly to the untrained observer. I would like to stress the ' untrained ' aspect. We feel that it is unrealistic to expect the professional worker to acquire any new skill as the admission price to our system : that is, our system must be designed for the user, with full knowledge of what he is prepared to accept and most definitely not for what the ' computer expert ' would like. This point can be further amplified : the average G.P. consultation time at present is short ; some of our own observations indicate times as low as $2\frac{1}{2}$ minutes/patient. What can we usefully do in such a short time ? Obviously if our methods of entering into the medical record are cumbrous and slow they just will not be used—whatever the ultimate advantages might be.

Keeping in mind this time limitation, let us now turn to considering the various segments of the medical record. We have made provisional calculations of the amount of storage space needed, and in order to avoid machine dependence in our sums, we have expressed our answers as ' bits ' (Fig. 1). Let me stress at this point that though we have indicated the various parts of the record as being contiguous, this does not necessarily mean that this is how they would be stored : this is how they would appear to the user. Figure 1A is our estimate of the information load which a new patient at a first visit could generate. As you will see it looks as though, with the exception of the signs and symptoms, the information load is quite manageable.

How do we intend to enter information into the record ? We have started work on a system which will permit the doctor to enter his findings via a visually displayed check list, with the facility of using free language in addition. A check list of course has the immense advantage of drastically reducing the amount of labour needed by the user. We hope that by the time we go into action it will be economically possible to use devices that will allow the doctor merely to touch the screen with his finger to enter data (a prototype of this ' Digiscribe ' has been made by Control Data Ltd.). Failing this, we should have to get the doctor to depress a key. But however attractive the check list approach may be, we feel that it is impossible for it to allow for all the comments which it may be appropriate to record. Therefore, we have to allow free language input : here we have a dilemma. Do we persuade the doctor to type his comment in (assuming that it will be short) or do we transcribe it after the event— and thus admit we cannot do what we set out to do ? Rather than plump for one solution we intend to arrange trials to try to find out which approach is more acceptable to the user. There is, of course, enormous latitude in our calculations for the amount of personal medical data collected at the interview : this is in effect a reflection of the spread of expected consultation times.

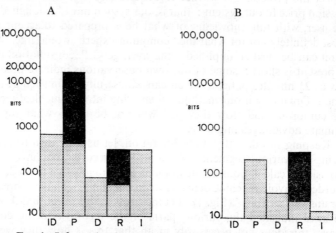

FIG. 1. Information load generated at a patient's

A. first visit with a new complaint
B. second and subsequent visits

ID : Identification
P : Physical examination including signs and symptoms
D : Diagnosis
R : Treatment
I : Investigations
Dark hatchings : estimated upper limits of information to be stored.

Let us now consider another of the record entities : treatment. We feel that this is perhaps the most important set of facts to be recorded about the patient : what better indication is there of what the doctor thought about his patient than the treatment he prescribed ? For this reason we are concentrating our efforts on drawing up a therapeutic index for use by visual display. (Perhaps I should make it clear here that for us treatment includes all the branches of therapeutics and is not restricted to drugs.) Using such sources as the National Formulary and MIMS we think that something like 1,000,000 bits of store will be needed for our therapeutic dictionary—for this of course has to include not only the treatment, but for example for a drug, its route of administration, tablet size, dose, frequency of administration and duration of use. We would very much like—legal considerations permitting—actually to have the computer draw up and print the prescription. Thus at one step we would have our electronic record together with a highly legible printed prescription which the doctor would need only to date and sign. On return visits—when many patients are really only coming for a new prescription—the saving in time and effort should be enormous as we would have the current treatment(s) displayed on the visual display unit. All the doctor would have to do is to depress the ' repeat ' key. This detailed record of treatment would also of course enable us to study the economics of prescribing far more satisfactorily than at present and would also allow us to investigate the pattern of prescription and diagnosis.

So far I have considered only the information generated from a first visit. Let us now examine the further additions made on second and subsequent visits to our record (Fig. 1B). We can readily see two important facts. Firstly, the total amount of information is now much smaller and secondly the treatment sector is now becoming the most important one. Thus it is clear to us that if we can deal with the input problem, and information load for ' first ' visits, we will have no real problems on second and subsequent visits.

In closing I would like to put to you a question that is causing us no little anxiety : this concerns the cost and effort involved in the programming of our system. We currently feel that fully to implement our system, naturally over a number of years, is going to involve approximately 200,000 programme instructions. Commercial firms do not expect their programmers to complete more than 5000 instructions annually. Thus there is something like 40 man-years of effort to be put into our system—which in salaries alone could cost over £80,000. Can such a costly system be justified to assist in giving general practitioner services to a community whose population will rise to about 70,000 in 15 years time ?

DISCUSSION

Dr Bennett : The Thamesmead project is one of the most fascinating projects at present being developed in this country. As such it is being watched with great interest by many people and this interest will be stimulated by the knowledge that the problems of record keeping are being considered in such a forward looking manner.

The recording of clinical case notes to serve the purposes of patient care, research and administration presents considerable difficulties in any situation and these difficulties are I think accentuated in general practice. One must however challenge the statement that doctors cannot be asked to develop new skills. We are continually developing new skills and as Dr Deans Weir said yesterday what is obviously relevant to practice, and I hope research should prove readily acceptable. A small piece of evidence to support this is that we asked house officers to code discharge diagnoses on mark-sense forms for an experimental project. They were able to do this easily and quickly and proved more accurate than coding clerks ! If we are to realize the immense potential of an automated system of recording then I think it is unrealistic to say that this can be done without requiring new skills and learning.

A problem with check lists that will be used for visual display on an on-line system is defining their content. I wonder if you could tell us more about your thinking on this problem and the methods you may be using.

Dr Abrams : All I can say about check lists is that we are working on them and will be happy to show them to you. It is quite impossible for us to display anything at a meeting like this. I would like to add that the advantage of using a visual display unit for a check list is that it is possible to go through an enormous amount of formated information very rapidly. If you do the same thing on pieces of printed paper you may have to have a book with so many pages that I don't think anyone would dream of using it.

Dr Bahn : Could you explain a bit more how the visual display would help you find your way through a check list of symptoms which you could not do through a book. I don't understand this.

Dr Abrams : It is difficult to explain without actually having a visual display unit in front of you, but one of the problems of looking at a printed check list is that they usually have a page of foolscap size with up to 200 or 300 boxes on it. I for one am daunted at the idea of making a mark in up to 300 boxes on a page and reading the miniscule print that goes along with it. You may have a great number of pages to work through. If you want to display this sort of information visually you can restrict each page to 16 or 20 pieces of information at a time. Thus the questions can be very large and it is very much easier to fill in what you want and to skip the pages you don't want than it is with printed pieces of paper. I have seen this in action and it seems to work but perhaps I ought to stress that we do intend to do trials on this to see that what we feel is right is in fact right. It may of course be quite wrong.

Mr Sunter : Would you expect to see an increase in the incidence of the symptoms which are check-listed and an increase in prescriptions which are check-listed? Does the question make sense? I would expect to see an increase in those symptoms on the check list because it is easier to do that. I am cynical about this sort of thing. We observe this in survey questionnaires.

Professor Butterfield : The people who are going to live at Thamesmead will come from south of the Thames. We have just finished a survey of how people in Bermondsey, south of the Thames, obtain their medical care. From the results, I do not think our arrangements will produce more symptoms but I expect that more symptoms would be recognized and treated in the National Health Service. As it is, people shop for relief for many symptoms they have at the chemists. However, while the population is becoming highly educated about symptoms—for example, they know what dyspepsia is—their education in therapeutics is far from good. They will take cough medicine for dyspepsia and stomach medicines for a cough. However, I agree with you that there may well be a great demand for medical care at the beginning ; we only hope it will prove generally less wasteful than obtains at the moment.

Dr Abrams : I would agree with Mr Sunter, but we have to make a start with something. We feel that whatever we start off with is going to be wrong. We hope it won't be 100 per cent. wrong. One of the advantages of using visual display units is that we use software to display our check list: it is thus relatively easy to replace. We envisage starting off with one sort of symptom-sign check list and modifying this as we go along to suit what is needed. We can think of no other way of coming out with an answer that is appropriate to our system.

Mr Sunter : Well do you think there will be a tendency to bias in the system, i.e. that people tend to check those things that are easy to check. You can have check-list status or a write-in status. My guess would be that you would expect a biassed situation in favour of the check-list.

Dr Abrams : That may well be true, but we are also allowing free language in which they can write in what they like.

Mr Sunter : That is more difficult.

Mr Smythe : You mention the cost of £80,000 for developing a programme to do this work. Presumably once this is written it would be available for areas other than Thamesmead, and I think what might be a more important cost would be the capital cost of the equipment that would need to be provided at each of the centres which were going to use this service, if in fact you are designing a service that could be used by other folk.

Dr Abrams : I can perhaps best answer that by saying that our estimated running costs for the predicted population of Thamesmead would be £1 to £2 per head of population per year.

PART 9

GENERAL DISCUSSION AND SUMMING UP

Chairman: DR W. R. S. DOLL (London)

GENERAL DISCUSSION AND SUMMING UP

Dr Brotherston : I must be brief and I may sound didactic. I never felt less didactic in my life. I am looking at this from the point of view of the requirements of a medical care system. Is record linkage on ? Of course it is. To some extent it is an inevitable by-product of the computer era. The only questions are : How far and how fast do we take it ? What are challenges to the medical care system which make record linkage relevant ? Many of these have been mentioned in our discussion.

Two of the main challenges at the present time in medical care systems are trends in demand and trends in medical science and technology. Trends in demand from changing patterns of disease, from age structure, from public expectation and attitude are well known ; these create increasing demand, and an increasing need to make best use of scarce resources in meeting these demands. Therefore, for example, we must try to achieve economy of resources and an avoidance of overlap in our divided type of service organization ; record linkage can clarify the problems, as for example in the maternity service analysis which we heard about. Communication of data between the different parts of the service is vital if we are to achieve better results. Assessment and evaluation are necessary activities of an intelligent system, and here record linkage offers us the opportunity of checking the system as a whole (and not merely checking part by part), by using one part of the system as a check against another. We have to get maximum return for effort expended. We are not always good at this. Our knowledge of outcome from our treatment efforts is poor despite the work of Professor Witts (Beck, Gardner & Witts, 1947) and Professor Ferguson and his colleagues (Ferguson & McPhail, 1954), to clarify this and we pay little enough attention to their findings. We require to know much more about outcome, in terms of further hospital experience, of what happens after hospital discharge, of time and cause of death and so on ; these things as we have been shown can be clarified by record linkage and fed back into the system.

We must prevent where possible, and Professor Case has talked about this and Dr Carter will talk again ; we must move over to the initiative in our attack on degenerative disease. Our recent experience with screening programmes reveals our ignorance of the early beginnings in the natural history of disease processes ; we are familiar only with the tip of the iceberg. Sir James Mackenzie said everything that was to be said about this in 1920 (Mair, 1962) and if he had been alive he would have been here to-day and pressing hard for a record linkage set-up in his institute in St. Andrew's. We have to define the vulnerable, to concentrate our resources on those who need them most, and again record linkage can help with delineation. We have to learn how to manipulate populations and services one to the other and the pioneer experiments of Dr Tom Galloway in West Sussex in relation to immunization indicate the way ahead (p. 80). Pressure is on us in terms of trends in medical science and the complexity of provision that derives from these trends. The ramification, the specialization of our services increases the need for orchestration of all, and here I think the linking potential of the computer can help very materially eventually in this type of management.

We are dealing, as we are well aware, with increasingly potent two-edged weapons in our treatment. Dr Doll, for example, talked about the need to have record linkage systems to monitor the effects of our drugs. We have in the Health Service to abide by the principle of *primum non nocere*. At least we must know what we are doing to learn about any ill effects from our efforts and to avoid them in the future.

How to get ahead : What are the roles respectively of the research worker and what might be called ' the System '? Clearly any large-scale record linkage must be taken over by ' the System '. Why ? The scale is too large for the individual research worker or even the largest type of private research group one could think of. It is too routine and too long-term. One cannot count on this sort of en-deavour attaching to itself the total allegiance through lifetimes and generations of private research workers. So what is the assignment for the research worker and pioneer ? To pioneer, of course, and to keep pioneering new possibilities. To sell to the system, bit by bit, as he has proved the value ; to the Registrar General, to the National Health Service and to both. To ensure that the system as it pro-gressively takes over makes the right opportunities and technical arrangements for the research workers to mesh in. To make efforts to get ' the System ' and others to put in sufficient effort to exploit the resources.

Who are to be the William Farrs of multiple source data ? This is one of the big questions hanging over us today. What are the prospects of selling to ' the System ', which is not notoriously either rash or quixotic ? There is the by-product effect. After all our present set-up of vital statistics is a kind of by-product of census and vital registration. Imagine, for example, a century and a half ago William

Farr making the theoretical case for a national system of medical statistics. Imagine the raspberry that would have greeted him if he had tried. But we have it ; it was sensible to bring this in as a by-product and it developed into magnificent scale and scope as we know.

The by-product principle is still operating. We see it in terms of certain kinds of medical computer developments currently taking place which derive from the fact that treasurers in regional boards and in local health authorities need these instruments and have a vested interest in them being used. There are demographic pressures, as we have been told, a need for more sophisticated forecasts. There are social security and educational pressures and the like. The National Health Service generates its own pressures in this ; the need to have its resources, its costs, its expenditure assessed with maximum efficiency.

We have come to the point in our arrangements in the National Health Service where research and intelligence are vital activities. We are also beginning to come to the point where every operator, every doctor for example, has to see his place clearly in the scheme of things. I just want to make the point here that research and intelligence, computers and record linkage are intimately bound together. In the last resort it is the extent to which research and intelligence is a driving force in the service which will make the place for computers and record linkage. Of course there is a chicken and egg phenomenon which Dr Logan talked about. I am always in favour of backing both the chicken and the egg.

The computer can create new research opportunities by forcing clearer and sharper thinking about records systems. So too can record linkage, as Professor Cheeseman has told us. Step by step we have to go forward, taking the principle of trying to show pay-off throughout and relevance to patient care. The pioneers have already reached first base. The basic linkage of hospital and death data is to be picked up by the service. We have now to pioneer possible extensions of effective recording systems in other fields such as outpatients, general practice and so on, and we have to pioneer the possibilities of total linkage on a small community basis such as Thamesmead and Livingstone as we are doing.

Dr Mosbech : Mr Chairman, Ladies and Gentlemen : If I may introduce myself, I am a hospital clinician with an interest in medical statistics and in epidemiology. I work in the Department of Medical Statistics in the Danish Ministry of Health. At present I am primarily concerned with hospital statistics.

At this stage of the meeting I only want to draw attention to a few points which appear to me to be essential and perhaps deserve further consideration and discussion. I think that we are all now convinced of and ' converted ' to the necessity of some sort of automation of medical records and that in the computer we have a wonderful tool, continuously developing with almost unlimited possibilities. We have heard a great deal about linkage of hospital records and the trend now is for other medical records to be included in an integrated system but we also are aware that very careful planning is needed. The many new possibilities for research in epidemiology and genetics have been dealt with extensively by many speakers, but perhaps these possibilities are not sufficiently realized. I remember Dr Benajmin stating that he had difficulty in persuading research workers in the field of demography to use linkage possibilities although they are cheap and simple. This is a problem of communication.

In hospital record linkage it is very important to have standardization of the format of the records. I think that if you are going in for linkage of medical records it is most important and often indispensable to start with the standardization of the paper. In principle all essential information might be placed on the front page of the medical record so that a photocopy could serve as a direct basis for punching.

I feel that what has been said about selling the idea of record linkage is crucial and this fact should never be underestimated. In the medical profession the clinicians as I know them are generally rather slow to accept new ideas concerning the procedure of record handling. They think that the way they have been working for many years should be good enough. This is the general attitude. But record linkage gives them more work in the first period, therefore the process of establishing a feedback to hospitals and institutions going in for this is most important. The fact mentioned that they have closed the manual diagnostic indices in five big hospitals in the Oxford region is a good sign of approval by the medical profession. To produce the feedback in a readable and easily understandable form is also important to establish general acceptance of a given system. There is also here a problem of data reduction. The cost of systems has been mentioned but perhaps not enough. We need precise economic figures to persuade health authorities and I think that it would be interesting to know the price per patient included in, for instance, the Oxford Linkage Study. When we are dealing with economics also the point of exchange of programmes comes in as important.

A personal identification number is a considerable advantage in linkage and it is my feeling that the advantages outweigh the disadvantages. However, there are political problems in this. Different attitudes prevail in different countries. I only want to mention here that the personal identification number has been in existence in Sweden and Norway for a couple of years virtually without any negative reactions.

Finally a practical point ; considering the multiple activities and quick development in the field of record linkage in medicine another symposium like this one would be most useful in a couple of years. I wouldn't dare to suggest Oxford as the next meeting place, although I would certainly like to come here again, as I should imagine that Dr Acheson at the moment feels rather fed-up with arranging symposia, but it might be possible that the World Health Organization which is represented here could be persuaded to take an initiative.

Dr Carter : I have been asked to say something about the genetic aspects of record linkage and I will divide my short contribution up into two sections—one on research and one on applications.

First, research : What can record linkage do that ordinary genetic studies cannot, assuming that we do have family record linkage and the necessary changes are made in certificates so that what Dr Howard Newcombe has done will also be done here on a national scale ? There are many things I think, where magnitude of operations puts all the odds in favour of record linkage. For example, for genetic counselling we need to know the recurrence risks within sibships of conditions such as spina bifida and anencephaly and we need to know them for each area. In South Wales the recurrence risk after a major neurological malformation of this sort is over one in 20. In Liverpool it is about one in 20. I am sure it is appreciably less in South-East England but we haven't got data. This kind of thing will just roll off.

We do need perhaps rather better classification of certain congenital malformations. The neurological malformations are all right except that some cases of hydrocephalus secondary to spina bifida get labelled as hydrocephalus. Heart malformations are inadequately classified at present for the estimation of recurrence risks. Genetic predispositions are highly specific and the recurrence risk is for a specific type of heart malformation. If congenital heart malformations are inadequately classified, you may underestimate the familial concentration and therefore underestimate the heritability.

Another situation where record linkage is going to be extremely valuable is for the mapping of chromosomes, the kind of thing that Dr Renwick and Dr John Edwards do. This needs complex mathematics, complex calculations and record linkage is the obvious way to do it. It will take years to build up but it can be allowed to run on.

383

Also the conditions of particular genetic interest at present are the complex common diseases where you have genetic predisposition and environmental factors interacting. Here again computers obviously have a lot to offer. For example ischaemic heart disease certainly has some important genetic factors and is heritable perhaps to an extent of 50 per cent through factors influencing blood cholesterol, blood triglycerides, glucose tolerance and so on : but there are also important environmental factors—smoking habits, exercise habits and diet.

Now to come to applications : Professor Brotherston and Professor Alwyn Smith (1966) said in a recent paperback that in future preventive medicine is going to be more and more recognizing those who are vulnerable, genetically vulnerable, for specific and common disorders and protecting them from the additional environmental triggers that are also required. Record linkage perhaps is going to be the way to do this. One can perhaps see the family doctor of the future—when a young couple come to see him, he will not only call up the past information on their medical history, he will also call up the family history. He might see perhaps, that the mother's sister had schizophrenia, that the father's brother died early of ischaemic heart disease, and that the mother's mother lost one child with spina bifida. By then it may perhaps be known that carotene early in pregnancy is one of the environmental triggers for spina bifida : he may make sure that the mother does not have too much carotene in the first pregnancy. It may be that when the child is born he will test for whatever is the future equivalent of the pink spot test for schizophrenia. He may want to do the blood cholesterol on the cord blood to see if the baby has hypercholesterolaemic xanthomatosis with its high risk of ischaemic heart disease. Perhaps if the mother has been picked up as a heterozygous carrier in the school medical service for cystic fibrosis of the pancreas, as one in 20 of us are, and if there is no information on the father, he may want to check the child. The effect of a drop of cord blood on the ciliary system of a freshwater mussel, a very simple test of this type may show if the child has cystic fibrosis or not. One can see this happening.

Something I'm not sure about, and this is a thing we will have to work out, is the extent to which one will use the family history to point to the particular types of screening procedures that are needed, or whether it would be more economical to screen the whole population anyhow. I suspect that in the case of cholesterol in cord blood—a test which is easily automated—it will be done in every child and we won't bother too much about leads from family history. But this will differ from condition to condition. Obviously we are going to get some very nice prototypes on smaller scales—the Amish, Icelandic, Northern Irish, Scottish projects before we have to put something into operation on a rather bigger scale for England and Wales. They are going to help us determine which is the most useful method of screening for vulnerability.

Dr Doll : Would Mr Reed care to open the general discussion ?

Mr Reed : Thank you, sir. I am grateful to you for giving me the opportunity to speak, very briefly indeed, because there are just two things I would like to say. One of them is to re-emphasize a point which I am glad that Professor Alwyn Smith (p. 340) and Professor Schilling (p. 214) have made during the earlier discussions today : That is, the extent to which that Dickensian outfit at Southport with its quill pen behind its ear is in fact now, with the resources that we have, able to carry out linkage exercises for specific research projects which are being set up. Without going so far as the routine comprehensive linkage schemes which have been planned for both Scotland and Northern Ireland, with of course their very much smaller populations, I don't think it is widely known just how much we can do to meet requests for specific exercises for particular research projects. If it were more widely known, I think we should be asked to do more and that I would welcome. I hope that the extent to which we are asked to help in this kind of way will steadily increase while the prospect of any kind of nation-wide scheme for a population of 50 million—a routine nation-wide scheme—is being perhaps more closely examined.

The other thing I would like to mention is to refer to some recommendations which were pressed upon us some little while ago by the Medical Research Council that we should include in the information which is collected at birth, marriage and death registration some additional data about the people involved. We have been asked to put in at birth registration the date of birth of both parents—at present we collect age only—the date of birth and the place of birth of the parents and the full date of marriage. This we propose to do. When I say propose, propose is exactly what I mean because this will not require legislation but will mean making regulations which will have to be approved by the Minister and we have not yet got the political authority to do this. But I don't myself anticipate that there should be any great difficulty about it. The age of the parents and the date of their marriage are at present collected under the Population Statistics Act and, as Mr Glazebrook said earlier this afternoon (p. 331), this must remain confidential unless there were legislation to alter that, and my own feeling about that is that it is legislation

2c

for which Parliament would show no very marked enthusiasm. We intend to include also the place of birth of the parents at birth registration. At marriage we at present get the age of the parties, though when they are married in church it is still fairly common simply to get the statement by the incumbent that they are ' of full age ' and we intend now to ask for date of birth instead. At death registration we intend to get the date and place of birth of the deceased and, in the case of married women, their maiden name. Some of these particulars are already collected in Scotland.

We have been faintly sceptical of the extent to which we shall get accurate information, at any rate in the early years of a new requirement of this kind, and we are at the moment carrying out some tests in the field to find out just how much information people can give. For example with the old lady who dies in hospital, it may well be that there isn't anybody easily available who knows her maiden name. This is the kind of thing that we are proceeding with. In addition to the vital records that we have ourselves, the Registrar General for Scotland and I of course are able to bring in a completely new dimension as custodians of the census records, and although, as I did mention in reply to Mr Glazebrook, there are very special considerations of confidentiality here, it is possible to use the census as a means of picking out samples of the population with any given characteristics that anybody wants. As, on the hospital side, the Hospital Activity Analysis on a 100 per cent. basis develops and takes hold in this country it will of course be possible to do a great deal more in the way of record linkage.

Mr Ford : I mentioned earlier today that, with the proper modesty of a Registrar General of nine months' standing, I came here not to contribute but to sit at the feet of wisdom, and at the risk of some breach of confidentiality I think I could report that you seemed inclined to doubt whether I had caught the right train. Professor Alwyn Smith has referred to the record linkage study which he initiated during his term as medical statistician in the General Register Office in Scotland (p. 340), and Dr Heasman has fairly fully described the new record linkage project (p. 251). There is really nothing that I can add to what these gentlemen have said. Nor need I add anything to what Mr Reed has just said. Although he was speaking in detail for England and Wales, the general import of his remarks applied equally to Scotland.

Mr White : Dr Doll asked me to say something about how record linkage looks from the Ministry. This is not my personal responsibility, but my personal view is that the Ministry is not yet fully informed on record linkage. Sir George Godber said yesterday that there was no doubt any longer about whether record linkage is supported, whether it should go on. His only question was ' when ?'. I think if he were here he would agree that there is another question, and that is, ' how ? '. This is where probably some of us in the Ministry—I am speaking of England and Wales now ; I would except Scotland from all this—would take the view that we should be unlikely to get record linkage pursued on a national basis for its own sake.

I tried to show yesterday why I thought it would entail some very heavy capital expenditure to do so. Dr Abrams this afternoon showed that records in themselves can be a very costly exercise—getting records on to computers can be a very costly exercise when it is done for ordinary day-to-day routine processes. That was for a very limited community in fairly limited circumstances. It did not even go into the hospital. So that records on computers, as I say, are going to be a heavy capital expenditure ; but I am very much more optimistic about the possibilities of introducing computers into the Health Service on a fairly large scale over the next few years, and, as I said yesterday, firmly believe that almost every major computer application will have to start with patient or population records as its nucleus.

Now this means that if one is getting records on to computers for reasons of efficiency, improving patient care directly, improving hospital management directly, improving clinical efficiency directly it is very much easier to justify the heavy capital expenditure, much easier than it would be for just research purposes. So I think this is the most likely way that it will succeed, giving this just as my personal view at the present moment.

Certainly we are agreed on objectives here for record linkage. We are agreed that the full medical record of an individual from birth onwards would offer substantial contributions to general health, to patient care ; it would provide much better opportunities of investigating the personal and environmental circumstances in which disease and illness occur, and doing something about preventing them. So I don't think there is any dispute over any of this. We are, as Sir George implied, concerned with how soon we can get on with it and the methods that we adopt.

I am not convinced that we could do very much of this except by these expensive computer methods. What is possible for a small group, I don't think is feasible on a national scale. I think the simple methods used in Oxford would become too cumbersome to support. But again, this is a personal opinion. Maybe we shall find that the extension of relatively simple methods, particularly in areas where there are not going to be computers for some time, will give us some advance in record linkage that we might not otherwise expect for some while. But, as I say, thinking in the Ministry on this isn't finally formed.

Dr Acheson : Until the beginning of this last discussion I had been overtaken by somewhat unwarranted optimism that the first round of the battle for a national system of linked medical records involving births, deaths and hospital admissions had been won. But having heard the words of officialdom I see that we have scarcely joined action.

I am going to confine my remarks to the matter of the cost of record linkage as I believe this is widely overestimated. In the calendar year 1966 the expenditure of the Oxford Record Linkage Study was in round figures £36,000 and this included the cost of all professional and clerical staff, of machine room rentals, computer time, and all the clerical expenses of transcribing, photocopying and coding the data in the hospitals. On the basis of a population covered of 750,000 people this works out at slightly less than one shilling per head per annum, or on the basis of the records of about 100,000 events processed in that year, a little more than seven shillings per event. Of these costs we reckon about 75 per cent. go in data preparation—transcription, coding, punching, and reading onto tapes, and the remaining 25 per cent. on linking the records ; so the cost of record linkage additional to data preparation is about 3d per head per annum.

But these estimates take no acount of the fact that the Record Linkage system in Oxford is currently additional to and superimposed upon a number of medical data processing systems *which require the preparation of closely similar data for computers in any case, and for which public money is already available or earmarked.* I refer to the Registrar General's vital statistics system and the Hospital Activity Analysis. These would be incorporated in any national system proposed and the bulk of the cost is already met.

Furthermore, of course, a national system would lead to substantial savings. An example from our own small study is the projected closure of two large manual diagnostic and operations indices in our area, as the indices in future will be provided centrally by us. This will save the hospitals concerned £5,000 between them in clerical salaries.

My point is not that medical records procedures are cheap—they are expensive—but that they are going on any way on a huge scale. The aim should be to try and get more productivity out of the money that is already being spent. A system of linked records, as envisaged,

388

would add greatly to the flexibility of the types of analysis possible and to the potentialities of the data on patient care. I will leave the point there.

Mr Sunter : It is not impossible to get around Australia by train but it's very expensive and difficult, and the reason is that all the States have different railway gauges. Now I suspect that the same thing may happen with record linkage systems, and I think that before very long people should start worrying about the compatibility of these systems—compatibility with respect to content which seems to be a medical matter, compatibility with respect to format which seems to be a matter for systems analysts, and compatibility with respect to statistical standards which I think is a matter for statisticians. I think someone should start worrying about these things fairly soon. The answer, the sort of compatibility you need, on standards anyway, is to some extent a matter of what the system is supposed to do. Are these statistical systems or intelligence systems ? That is do you want to do statistical research in the system or do you want to provide patient information ? I have a feeling that it would probably be best to start off with statistical systems and raise the standards to the point where you have an intelligence system.

Dr Kennedy : I find my worries are the opposite of Dr Acheson's about this. I get perturbed as I listen this afternoon to the Orwellian overtones of it. I believe that this year marks the halfway point between the writing of the book ' 1984 ' and the year 1984 itself. I feel that we seem to be well on the way towards the society of ' 1984 ' in that the technology is becoming available for these large data banks and it is becoming apparent that they are not going to appear economically feasible unless they are used for a wide variety of diverse purposes. We will agree, for the purposes of this meeting I am sure, that medical research with these files is good, but the demographers would like to see a lot of social data included in them as well. Both in the United States and in Canada there are other national systems of record linkage connected with the income tax system, in which files of successive income tax returns are automatically collated by the computer and financial history of individuals is kept. We often find ourselves in North America hearing talk of the chequeless economy which is soon going to be with us, using a national system of on-line computers. Much of this we won't see before this next conference two years hence. But I think within 10 years a good deal of it will be upon us and much of it in the hands of people, perhaps like myself as a computer manager, whose interests are often in means rather than in ends. I find myself as a layman and a citizen perturbed that Professor Smith's Ombudsman may not be appointed in time to save us from some of the dire consequences that will come from a fully linked system for all the population.

Professor Schilling : I just wanted to say a brief word about an era long before Orwell ; that of Dickens. Much of the research mentioned in connection with record linkage is concerned with genetic studies, and I am sure this is right. This is an attractive field, but I am sure that a lot needs to be done in terms of linking environmental factors to disease. Even in our society we've got any number of hazards which I think have been missed through lack of record linkage and I hope that in the systems that are evolved in the next year or so some attention will be paid to the possibility of getting more information on occupational groups and social class groups.

Miss Jones : In case it was I who caused Dr Acheson's rather gloomy contribution just recently about the official attitude, I should like to emphasize the sympathy which we have with the idea of a common number. The point I want to make is that it is best to hasten slowly ; it is no good trying to introduce a common number which doesn't fulfil all the functions of the number it supersedes. I am not responsible for confidentiality policy in the Ministry but I am responsible for co-operation in research, and I should particularly like to emphasize the pleasure I have had in being present at this meeting and to congratulate Dr Acheson on all that he has achieved in calling it and in the experimental work which he has carried out and which I am sure in the future will go a long way. I would remind Dr Doll of the example of record linkage for a sample population (1965) which we did with his advice and that of Dr Heasman and Professor Reed in linking the sickness experience over a year of a sample of about three-quarters of a million population. Having obtained information about occupation in such a way as to enable it to be analysed by social class and by occupational group, we brought together the records of incapacity of those people over the succeeding year to compare both area and occupation groups. This brought into account every bit of sickness, no matter where in Great Britain it occurred, no matter what hospital treated them and no matter what general practitioner gave the follow-up treatment, provided there was at least four days of incapacity. It also took into account the environmental factor of atmospheric pollution. This was done through a common number and through a simple system of standardized records. I therefore have particular sympathy with the idea of developing standardized records and a common number. But knowing that the common number will not solve all the linking problems I have been glad to hear that the development of other means of linking will

390

probably get over what would otherwise be a pretty sticky interim period.

Professor Alwyn Smith : I'd like to say that it seems to me that there can now be no reasonable doubt that an operation on the scale of the Oxford Record Linkage Study is highly desirable and reasonably practicable and not so expensive that we ought not to be able to afford it. I think Acheson has proved and demonstrated beyond any reasonable doubt that we ought to have something on that scale at a very much larger level. I also think it is highly desirable that in order to extend this scale to ad hoc procedures, it would be good if we developed the facility of linkability in respect of a very large number of other kinds of records which I think neither Acheson nor anyone else has ever suggested should be part of a huge compendium file. These two things are separate. The linking of records which are already collected and already processed could, I am quite sure, be streamlined to the point where it is practical. In addition we could have suitable linkage codes transcribed onto all kinds of other documents.

Mr Seymour Jablon : I merely wanted to say in connection with the question of a single-number system that in the United States the Social Security number is being used widely by a great many agencies. In point of fact the Veterans Administration is now using this number as an indexing device for their clinical records, the Army and Navy have just begun to use the Social Security number in place of their own military identifying numbers, many States are beginning to use the Social Security number as an identifying number on drivers' licences, and I feel quite sure that this trend will accelerate.

Mr Weber : First, Mr Chairman, I would like to express my gratitude to the organizers for having arranged this very interesting symposium. The World Health Organization was mentioned by the previous speaker and as one of its staff members I can assure you that the Organization is interested in record linkage. In the Regional Office for Europe we have had several meetings at which record linkage was proposed as a major solution to the problems under consideration. I may mention, for instance, recent discussions on the establishment of registers of persons suffering from ischaemic heart disease by using multiple sources of information.

I am confident that medical record linkage is going to receive much attention at future conferences both at the European level and, under the auspices of our Headquarters, at the world level.

Dr Newcombe : I detect a difference in practice and thought on the two sides of the Atlantic concerning the matter of costs. My own experience in Canada has been with systems in which punch cards have already been used for a long time. For example in order to prepare alphabetic indexes of the birth, death and marriage registrations by machine rather than by hand, punch cards are prepared with names in them and these are sorted and listed. In order to run schemes of hospital insurance the accounting is done with punch cards for reasons of economy. The payroll at the organization for which I work is also mechanized and makes use of punch cards and computers. We do have organizations that do not do this, like our Family Allowance Administration, but I am sure they are spending more money because of their lack of mechanization. There is a feeling which I have detected at this meeting that mechanized methods cost more, rather than less, than their manual counter parts. I wonder whether any of the participants have hard facts bearing on the matter.

Dr Doll : This session is described as General Discussion and Summing-up and, although summing is the only mathematical procedure of which I am capable I don't think that I can possibly sum the discussions that we have had in the last two days. I would, however, like to put before you very briefly half a dozen conclusions that I have drawn personally from the meeting. The first is that people who are interested in record linkage are a remarkably amiable group with a highly developed sense of humour. The second is that the linkage of medical records has developed over a long period, has a respectable history, and is now going through a qualitative change which will eventually lead to the linkability of all vital statistic and medical data relating to the individual and his family. Thirdly, that in British circumstances linked data should be confined to health material and available only to people wishing to use them for health purposes. Whether other sets of data should be linked for other purposes—tax office or police—is outside our province ; but health data should be linked only to health data and utilized only by people interested in using them for purposes related to health. If this principle is accepted the medical ethical problem of confidentiality can be solved.

Fourthly, that the identification of individuals is extremely difficult and is greatly simplified by the use of a widely used identity number, but that without such a number linkage is still possible. We must, however, continue to hope that if Scandinavia and the United States can come to use a single number for a very wide range of Government purposes, it is not thereby necessarily proved to be impossible to do it in Britain. Meanwhile we can make some attempt to get the National Health Service number used more widely on medical forms. One way of doing this would be to issue medical cards to the public. That many people would like this is indicated by the existence of a private organization set up to provide people with medical cards on which they can state that they have an allergy, or are liable to become comatose from diabetes, and if they go into hospital it is to their benefit that they should have this card with them to provide this information. And of course if they had such a card one could surreptitiously put the National Health Service number on it. Fifthly, that the value of linking medical records is not confined to medical research but has major contributions to make to patient care and to the efficient running of the health services. Sixthly, and finally, that Government departments that are concerned in this problem are actively interested in developing a system of record linkage and it is up to us who say we want to use it to provide them and provide them repeatedly with examples of the way in which it can and will be used.

All that remains for me to do now is to thank the many people who have made this symposium such a great success. Dr Acheson's work in organizing it has been referred to on several occasions during this symposium but I am sure you would all wish me to thank him again for having initiated it, organized it and carried it through so delightfully. Secondly, to thank the Nuffield Foundation for the financial support that they have given which has enabled the symposium to be held and has enabled some of our foreign visitors to attend. Thirdly, to thank the Oxford Regional Hospital Board for the use of the premises, for the sherry at lunchtime, and for the reception which is to come. Fourthly, to thank the Provost and the Fellows of The Queen's College for allowing us the use of their beautiful college and to see the improvements which are being put into the basements, something which those of us who have lived in England for a long time hadn't always associated with the older Universities. Fifthly, I should like to thank the speakers for the very carefully prepared papers which they have presented and particularly to thank our European colleagues for having used English throughout ; they have presented their papers most clearly and beautifully. Finally I would like to thank the staff of the Oxford Record Linkage Study for the extremely efficient way they have attended to our every want and for disciplining us so pleasantly but effectively when we tended to talk for too long.

REFERENCES

BECK, I. F., GARDNER, F. V. & WITTS, L. J. (1947). Social service for a medical ward. *Br. J. soc. Med.* **1**, 197.

FERGUSON, T. & MACPHAIL, A. N. (1954). *Hospital and Community*. London : Nuffield Provincial Hospitals Trust.
MAIR, A. (1962). MacKenzie on records in medical practice, *Br. med. J.* **1**, 1331.
SMITH, A. (1966). *Genetics in Medicine*. Edinburgh : Livingstone.

Report on an Enquiry into the Incidence of Incapacity for Work. Part II : Incidence of Incapacity for Work in Different Areas and Occupations. HMSO, 1965.

INDEX

Printed by Neill & Co. Ltd., Edinburgh